Frommer's®

Tahiti & French Polynesia

3rd Edition

by Bill Goodwin

WILEY

Wiley Publishing, Inc.

Published by:
WILEY PUBLISHING, INC.
111 River St.
Hoboken, NJ 07030-5774

ISBN 978-0-470-61828-8 (paper); ISBN 978-0-470-94738-8 (ebk); ISBN 978-0-470-94736-4 (ebk); ISBN 978-0-470-94737-1 (ebk)

Editor: Christine Ryan
Production Editor: Eric T Schroeder
Cartographer: Guy Ruggiero
Photo Editor: Richard Fox
Production by Wiley Indianapolis Composition Services
Front Cover Photo: Le Meridien Resort, Bora Bora ©Jon Arnold Images / DanitaDelimont.com.
Back Cover Photo: Stone tikis at Taiohae, Marquesas Islands ©Ken Gillham / Robert Harding Picture Library.

For information on our other products and services or to obtain technical support, please contact our Customer Care Department within the U.S. at 877/762-2974, outside the U.S. at 317/572-3993 or fax 317/572-4002.

Wiley also publishes its books in a variety of electronic formats. Some content that appears in print may not be available in electronic formats.

CONTENTS

4 SUGGESTED TAHITI & FRENCH POLYNESIA ITINERARIES 76

5 TAHITI 87

6 MOOREA 128

7 HUAHINE 156

8 RAIATEA & TAHAA 167

LIST OF MAPS

*To my father,
with love and grateful thanks for supporting my being a writer
rather than a lawyer*

ACKNOWLEDGMENTS

I owe a debt of gratitude to many individuals and organizations for their assistance, information, and advice without which it would have been impossible to research and write this book. You will become acquainted with many of them in these pages, and it will be your good luck to meet them in the islands.

I am particularly grateful to Al Keahi, Jonathan Reap, Hinata Pea, Céline Teihotaata, Vaini Roloux, and Tina Karimi of Tahiti Tourisme, French Polynesia's tourist information bureau.

It was my good fortune to be accompanied on the research trip for this edition by my dear friend and colleague Muriel Weber of Nancy, France. I met Muriel during a cruise to the Marquesas Islands on the *Aranui 3,* during which I was greatly impressed by her skill behind a camera. As I point out in chapter 1, she also is gifted at discovering and evaluating places to stay (never again will I complain about the French not caring where they sleep!). That ability and her fluency in both English and French were of immense help to me in gathering information for this book. When my schoolboy French fumbled, Muriel was there to translate—and to ask just the right question at just the right time.

My deep personal thanks go to my sister, Jean Goodwin Santa Maria, who has consistently given much-needed moral support; to Curtis and Judy Moore, Vic and Kathy Mortenson, Connie Haeder, Anne Simon, Suzanne McIntosh, Nancy Monseaux, and Max Parrish, all of whom have doused the home fires while I was away in the islands at one time or another; and to Bill and Donna Wilder, who introduced me to the intricacies of Tahiti and who once let me chill out in their home on Moorea. I am truly blessed to have these wonderful folks in my life.

—Bill Goodwin

HOW TO CONTACT US

In researching this book, we discovered many wonderful places—hotels, restaurants, shops, and more. We're sure you'll find others. Please tell us about them, so we can share the information with your fellow travelers in upcoming editions. If you were disappointed with a recommendation, we'd love to know that, too. Please write to:

Frommer's Tahiti & French Polynesia, 3rd Edition
Wiley Publishing, Inc. • 111 River St. • Hoboken, NJ 07030-5774
frommersfeedback@wiley.com

AN ADDITIONAL NOTE

Please be advised that travel information is subject to change at any time—and this is especially true of prices. We therefore suggest that you write or call ahead for confirmation when making your travel plans. The authors, editors, and publisher cannot be held responsible for the experiences of readers while traveling. Your safety is important to us, however, so we encourage you to stay alert and be aware of your surroundings. Keep a close eye on cameras, purses, and wallets, all favorite targets of thieves and pickpockets.

ABOUT THE AUTHOR

Bill Goodwin began his writing career as an award-winning newspaper reporter and then served as legal counsel and speechwriter for two influential U.S. senators—Sam Nunn of Georgia and the late Sam Ervin of North Carolina. In 1977 he and a friend took a long break from office life and sailed a 41-foot yacht from Annapolis, Maryland, through the Panama Canal to the Marquesas Islands, the Tuamotu Archipelago, and Tahiti. He left the boat in Papeete and, with a girlfriend and backpack, explored Tahiti, Moorea, and the Society Islands for as long as the local immigration authorities would allow. He has returned for extended visits many times since, most devoted to researching and writing this book and its forerunner, *Frommer's South Pacific*. He also is author of *Frommer's Fiji* and at home, *Frommer's Virginia*. Find out more at www.billgoodwin.com.

FROMMER'S STAR RATINGS, ICONS & ABBREVIATIONS

Every hotel, restaurant, and attraction listing in this guide has been ranked for quality, value, service, amenities, and special features using a star-rating system. In country, state, and regional guides, we also rate towns and regions to help you narrow down your choices and budget your time accordingly. Hotels and restaurants are rated on a scale of zero (recommended) to three stars (exceptional). Attractions, shopping, nightlife, towns, and regions are rated according to the following scale: zero stars (recommended), one star (highly recommended), two stars (very highly recommended), and three stars (must-see).

In addition to the star-rating system, we also use seven feature icons that point you to the great deals, in-the-know advice, and unique experiences that separate travelers from tourists. Throughout the book, look for:

special finds—those places only insiders know about

fun facts—details that make travelers more informed and their trips more fun

kids—best bets for kids and advice for the whole family

special moments—those experiences that memories are made of

overrated—places or experiences not worth your time or money

insider tips—great ways to save time and money

great values—where to get the best deals

The following abbreviations are used for credit cards:

AE	American Express	DISC	Discover	V	Visa
DC	Diners Club	MC	MasterCard		

TRAVEL RESOURCES AT FROMMERS.COM

Frommer's travel resources don't end with this guide. Frommer's website, www.frommers.com, has travel information on more than 4,000 destinations. We update features regularly, giving you access to the most current trip-planning information and the best airfare, lodging, and car-rental bargains. You can also listen to podcasts, connect with other Frommers.com members through our active-reader forums, share your travel photos, read blogs from guidebook editors and fellow travelers, and much more.

THE BEST OF TAHITI & FRENCH POLYNESIA

Tahiti and her sister islands in French Polynesia have conjured up romantic images of an earthly paradise since European sailors brought home tales of their tropical. splendor and uninhibited people in the 1760s. My own love affair with these remote outposts doesn't go back quite that far, but when I did wash ashore more than 3 decades ago, I quickly understood why they came to have such a reputation. In fact, I was so smitten that I stayed for 7 months, as long as the gendarmes would allow.

You may wish to plan a longer trip yourself, for these are the most beautiful islands in the world—an opinion I share with many others, including the late James A. Michener. They are blessed with gorgeous beaches, and their lagoons allow for spectacular diving and snorkeling.

Then there are the Polynesian islanders who live here. Their fabled history has provided fodder for famous books and films, their storied culture inspires hedonistic dreams, and their big, infectious smiles add charm to any visit.

Your choice of where you go and what you do will depend on why you are coming here, and on how much money you have to spend. French Polynesia has a well-earned reputation as an expensive destination. An unforgettable honeymoon spent in a romantic bungalow standing over a lagoon may cost a small fortune. But by foregoing such niceties as air conditioners and televisions, you can have an enjoyable vacation at a small hotel or a charming pension without hocking all of the family jewels.

In this chapter, I point out the best of the best—not necessarily to pass qualitative judgment, but to help you choose among the surprisingly many options in the islands. They're listed here in the order in which they appear in the book. For a preview of the islands, see "The Islands in Brief" in chapter 4.

THE most beautiful
ISLANDS

"In the South Seas," the poet Rupert Brooke wrote in 1914, "the Creator seems to have laid himself out to show what He can do." How right the poet was, for here lie some of the world's most dramatically beautiful islands. The best of the lot have jagged mountain peaks plunging into aquamarine lagoons, and often appear on travel posters and brochures.

o **Moorea:** To my mind, Moorea is the most beautiful island in the world. Nothing compares with its saw-toothed ridges and the great dark-green hulk of Mount Rotui separating glorious Cook's and Opunohu bays. The view from Tahiti of Moorea's dinosaur-like skyline is unforgettable. See chapter 6.

o **Huahine:** Although Moorea and Bora Bora get most of the ink, Huahine is almost as gorgeous. Its bays are surrounded by mountains that almost rival Moorea's. But since it is off the well-beaten tourist track, it still retains an air of old Polynesia. Because it hasn't yet been taken over by tourists or the pressures of modern life, its residents still greet you with a big smile and have time to sit and chat. See chapter 7.

o **Bora Bora:** James Michener thought Bora Bora was the most beautiful island in the world. Although tourism has turned this gem into a sort of expensive South Seas Disneyland, development hasn't altered the incredible beauty of Mount Otemanu, the basaltic tombstone towering over Bora Bora's lagoon, which ranges in color from bright yellow to deep blue. See chapter 9.

o **Maupiti:** An unspoiled jewel, Maupiti is like nearby Bora Bora in miniature, but without any modern hotels or resorts. Like Bora Bora, its mountainous central island hovers over a crystal-clear lagoon. See chapter 10.

o **Rangiroa, Tikehau, Manihi, & Fakarava:** These atolls are lumped together because they are equally beautiful. Each has a string of islets enclosing large lagoons, like giant lakes in the middle of the ocean. See chapter 11.

o **Ua Pou:** In the far-off Marquesas Islands, Ua Pou's mountain ridges are topped by stovepipe spires, which inspired Jacques Brel to write his song, "La Cathédrale." See chapter 12.

o **Fatu Hiva:** Virgin's Bay on Fatu Hiva is one of the world's most gorgeous yacht anchorages, especially at sunset when golden light plays off two stone pillars guarding the entrance to the island's gorgelike central valley. See chapter 12.

THE best BEACHES

Because all but a few of the islands are surrounded by coral reefs, there are few surf *plages* here (the French word for "beach" being *plage*). Most of those on Tahiti have heat-absorbing black volcanic sand. Except in the Marquesas, which are almost devoid of coral, most islands (and all but a few resorts) have bathtub-like lagoons that lap on white-coral sands draped by coconut palms. Here are a few that stand out from the many:

o **La Plage de Maui** (Tahiti): Bordering the southern shore of Tahiti Iti, the main island's peninsula, this strip of white sand is far and away the best beach on Tahiti. The lagoon is suitable for swimming, and there's an excellent snack bar beside the beach. See chapter 5.

- **Mareto Plage Publique** (Moorea): Although it isn't as picturesque as Moorea's Temae Plage Publique (see below), this beach between Cook's and Opunohu bays sits between a coconut grove and the lagoon. See chapter 6.
- **Temae Plage Publique** (Moorea): The northeastern coast of Moorea is fringed by a nearly uninterrupted stretch of white-sand beach that commands a glorious view: across a speckled lagoon to Tahiti, sitting on the horizon across the Sea of the Moon. See chapter 6.
- **Avea Beach** (Huahine): My favorite resort beach is at Relais Mahana, a small hotel on Auea Bay near Huahine's southern end. Trees grow along the white beach, which slopes into a lagoon deep enough for swimming at any tide. The resort's pier goes out to a giant coral head, a perfect and safe place to snorkel, and the lagoon here is protected from the trade winds, making it safe for sailing. See chapter 7.
- **Matira Beach** (Bora Bora): Although metal boat lifts in the lagoon now mar its beauty, this fine ribbon of sand stretches around skinny Matira Point, which forms the island's southern extremity. The eastern side has views of the sister islands of Raiatea and Tahaa. See chapter 9.
- **Plage Tereia** (Maupiti): Like Matira Beach on Bora Bora, this white-sand beach wraps around a peninsula on Maupiti's main island. It's so lovely that locals are building homes next to it, so you aren't likely to have this one all to yourself, especially on weekends. Almost as beautiful is the beach at the northern end of Motu Tiapaa, where you have a view of Maupiti's central mountain, and no one seems to care if you discretely skinny-dip. See chapter 10.
- **Les Sables Rose/The Pink Sands** (Rangiroa): At a remote corner of Rangiroa's lagoon, the world's second largest, lies a gorgeous beach made up of pink sand. There is no shade, but it's well worth the hour-long boat ride from Rangiroa's hotels. See chapter 11.
- **Motu Tuherahera** (Tikehau): The eastern half of Tikihau's main island is skirted by a beautiful stretch of white sand, much of it flanked by the atoll's pensions. See chapter 11.

THE best HONEYMOON RESORTS

Whether you're on your honeymoon or not, French Polynesia is a marvelous place for romantic escapes. After all, romance and the islands have gone hand-in-hand since the young women of Tahiti gave rousing, bare-breasted welcomes to the 18th-century European explorers.

Back in those days, everyone here lived in a proverbial little grass shack by the beach. The modern resorts have elevated that concept into luxurious guest bungalows, many built on stilts out over the lagoons. I've never stayed anywhere as romantic as these thatched-roof overwater units, most with glass panels in their floors for viewing fish swimming below. If their indoor luxuries aren't enough, you can climb down the steps leading from your front deck and go skinny-dipping in the warm waters below. The overwater bungalows help make French Polynesia—especially Bora Bora—one of the world's most famous honeymoon destinations. Naturally, they are the most expensive accommodations here.

One caveat is in order: Many overwater bungalows are relatively close together, meaning that your honeymooning next-door neighbors will be within earshot. ("It can be like watching an X-rated video," a hotel manager once confessed, "but without the video.") Therefore, if you're seeking a high degree of privacy and seclusion, these won't necessarily be your best choice.

The top resorts are variations on the same theme: a beachside central complex with a restaurant, bar, and other public facilities flanked by individual guest bungalows in a coconut grove. From the shoreline, piers reach out to the overwater units. I point out the top resorts island-by-island in the paragraphs below, but please read the reviews in the chapters that follow before making your choice.

o **Tahiti:** Most visitors now consider Tahiti to be a way station to the other islands, but the **InterContinental Resort Tahiti** (p. 114) has overwater bungalows that face the dramatic outline of Moorea across the Sea of the Moon. Some of those at **Le Meridien Tahiti** (p. 116) also have this view.

o **Moorea:** The units at the **Club Bali Hai** (p. 144) are among the oldest—and the least expensive—overwater bungalows in the islands, but they enjoy an unparalleled view of the jagged mountains surrounding Cook's Bay. Some overwater units at the **Sofitel Moorea Ia Ora Beach Resort** (p. 142) actually face Tahiti across the Sea of the Moon, and they're built over Moorea's most colorful lagoon. The **Moorea Pearl Resort & Spa** (p. 142) has a few bungalows perched on the edge of the clifflike reef, making for superb snorkeling right off your front deck. You'll have more of these luxurious cabins at the **InterContinental Resort and Spa Moorea** (p. 146).

o **Huahine:** After a few days on Bora Bora, many couples today are opting to end their honeymoons by decompressing on Huahine or Tahaa (see below). On Huahine, **Te Tiare Beach Resort** (p. 163) is one of the smallest and most intimate retreats in French Polynesia. Its units have some of the largest decks of any overwater bungalows (one side is completely shaded by a thatched roof).

o **Tahaa:** The most charmingly Polynesian of all overwater units are at the **Le Taha'a Private Island & Spa** (p. 177), a luxurious resort on a small islet off Tahaa. Some of these have views of Bora Bora on the horizon.

o **Bora Bora:** This most famous—and crowded—of French Polynesia's honeymoon islands has several hundred overwater bungalows. Some at the superluxe **St. Regis Resort Bora Bora** (p. 194) have swimming pools set in their overwater decks. Not only does the **InterContinental Resort and Thalasso Spa Bora Bora** (p. 193) have overwater units for its guests, but three treatment rooms at its extraordinary spa also extend out over the lagoon (you can watch the fish through a glass floor panel while getting a massage). The **Hilton Bora Bora Nui Resort & Spa** (p. 193) has large, two-room overwater units, but only a few look out to tombstonelike Mount Otemanu, one of the most photographed scenes in the entire South Pacific. You will have that awesome view at the **Sofitel Bora Bora Marara Beach and Private Island** (p. 195), where some bungalows directly face the tombstone mountain. You'll see the mountain from its other side from the **Four Seasons Resort Bora Bora** (p. 192), the newest resort here. Among the most private units are the garden units at the **Bora Bora Pearl Beach Resort** (p. 192); you can cavort to your heart's content in their wall-enclosed patios, which have sun decks and splash pools. The smaller but well-appointed overwater units at the friendly **Le Maitai Polynesia Bora Bora** (p. 195) are the least expensive on Bora Bora. You'll be up on a hillside rather than by the beach, but the three units at the inexpensive **Rohutu Fare Lodge** (p. 196) are the most suggestively decorated in French Polynesia.

○ **Tuamotu Archipelago:** Most beaches in the Tuamotu atolls have more coral gravel than sand, but not so at the **Tikehau Pearl Beach Resort** (p. 222), where some overwater bungalows actually sit over the riptides in a pass that lets the sea into the lagoon. Although its bungalows are all ashore, the charming **Relais Royal Tikehau** (p. 222) is a less expensive alternative, and it also has a very fine beach. On Manihi atoll, units at the **Manihi Pearl Beach Resort** (p. 226) are cooled by the almost constantly blowing trade winds.

THE best FAMILY RESORTS

There are no Disney Worlds or other such attractions in the islands. As I point out in the "Family Travel" section in chapter 3 (p. 62), most tourism here is geared toward honeymooners and other couples. In fact, most resorts in French Polynesia are designed specifically for romance. Accordingly, most resorts house their guests in individual bungalows best occupied by two people. That's not to say that children won't have a fine time here, for more and more resorts are making provisions for families as well as honeymooners. Kids who like being around the water will enjoy themselves the most.

Here are a few family-friendly resorts:

○ **InterContinental Resort Tahiti** (Tahiti): Tahiti's best all-around resort has a few overwater bungalows, but most units are hotel rooms that interconnect, thus giving families who can afford them two or more units in which to roam. See p. 114.

○ **Radisson Plaza Resort Tahiti** (Tahiti): The lagoon off the black-sand beach at the Radisson Plaza is subject to dangerous riptides, but kids can play in the walk-in swimming pool. Parents who don't mind letting their youngsters bunk on the living-room sofa can sleep upstairs in a two-story "duplex" suite. The Radisson occasionally offers special deals for families, such as letting kids stay and eat free. See p. 118.

○ **Legends Resort** (Moorea): Sitting high on a mountainside, Legends Resort does not offer a program for kids, but all of its modern villas have fully-equipped kitchens, and some have two and three bedrooms. See p. 146.

○ **Bora Bora Nui Resort & Spa** (Bora Bora): This large and swanky resort has a variety of accommodations, including hotel-style units that interconnect. See p. 193.

Getting Hitched in the Islands

The islands are marvelous places for a honeymoon. Thanks to a recent change in the law, visitors can now get legally hitched in French Polynesia without being here for 30 days beforehand. The rules are a bit complicated, and everything must be done in French, so it's best to let your choice of resort handle the details. Most of them have romantic wedding packages including traditional ceremonies, often right on the beach.

---

o **Four Seasons Resort Bora Bora** (Bora Bora): Although the swanky Four Seasons attracts mainly couples, during holiday periods a marine biologist is on duty at its "Chill Island" kids club. Some of the resort's villas have bedrooms designed especially for children. See p. 192.

o **Le Meridien Bora Bora** (Bora Bora): Although it doesn't have a children's center, I think this Meridien is the top family resort in French Polynesia. The youngsters can both play and learn in the resort's award-wining sea turtle rescue and breeding program. Family-size units sit beside a shallow, man-made lagoon, a safe haven for kids. See p. 194.

THE best PENSIONS & GUEST HOUSES

I had the great fortune to be accompanied on my research trip for this edition by my dear French friend Muriel Weber, who not only has an extraordinary eye behind the camera but a wonderful nose for sniffing out *bonnes adressees,* which is her way of saying charming places to stay. It's a useful talent in a country whose pensions and guest houses run the gamut from cold-water basic to charmingly comfortable.

Common in Europe, pensions are comparable to bed-and-breakfasts in the United States, to home-stays in other English-speaking countries. Many pensions include breakfast and dinner in their rates, which makes them very good value.

Here are best of those Muriel and I found. Others are in chapters 5 through 12. Also see "Tips on Accommodations" in chapter 3 (p. 73).

o **Hiti Moana Villa** (Tahiti): In rural Papara on Tahiti's south coast, the bungalows at this little pension sit beside the lagoon. There's also a swimming pool. See p. 117.

o **Fare Suisse** (Tahiti): This modern home with motel-style rooms is just 3 blocks inland from the Papeete waterfront. See p. 120.

o **Fare Vaihere** (Moorea): The owner of this 4-bungalow bed-and-breakfast on the shores of spectacular Opunohu Bay is a dive instructor. His wife is a terrific cook. See p. 145.

o **Fare Manuia** (Moorea): More of a cottage rental place than pension, the fully-equipped units here are beside a very good beach. See p. 147.

o **Pension Mauarii** (Huahine): Built of thatch, bamboo, and tree trunks, Pension Mauarii's rustic bungalows sit beside one of French Polynesia's best beaches. The restaurant is both good and charming. See p. 165.

o **Sunset Beach Motel** (Raiatea): This collection of Western-style cottages occupies a coconut grove skirting Raiatea's lagoon. Every unit has a kitchen and a view of Bora Bora. See p. 177.

o **Rohutu Fare Lodge** (Bora Bora): On a hillside overlooking the Bora Bora's fabulous lagoon, this little charmer's bungalows are cleverly—and suggestively—designed. See p. 196.

o **Le Kuriri** (Maupiti): This small hotel is the most charming and sophisticated accommodation on a beautiful island whose residents have rejected big resorts. See p. 206.

o **Poe Iti Guest House** (Maupiti): They lack the Polynesian charm of Le Kuriri's, but Poe Iti's bungalows have TVs and air conditioners, a rarity for a French Polynesian pension. See p. 207

- **Les Relais de Josephine** (Rangiroa): You can watch the dolphins frolic in Tipua Pass from the Mediterranean-style villa and three of the six bungalows of this little charmer. See p. 217.
- **Raira Lagon** (Rangiroa): The bungalows are air-conditioned at this pension beside Rangiroa's huge lagoon. See p. 219.
- **Relais Royal Tikehau** (Tikehau): Unlike most accommodations in the atolls of the Tuamotu Archipelago, this small hotel has a great beach of pinkish sand. See p. 222.
- **Pension Kiria** (Fakarava): On an island with several good pensions, this one stands out for its bungalows built entirely of native materials. See p. 230.

THE best HISTORICAL & CULTURAL EXPERIENCES

The people of Tahiti and French Polynesia are justly proud of their ancient culture, as well as the unique modern history that sets them apart from all other Pacific Islanders. Below are the best ways to learn about the people, their lifestyle, and their history.

- **La Maison de James Norman Hall/James Norman Hall's Home** (Tahiti): The coauthor of *Mutiny on the Bounty* and other books set in the South Pacific lived most of his adult life on Tahiti. His family maintains his former home as a fascinating museum. See p. 93.
- **Marché Municipal/Municipal Market** (Tahiti): Papeete's large, teeming market is a wonderful place to examine tropical foodstuffs as well as to buy handicrafts. It's especially busy before dawn on Sunday. See p. 94.
- **Musée de Tahiti et Ses Isles/Museum of Tahiti and Her Islands** (Tahiti): This terrific lagoonside museum recounts the geology, history, culture, flora, and fauna of French Polynesia. It's worth a stop just for the outstanding view of Moorea from its coconut-grove setting. See p. 94.
- **Musée Gauguin/Gauguin Museum** (Tahiti): The great French painter Paul Gauguin lived and worked on Tahiti's south coast from 1891 until moving to Hiva Oa in the Marquesas Islands, where he died. This museum has a few of his original works, but is best at tracing his adventures in French Polynesia. See p. 95.
- **Tiki Theatre Village** (Moorea): Built to resemble a pre-European Tahitian village, this cultural center has demonstrations of handicrafts making and puts on a nightly dance show and feast. It's a bit commercial, and the staff isn't always fluent in English, but this is the only place in French Polynesia where one can sample the old ways. See p. 137.
- **Maeva Maraes** (Huahine): The ancient Tahitians gathered to worship their gods and hold other ceremonies at stone temples known as *maraes*. More than 40 of these structures have been restored near the village of Maeva and are a highlight of any visit to Huahine. See p. 158.
- **Taputapuatea Marae** (Raiatea): French Polynesia's largest and most important *marae* sits beside the lagoon on Raiatea. Archaeologists have uncovered bones apparently from human sacrifices from beneath its 45m-long (150-ft.) grand altar. See p. 171.
- **Tohua Papa Nui/Paul Gauguin Cultural Center** (Hiva Oa): This small museum recounts Paul Gauguin's last days on Hiva Oa, where he died in 1903. It's worth a visit to see the exact replicas of his original paintings executed by a team of French artists. See p. 257.

THE best OF THE OLD SOUTH SEAS

The islands are developing rapidly, with modern, fast-paced cities like Papeete replacing what were once sleepy backwater ports. But there are still remnants of the old South Seas days of coconut planters, beach bums, and missionaries.

- **Huahine:** Of the major French Polynesian islands, Huahine has been the least affected by tourism, and its residents are still likely to give you an unprompted Tahitian greeting, *"Ia orana!"* Agriculture is still king on Huahine, which makes it the "Island of Fruits." There are ancient *maraes* (temples) to visit, and the only town, tiny **Fare,** is little more than a collection of Chinese shops fronting the island's wharf, which come to life when ships pull in. See chapter 7.
- **Tahaa:** With no towns and barely a village, Tahaa is still predominately a vanilla-growing island—as sweet aromas will attest. One of French Polynesia's top resorts is on a small islet off Tahaa, but otherwise this rugged little island takes you back to the way Moorea used to be. See chapter 8.
- **Maupiti:** Not long ago, residents of Maupiti voted down a proposal to build an upscale resort on their gorgeous little island, thus leaving it as a day trip from Bora Bora or as an unspoiled retreat for those who can do without maximum luxuries—or the English language. Maupiti looks like Bora Bora; locals boast that it's how Bora Bora used to be. See chapter 10.
- **The Tuamotu Archipelago:** Whether you choose to visit Rangiroa, Tikehau, Manihi, or Fakarava, you will find modern Polynesian life relatively undisturbed by modern ways, except for the many black-pearl farms in their lagoons. See chapter 11.
- **The Marquesas Islands:** Best visited on the cruise ship *Aranui 3,* the Marquesas hearken back to the early 19th century, when Herman Melville and others jumped off whaling ships and disappeared into the islands' haunting valleys. See chapter 12.

THE best DINING EXPERIENCES

Wherever the French go, fine food and wine are sure to follow, and French Polynesia is no exception. You will get good food everywhere here, but these are a few of the best places to sample fine fare.

- **Le Coco's** (Tahiti): On Tahiti's west coast, you'll have a fine view of Moorea from the patio at Le Coco's, specializing in light nouvelle cuisine. See p. 122.
- **Le Lotus** (Tahiti): The most romantic setting of any French Polynesian restaurant is in this overwater dining room at the InterContinental Resort Tahiti. The food is gourmet French and the service highly efficient and unobtrusive, but even if they weren't, the view of Moorea on a moonlit night would still make an evening here special. See p. 122.
- **Restaurant Pink Coconut** (Tahiti): Also with a spectacular view of Moorea from Marina Taina, the Pink Coconut is my favorite place for a romantic lunch. See p. 122.

- **Le Belvédère** (Tahiti): The fondue isn't worth writing home about, but the spectacular view of Papeete and Moorea from high in the hills above the city is worth a postcard. See p. 123.
- **L'O a la Bouche** (Tahiti): This stylish bistro, emphasizing fusion cooking and fine wines, serves the best food in downtown Papeete. See p. 123.
- **Les Roulottes** (Tahiti): Dining in a parking lot is far from romantic, but the meal wagons on the Papeete waterfront after dark are the best food value in French Polynesia. The carnival-like scene itself is worth seeing. See p. 125.
- **Le Mahogany** (Moorea): After 30 years at the former Hotel Bali Hai, Chef François Courtien now works his magic at Le Mahogany, one of the best food values on Moorea. See p. 150.
- **Le Mayflower** (Moorea): Mainly locals in the know frequent this roadside restaurant, Moorea's best. The sauces are delightfully light, as are the prices for such good food. See p. 153.
- **Painapo (Pineapple) Beach** (Moorea): This beachside pavilion is my favorite place for an authentic Sunday buffet of traditional Tahitian food. It's one of French Polynesia's best values, too. See p. 153.
- **Bloody Mary's Restaurant & Bar** (Bora Bora): A fun evening at French Polynesia's most famous restaurant is a must-do when on Bora Bora. That's because Bloody Mary's provides the most unique and charming dining experience in the islands. Come early for a drink at the friendly bar, and then pick your fresh seafood from atop a huge tray of ice. After eating heavy French fare elsewhere for a few days, the sauceless fish from the grill will seem downright refreshing. See p. 198.
- **La Villa Mahana** (Bora Bora): Corsican chef Damien Rinaldi Dovio also provides relief from traditional French sauces at his romantic little restaurant, where he uses "exotic" spices to enliven fresh fish and beef dishes. See p. 199.

THE best ISLAND NIGHTS

Don't come to the islands expecting opera and ballet, or Las Vegas–style floor shows either. Other than pub-crawling to bars and nightclubs in Papeete, evening entertainment here consists primarily of feasts of island foods followed by traditional dancing—and whatever else you and your companion can concoct in these extraordinarily romantic islands.

Of course, the Tahitian hip-swinging traditional dances are world-famous. They are not as lewd and lascivious today as they were in the days before the missionaries arrived, but they still have plenty of suggestive movements to the primordial beat of drums; see "A Most Indecent Song & Dance" (p. 36).

Every hotel will have at least one dance show a week. The best are on Tahiti, especially the thrice-weekly performances at the InterContinental Resort Tahiti that feature one of the best troupes, the **Grande Danse de Tahiti** (p. 126).

Moorea has one of the best shows at **Tiki Theatre Village,** where the dancers wear traditional costumes (p. 137). Among Moorea's hotels, the **InterContinental Resort and Spa Moorea** (p. 146) stages a spectacular beachside show on Saturday nights, and the **Club Bali Hai** (p. 144) has a free performance at 6pm on Wednesday, followed by an à la carte barbecue, making it also a very good value.

If you want to see the very best Tahitian dancing, come here in July during the annual **Heiva Nui** festival, when the top troupes compete on the Papeete waterfront. Plan early, since tickets can be hard to come by if you wait until the last minute. See the "French Polynesia Calendar of Events" (p. 42) for details.

THE best BUYS

Take some extra money along, for you'll likely spend it on black pearls, handicrafts, and tropical clothing.

See "Shopping," in chapter 5, for an overall discussion and the "Shopping" sections in the individual destination chapters for the best shops on each island.

o **Black Pearls:** Few people will escape French Polynesia without buying at least one black pearl. That's because the shallow, clear-water lagoons of the Tuamotu Archipelago are the world's largest producers of the beautiful dark orbs. The seemingly inexhaustible supply has resulted in fierce competition by vendors ranging from market stalls to high-end jewelry shops.

o **Handicrafts:** Although many of the items you will see in island souvenir shops are actually made in Asia, locally produced handicrafts are among the best buys. The most widespread are hats, mats, and baskets woven of pandanus leaves or other fibers, usually by women who have maintained this ancient art to a high degree. Woodcarvings are also popular, especially those from the Marquesas Islands. Many carvings in some large stores, however, tend to be produced for the tourist trade and often lack the imagery of bygone days; some may also be machine-produced these days.

o **Tropical Clothing:** Colorful hand-screened, hand-blocked, and hand-dyed fabrics are very popular in the islands for making dresses or the wraparound skirt known as *pareu*. Many *pareus* are hand-painted, some almost works of art. Others are produced when heat-sensitive dyes are applied by hand to gauzelike cotton, which is then laid in the sun for several hours. Flowers, leaves, and other designs are placed on the fabric, and as the heat of the sun darkens and sets the dyes, the shadows from these objects leave their images behind on the finished product.

THE best DIVING & SNORKELING

All the islands have excellent scuba diving and snorkeling, and all but a few of the resorts have their own dive operations or can easily make arrangements with a local company.

The lagoons in French Polynesia are known less for colorful soft corals than for the wide variety of sea life they contain. Both the number and variety of colorful tropical fish are astounding. Stingrays and manta rays are prevalent, and some in the Society Island lagoons are quite friendly to humans, the result of having been hand-fed (you'll see them hanging around the waterside restaurants after dark, hoping for handouts).

Rare is the diver who doesn't encounter sharks here, though most will be of the relatively harmless reef varieties—blacktip, silvertip, whitetip, and gray. The most visited islands now have shark-feeding encounters (see "The Best Offbeat Travel Experiences" at the end of this chapter). Hammerheads and other large sharks live outside the reef and in the passes leading into the lagoons.

Most dive sites are along or just outside the barrier reefs and within short boat rides of the resorts.

If you like to snorkel, you're in for a few treats, whether on a shark-feeding excursion with other tourists or just swimming off your hotel beach. In some cases, snorkelers can go out with scuba divers.

The best diving and snorkeling are at **Rangiroa, Tikehau, Manihi,** and **Fakarava** in the Tuamotu Archipelago, where the huge lagoons harbor an incredible variety of fish and sharks. Go to Rangiroa to see sharks; go to the others to see more fish than you ever imagined existed. See chapter 11.

The atolls are also home to heart-stopping "ride the rip" dives and snorkeling trips, on which you literally ride the tidal current through the passes into the lagoons. See "The Best Offbeat Travel Experiences," below.

THE best SAILING

Sailboats based on Tahiti and Moorea will take you out for a spin, or even to the late Marlon Brando's island of Tetiaroa, but the best sailing here is among the Leeward Islands of Raiatea, Tahaa, Bora Bora, and Huahine. Having arrived here originally via yacht from the East Coast of the United States, I can say without qualification that the sailing among the Leeward Islands is world-class.

French Polynesia's center for charter-yacht sailing is **Raiatea,** where rentals are available from several companies (including The Moorings, the outstanding American company).

Raiatea shares a lagoon with **Tahaa,** its rugged sister island. Tahaa is indented with long bays sheltering numerous picturesque anchorages, and you can sail completely around it without leaving the lagoon.

If you are reasonably skilled at "blue water" offshore sailing, both Bora Bora and Huahine are just 32km (20 miles) away, albeit in opposite directions. Most of the charter-boat companies will let you leave the boat in either Huahine or Bora Bora, so you won't have to beat back to Raiatea after your week or so of knocking around the islands.

Details are in "Sailing" under "The Active Traveler" in chapter 3.

THE best OFFBEAT TRAVEL EXPERIENCES

Some cynics might say that a visit to French Polynesia itself is an offbeat experience, but there are three things to do here that are really unusual.

o **Getting Asked to Dance** (everywhere): I've seen so many traditional dance shows that I now stand by the rear door, ready to beat a quick escape before those lovely young women in grass skirts can grab my hand and force me to make a fool of myself trying to gyrate my hips up on the stage. It's part of the tourist experience at all resorts, and it's all in good fun.

o **Swimming with the Sharks** (Bora Bora): A key attraction in Bora Bora's magnificent lagoon is to snorkel with a guide, who actually feeds a school of sharks as they thrash around in a frenzy. I prefer to leave this one to the Discovery Channel. See p. 188.

o **Riding the Rip** (Rangiroa and Manihi): Divers and snorkelers will never forget the flying sensation as they ride the strong currents ripping through passes into the lagoons at Rangiroa and Manihi. See "Rangiroa" and "Manihi" in chapter 11.

TAHITI & FRENCH POLYNESIA IN DEPTH

One of my editors once commented that I mention several bars and nightclubs in Papeete, French Polynesia's busy capital city, but not on Bora Bora, Moorea, and elsewhere. "Isn't there nightlife on the other islands?" she queried.

"Not really," I answered. "Here's how it works in French Polynesia: You get up in the morning, you look at an unbelievably beautiful island over breakfast, you play in the blue lagoon all day, you come back to your thatched-roof bungalow for a shower, and you have a fine French meal followed by a hip-swinging Tahitian dance show. It's all over by 9pm. If you don't know how to occupy yourselves between 9pm and midnight on your honeymoon, you need more than travel advice."

My reply may have been in jest, but many people do choose to honeymoon on these gorgeous islands, and for good reason. These perpetually warm, languid specks of land on a vast ocean are the perfect places for passion—as I can vouch from personal experience!

Romance is inspired not only by the beauty of the islands but by the prevailing attitude here. You are likely to encounter women with bare breasts on the beaches, for these islands are French as well as Polynesian. Unlike other South Pacific island countries, where the preaching of puritanical 19th-century missionaries took deeper root, here you will discover a marvelous combination of French laissez faire and Tahitian *joie de vivre* born of a hedonistic Polynesian past.

Understanding that storied past, the culture and language of the marvelous people, and the fascinating flora and fauna will add an immeasurable richness to your visit. That's especially true of Tahiti, the first South Pacific island to be examined in detail by Europeans and historically the most significant island in the region.

The material in this chapter will give you an in-depth look at the islands. I strongly recommend you read it before beginning your own exploration of these most intriguing destinations.

FRENCH POLYNESIA TODAY

One reason there is so little nightlife in the islands is that Polynesians traditionally go to bed early so they can get up with the sun. This lifestyle comes in handy on Tahiti, where they rise before the crack of dawn to make the 2-hour-plus commute to work in Papeete. That's right: While you're sleeping late on your honeymoon, many thousands of islanders are sitting in Tahiti's choking traffic.

Therein lies one of the paradoxes of French Polynesia today. On the one hand are the outer islands with their small populations, crystal-clear lagoons, and resorts designed with love (or at least sex) in mind. On the other are Papeete and its suburbs, a busy metropolitan area that—except for the phenomenal scenery surrounding it—could be on the French Riviera.

On another hand, wealthy French expatriates build luxury homes high into the hills overlooking the city, while many Tahitians live in homes of plywood and tin jammed into crowded neighborhoods. French Polynesia is governed by France, but about half of the local population consistently votes for politicians favoring independence from France.

Although those are the realities, they bear little resemblance to the fantasy world most of us experience while here. Instead, we're whisked away to resorts designed to make us forget our own realities back home, while barely seeing the real world around us here.

However, one thing we all do experience is the warmth and friendliness of the Polynesian people, which no amount of money, vehicles, or political bickering has managed to change.

Government

French Polynesia is an overseas territory of France, which sends a high commissioner from Paris and controls foreign affairs, defense, justice, internal security, and currency. French Polynesians have considerable autonomy over their internal affairs through a 49-member Assembly, which selects a president, the country's highest-ranking local official. The local legislature decides all issues that are not reserved for the metropolitan French government.

Local voters also cast ballots in French presidential elections and send two deputies and two senators to the French parliament in Paris.

The city of Papeete and a few other communities have local police forces, but the French gendarmes control most law enforcement (they are as likely to be from Martinique as from Moorea).

Local politics breaks down generally into two camps: those who favor remaining under French control, but with increased local autonomy (that is, pro-autonomy), and those who seek complete independence from France (pro-independence). The two sides have swapped control of the local government several times in recent years, and the "musical chairs" is likely to continue until France changes the electoral system. Except for an occasional demonstration or labor stoppage, the instability has had little effect on visitors. See "A Look at the Past," below.

The Economy

French Polynesia has only two significant industries: tourism and black pearls, and both have suffered since the worldwide Great Recession began with the crash of September 2008.

Tourism has been especially hard hit. More than 200,000 visitors arrived in these islands each year before the crash, making it the largest earner. That number has dropped by as much as 30%, sending the industry into a tailspin. The islands experienced a hotel building boom a decade ago, mostly high-end luxury resorts designed to attract millionaire tourists. But with fewer millionaires roaming the globe, some of those new properties—and some venerable ones, too—have shut their doors, either temporarily or for good. Others may be closed by the time you plan your trip.

Some US$150 million worth of black pearls are exported annually, mostly to Japan. The gorgeous little orbs are on every visitor's shopping list (see "Buying Your Black Pearl," in chapter 5).

Vanilla, copra, coconut-oil cosmetics (you will see the *Monoi* brand everywhere), and an elixir made from the *noni* fruit are minor exports (most of the *noni* processed here is imported from Fiji).

Likewise, about 80% of all food consumed here is imported, which helps explain why prices are so high in the grocery stores.

A better explanation is the more than 20€ billion France pours in each year. That includes some 150€ million a year from an economic restructuring fund, set up after France closed its nuclear testing facility in 1996, to foster self-sufficiency by developing the local infrastructure. The fund has paid for public-works projects that have transformed the waterfronts in Papeete and on Raiatea, improved the roads, and built new schools, hospitals, and docks.

> ### Bougainville & *Bougainvillea*
>
> After leaving Tahiti, the French explorer Antoine de Bougainville discovered several islands in Samoa and the Solomon Islands, of which the island of Bougainville—now part of Papua New Guinea—still bears his name. So does the bright tropical shrub known as bougainvillea.

In addition, the local government set up highly favorable tax and investment laws that have spurred hotel construction. Bora Bora got most of the new properties, but islands such as Tahaa and Fakarava also have major resorts for the first time.

All this money translates into an artificially high standard of living. The *minimum* wage here is more than US$1,500 a month plus benefits, compared to about US$850 not including benefits in the U.S. Consequently, prices are high for everyone.

If there is a saving grace for us visitors, it's the lack of both required tipping and a direct sales tax, which together can add 25% or more to your bill in Hawaii and elsewhere.

A LOOK AT THE PAST

The South Pacific Ocean came to Europe's attention during the latter half of the 18th century with the theory that an unknown southern land—a *terra australis incognita*—lay somewhere in the Southern Hemisphere. It must be there to balance the northern continents, the theory went, for otherwise the unbalanced earth would wobble off into space.

King George III of Great Britain took interest in the idea and, in 1764, sent Capt. John Byron (the poet's grandfather) to the Pacific in HMS *Dolphin*. When Byron came home without discovering *terra australis incognita* (though he found some Tuamotu atolls), King George immediately dispatched Capt. Samuel Wallis in the *Dolphin*.

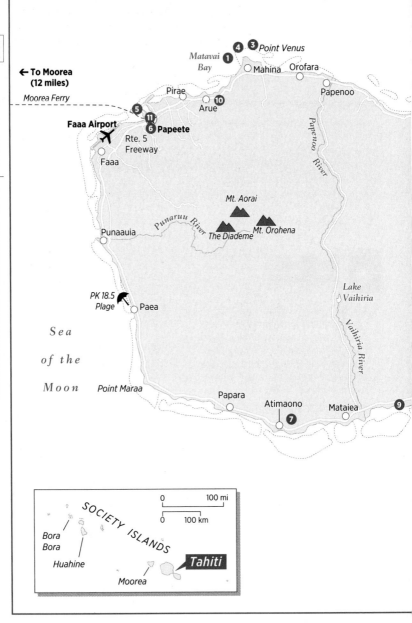

← **To Moorea**
(12 miles)

Moorea Ferry

Pirae

⑩ **Arue**

⑤

⑪

⑥ **Papeete**

Faaa Airport ✈

Rte. 5
Freeway

Faaa

① *Matavai
Bay*

④

③ *Point Venus*

Mahina   **Orofara**

Papenoo

*Papenoo
River*

Mt. Aorai

The Diademe   *Mt. Orohena*

Punaauia

Punaruu River

*Lake
Vaihiria*

Vaihiria River

*PK 18.5
Plage*   **Paea**

Sea

of the

Moon

Point Maraa

Papara

Atimaono

⑦

Mataiea

⑨

0   100 mi

0   100 km

SOCIETY ISLANDS

*Bora
Bora*

Huahine

Moorea

Tahiti

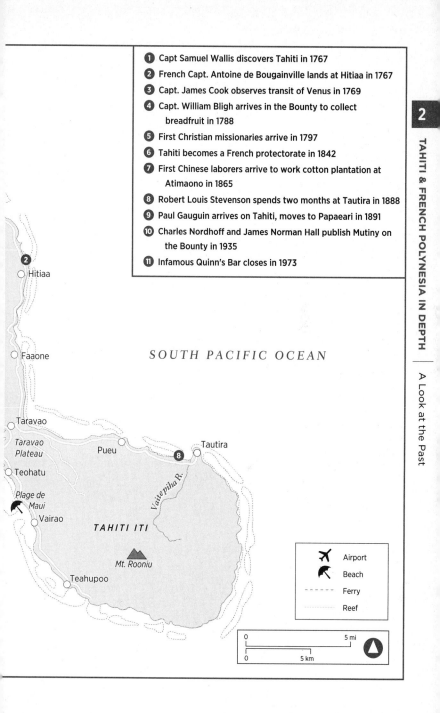

1. Capt Samuel Wallis discovers Tahiti in 1767
2. French Capt. Antoine de Bougainville lands at Hitiaa in 1767
3. Capt. James Cook observes transit of Venus in 1769
4. Capt. William Bligh arrives in the Bounty to collect breadfruit in 1788
5. First Christian missionaries arrive in 1797
6. Tahiti becomes a French protectorate in 1842
7. First Chinese laborers arrive to work cotton plantation at Atimaono in 1865
8. Robert Louis Stevenson spends two months at Tautira in 1888
9. Paul Gauguin arrives on Tahiti, moves to Papaeari in 1891
10. Charles Nordhoff and James Norman Hall publish Mutiny on the Bounty in 1935
11. Infamous Quinn's Bar closes in 1973

2 Hitiaa

SOUTH PACIFIC OCEAN

Faaone

Taravao

Taravao Plateau

Pueu

Tautira

8

Teohatu

Vaitepiha R.

Plage de Maui

Vairao

TAHITI ITI

Mt. Rooniu

Teahupoo

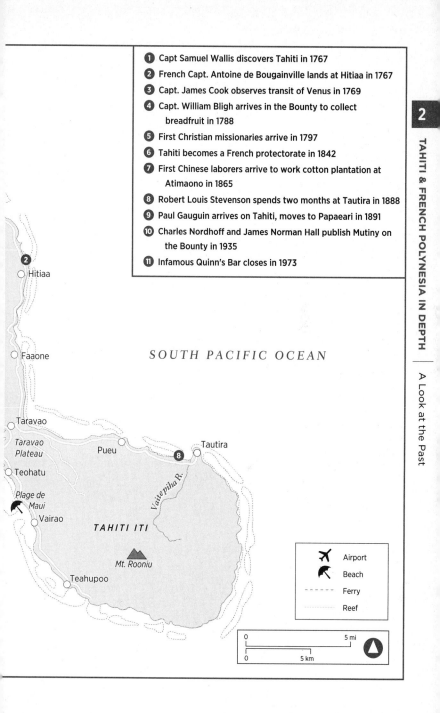

✈ Airport

🏄 Beach

----- Ferry

········· Reef

| 0 | | 5 mi |
| 0 | 5 km | |

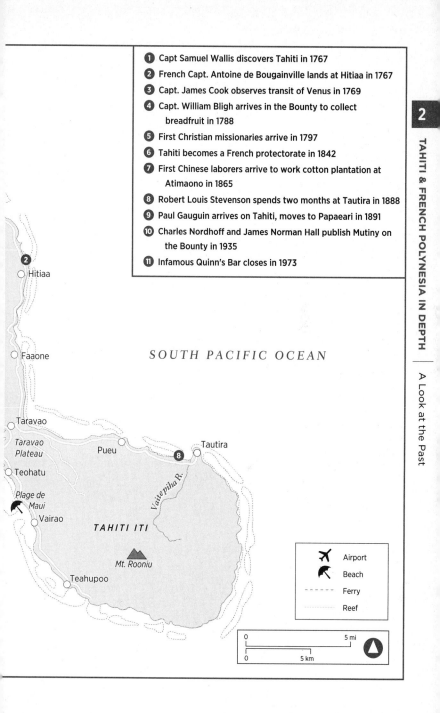

2

 TAHITI & FRENCH POLYNESIA IN DEPTH | A Look at the Past

Instead of a southern continent, Wallis discovered Tahiti. Surely he and his crew could hardly believe their eyes when they sailed into Matavai Bay in 1767 and were greeted by Tahitians in more than 500 canoes, many loaded with pigs, chickens, coconuts, fruit, and topless young women. The latter, Wallis reported, "played a great many droll and wanton tricks" on his scurvy-ridden crew.

Less than a year later, the Tahitians similarly welcomed French explorer Louis Antoine de Bougainville. Although he stayed at Hitiaa, on Tahiti's east coast, for just 10 days, Bougainville was so enchanted by the Venus-like quality of Tahiti's women that he named their island New Cythère—after the Greek island of Cythera, associated with the goddess Aphrodite (Venus).

Bougainville took back to France a young Tahitian named Ahutoru, who became a sensation in Paris as living proof of Jean-Jacques Rousseau's theory that man was, at his best, a "noble savage." Indeed, Bougainville and Ahutoru contributed mightily to Tahiti's hedonistic image.

Captain Cook's Tours

After Wallis returned to England, the Lords of the Admiralty put a young lieutenant named James Cook in command of a converted collier and sent him to Tahiti. A product of the Age of Enlightenment, Cook was a master navigator, a mathematician, an astronomer, and a practical physician who became the first captain of any ship to prevent scurvy among his crewmen by feeding them fresh fruits and vegetables. His ostensible mission was to observe the transit of Venus—the planet, that is—across the sun, an astronomical event that would not occur again until 1874, but which, if measured from widely separated points on the globe, would enable scientists for the first time to determine longitude on the earth's surface. Cook's second, highly secret mission was to find the elusive southern continent.

Cook set up an observation point at the end of a sandy peninsula on Tahiti's north shore, a locale he appropriately named Point Venus. His measurements of Venus

DATELINE

6th century Polynesians arrive
A.D. (estimated time).

1595 Alvaro de Mendaña discovers the Marquesas Islands.

1606 Pedro Fernández de Quirós sails through the Tuamotus.

1765 Searching for *terra australis incognita,* Capt. John Byron on HMS *Dolphin* finds some Tuamotu islands, but misses Tahiti.

1767 Also on HMS *Dolphin,* Capt. Samuel Wallis discovers Tahiti and claims it for King George III.

1768 French Capt. Antoine de Bougainville arrives on Tahiti.

1769 Capt. James Cook arrives to observe the transit of Venus on the first of his three voyages of discovery.

1788 HMS *Bounty* under Capt. William Bligh arrives and then takes breadfruit to the Caribbean.

1789 Lt. Fletcher Christian leads the mutiny on the *Bounty.*

1797 London Missionary Society emissaries arrive, looking for converts.

were somewhat less than useful, but his observations of Tahiti, made over 6 months, were of immense importance in understanding the "noble savages" who lived there.

Using Tahiti as a base, Cook went on to discover the Society Islands northwest of Tahiti and the Australs to the south, and then fully explored the coasts of New Zealand and eastern Australia. After nearly sinking his ship on the Great Barrier Reef, he left the South Pacific through the strait between Australia and Papua New Guinea, which he named for his ship, the *Endeavor*. He returned to London in 1771.

During two subsequent voyages, Cook discovered several other islands, among them what are now known as Fiji, the Cook Islands, Tonga, Niue, New Caledonia, and Norfolk Island. His ships were the first to sail below the Antarctic Circle. On his third voyage in 1778–79, he traveled to the Hawaiian Islands and explored the northwest coast of North America until ice in the Bering Strait turned him back. He returned to the Big Island of Hawaii, where, on February 14, 1779, he was killed during a petty skirmish with the islanders.

With the exception of the Hawaiians who smashed his skull, Captain Cook was revered throughout the Pacific. He treated the islanders fairly and respected their traditions. The Polynesian chiefs looked upon him as one of their own. Cook's Bay on Moorea bears his name.

Mutiny on the Bounty

Based on reports by Cook and others about the abundance of breadfruit, a head-size, potato-like fruit that grows on trees throughout the islands, a group of West Indian planters asked King George III if he would be so kind as to transport the trees from Tahiti to Jamaica as a cheap source of food for the slaves. The king dispatched Capt. William Bligh, who had been one of Cook's navigators and was later in command of HMS *Bounty* in 1787. One of Bligh's officers was a former shipmate named Fletcher Christian.

Their story is one of history's great sea yarns.

1827	Queen Pomare IV succeeds to the throne.		He later writes *Omoo* about his adventures.
1837	Protestants deny French Catholic priests permission to land. Irate France demands full reparations.	1844–48	Tahitians wage guerrilla war against the French.
1838	Queen reluctantly signs ultimatum of French Adm. du Petit-Thouars.	1847	Queen Pomare acquiesces to full French protection.
1841	French traders trick Tahitian chiefs into asking for French protection. They later disavow it.	1862	Irish adventurer William Stewart starts a cotton plantation at Atimaono.
1842	Tahiti becomes a French protectorate. Herman Melville jumps ship, spends time in the *Calaboosa Beretane* (British jail).	1865	The first 329 Chinese people arrive from Hong Kong to work Stewart's plantation, which fails. Most of the Chinese people stay.

continues

The *Bounty* was late arriving in Tahiti, so Christian and the crew frolicked on Tahiti for 6 months, waiting for the next breadfruit season. Christian and some of the crew apparently enjoyed the island's women and easygoing lifestyle, for on the way home they staged a mutiny on April 28, 1789, off the Ha'apai islands in Tonga. Christian set Bligh and 18 of his loyal officers and crewmen adrift with a compass, a cask of water, and a few provisions. Bligh and his men miraculously rowed the *Bounty's* longboat some 4,830km (3,000 miles) to the Dutch East Indies, where they hitched a ride back to England.

> ### Recovering the *Bounty's* Rudder
>
> Sunk by the mutineers in 1789, HMS *Bounty* remained in its watery grave until it was discovered by a *National Geographic* expedition in the 1950s. The *Bounty's* rudder is now on display at the Fiji Museum in Suva.

Meanwhile, Christian sailed the *Bounty* back to Tahiti, where he put ashore 25 Bligh loyalists. Christian, eight mutineers, their Tahitian wives, and six Tahitian men then disappeared.

The Royal Navy's HMS *Pandora* eventually rounded up the *Bounty* crewmen still on Tahiti and returned them to England. Three were hanged, four were acquitted, and three were convicted but pardoned.

In 1808, the captain of an American whaling ship happened upon remote Pitcairn Island, between Tahiti and South America, and was astonished when some mixed-race teenagers rowed out and greeted him not in Tahitian but in perfect English. They were the children of Christian and several other mutineers, only one of whom was still alive. The mutineers had fled to the island to avoid the British, bringing a number of Tahitian women with them. About 50 of the mutineers' descendants live on Pitcairn to this day.

Bligh later collected more breadfruit on Tahiti, but his whole venture went for naught when the slaves on Jamaica insisted on rice.

1872 Pierre Loti (Julien Viaud) spends several months on Tahiti. His *The Marriage of Loti* is published 8 years later.	**1903** Paul Gauguin dies at Hiva Oa in the Marquesas. All of eastern Polynesia becomes one French colony.
1877 Queen Pomare IV dies at age 64.	**1914** Two German warships shell Papeete, sinking the French navy's *Zélée*.
1880 King Pomare V abdicates in return for pensions for himself, his family, and his mistress. Tahiti becomes a French colony.	
1888 Robert Louis Stevenson spends 2 months at Tautira, on Tahiti Iti.	**1917** W. Somerset Maugham spends several months on Tahiti.
1891 "Fleeing from civilization," the painter Paul Gauguin arrives.	**1933** Charles Nordhoff and James Norman Hall publish *Mutiny on the Bounty,* an instant bestseller.
	1935 Clark Gable and Charles Laughton star in the movie *Mutiny on the Bounty.*

Guns & Whiskey

The *Bounty* mutineers hiding on Tahiti loaned themselves and their guns to rival chiefs, who for the first time were able to extend their control beyond their home valleys. With the mutineers' help, a chief named Pomare II came to control half of Tahiti and all of Moorea.

The U.S. ship that found the mutineers' retreat at Pitcairn was one of many whalers roaming the South Pacific in the early 1800s. Their ruffian crews made dens of iniquity of several South Pacific ports, including Papeete and Nuku Hiva in what is now French Polynesia. Many crewmen jumped ship and lived on the islands, some of them even casting their lots—and their guns—with rival chiefs during tribal wars. With their assistance, some chiefs were able to extend their power over entire islands or groups of islands.

Along with the whalers came traders in search of sandalwood, pearls, shells, and sea cucumbers (known as *bêches-de-mer*), which they traded for beads, cloth, whiskey, and guns and then sold at high prices in China. Some established stores, which became the catalysts for Western-style towns. The merchants brought more guns and alcohol to people who had never used them before.

While the traders were building towns, other arrivals were establishing coconut and cotton plantations. With the native islanders disinclined to work, Chinese indentured laborers were brought to a cotton plantation in Tahiti in the 1860s. After it failed, some of the Chinese stayed

> ### First Novels
>
> One deserter who jumped ship in the Marquesas Islands and later went to Tahiti, in the early 1820s, was Herman Melville. He returned to New England and wrote two books, *Typee* and *Omoo*, based on his exploits. They were the start of his illustrious literary career.

1942 U.S. Marines build the territory's first airstrip on Bora Bora.

1960 Tahiti-Faaa International Airport opens, turning Tahiti into a jet-set destination. Marlon Brando arrives to film a second movie version of *Mutiny on the Bounty.*

1963 France chooses Mururoa as its nuclear testing site.

1966 France explodes the first nuclear bomb aboveground at Mururoa.

1973 Infamous Quinn's Bar closes and is replaced by a shopping center.

1977 France grants limited self-rule to French Polynesia.

1984 Local autonomy statute enacted by French parliament.

1992 France halts nuclear testing, hurting local economy.

1995 Conservative French Pres. Jacques Chirac permits six more underground nuclear explosions; antinuclear riots take place in Papeete; Japanese boycott Tahiti tourism.

1996 France halts nuclear testing, signs Treaty of Rarotonga (declaring South Pacific to be nuclear-free), and tells French Polynesia to start earning its own way.

continues

and became farmers and merchants. Their descendants now form the commercial class of French Polynesia.

The Fatal Impact

The European discoverers brought many changes to the islands, starting with iron, which the Tahitians had never seen. The Tahitians figured out right away that iron was much harder than stone and shells, and that they could swap pigs, breadfruit, bananas, and the affections of their young women for it. So many iron nails soon disappeared from the *Dolphin* that Captain Wallis restricted his men to the ship out of fear it would fall apart in Matavai Bay. A rudimentary form of monetary economy was introduced to Polynesia for the first time, and the English word "money" entered the Tahitian language as *moni*.

Much more devastating European imports were diseases such as measles, influenza, pneumonia, and syphilis, to which the islanders had no resistance. Captain Cook estimated Tahiti's population at some 200,000 in 1769. By 1810, it had dropped to fewer than 8,000.

Bringing the Word of God

The reports of the islands by Cook and Bougainville may have brought word of noble savages living in paradise to some people in Europe; to others, they heralded heathens to be rescued from hell. So while alcohol and diseases were destroying the islanders' bodies, a stream of missionaries arrived on the scene to save their souls.

The "opening" of the South Pacific coincided with a fundamentalist religious revival in England, and it wasn't long before the London Missionary Society (LMS) was on the scene in Tahiti. Its missionaries, who arrived in 1797, were the first Protestant missionaries to leave England for a foreign country. They chose Tahiti because there "the difficulties were least."

1997 Spurred by economic restructuring funds from Paris, the first of several new hotels are built, and Papeete waterfront reconstruction begins.

1999 Local officials propose increased autonomy from France.

2001 Longtime pro-autonomy Gaston Flosse is reelected as president, continuing 20-year control of local government.

2004 French Polynesia becomes an overseas "collective" of France with new legislative assembly. Pro-independence leader Oscar Temaru is elected president by a narrow margin, holds office for 4 months until no-confidence vote returns Flosse to power.

2005 Special elections on Tahiti and Moorea return Temaru to the presidency. He calls for independence from France over 15- to 20-year period.

2006 Votes of no confidence replace Temaru with Gaston Tong Sang, pro-autonomy mayor of Bora Bora.

2007 French Polynesia becomes an "overseas community" of France.

Already believing in a supreme being at the head of a hierarchy of lesser gods, many Polynesians quickly converted to Christianity. With the exception of Roman Catholic priests serving in the Marquesas Islands, the puritanical missionaries demanded the destruction of all tikis, the stylized statues representing ancestors, which they regarded as idols. With the exception of authentic Marquesan carvings, most tikis carved for the tourist souvenir trade today resemble those of New Zealand, where the more liberal Anglican missionaries were less demanding.

The missionaries in French Polynesia also insisted that most heathen temples (known as *maraes*) be abandoned. Many have now been restored, however, and can be visited.

The Tricked Queen

The Protestant missionaries enjoyed a monopoly until the first Roman Catholic priests arrived from France in the 1830s. The Protestants immediately saw a threat, and in 1836 they engineered the interlopers' expulsion by Queen Pomare IV, the illegitimate daughter of Pomare II, who had succeeded to her father's throne.

> ### Impressions
>
> *It would have been far better for these people never to have known us.*
> —Capt. James Cook, 1769

When word of this outrage reached Paris, France demanded a guarantee that Frenchmen would thereafter be treated as the "most favored foreigners" on Tahiti. Queen Pomare politely agreed, but as soon as the warship left Papeete, she sent a letter to Queen Victoria, asking for British protection. Britain declined to interfere, which in 1842 opened the door for a Frenchman to trick several Tahitian chiefs into signing a document that in effect made Tahiti a French protectorate.

2008	Gaston Flosse is briefly returned to presidency in coalition with Temaru, who serves as assembly speaker, before Tong Sang is restored to power.
2009-2010	Control of local government seesaws between Tong Sang and Temaru. Neither is able to stem a depression in the tourism industry.

SEXY skin

The United States isn't the only place where it's cool to have a tattoo. With their increasing interest in ancient Polynesian ways, known as *maohi,* many young Tahitian men and women are getting theirs—but not necessarily with modern electric needles.

The 18th-century explorers from Europe were amazed to find many Polynesians on Tahiti and throughout the South Pacific who were covered from face to ankle with a plethora of geometric and floral designs. In his journal, Capt. James Cook described in detail the excruciatingly painful tattoo procedure, in which natural dyes are hammered into the skin by hand. The repetitive tapping of the mallet gave rise to the Tahitian word *tatau,* which became "tattoo" in English.

Members of the opposite sex rejected anyone with plain skin, which may explain why members of Cook's crew were so willing to endure the torture to get theirs. At any rate, thus began the tradition of the tattooed sailor.

Appalled at the sexual aspects of tattoos, the missionaries prohibited the practice on Tahiti in the early 1800s. Although the art continued in the remote Marquesas and in Samoa, by 1890 there were no tattooed natives left in the Society Islands.

When a British anthropologist undertook a study of tattooing in 1900, the only specimen he could find was on the skin of a Tahitian sailor, who died in England in 1816. Before he was buried, an art-loving physician removed his hide and donated it to the Royal College of Surgeons.

Queen Pomare retreated to Raiatea, which was not under French control, and continued to resist. On Tahiti, her subjects launched an armed rebellion against the French. This French-Tahitian war continued until 1846, when the last native stronghold was captured and the remnants of their guerrilla bands retreated to Tahiti Iti, the island's eastern peninsula. A monument to the fallen Tahitians now stands beside the round-island road near the airport at Faaa, the village still noted for its strong pro-independence sentiment.

Giving up the struggle, the queen returned to Papeete in 1847 and ruled as a figurehead until her death 30 years later. Her son, Pomare V, remained on the throne for 3 more years until abdicating in return for a sizable French pension for himself, his family, and his mistress. In 1903, all of eastern Polynesia was consolidated into a single colony known as French Oceania. In 1957, its status was changed to the overseas territory of French Polynesia.

A Blissful Backwater

French Polynesia remained an idyllic backwater until the early 1960s, except for periodic invasions by artists and writers. French painter Paul Gauguin gave up his family and his career as a Parisian stockbroker and arrived in 1891; he spent his days reproducing Tahiti's colors and people on canvas until he died in 1903 on Hiva Oa, in the Marquesas Islands. W. Somerset Maugham, Jack London, Robert Louis Stevenson, Rupert Brooke, Zane Grey, and other writers added to Tahiti's romantic reputation during the early years of the 20th century.

In 1932, two young Americans—Charles Nordhoff and James Norman Hall—published *Mutiny on the Bounty,* which quickly became a bestseller. Three years later, MGM released the first movie version, with Clark Gable and Charles Laughton in the roles of Christian and Bligh, respectively. Hall's homestead is now a museum on Tahiti (p. 93)

In 1942, some 6,000 U.S. sailors and marines quickly built the territory's first airstrip on Bora Bora and remained there throughout World War II. A number of mixed-race Tahitians claim descent from those American troops.

Movies & Bombs

The backwater years ended in 1960, when Tahiti's new international airport opened at Faaa. Marlon Brando and a movie crew arrived shortly thereafter to film a remake of *Mutiny on the Bounty.* This new burst of fame, coupled with the ability to reach Tahiti overnight, transformed the island into a jet-set destination, and hotel construction began in earnest.

Even more changes came in 1963, when France established the *Centre d'Experimentation du Pacifique* and began exploding nuclear bombs on Moruroa and Fangataufa atolls, in the Tuamotus, about 1,127km (700 miles) southeast of Tahiti. A huge support base was constructed on the eastern outskirts of Papeete. Thousands of Polynesians flocked to Tahiti to take the new construction and hotel jobs, which enabled them to earn good money and to experience life in Papeete's fast lane. (Locals joke that so much money was floating around that Papeete had the world's highest per capital consumption of champagne.)

Between 1966 and 1992, the French exploded 210 nuclear weapons at Moruroa and Fangataufa, first in the air and then underground. Their health repercussions are still being debated.

Led by New Zealand, where French secret agents sank the Greenpeace protest ship *Rainbow Warrior* in 1985, many South Pacific island nations vociferously complained about the blasts. That same year, the regional heads of government, including the prime ministers of New Zealand and Australia, adopted the Treaty of Rarotonga, calling for the South Pacific to become a nuclear-free zone.

After a lull, French Pres. Jacques Chirac decided in 1995 to resume nuclear testing, a move that set off worldwide protests, a day of rioting in Papeete, and a Japanese tourist boycott of French Polynesia. After six underground explosions, the French halted further tests, closed their testing facility, and signed the Treaty of Rarotonga.

Picking Up a Few Extra Bucks

Neither Clark Gable nor Charles Laughton came to Tahiti to film the 1935 version of *Mutiny on the Bounty.* While background scenes were shot on Tahiti, they actually performed on Catalina Island, off Southern California. The Mexican actress Maria "Movita" Castenada, who played the chief's young daughter, was later married to Marlon Brando, star of the 1962 version. A young actor named James Cagney, who was vacationing on Catalina at the time, picked up a few extra bucks by playing a sailor for a day.

To Be—or Not to Be—Independent

In 1977, the French parliament created the elected Territorial Assembly with powers over the local budget. A high commissioner sent from Paris, however, retained authority over defense, foreign affairs, immigration, the police, civil service, communications, and secondary education.

Local politics have long centered on the question of whether the islands should have even more autonomy while remaining French, or whether they should become an independent nation. Politicians have been equally divided roughly into "pro-autonomy" and "pro-independence" camps. On the other hand, neither side wants to give up all that money from Paris!

An additional grant of local control followed in 1984, and in 2004 the local Assembly gained increased powers over land ownership, labor relations, civil aviation, immigration, education, and international affairs; that is, within the South Pacific region. The legal status changed again in 2007, this time to an "overseas community," primarily so that France could enact laws specific to its territories and not have them apply equally in metropolitan France.

The 2004 law called for fresh Assembly elections. In a surprise upset, a coalition led by Oscar Temaru, the mayor of independence-leaning Faaa, narrowly ousted longtime pro-autonomy President Gaston Flosse, who had ruled with an iron fist for more than 20 years—during which he also made several fortunes.

Temaru, who espouses independence over a 15- to 20-year period, was in office less than 5 months before being toppled by Flosse, who ruled for only 4 months until special elections on Tahiti and Moorea returned Temaru to the presidency. Temaru hung on until ousted at the end of 2006 by Gaston Tong Sang, the mayor of Bora Bora and then an ally of Gaston Flosse (they have since split). The presidency again became a game of musical chairs in 2008, when Flosse and Temaru teamed up to boot Tong Sang, only to see him return less than 2 months later. Since then control has gone back and forth like a ping pong ball. As I write, the mayor of Bora Bora is once again the president of French Polynesia.

THE LAY OF THE LAND & SEA

A somewhat less-than-pious wag once remarked that God made the French Polynesian islands on the sixth day of creation so He would have an extraordinarily beautiful place to rest on the seventh day. Modern geologists have a different view, but the fact remains that the islands and the surrounding sea are possessed of heavenly beauty and a plethora of life forms.

All these islands were formed by molten lava escaping upward through cracks in the earth's crust as it has inched northwestward over "hot spots" of molten magma, which escaped through the crust and built great seamounts. Tahiti and the other Society Islands, as well as the Marquesas, are called "high islands" because they have mountains soaring into the clouds. In contrast, the atolls of the Tuamotu Archipelago are pancake-flat because they were formed when the islands sank back into the sea, leaving only a thin necklace of coral islets to circumscribe their lagoons and mark their original boundaries. Bora Bora and Maupiti are examples of partially sunken islands, with the remnants of mountains sticking up in their lagoons.

Flora & Fauna

Most species of plants and animals native to the islands originated in Southeast Asia and worked their way eastward across the Pacific, by natural distribution or in the company of humans. The number of native species diminishes the farther east one goes, so French Polynesia has fewer species than Fiji and other islands to the west.

Very few local plants or animals came from the Americas, the one notable exception being the sweet potato, which may have been brought back from South America by voyaging Polynesians.

PLANTS

In addition to the west-to-east differences, the flora changes according to each island's topography. The mountainous islands make rain from the moist trade winds and thus possess a greater variety of plants. Their interior highlands are covered with ferns, native bush, or grass. The low atolls, on the other hand, get sparse rainfall and support little other than scrub bush and coconut palms.

Ancient settlers brought coconut palms, breadfruit, taro, paper mulberry, pepper (*kava*), and bananas to the isolated mid-ocean islands because of their usefulness as food or fiber. Accordingly, they are generally found in the inhabited areas of the islands and not so often in the interior bush.

With a few indigenous exceptions, such as the *tiare* (Tahiti gardenia), tropical flowers also worked their way east in the company of humans. Bougainvillea, hibiscus, *allamanda*, poinsettia, poinciana (the flame tree), croton, frangipani (plumeria), ixora, canna, and water lilies all give colorful testament to the islanders' love for flowers of every hue in the rainbow. The aroma of the white, yellow, or pink frangipani is so sweet, it's used as perfume here.

ANIMALS & BIRDS

The fruit bat, or "flying fox," and some species of insect-eating bats are the only mammals native to the islands. The early settlers introduced dogs, chickens, pigs, rats, and mice. There are few land snakes or other reptiles in the islands. The notable exceptions are geckos and skinks, those little lizards that seem to be everywhere.

The number and variety of species of bird life also diminish as you go eastward. Most land birds live in the bush away from settlements and the accompanying cats, dogs, and rats. For this reason, the birds most likely to be seen are terns, boobies, herons, petrels, noddies, and others that earn

> ### Useful Little Lizards
>
> Don't go berserk when a gecko walks upside-down across the ceiling of your bungalow: These little lizards are harmless and actually perform a valuable service by eating mosquitoes and other insects.

their livelihoods from the sea. Of the introduced birds, the Indian myna exists in the greatest numbers. Brought to the South Pacific in the early 20th century to control insects, the myna quickly became a noisy nuisance in its own right. Mynas are extremely adept at stealing the toast off your breakfast table.

Sea Life

The tropical South Pacific Ocean teems with sea life. More than 600 species of coral—10 times the number found in the Caribbean—form the great reefs that make the islands a mecca to divers. Billions of tiny coral polyps build their own skeletons on top of those left by their ancestors, until they reach the level of low tide. Then they grow outward, extending the edge of the reef. The old skeletons are white, and the living polyps present a rainbow of colors; they grow best and are most colorful in the clear, salty water on the outer edge or in channels, where the tides and waves wash fresh seawater along and across the reef. A reef can grow as much as 2 inches a year in ideal conditions. Although pollution, rising seawater temperature, and a proliferation of crown-of-thorns starfish have greatly hampered reef growth—and beauty—in parts of the South Pacific, there are still many areas where the color and variety of corals are unmatched.

Like gigantic aquariums, a plethora of tropical fish and other marine life fill most of the lagoons. Many hotel boutiques and bookstores in the main towns sell pamphlets containing photographs and descriptions of the creatures that will peer into your face mask. Not all sea creatures are harmless, so be sure to read "Be Careful in the Water," (p. 61).

Humpback whales migrate to the islands from June to October, and sea turtles lay their eggs on some beaches from November through February. Sea turtles and whales are on the list of endangered species, and many countries, including the United States, prohibit the importation of their shells, bones, and teeth.

THE ISLANDERS

Polynesians had been living on these tiny outposts for hundreds of years before Europeans had the foggiest notion that the Pacific Ocean existed. Even after Vasco Nuñez de Balboa crossed the Isthmus of Panama and discovered this largest of oceans in 1513, and Ferdinand Magellan sailed across it in 1521, more than 250 years went by before Europeans paid much attention to the islands that lay upon it.

The early European explorers were astounded to find the far-flung South Pacific islands inhabited by peoples who shared similar physical characteristics, languages, and cultures. How had these people—who lived a late–Stone Age existence and had no written languages—crossed the vast Pacific to these remote islands long before Christopher Columbus had the courage to sail out of sight of land? Where had they come from? Those questions baffled the early European explorers, and they continue to intrigue scientists and scholars today.

The First Settlers

The late Thor Heyerdahl drifted in his raft *Kon Tiki* from South America to French Polynesia in 1947, to prove his theory that the Polynesians came from the Americas. Bolstered by recent DNA studies linking the Polynesians to Taiwan, however, experts now believe that the Pacific Islanders have their roots in eastern Asia. The generally accepted view is that during the Ice Age, a race of early humans known as Australoids migrated from Southeast Asia to Papua New Guinea and Australia, when those two countries were joined as one landmass. Another group, the Papuans, arrived from Southeast Asia between 5,000 and 10,000 years ago. Several thousands of years later, a lighter-skinned race known as Austronesians pushed the Papuans inland and out into the more eastern South Pacific islands.

The most tangible remains of the early Austronesians are remnants of pottery, the first shards of which were found during the 1970s in Lapita, a village in New Caledonia. Probably originating in Papua New Guinea, Lapita pottery spread east as far as Tonga, but by the time European explorers arrived in the 1770s, gourds and coconut shells were the only crockery used by the Polynesians, who cooked their meals underground and ate with their fingers off banana leaves.

The Polynesians

The Polynesians' ancestors stopped in Fiji on their migration from Southeast Asia, but later pushed on into the eastern South Pacific. Archaeologists now believe that they settled in Tonga and Samoa more than 3,000 years ago and then slowly fanned out to colonize the vast Polynesian triangle stretching from New Zealand in the south to Hawaii in the north and to Easter Island to the east. In French Polynesia, they landed first in the Marquesas (where the language and culture still have Samoan traces), and then backtracked to Raiatea and the other islands before eventually arriving in Hawaii and New Zealand.

These extraordinary mariners crossed thousands of miles of ocean in large, double-hulled canoes capable of carrying hundreds of people, animals, and plants. They navigated by the stars, the wind, the clouds, the shape of the waves, and the flight pattern of birds—a remarkable achievement for a people who had no written languages.

Their ancestors fought each other with war clubs for thousands of years, and it stands to reason that the biggest, strongest, and quickest survived (many modern Polynesians have become professional football and rugby players). The notion that all Polynesians are fat is incorrect. In the old days, body size did indeed denote wealth and status, but obesity today is more likely attributable to poor diet. On the other hand, village chiefs are still expected to partake of food and drink with anyone who visits to discuss a problem; hence, great weight remains an unofficial marker of social status.

> ## Impressions
>
> *You who like handsome men would find no shortage of them here; they are taller than I, and have limbs like Hercules.*
> —Paul Gauguin, 1891

Tahitian Society

Polynesians developed highly structured societies. On Tahiti, they were highly stratified into three classes: chiefs and priests, landowners, and commoners. Among the commoners was a subclass of slaves, mostly war prisoners. One's position in society was hereditary, with primogeniture the general rule. In general, women were equal to men, although they could not act as priests.

A peculiar separate class of wandering dancers and singers, known as the *Arioi,* traveled about the Society Islands, performing ritual dances and shows—some of them sexually explicit—and living in a state of total sexual freedom. Family values were the least of their concerns; in fact, members immediately killed any children born into their clan.

> ### Impressions
>
> *Now the cunning lay in this, that the Polynesians have rules of hospitality that have all the force of laws; an etiquette of absolute rigidity made it necessary for the people of the village not only to give lodging to the strangers, but to provide them with food and drink for as long as they wished to stay.*
>
> —W. Somerset Maugham, 1921

The Tahitians had no written language, but their life was governed by an elaborate set of rules that would challenge modern legislators' abilities to reduce them to writing. Everyday life was governed by a system based on *tabu,* a rigid list of things a person could or could not do, depending on his or her status in life. *Tabu* and its variants *(tapu, tambu)* are used throughout the South Pacific to mean "do not enter"; from them derives the English word "taboo."

Western principles of ownership have made inroads, but by and large almost everything in Polynesia—especially land—is owned communally by families. In effect, the system is pure communism at the family level. If your brother has a crop of taro and you're hungry, then some of that taro belongs to you. The same principle applies to a can of corned beef sitting on a shelf in a store, which helps explain why most of the grocery shops in French Polynesia are owned by the Chinese. It also explains why you should keep a wary eye on your valuables.

Although some islanders would be considered poor by Western standards, the extended family system insures that few go hungry or sleep without a roof over their head. Most of the thatched roofs in Polynesia today are actually bungalows at the resort hotels; nearly everyone else sleeps under tin. It's little wonder, therefore, that the islands are inhabited for the most part by friendly, peaceable, and extraordinarily courteous people.

A Hierarchy of Gods

The ancient Tahitians worshiped a hierarchy of gods. At its head stood Taaroa, a supreme deity known as Tangaroa in the Cook Islands and Tangaloa in Samoa. *Mana,* or power, came down from the gods to each human, depending on his or her position in society. The highest chiefs had so much *mana* that they were considered godlike, if not actually descended from the gods.

The Tahitians worshipped their gods on *maraes* (ancient temples or meeting places) built of stones. Every family had a small *marae,* which served the same functions as a chapel would today, and villages and entire districts—even islands—built large *maraes* that served not only as places of worship but also as meeting sites. Elaborate religious ceremonies were held on the large central *marae*. Priests prayed that the gods would come down and reside in carved tikis and other objects during the ceremonies (the objects lost all religious meaning afterward). Sacrifices were offered to the gods, sometimes including humans, mostly war prisoners or trouble-makers. Despite the practice of human sacrifice, cannibalism apparently was never practiced in the Society Islands, although it was fairly widespread in the Marquesas.

The souls of the deceased were believed to return to Hawaiki, the homeland from which their Polynesian ancestors had come. In all Polynesian islands, the souls departed for it from the northwest corner of each island. That's in the direction of Asia, from whence their ancestors came.

The Chinese

The outbreak of the American Civil War in 1861 resulted in a worldwide shortage of cotton. In September 1862, an Irish adventurer named William Stewart founded a cotton plantation at Atimaono, Tahiti's only large tract of flat land. The Tahitians weren't the least bit interested in working for Stewart, so he imported a contingent of Chinese laborers. The first 329 of them arrived from Hong Kong in February 1865. Stewart ran into financial difficulties, which were compounded by the drop in cotton prices after the American South resumed production after 1868; this led to the collapse of his empire.

Nothing remains of Stewart's plantation at Atimaono (a golf course now occupies most of the land), but many of his Chinese laborers decided to stay. They grew vegetables for the Papeete market, saved their money, and invested in other businesses. Their descendants and those of subsequent immigrants from China now influence the economy far in excess of their numbers. They run nearly all of French Polynesia's grocery and general merchandise stores, which in French are called *magasins chinois,* or Chinese stores.

THE TAHITIAN LANGUAGE

With the exception of some older Polynesians, everyone speaks **French,** the official language. **Tahitian,** the indigenous language originally of Tahiti and the other Society Islands, is widely spoken by the local Polynesians. Many residents of the Tuamotu Archipelago also speak **Puamotuan,** a dialect similar to Tahitian, and those in the Marquesas have their own language, known as **Marquesasan.**

English is taught as a third language in most schools (and all of those operated by the Chinese community), and it's a prerequisite for getting a hotel job involving

---

A Flower Behind the Ear

Tahitians love to wear flowers tucked behind their ears, which signals the status of their love lives. Behind the left ear means your heart is taken and you are unavailable, while behind the right ear signals you are unattached and available. Flowers behind both ears announce you are married but available, while a backward flower declares you are available immediately!

SEX & THE single polynesian

The puritanical Christian missionaries who began arriving in Tahiti during the late 18th century convinced the islanders that they should clothe their nearly naked bodies. They had less luck, however, when it came to sex. To the islanders, sex was as much a part of life as any other daily activity, and they uninhibitedly engaged in it with a variety of partners from adolescence until marriage.

Even today, they have a somewhat laissez-faire attitude about premarital sex. Every child, whether born in or out of wedlock, is accepted into one of the extended families that are the bedrock of Polynesian society. Mothers, fathers, grandparents, aunts, uncles, and cousins of every degree are all part of the close-knit Polynesian family. Relationships sometimes are so blurred that every adult woman within a mile is known as a child's "auntie"—even the child's mother.

Male transvestitism, homosexuality, and bisexuality are facts of life in Polynesia, where families with a shortage of female offspring will raise young boys as girls. Some of these youths grow up to be heterosexual; others become homosexual or bisexual and, often appearing publicly in women's attire, actively seek out the company of tourists. In Tahitian, these males are known as *mahus*.

guest relations. You can converse in English with your hotel's professional and activities staff, but not necessarily with the housemaids.

Many young Tahitians are eager to learn English, if for no other reason than to understand the lyrics of American songs, which dominate the radio airwaves in French Polynesia. Accordingly, you will find English spoken in shops, restaurants, and other businesses, especially those frequented by tourists. Many French residents here also speak English.

Once you get off the beaten path, however, an ability to speak what I call *français touristique*—tourist French, as in asking directions to the loo—will be very helpful if not outright essential. I really need my schoolbook French on Maupiti and in the Tuamotu and Marquesas islands, where English is not widely spoken.

Not to fear: Tahitians are enormously friendly folk, and most will immediately warm to you when they discover you don't speak French, or that you speak it haltingly or with a pronounced accent.

Tahitian Pronunciation

A little knowledge of Tahitian will also help you correctly pronounce the tongue-tying place names here.

All Polynesian languages, including Tahitian, consist primarily of vowel sounds, which are pronounced in the Roman fashion—that is, *ah, ay, ee, oh,* and *ou,* not *ay, ee, eye, oh,* and *you,* as in English. Almost all vowels are sounded separately. For example, Tahiti's airport is at Faaa, which is pronounced Fah-*ah*-ah, not Fah. Papeete is Pah-pay-*ay*-tay, not Pa-*pee*-tee. Paea is Pah-*ay*-ah.

The consonants used in Tahitian are *f, h, m, n, p, r, t,* and *v.* There are some special rules regarding their sounds, but you'll be understood if you say them as you would in English. One exception is *r,* which is pronounced with a slight click of the tongue at the top of the mouth behind the top front teeth, like an abbreviated version of the rolled *r* in Spanish.

Useful Tahitian Words

To help you impress the locals with what a really friendly tourist you are, here are a few Tahitian words you can use on them:

ENGLISH	TAHITIAN	PRONUNCIATION
hello	ia orana	ee-ah oh-rah-na (sounds like "your honor")
welcome	maeva	mah-ay-vah
goodbye	parahi	pah-rah-hee
good	maitai	my-tie
very good	maitai roa	my-tie-row-ah
thank you	maruru	mah-roo-roo
thank you very much	maruru roa	mah-roo-roo row-ah
good health!	manuia	mah-new-yah
woman	vahine	vah-hee-nay
man	tane	tah-nay
sarong	pareu	pah-ray-oo
small islet	motu	moh-too
take it easy	hare maru	ha-ray mah-roo
fed up	fiu	few

TAHITI IN POPULAR CULTURE

Tahiti and her islands have supplied inspiration for bestselling books since shortly after the first European explorers reported the islands' existence. The number of writers who have penned island stories reads like a who's who of letters: Herman Melville, Robert Louis Stevenson, W. Somerset Maugham, Pierre Loti, Jack London, Zane Grey, James A. Michener, Charles Nordhoff, and James Norman Hall. Several of their novels were turned into movies. Also, television programs have been produced here, including *Survivor: Marquesas* in 2002.

 "Oh-oh"—How to Spell Like a Tahitian

When spelling Tahitian words, many cultural activists advocate the use of apostrophes to indicate glottal stops—those slight pauses between some vowels similar to the tiny break between "Oh-oh!" in English. Moorea, for example, is pronounced Moh-*oh*-ray-ah, with a glottal stop between *Moh* and *oh,* and thus is often spelled Mo'orea. Likewise, you may see Papeete spelled Pape'ete.

Abundant apostrophes already appear in written Tongan and Samoan, but in this book I have used the traditional spellings, with apostrophes appearing for some common nouns and also where they are used in an establishment's name, such as Le Taha'a Private Island & Spa. If you want to spell like a Tahitian, look for a handbook such as D. T. Tyron's *Say It in Tahitian.*

> ### Jotting It Down
>
> No Polynesian language was written until Peter Heywood jotted down a Tahitian vocabulary while awaiting trial for his part in the mutiny on the *Bounty* (he was convicted, but pardoned). The early missionaries who later translated the Bible into Tahitian decided which letters of the Roman alphabet to use to approximate the sounds of the Polynesian languages. These tended to vary from place to place. For example, they used the consonants *t* and *v* in Tahitian. In Hawaiian, which is similar, they used *k* and *w.* The actual Polynesian sounds are somewhere in between.

Artists have been here, too, the most famous being Paul Gauguin, who spent the final years of his life in French Polynesia and whose paintings are almost synonymous with French Polynesia.

Although local youths prefer Polynesian versions of reggae and hip-hop, traditional music is like that played in Hawaii—a blend of the guitar, ukulele, and drums. Most hotels and many restaurants will engage a small band to play traditional music during happy hour and dinner.

Of all the arts, Tahiti is most famous for its hip-swinging traditional dance, the most suggestive performed in all of Polynesia except the nearby Cook Islands (see "A Most Indecent Song & Dance" box, p. 36).

Books

Rather than list the hundreds of books about Tahiti and French Polynesia, I have picked my favorites. A few out-of-print island classics have been reissued in paperback by **Mutual Publishing, LLC,** 125 Center St., Ste. 210, Honolulu, HI 96816 (© **808/732-1709;** fax 808/734-4094; www.mutualpublishing.com).

GENERAL

If you have time for only one book, read *The Lure of Tahiti* (1986). Editor A. Grove Day, himself an islands expert, includes 18 short stories, excerpts from other books, and essays. There is a little here from many of the writers mentioned below, plus selections from captains Cook, Bougainville, and Bligh.

The National Geographic Society's book, *The Isles of the South Pacific* (1971), by Maurice Shadbolt and Olaf Ruhen, and Ian Todd's *Island Realm* (1974) are somewhat out-of-date coffee-table books, but they have lovely color photographs. *Living Corals* (1979), by Douglas Faulkner and Richard Chesher, shows what you will see underwater.

HISTORY & POLITICS

Several early English and French explorers published accounts of their exploits, but *The Journals of Captain James Cook* stand out as the most exhaustive and even-handed. Edited by J. C. Beaglehole, they were published in three volumes (one for each voyage) in 1955, 1961, and 1967. A. Grenfell Price edited many of Cook's key passages and provides short transitional explanations in *The Explorations of Captain James Cook in the Pacific* (1971).

The explorers' visits and their consequences in Tahiti, Australia, and Antarctica are the subject of Alan Moorehead's excellent study *The Fatal Impact: The Invasion of the South Pacific, 1767–1840* (1966), a colorful tome loaded with sketches and paintings of the time.

Three other very readable books trace Tahiti's post-discovery history. Robert Langdon's *Tahiti: Island of Love* (1979) takes the island's story up to 1977. David Howarth's *Tahiti: A Paradise Lost* (1985) covers more thoroughly the same early ground covered by Langdon, but stops with France's taking possession in 1842. *The Rape of Tahiti* (1983), by Edward Dodd, covers the island from prehistory to 1900.

Mad About Islands (1987), by A. Grove Day, follows the island exploits of literary figures Herman Melville, Robert Louis Stevenson, Jack London, and W. Somerset Maugham. Also included are Charles Nordhoff and James Norman Hall, coauthors of the so-called Bounty Trilogy and other works about the islands (see "Fiction," below). *A Dream of Islands* (1980), by Gavan Dawes, tells of the missionary John Williams as well as Melville, Stevenson, and the painter Paul Gauguin.

PEOPLES & CULTURES

The late Bengt Danielsson, a Swedish anthropologist who arrived in Tahiti on Thor Heyerdahl's *Kon Tiki* raft in 1947 and spent the rest of his life there, painted a broad picture of Polynesian sexuality in *Love in the South Seas* (1986). Heyerdahl tells his tale and explains his theory of Polynesian migration (since debunked) in *Kon Tiki* (1950). In 1936, Heyerdahl and his wife lived for a year in the Marquesas; his book *Fatu-Hiva: Back to Nature* (1975) provides an in-depth look at Marquesan life at the time. Robert Lee Eskridge spent a year on Mangareva; his charming book is titled, appropriately, *Manga Reva* (1931; reprinted by Mutual in 1986).

FICTION

Starting with Herman Melville's *Typee* (1846) and *Omoo* (1847)—semifictional accounts of his adventures in the Marquesas and Tahiti, respectively—the islands have spawned a wealth of fiction. (Though set in the South Pacific Ocean, Melville's 1851 classic, *Moby-Dick,* does not tell of the islands.)

After Melville came Julien Viaud, a French naval officer who fell in love with a Tahitian woman during a sojourn in Tahiti. Under the pen name Pierre Loti, he wrote *The Marriage of Loti* (1880; reprinted by KPI in 1986), a classic tale of lost love.

W. Somerset Maugham's *The Moon and Sixpence* (1919) is a fictional account of the life of Paul Gauguin. Maugham changed the name to Charles Strickland and made the painter English instead of French. (Gauguin's own novel, *Noa Noa,* was published in English in 1928, long after his death.) Maugham also produced a volume of South Pacific short stories, *The Trembling of a Leaf* (1921; reprinted by Mutual in 1985). My favorite is "The Fall of Edward Bernard," about a

> ## Impressions
>
> *I have often been mildly amused when I think that the great American novel was not written about New England or Chicago. It was written about a white whale in the South Pacific.*
> —James A. Michener, *Return to Paradise,* 1951

Chicagoan who forsakes love and fortune at home for "beauty, truth, and goodness" in Tahiti.

Next on the scene were Charles Nordhoff and James Norman Hall (more about them in chapter 5). Together they wrote the most famous of all South Pacific novels, *Mutiny on the Bounty* (1932). They followed that enormous success with two other novels: *Men Against the Sea* (1934), based on Captain Bligh's epic longboat voyage after the mutiny, and *Pitcairn's Island* (1935), about Lt. Fletcher Christian's demise on the mutineers' remote hideaway. (For a nonfiction retelling of the great tale, see Caroline Alexander's *The Bounty: The True Story of the Mutiny on the Bounty* 2003.)

💬 A MOST indecent SONG & DANCE

The young girls whenever they can collect 8 or 10 together dance a very indecent dance which they call Timorodee singing most indecent songs and useing most indecent actions in the practice of which they are brought up from their earliest Childhood.
—Capt. James Cook, after seeing his first Tahitian dance show in 1769

The Tahitian dances described by the great explorer in 1769 left little doubt as to the temptations that inspired the mutiny on the *Bounty* a few years later. At the time Cook arrived, the Tahitians would stage a *heiva* (festival) for almost any reason, from blessing the harvest to celebrating a birth. After eating meals cooked in earth ovens, they would get out the drums and nose flutes and dance the night away. Some of the dances involved elaborate costumes, and others were quite lasciviously and explicitly danced in the nude or semi-nude, which added to Tahiti's reputation as an island of love.

The puritanical Protestant missionaries would have none of that and put an end to dancing in the early 1820s. Of course, strict prohibition never works, and Tahitians—including a young Queen Pomare—would sneak into the hills to dance. Only after the French took over in 1842 was dancing permitted again, and then only with severe limitations on what the dancers could do and wear. A result of these varied restrictions was that most of the traditional dances performed by the Tahitians before 1800 were nearly forgotten within 100 years.

You'd never guess that Tahitians ever stopped dancing, for after tourists started coming in 1961, they went back to the old ways. Today, traditional dancing is a huge part of their lives—and of every visitor's itinerary. No one goes away without vivid memories of the elaborate and colorful costumes, the thundering drums, and the swinging hips of a Tahitian *tamure* in which young men and women provocatively dance around one another.

The *tamure* is one of several dances performed during a typical dance show. Others are the *o'tea,* in which men and women in spectacular costumes dance certain themes, such as spear throwing, fighting, or love; the *aparima,* the hand dance, which emphasizes everyday themes, such as bathing and combing one's hair; the *hivinau,* in which men and women dance in circles and exclaim *"hiri haa haa"* when they meet each other; and the *pata'uta'u,* in which the dancers beat the ground or their thighs with their open hands. It's difficult to follow the themes without understanding Tahitian, but the color and rhythms (which have been influenced by faster, double-time beats from the Cook Islands) make the dances thoroughly enjoyable.

Nordhoff and Hall later wrote *The Hurricane* (1936), a novel set in American Samoa that has been made into two movies filmed in French Polynesia. Hall also wrote short stories and essays, collected in *The Forgotten One* (1986).

The second-most famous South Pacific novel appeared just after World War II—*Tales of the South Pacific* (1947), by James A. Michener. A U.S. Navy historian, Michener spent much of the war on Espiritu Santo, in the New Hebrides (now Vanuatu). Richard Rodgers and Oscar Hammerstein turned the novel into the musical *South Pacific,* a huge Broadway hit; it was later made into the blockbuster movie.

Michener toured the islands a few years later and wrote *Return to Paradise* (1951), a collection of essays and short stories. He describes the islands as they were after World War II, but before tourists began to arrive via jet aircraft—in other words, near the end of the region's backwater, beachcomber days.

Film

The most famous of many movies about Tahiti are the two *Mutiny on the Bounty* films based on the novel by Charles Nordhoff and James Norman Hall. The 1935 version starred Clark Gable as Fletcher Christian and Charles Laughton as a tyrannical Captain Bligh. (It was actually the second film based on the *Bounty* story; the first was an Australian production, starring Errol Flynn in his first movie role.) Although the 1935 version contained background shots of 40 Tahitian villages, most of the movie was filmed on Santa Catalina, off the California coast; neither Gable nor Laughton visited Tahiti. The 1962 remake with Marlon Brando and Trevor Howard in the Gable and Laughton roles, however, was actually filmed on Tahiti. It was the beginning of Brando's tragic real-life relationship with Tahiti (see "Marlon's Mana," p. 108). A 1984 version, *The Bounty,* not based on Nordhoff and Hall, was filmed in Opunohu Bay on Moorea and featured Mel Gibson as Christian and Anthony Hopkins as a more sympathetic (and historically accurate) Bligh.

Another Nordhoff and Hall novel, *The Hurricane* (1936), was turned into two movies set in French Polynesia (the novel was about a hurricane striking American Samoa). The 1937 version starring Dorothy Lamour and Jon Hall (a relative of the coauthor) was a hit, while the 1977 remake, starring Mia Farrow and filmed on Bora Bora, was a classical bomb.

Also a bomb was 1994's *Love Affair* starring Warren Beatty, Annette Bening, and Katherine Hepburn. The best things about it are the scenes shot on the *Aranui 2* and in Opunohu Bay on Moorea.

EATING & DRINKING

French Polynesia has a plethora of excellent restaurants. I've seldom had a really bad meal here. You are in for a special treat when ordering tomatoes and other locally grown vegetables, for more than likely they will be as fresh as if they had come from your own garden.

Many visitors are shocked at the high prices on the menus and in the grocery stores. Most foodstuffs are imported, and except for sugar, flour, and a few other necessities, are subject to stiff duties. On the other hand, you won't have sales tax added to your bill, and although the practice is widespread here these days, you will not be expected to add 20% to the cost of your meals to tip the waitstaff, as in the United States. See below for how I save more money on food here.

Except for breakfast buffets, prices in hotel and resort dining rooms are now comparable to those in the better outside restaurants.

Local Fare: Ma'a Tahiti

As would be expected, French is the dominant cuisine in these islands. Local French residents demand their steaks in red-wine sauces, mahimahi under a vanilla sauce, and *canard* (duck) with orange sauce, which seem to appear on every menu, as does carpaccio (thinly sliced raw beef or tuna) and sashimi (especially good when it's fresh yellowfin tuna).

While the Tahitians have adopted many of these dishes as well as Chinese ones, they still consume copious quantities of **ma'a Tahiti** (traditional Tahitian food), especially at midday on Sunday. Like their Polynesian counterparts elsewhere, Tahitians still cook meals underground in an earth oven, known here as an *himaa*. Pork, chicken, fish, shellfish, leafy green vegetables such as taro leaves, and root crops such as taro and yams are wrapped in leaves, placed on a bed of heated stones, covered with more leaves and earth, and left to steam for several hours. The results are quite tasty, since the steam spreads the aroma of one ingredient to the others, and liberal use of coconut cream adds a sweet richness.

Many restaurants serving primarily French, Italian, or Chinese cuisine also offer Tahitian dishes. One you will see virtually everywhere is **poisson cru,** French for "raw fish." It's the Tahitian-style salad of fresh tuna or mahi-mahi marinated in lime juice, cucumbers, onions, and tomatoes, all served in coconut cream. Chili is added to spice up a variation known as Chinese *poisson cru.*

Most of Tahiti's big resort hotels have at least one **tama'ara'a** (Tahitian feast) a week, followed by a traditional, hip-swinging dance show (see the box "A Most Indecent Song & Dance," p. 36).

Snack Bars & Les Roulottes

Tahiti has two McDonald's, but locals still prefer their plethora of snack bars, which they call "snacks." You can get a hamburger and usually *poisson cru,* but the most popular item is the *casse-croûte,* a sandwich made from a crusty French baguette and ham, tuna, *roti* (roast pork), or *hachis* (hamburger), with lettuce, tomatoes, and cucumbers—or even spaghetti. A *casse-croûte* usually costs about 300CFP or less.

Also in this category are *les roulottes*—or portable meal wagons. A friend of mine says he hates the idea of dining in a parking lot, but *les roulottes* are one of the best values here, with meals seldom topping 2,000CFP. They roll out after dark on most islands. The carnival-like ambience they create on the Papeete waterfront makes them a highlight of any visit to the city (see "Don't Miss *Les Roulottes*," p. 125).

Money-Saving Tips

Despite the high prices, you don't have to go broke dining here. In addition to finding the nearest "snack," here are some ways to eat well for the least money:

o Unless you have no choice, do not have breakfast at the resort hotel dining rooms, which charge 3,000CFP or more per person. You can have a perfectly good breakfast for less than half that at a snack bar or patisserie.

- Likewise, do not buy a hotel meal package except on remote islands, where your resort's restaurant is your only choice. Dining out is as much a part of the French Polynesian experience as is snorkeling.

- Order breakfast from room service if you don't want to go out and your hotel restaurant serves only an expensive buffet. Room service menus usually are a la carte, meaning you can order individual items whose total may be much less than the full buffet price.

- Dine at *restaurants conventionné*, which get breaks on the government's high duty on imported alcoholic beverages. Wine and mixed drinks in these establishments cost significantly less than elsewhere. They can charge no more than 700CFP for spirits served on the rocks, but cocktails can be more than twice that amount. I buy rum on the rocks and then add my own Coke to it. You can also order *vin ordinaire* (table wine) served in a carafe to save money. The chef buys good-quality wine in bulk and passes the savings on to you.

- Take advantage of *plats du jour* (daily specials), especially at lunch. Many people in Papeete eat on the run at midday in the American fashion, but my French friends typically follow a very light breakfast with a long, substantial lunch. *Plats du jour* are especially appealing to them since they usually are made with fresh produce direct from the market.

- Look for prix-fixe (fixed-price) "tourist menus." You will not necessarily get the chef's most creative efforts, but the offerings will be less expensive than ordering three or four courses separately.

- Consider sharing a starter course, which usually are more substantial servings than American appetizers. If you have a light appetite, an entree could suffice as your only course, or you can share one with your mate or a friend. I discreetly glance at other tables to check portion sizes before ordering.

- Make your own snacks or perhaps a picnic lunch to enjoy at the beach. Every village has at least one grocery store. Fresh loaves of French bread cost about 50CFP each, and most stores carry cheeses, deli meats, vegetables, and other sandwich makings, many imported from France. Locally brewed Hinano beers sell for about 300CFP or less in grocery stores, versus 500CFP or more at the hotel bars, and bottles of decent French wine cost a fraction of restaurant prices.

PLANNING YOUR TRIP TO TAHITI & FRENCH POLYNESIA

Thanks to tons of euros pouring in from Paris, French Polynesians enjoy a relatively high standard of living. The flip side of that coin is that everyone pays high prices for almost everything, locals and visitors alike. As one resident of these gorgeous islands once told me, "You must pay for paradise."

Indeed, you can pay a king's ransom to vacation here, but French Polynesia doesn't have to cost you both arms and both legs. In this chapter, I will advise you on how to plan your trip, hopefully so that you won't have to declare bankruptcy after visiting this modern paradise.

In planning your trip, keep in mind why you are coming here and what your priorities are. You can go scuba diving to exhaustion or just sit on the beach with a trashy novel. You can share a 200-room hotel with package-tour tourists or get away from it all in an overwater bungalow. You can hide away with your lover or join your fellow guests at lively dinner parties. You can totally ignore the islanders around you or enrich your own life by learning about theirs. You can listen to the day's events on CNN International or see what the South Seas were like a century ago. Lacking the ability to read minds, I must leave those decisions to you.

WHEN TO GO

There is no bad time to go to French Polynesia, but some periods are better than others. The weather is at its best—comfortable and dry—in July and August, but this is the prime vacation and festival season. July is the busiest month because of the *Heiva Nui* festival (see "French Polynesia Calendar of Events," below). Hotels on the outer islands are at

Impressions

It is no exaggeration to say, that to a European of any sensibility, who, for the first time, wanders back into these valleys—away from the haunts of the natives—the ineffable repose and beauty of the landscape is such, that every object strikes him like something seen in a dream; and for a time he almost refuses to believe that scenes like these should have a commonplace existence.

—Herman Melville, 1847

their fullest during August, the traditional French vacation month, when many Papeete residents head for the outer islands to get away from it all. In other words, book your air tickets and hotel rooms for July and August as far in advance as possible.

May, June, September, and October have the best combination of weather and availability of hotel rooms.

Although the weather usually is hot and humid, Christmas through the middle of January is a good time to get a hotel reservation in the islands, but airline seats can be hard to come by, since thousands of islanders fly home from overseas.

The Climate

Tahiti and the rest of the Society Islands enjoy a balmy tropical climate. Rain showers can pass overhead at any time of the year. Humidity averages between 77% and 80% throughout the year.

The most pleasant time of year is the May-through-October austral winter, or **dry season,** when midday maximum temperatures average a delightful 82°F (28°C), with early morning lows of 68°F (20°C) often making a blanket necessary. Some winter days, especially on the south side of the islands, can seem quite chilly when a strong wind blows from Antarctica.

November through April is the austral summer, or **wet season,** when rainy periods can be expected between days of intense sunshine. The average maximum daily temperature is 86°F (30°C) during these months, while nighttime lows are about 72°F (22°C). An air-conditioned hotel room or bungalow will feel like heaven during this humid time of year.

The central and northern Tuamotus have somewhat warmer temperatures and less rainfall. Since there are no mountains to create cooling night breezes, these islands can experience desertlike hot periods between November and April.

The Marquesas are closer to the Equator, and temperatures and humidity tend to be slightly higher than in Tahiti. Rainfall in the Marquesas is scattered throughout the year, but is most likely from June through August, exactly opposite that of the rest of French Polynesia. The trade winds reach that far north and temper the climate from April to October, but the Marquesas can see hot and sticky days the rest of the year.

The climate in the Austral and Gambier islands, which are much farther south, is more temperate year-round.

French Polynesia is on the far eastern edge of the South Pacific cyclone (hurricane) belt, and storms can occur between November and March.

Another factor to consider is the part of an island that you'll visit. Because the moist trade winds usually blow from the east, the eastern sides of the high, mountainous islands tend to be wetter all year than the western sides.

Also bear in mind that the higher the altitude, the lower the temperature. If you're going up in the mountains, be prepared for much cooler weather than you'd have on the coast.

The local office of **Météo France,** the national weather service, posts the forecasts and climatic observations in French on **www.meteo.pf**.

Average Daytime Temperatures in Tahiti

	JAN	FEB	MAR	APR	MAY	JUNE	JULY	AUG	SEPT	OCT	NOV	DEC
Temp °F	80.6	80.8	81.3	80.8	79.5	77.4	76.5	76.3	77	78.1	79.3	79.9
Temp °C	27	27.1	27.4	27.1	26.4	25.2	24.7	24.6	25	25.6	26.3	26.6

Holidays

Like all Pacific Islanders, the Tahitians love public holidays and often extend them past the official day. For example, if Ascension Day falls on a Thursday, don't be surprised if some stores and even banks are closed through the weekend. Plan your shopping forays accordingly.

Public holidays are New Year's Day (government offices are also closed on Jan 2), Good Friday and Easter Monday; Ascension Day (40 days after Easter); Whitmonday (the seventh Mon after Easter), Missionary Day (Mar 5), Labor Day (May 1), Internal Autonomy Day (June 29), Bastille Day (July 14), Assumption Day (Aug 15), All Saints' Day (Nov 1), Armistice Day (Nov 11), and Christmas Day (Dec 25).

Tahiti Tourisme publishes an annual list of the territory's leading special events on its website (see "Visitor Information," later in this chapter).

French Polynesia Calendar of Events

JANUARY

Chinese New Year. Parade, musical performances, demonstrations of martial arts, Chinese dances, and handicrafts. Between mid-January and mid-February. Call ℰ **42.74.18** for information.

Oceania International Documentary Film Festival (FIFO). Films produced by Pacific islanders are shown and judged in Papeete. Last weekend. www.fifo-tahiti.com.

FEBRUARY

Moorea Marathon. Prizes worth up to US$15,000 entice some of the world's best runners to trot 42km (26 miles) around Moorea. Second Saturday. Call ℰ **56.25.79** for information.

MARCH

Moorea Golf ProAm. Professional and amateur golfers tee off at Moorea Green Pearl Golf Course. Mid-month. www.moorea-golf-resort.com.

APRIL

Polynesian Traditional Sports Championship. Stone lifting, coconut tree climbing, javelin throwing, other pre-European sports. Call ℰ **50.31.11** for information.

MAY

Billabong Pro Surfing. World-class surfers compete on the waves off Teahupoo on Tahiti Iti. First 2 weeks (but note, the dates can change from year to year). www.billabong pro.com.

Tahiti Pearl Regatta. Yachts sail among Raiatea, Tahaa, Huahine, and Bora Bora. Mid-May. www.tahitipearlregatta.org.pf.

JUNE

Miss Tahiti, Miss Heiva, Miss Moorea, and Miss Bora Bora Contests. Candidates from around the islands vie to win the titles. It is among the biggest annual events on outer islands. Early to mid-June.

The islands are extraordinarily beautiful anytime, especially so at equinox time in late September and late March, when the sun's rays hit the lagoons at just the right angle to highlight the gorgeous colors out in the lagoons. The play of moonlight on the water and the black silhouettes the mountains cast against the sky, make them even more magical when the moon is full. Keep that in mind when planning your trip—especially if it's your honeymoon.

Tahiti International Golf Open. Local and international golfers vie at Atimaono Golf Course, Tahiti. Mid-June.

Heiva Nui. This is the festival to end all festivals in French Polynesia. It was originally a celebration of Bastille Day on July 14, but the islanders have extended the shindig into a nearly 2-month-long blast. They pull out all the stops, with parades, outrigger canoe races, javelin-throwing contests, fire walking, games, carnivals, festivals, and reenactments of ancient Polynesian ceremonies at restored *maraes*. While still the largest, the *Heiva I Tahiti* in Papeete is almost overshadowed by smaller versions on Bora Bora and other islands, especially the annual dance contests. Airline and hotel reservations can be difficult to come by, so book early and take your written confirmation with you. First week in June through July. www.heivanui.com.

JULY

Heiva Va'a I Tahiti. A great outrigger canoe race in Papeete Harbor and on the Sea of the Moon between there and Moorea is a highlight of the overall *Heiva Nui* celebrations. First week in July. www.heivanui.com

AUGUST

Mini Fêtes. Winning dancers and singers from the *Heiva Nui* perform at hotels on the outer islands. All month.

SEPTEMBER

World Tourism Day. Islanders pay homage to overseas visitors, who get discounts. Last weekend.

OCTOBER

Rotui's Tour. Runners race 15km (9 miles) around Moorea's Mount Rotui. Late October.

Tahiti Carnival. Parades, floats, and much partying on the Papeete waterfront. Last week.

NOVEMBER

Tatoonesia. Local and foreign tattoo artists gather in Papeete to share designs and techniques. Early November. Followed by Exhibition "Tattoo" in late November. www.tattoonesia.com.

Hawaiki Nui Va'a. Outrigger canoe racing, the national sport, takes center stage as international teams race from Huahine to Raiatea, Tahaa, and Bora Bora over 3 days. www.hawaikinuivaa.pf. Late October to early November.

All Saints' Day. Flowers are sold everywhere to families who put them on graves after whitewashing the tombstones. November 1.

DECEMBER

Tiare Tahiti Flower Festival (The Tiare Days on Tahiti). Everyone on the streets of Papeete and in the hotels receives a *tiare Tahiti*, the fragrant gardenia that is indigenous to Tahiti. Dinner and dancing later. First week in December.

Hura Tapairu. Traditional dance competition at Maison de la Culture (cultural center) in Papeete is second only to Heiva Nui in July. Early December. www.maisondelaculture.pf.

New Year's Eve. A big festival in downtown Papeete leads territory-wide celebrations. December 31.

ENTRY REQUIREMENTS
Passports & Visas

All visitors except French nationals are required to have a **passport** that will be valid for 6 months beyond their intended stay, as well as a **return or ongoing ticket.**

For information on how to get a passport, see "Passports" in chapter 13.

Nationals of the United States, Canada, Andorra, Australia, the European Union countries, Monaco, Switzerland, Iceland, Liechtenstein, Norway, St. Martin, and the Vatican can stay up to 3 months without a visa.

Citizens and nationals of Argentina, Bermuda, Bolivia, Brunei, Chile, Costa Rica, Croatia, the Czech Republic, Ecuador, El Salvador, Estonia, Guatemala, Honduras, Hungary, Japan, Latvia, Lithuania, Malaysia, Mexico, New Zealand, Nicaragua, Panama, Paraguay, Poland, Singapore, Slovakia, Slovenia, South Korea, and Uruguay may visit for up to 30 days without a visa.

Citizens from all other countries (including foreign nationals residing in the U.S.) must get a visa before leaving home.

French embassies and consulates overseas can issue "short stay" visas valid for 1 to 3 months, and they will forward applications for longer visits to the local immigration department in Papeete. *Note:* Visas issued by French embassies and consulates do not entitle you to visit Tahiti without being stamped *"valable pour la Polynésie Française"*—valid for French Polynesia.

TRANSITING THE U.S.

Nearly all travelers to Tahiti from the U.K. and Europe will stop in Los Angeles on the way and thus must comply with U.S. immigration procedures. Citizens of 27 countries (including the U.K., most European nations, Australia, and New Zealand) can visit and transit the U.S. without a visa, but they must register online at **https://esta.cbp.dhs.gov** more than 72 hours before leaving home under the Electronic System for Travel Authorization (ESTA) program administered by the U.S. Department of Homeland Security (www.dhs.gov). Citizens of all other countries without a visitor visa to the U.S. must obtain a C-1 transit visa from the U.S. State Department (www.unitedstatesvisas.gov), even if they don't leave the airport.

Medical Requirements

No vaccinations are required unless you are coming from a yellow fever, plague, or cholera area.

Customs
WHAT YOU CAN BRING INTO FRENCH POLYNESIA

French Polynesia's **Customs allowances** are 200 cigarettes or 50 cigars, 2 liters of spirits or 2 liters of wine, 50 grams of perfume, 250ml of toilet water, 500 grams of coffee, 100 grams of tea, and 30,000CFP worth of other goods. Narcotics, dangerous drugs, weapons, ammunition, and copyright infringements (that is, pirated videotapes and audiotapes) are prohibited. Pets and plants are subject to stringent regulations (don't even think of bringing your dog).

WHAT YOU CAN TAKE HOME FROM FRENCH POLYNESIA

U.S. citizens who have been in French Polynesia for at least 48 hours are allowed to bring back, once every 30 days, US$800 worth of merchandise duty-free. For

WHAT TO pack

I am not about to tell anyone exactly what to bring to the islands, but here are a few things I always bring with me, and which invariably come in handy.

The humid tropical weather and a scarcity of self-service laundries dictate lightweight, **easy-care clothing.** I have a strong personal preference for all-cotton clothing, which I find to be cooler than wash-and-wear polyester blends, even though it costs dearly to have them laundered commercially.

A **long-sleeve shirt** and my lightweight nylon **windbreaker** keep me warm during the chilly nights in July and August, and when I go high into the mountains.

A small **folding umbrella** is always in my backpack. It's much cooler than a raincoat during tropical showers.

I wear a **sun visor** most of the time and a broad-brim **hat** when I'm outdoors for extended periods.

I also carry **sunscreen** and **insect repellent.** I treat all cuts and scrapes immediately with my small tube of **antibacterial ointment** and a small package of **bandages.** (You can buy these at most stores in French Polynesia but not in small, easily packable sizes.)

I also wear comfortable **walking shoes** (cloth dries faster than leather), and I carry a pair of **aqua socks** (rubber-sole, nylon-mesh shoes) for walking on the reefs (plastic reef sandals are available at most general stores here). I was tramping around in **flip-flops** long before they became trendy.

My **inflatable neck cushion** is invaluable on the long flights here and back.

Only in the luxurious resorts will you always find a **face cloth** in the bathroom, so I bring one.

My small **flashlight** is often useful, since some public areas are not well lighted.

specifics contact the **U.S. Customs & Border Protection (CBP),** 1300 Pennsylvania Ave., NW, Washington, DC 20229 (© **877/287-8667;** www.cbp.gov).

Canadian Citizens: Canada Border Services Agency, Ottawa, Ontario, K1A 0L8 (© **800/461-9999** in Canada, or 204/983-3500; www.cbsa-asfc.gc.ca).

U.K. Citizens: HM Customs & Excise, Crownhill Court, Tailyour Road, Plymouth, PL6 5BZ (© **0845/010-9000;** from outside the U.K., 020/8929-0152; www.hmce.gov.uk).

Australian Citizens: Australian Customs Service, Customs House, 5 Constitution Avenue, Canberra City, ACT 2601 (© **1300/363-263;** from outside Australia, 612/6275-6666; www.customs.gov.au).

New Zealand Citizens: New Zealand Customs, The Customhouse, 17–21 Whitmore St., Box 2218, Wellington, 6140 (© **04/473-6099** or 0800/428-786; www.customs.govt.nz).

GETTING TO TAHITI & FRENCH POLYNESIA

A few cruise ships stop in the islands on their way across the Pacific Ocean (see "By Cruise Ship" below), yet today, all but a handful of visitors arrive by air at **Tahiti-Faaa International Airport (PPT),** on Tahiti's northwest corner, about 11km

(7 miles) west of downtown Papeete. It is the only international airport here. See "Getting Around Tahiti & French Polynesia" below, for details on getting from the airport to Papeete and other points on Tahiti.

The Airlines

- **Air Tahiti Nui** (© 877/824-4846; www.airtahitinui-usa.com), French Polynesia's award-winning national airline, has more flights—all on relatively new Airbus planes—to and from Tahiti than any other airline. Some of Air Tahiti Nui's flights depart Los Angeles in the afternoon California time and arrive in Papeete in the evening local time, thus enabling Americans and Canadians to make connections to Moorea or to get a good night's sleep on Tahiti before tackling the islands the next morning. Most of its return flights are overnight, but you arrive in Los Angeles early enough in the morning to make convenient connections to other cities. Air Tahiti Nui also links Paris (with stops in Los Angeles), Tokyo, Auckland, and Sydney (with stops in Auckland) to Papeete.

- **Air New Zealand** (© 800/262-1234 or 310/615-1111; www.airnewzealand. com) flies its own planes between Auckland and Papeete, and it code-shares with Air Tahiti Nui between Los Angeles and Papeete. That means you will fly in an Air Tahiti Nui plane even if you bought your ticket from Air New Zealand or one of its partners, such as United Airlines. It flies to several Australian cities, so Aussies can reach Tahiti through Auckland. It links Tokyo, Hong Kong, Singapore, Seoul, Taipei, and Beijing to Auckland, with connections on to Papeete. Air New Zealand is a member of the Star Alliance, which includes United Airlines and several other carriers, which means you can get to the islands from many cities in the United States, Canada, and Europe on an Air New Zealand ticket.

- **Air France** (© 800/321-4538; www.airfrance.com) flies between Tahiti and Paris, with stops in Los Angeles each way.

- **Hawaiian Airlines** (© 800/367-5320 in the continental U.S., Alaska, and Canada, or 808/838-1555 in Honolulu; www.hawaiianair.com) is the only direct link between Honolulu and Tahiti, usually once a week. You can fly from Los Angeles, San Francisco, Portland, or Seattle to Honolulu, and then change plans for Tahiti. *Beware:* The plane change can result in delays and even an unexpected Hawaiian holiday.

- **Lan Airlines** (© 800/735-5526; www.lan.com), the Chilean national airline, flies at least weekly between Santiago, Chile, and Tahiti by way of Easter Island.

- **Qantas Airways** (© 800/227-4500; www.qantas.com), the Australian carrier, code-shares flights to and from Papeete with Air Tahiti Nui.

Knowledgeable Travel Agents

In addition to searching for the lowest airfare in the usual ways, I contact travel agents who specialize in French Polynesia. Which is to say, one who actually has been here and is familiar with all it has to offer.

Following in alphabetical order are some reputable American companies specializing in French Polynesia. They don't turn as much profit from air tickets as they do from hotel rooms, but some will discount air fare and hotel rooms separately; that is, not as part of a package. Be sure to shop for the best deal among them, and remember, it never hurts to ask.

- **Costco Travel** (© 877/849-2730; www.costco.com) sells island packages to Costco members. The agency was a South Pacific specialist before Costco bought it.

- **Island Escapes** (℗ 800/983-0210; www.islandescapes.com) has packages to the Society Islands and to Rangiroa and Fakarava in the Tuamotu Archipelago, and it will arrange cruising and yachting vacations.
- **Islands in the Sun** (℗ 800/828-6877 or 310/536-0051; www.islandsinthesun.com), the largest and oldest South Pacific specialist, sells packages to all the islands.
- **Pleasant Holidays** (℗ 800/448-3333; www.pleasantholidays.com), a huge company best known for its Pleasant Hawaiian and Pleasant Mexico operations, offers packages to French Polynesia.
- **Qantas Vacations** (℗ 866/914-4359; www.qantasvacations.com) concentrates on Australia, home of Qantas Airways, but it has attractive packages to French Polynesia, too.
- **Swain Tahiti Tours** (℗ 800/227-SWAIN [79246]; www.swaintours.com) obviously knows a lot about Tahiti and French Polynesia.
- **Tahiti Discount Travel** (℗ 877/426-7262; www.tahiti-discounttravel.com) is owned by former employees of the defunct Discover Wholesale Travel, once the leader in budget packages. Today they arrange some of the lowest-priced packages to French Polynesia.
- **Tahiti Legends** (℗ 800/200-1213; www.tahiti-legends.com) is run by former officials of Islands in the Sun. It sells tours to French Polynesia, the Cook Islands, and Fiji under the name **Pacific Legends** (www.pacificlegends.com).
- **Tahiti Vacations** (℗ 800/553-3477; www.tahitivacation.com), a subsidiary of Air Tahiti, French Polynesia's domestic airline, specializes in French Polynesia but also has packages to Fiji, the Cook Islands, and Tonga. It frequently offers the least expensive packages available to Tahiti and Moorea.
- **Travel2** (℗ 888/801-6663; www.travel2-us.com) devises packages in all price ranges and offers discounted airfare.
- **True Tahiti Vacations** (℗ 310/464-1490 in the U.S.; www.truetahitivacation.com) is operated by American-born Laurel Samuela from her home on Moorea.

Tourisme Tahiti, the country's visitor information bureau, lists more knowledgeable travel agents in the U.S. and elsewhere on its Website (see "Visitor Information," in chapter 13).

Check the Airline Websites

Before buying your ticket elsewhere, open a new window or tab and go to the airline's own Website. The carriers occasionally have discounts not offered through other Websites and travel agents

Baggage Allowances

Pack carefully and bring evidence of your international ticket with you, as the baggage limit on both of French Polynesia's domestic airlines is 20 kilograms (44 lb.) per person if you're connecting with an international flight within 7 days, but it's 10 kilograms (22 lb.) per person if you're not. You will face a substantial extra charge for excess weight unless you buy a "Z Class" fare on Air Tahiti, which allows passengers to carry up to 50 kilograms (110 lb.) of luggage, as opposed to 20 kilograms under its economy fare. You can leave your extra belongings in the storage room at your hotel or at Tahiti-Faaa International Airport (see "Baggage Storage" under "Arriving & Departing," below).

French Polynesia & the South Pacific

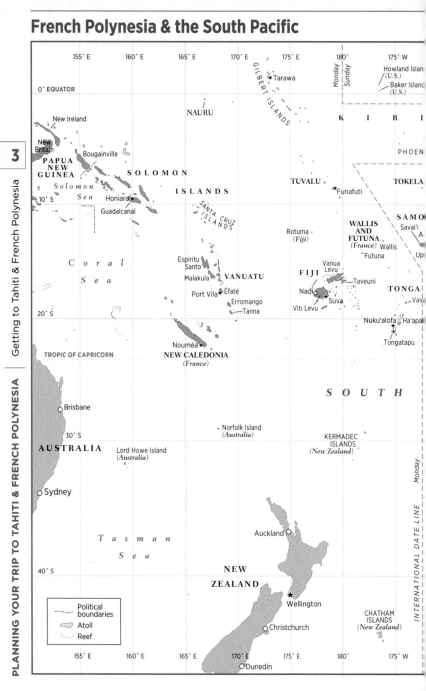

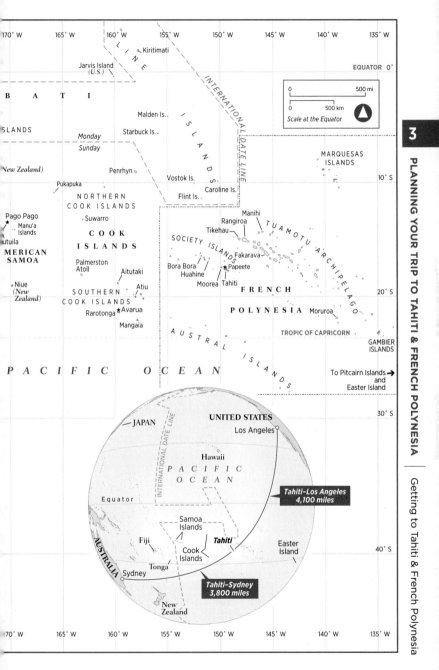

Arriving & Departing

All international flights arrive at, and depart from, **Tahiti-Faaa International Airport (PPT),** 7km (4 miles) west of downtown Papeete.

ARRIVING

Group tour operators will be holding signs announcing their presence. Pick up some pocket money at **Banque de Polynésie,** to the left as you exit Customs, or at **Banque Socredo** to the right. Banque de Polynésie opens its exchange window whenever international flights arrive and depart, while Banque Socredo's office is open only during normal banking hours. Both have ATMs, and Banque Socredo has a machine that will change U.S. dollars and other major notes to CFP (French Pacific francs, the local currency).

I have spent many hours waiting for flights at the open-air, 24-hour **snack bar** to the right. There's a **McDonald's** next to Air Tahiti's domestic departure lounge, also to the right.

GETTING TO YOUR HOTEL

Unless you're on a package tour or your hotel has arranged a transfer, your only choice of transportation to your hotel between 10pm and 6am will be a **taxi.** Official fares from 8pm to 6am are 1,500CFP to the hotels on the west coast, 2,500CFP to downtown. Add 100CFP for each bag.

Don't Forget to Reconfirm

Air Tahiti Nui requires that you reconfirm your return flight within 72 hours of departure. It's mainly so the airline will know how to contact you should the schedule change.

If you arrive when buses are running and you're in good physical condition, haul your baggage across the parking lot in front of the terminal, climb the stairs to the main road, and flag down a local bus.

If you're driving a rental car, take Route 1 west to the InterContinental Resort Tahiti, the Sofitel Tahiti Maeva Beach Resort, or Le Meridien Tahiti. Route 1 east passes the Sheraton Hotel Tahiti & Spa on its way to downtown Papeete. If you're going to downtown, watch for the Route 5 signs directing you to the expressway connecting Papeete to the west coast.

See "Getting Around Tahiti & French Polynesia," below, and "Getting Around Tahiti," in chapter 5, for more information.

BAGGAGE STORAGE

Most hotels will keep your baggage for free. The airport's **baggage storage room** (© **88.60.08;** hmoea@yahoo.fr) is in the rear of Fare Hei, the open-air pavilion where Tahitian women sell leis and flower crowns. It's in the parking lot in front of the international departures gate. Charges range from 640CFP per day for regular-size bags to 2,700CFP for large items such as surfboards and bicycles. The room opens 2 hours before every international flight departs. Regular hours are Monday 4am to 7pm, Tuesday to Thursday 5am to 11pm, Saturday 5am to 12:30am, Sunday and holidays 1pm to 12:30am. MasterCard and Visa credit cards are accepted for charges in excess of 1,200CFP.

DEPARTING

Check-in time for departing international flights is 3 hours before flight time; for domestic flights, be there 2 hours in advance. All of your bags must be screened for both international and domestic flights leaving Papeete. (There are no security procedures at the outer-island airstrips.)

There is no airport departure tax for either international or domestic flights.

Note: There is no bank or currency exchange bureau in the international departure lounge, so change your money before clearing immigration.

By Cruise Ship

Although the days of great liners plying the Pacific are long gone, a few lines still offer cruises that include French Polynesia and in addition, it may be possible to reach the islands on a cruise ship making an around-the-world voyage or being repositioned, say, from Alaska to Australia. In addition to Paul Gaugin Cruises (see "Cruising in the Islands," later in this chapter), other companies likely to have ships in the South Pacific include **Celebrity Cruises** (ⓒ 800/647-2251; *www.celebritycruises. com*); **Cunard Line** (ⓒ 800/528-6273; www.cunardline.com), and **Orient Lines** (ⓒ 800/333-7300; www.orientlines.com). Most sell tickets through travel agents, although some offer them directly to the public on their websites.

GETTING AROUND TAHITI & FRENCH POLYNESIA

By Plane

Having Air Tahiti Nui or another carrier book your domestic flights along with your international ticket will greatly simplify matters in case of a local cancellation, and you will avoid an extra fee if you have to change your flights once here.

AIR MOOREA

A subsidiary of Air Tahiti (see below), **Air Moorea** (ⓒ 86.41.41; fax 86.42.99; www.airmoorea.pf) provides shuttle service between Tahiti-Faaa International Airport and Temae Airport on Moorea. Its small planes (and I do mean small) leave Faaa on the hour and half-hour daily from 6 to 9am, then on the hour from 10am to 3pm, and on the hour and half-hour again from 4 to 6pm. Each plane turns around

---

Air Tahiti's Money-Saving Airpass

You can save by buying an **Air Tahiti Airpass** over the popular routes. For example, the "Bora Bora Pass" permits adults to travel over the popular Papeete–Moorea–Huahine–Raiatea–Bora Bora–Maupiti–Papeete route for about 33,000CFP. The "Bora Bora–Tuamotu Pass" costs 52,600 and adds Rangiroa, Tikihau, Fakarava, and Manihi. Whether you save anything will depend on how many islands you plan to visit, so add up the regular fares and compare that to the price of the passes (they're explained on Air Tahiti's website). All travel must be completed within 28 days of the first flight, and other restrictions apply. See **www.airtahiti.pf** for details.

on Moorea and flies back to Tahiti. The one-way fare for us visitors is about 4,000CFP if we pay in advance, 5,050CFP if we pay at the check-in counter. Round-trip fares are less. Children pay about half-fare.

Air Moorea's little terminal is on the east end of Tahiti-Faaa International Airport (that's to the left as you come out of Customs). Air Moorea will take you from the airport to your Moorea hotel for 600CFP each way, but *you must buy your transfer ticket in Papeete.* It is not available after you arrive on Moorea.

AIR TAHITI

Air Tahiti (✆ **86.42.42;** www.airtahiti.pf) provides daily flights between Papeete and all the main islands, most in modern ATR turboprop planes seating 44 or 72 passengers. It's wise to reserve your seats as early as possible, especially during vacation and school holiday periods.

Air Tahiti's central downtown Papeete walk-in reservations office is at the corner of rue du 22 Septembre and rue du Maréchal Foche (✆ **47.44.00**). It also has an office in the Tahiti-Faaa International Airport terminal (✆ **86.41.84**).

Check-in time is 2 hours in advance for domestic flights departing Papeete and Bora Bora, 1 hour at the other outer islands.

By Ferry to Moorea

Two companies—**Aremiti** (✆ **50.57.57;** www.aremiti.pf) and **Moorea Ferry** (✆ **86.87.47** on Tahiti, or 56.34.34 on Moorea; www.mooreaferry.pf)—run ferries between the Papeete waterfront and Vaiare, a small bay on Moorea's east coast.

Due to open in 2011, Papeete's new **Gare Maritime** (no phone; www.garemaritime2011.pf) should make it easier to find your ferry. Until then, it can seem like madness when the boats arrive and depart at the dock, so take your time and be sure to get on one of the two **fast catamarans,** which take 30 minutes to cover the 19km (12 miles) between the islands.

The *Aremiti V* is a larger, faster, and more comfortable catamaran than the *Moorea Express.* I try not to take the *Aremiti Ferry* or the *Moorea Ferry,* which take 1 hour or more.

> ### Breaking into Tahitian Song
>
> I was on the last ferry to Tahiti from Moorea when a Tahitian passenger, apparently on his way home from work, started playing a guitar. Within seconds, everyone onboard spontaneously began singing Tahitian songs. If you're lucky, you'll witness a very special moment like that one.

The one-way fare on any ferry, whether fast or slow, is about 1,400CFP for visitors. Local residents pay 1,050CFP.

Since the departure times change from day to day, I either print out the schedules from the websites before I leave home or get a copy at the ferry dock when I get here.

In general, one or another of the fast catamarans departs Papeete about 6am, 7:30am, 9am, noon, 2:40pm, 4:05pm, and 5:30pm Monday to Friday, with extra voyages on Friday and Monday (Moorea is a popular weekend retreat for Papeete residents). Weekend hours are slightly different on each ferry.

Buses meet all ferries at Vaire, except the midday departures from Papeete, to take you to your hotel or other destination on Moorea for 600CFP per person. From Vaiare, they take about 1 hour to reach the northwest corner of Moorea.

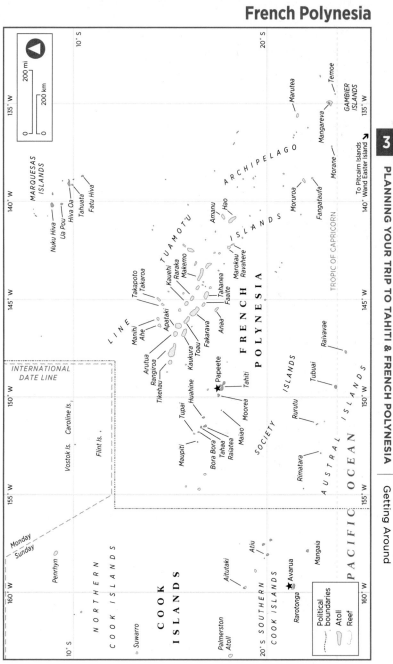

📎 **The Best Seats & Something to Eat**

It depends on the pilots and how much sightseeing they want to do, but usually you will have the best views of the islands by sitting on the left side of the Air Tahiti aircraft when you're flying from Papeete to the outer islands, on the right side returning.

Make sure you have your camera ready.

Most hotel dining rooms open for breakfast at 7am and close by 9:30am, so if you're catching an early morning flight to another island, stock up on some munchies the night before, and bring them along on the plane.

By Ferry to the Outer Islands

In the Leeward Islands, you can make the voyage between Bora Bora and Raiatea on the *Maupiti Express* (© **67.66.69** on Bora Bora, 66.37.81 on Raiatea; www.maupitiexpress.com). This small, fast passenger ferry departs Bora Bora for Tahaa and Raiatea at 7am on Monday, Wednesday, and Friday, returning to Bora Bora in the late afternoon. It stops at Tahaa in both directions. On Tuesday, Thursday, and Saturday, it sails from Bora Bora to Maupiti, departing at 8:30am and returning in late afternoon. In other words, it's possible to make day trips from Bora Bora to Raiatea or Maupiti. Fares on either route are 3,400CFP one-way, 5,000CFP return. See "Maupiti as a Day Trip from Bora Bora," p. 204.

Except for the excellent *Aranui 3,* which is as much cruise vessel as cargo ship (see "Cruising in the Islands," later in this chapter), ships to the Tuamotu, Marquesas, Gambier, and Austral island groups keep somewhat irregular schedules in terms of weeks or even months, not days. I do not recommend them. If you're interested, contact Tahiti Tourisme for a list of interisland schooners, their fares, and approximate schedules from Tahiti Tourisme. You'd best have a 3-month visa to stay in French Polynesia.

By Rental Car

Avis, Hertz, and **Europcar** have rental-car agencies (*locations de voiture* in French) here. See the "Getting Around" sections in the following chapters for details.

A valid **driver's license** from your home country will be honored in French Polynesia.

DRIVING RULES

Driving is on the **right-hand side** of the road, as in North America and continental Europe.

All persons in a vehicle must wear **seat belts.** If you drive or ride on a scooter or motorbike, **helmets** (*casques,* pronounced "casks") are mandatory.

Speed limits are 40kmph (24 mph) in the towns and villages, and 80kmph (48 mph) on the open road. The limit is 60kmph (36 mph) for 8km (5 miles) on either side of Papeete. The general rule on the Route 5 freeway between Papeete and Punaauia, on Tahiti's west coast, is 90kmph (54 mph), although there is one short stretch going down a hill where it's officially 110kmph (66 mph).

Drivers on the main rural roads have the right of way. In Papeete, priority is given to vehicles entering from the right side, unless an intersection is marked with a traffic light or a stop or yield sign. This rule differs from those of most other countries, so be especially careful at all intersections, especially those marked with a *priorité à droite* (priority to the right) sign, and give way accordingly.

Drivers are required to **stop for pedestrians** at marked crosswalks, but on busy streets, don't assume that drivers will politely stop for you when you try to cross.

Traffic lights in Papeete may be difficult to see, since some of them are on the far left-hand side of the street instead of on the driver's side of the intersection.

MONEY & COSTS

The cost of living in French Polynesia is high for local residents and visitors alike. You will be reminded on your first morning here when you come to breakfast and find that your hotel may charge more than 3,500CFP per person for its buffet. This is what I call waking up to "breakfast shock."

The flip side of the coin is that French Polynesia is a modern, First World place. You cannot drink the tap water on most islands, but the electricity is reliable, the airplanes and ferries ordinarily depart and arrive on time, the automated teller machines (ATMs) usually have cash to dispense, you can call anywhere in the world from a public phone, and access to the Internet is readily available. In other words, your visit should go as smoothly here as it would in any other developed country.

Drive Defensively!

Except for the four-lane expressways leading into Papeete, the roads here are narrow and winding. Add a penchant for speeding on the part of some locals, and you have the recipe for danger. If you rent a vehicle, keep your eyes on the road and drive defensively at all times.

WHAT THINGS COST IN TAHITI & FRENCH POLYNESIA	CFP
Taxi from airport into Papeete	2,500
Bus from airport into Papeete	130
Moderate hotel room for two	20,000
Inexpensive hotel room for two	15,000
Moderate lunch for two, without alcohol	5,000
Moderate three-course meal for two, without alcohol	9,000
Bottle of Coca-Cola	150
Bottle of Hinano beer in a bar	500
Cup of coffee	300

Converting in Your Head

No decimals are used with Pacific franc units, so prices at first can seem even more staggering than they really are. Although the value of the CFP varies with the European euro, many local residents think of 100CFP as US$1 (the historical benchmark, which explains the unusual 119.332 CFP value against the European euro), and they often express prices that way to visitors. For example, if the price of something is 1,000CFP, they might say it costs US$10. Using their method, you can make a quick conversion without a calculator by thinking of 100CFP as US$1, 500CFP as US$5, 1,000CFP as US$10, and so on. That is, drop the last two zeros, then add or subtract the percentage difference between the actual rate at the time of your visit and 100CFP. In the case of US$1 = 80CFP, for example, you would add 20%.

Currency

Although there have been proposals to switch to the euro, the local currency is still the *Comptoirs Français du Pacific franc,* or **French Pacific franc (CFP),** which comes in coins up to 100CFP and in colorful notes ranging from 500CFP into the millions.

The Pacific franc is abbreviated "XPF" by the banks, but in this book I use CFP, the local abbreviation.

A relic of France's colonial empire, the same franc is used in New Caledonia and Wallis and Futuna islands.

The value of the CFP is pegged directly to the European euro at a rate of **1€ = 119.332CFP.**

In other words, the value of the CFP goes up and down with the value of the euro against other currencies.

At this writing, US$1 = approximately 100CFP, which is the highest the U.S. dollar has been in several years. The table below gives the approximate values of the CFP against other currencies.

Note: International exchange rates fluctuate depending on economic and political factors. Thus, the values given in this table probably will not be the same when you travel to French Polynesia. Use the following table only as a guide. Find the current rates at **www.xe.com**.

U.S. dollar and European euro notes (but not coins) are widely accepted as cash in the islands, although at less favorable exchange rates than at banks.

You will probably get a more favorable rate if you change your money in French Polynesia rather than before leaving home.

THE VALUE OF THE PACIFIC FRANC VS. OTHER POPULAR CURRENCIES

CFP	US$	Can$	UK£	Euro (€)	A$	NZ$
100	$1.03	C$1.08	£.72	€.84	A$1.23	NZ$1.51

How to Get Local Currency

The easiest and best way to get local currency is from an ATM, known as a *billetterie* in French and sometimes referred to in English as a "cash machine" or "cashpoint." **Banque de Polynésie, Banque Socredo,** and **Banque de Tahiti** have offices with ATMs on the main islands, and many **post offices** have *billetteries* that dispense cash against MasterCard and Visa cards. See the "Fast Facts" sections in the following island chapters for bank and ATM locations (this is essential since some of the smaller islands do not have ATMs or even banks).

The ATMs operate in both French and English, and they usually are reliable at giving cash or cash advances. Nevertheless, I carry some cash or traveler's checks with me in case the local ATM runs out of cash or is out of service.

Be sure you know your four-digit **personal identification number (PIN)** for each credit and debit card—and find out your daily withdrawal limit before you leave home.

I carry two debit (that is, "cash" or "check") cards so there's a backup in case one doesn't work in a bank's ATM. You should use them to get local cash for two reasons: You get a better exchange rate than if you exchange traveler's checks, and you avoid the local banks' fees for changing cash and traveler's checks (see below).

Visa and MasterCard tack a 1% currency conversion fee to every debit card withdrawal, and many banks add up to 5% as their own "foreign transaction fee." In addition, many banks impose a fee every time you use a card at another bank's ATM, and that fee can be higher for international transactions (up to $5 or more) than for domestic ones.

How much you will pay depends entirely on your bank. Call your bank's customer service department for information on any applicable charges.

> ### Let Them Know You Will Be Away
>
> I always let my banks and credit unions know in advance that I will be using my ATM and credit cards in French Polynesia. Otherwise they might block my transactions as a means of preventing identity theft.

Also, ask if your bank levies a fee even if you pay in dollars, or when you charge a U.S. dollar amount to an overseas company or website and the vendor sends the transaction through a foreign bank. You may be able to avoid fees by paying for your airfare and hotel in U.S. dollars before leaving home, such as through a travel agent.

You can withdraw cash advances from your credit cards at banks or ATMs, but high withdrawal fees make credit card cash advances a pricey way to get cash. In addition to the fees, you'll pay interest from the moment of your withdrawal, even if you pay your monthly bills on time.

CREDIT CARDS

You can use MasterCard and Visa cards to charge your expenses at most island hotels, car-rental companies, restaurants, and large shops. Many also accept American Express. Only the major hotels and car-rental firms accept Diners Club, however, and none accept Discover cards. Always ask first, and when you're away from the main towns, don't count on putting anything on plastic.

💬 "TAHITI time"

There's an old story about a 19th-century planter who promised a South Pacific islander a weekly wage and a pension if he would come to work on his copra plantation. Copra is dried coconut meat, from which oil is pressed for use in soaps, cosmetics, and other products. Hours of backbreaking labor are required to chop open the coconuts and extract the meat by hand.

The islander was sitting by the lagoon, eating the fruit he had picked from nearby trees while hauling in one fish after another. "Let me make sure I understand correctly," said the islander. "You want me to break my back working for you for 30 years. Then you'll pay me a pension so I can come back here and spend the rest of my life sitting by

the lagoon, eating the fruit from my trees and the fish I catch? I may not be sophisticated, but I am not stupid."

The islander's response reflects an attitude still prevalent in Tahiti and French Polynesia, where many people don't have to work in the Western sense. Here life moves at a slow pace. The locals call it "Tahiti time."

Consequently, do not count on the same level of service in hotels and restaurants as you might expect back home. The slowness is not slothful inattention; it's just the way things are done here. Your drink will come in due course. If you must have it immediately, order it at the bar. Otherwise, relax with your friendly hosts and enjoy their charming company.

Beware of hidden credit-card fees while traveling. Check with your credit or debit card issuer to see what fees, if any, will be charged for overseas transactions. Recent reform legislation in the U.S., for example, has curbed some exploitative lending practices. But many banks have responded by increasing fees in other areas, including fees for customers who use credit and debit cards while out of the country—even if those charges were made in U.S. dollars. Fees can amount to 3% or more of the purchase price. Check with your bank before departing to avoid any surprise charges on your statement.

Personally, I use my Capital One credit card since it charges no foreign transaction fee, nor does it have an annual fee. Read your own card member agreement—or better yet, call your bank's customer service department—for charges.

Once you are here, merchants and other businesses cannot legally add to your final bill to cover their credit card costs. In other words, they cannot tack on a few percent points for the privilege of using your card.

STAYING HEALTHY
Doctors & Medication

Tahiti and French Polynesia pose no major health problem for most travelers, although it's a good idea to have your tetanus, hepatitis-A, and hepatitis-B vaccinations up-to-date.

If you have a chronic condition, you should consult your doctor before visiting the islands.

By and large, medical care is very good in Papeete. Every island also has a government clinic, and some have doctors in private practice. Should the need arise, your hotel or pension will recommend a qualified physician or dentist.

Overseas health-insurance plans are not accepted here, so you will likely have to pay all medical costs upfront and be reimbursed later. See "Insurance," in the "Fast Facts" in chapter 13.

Remember to pack **prescription medications** in your carry-on luggage, and carry them in their original containers, with pharmacy labels affixed—otherwise, they won't make it through airport security. Also bring along copies of your prescriptions in case you lose your pills or run out. Carry the generic name of prescription medicines, since local pharmacies primarily carry medications manufactured in France, and the brand names might be different here than in the United States.

And don't forget **sunglasses** and an extra pair of **contact lenses** or **prescription glasses.**

Common Ailments

Minor illnesses on the islands include the common cold and the occasional outbreaks of influenza and conjunctivitis (pinkeye).

Cuts, scratches, and all open sores should be treated promptly in the Tropics. I always carry a tube of antibacterial ointment and a small package of adhesive bandages.

TROPICAL ILLNESSES

There are plenty of mosquitoes, but they do not carry deadly endemic diseases such as malaria. From time to time, the islands will experience an outbreak of **dengue fever,** a viral disease borne by the *Adès aegypti* mosquito, which lives indoors and bites only during daylight hours. Dengue seldom is fatal in adults, but you should take extra precautions to keep children from being bitten by mosquitoes if the disease is present. (Other precautions should be taken if you are traveling with **children;** see "Specialized Travel Resources," below.)

BUGS, BITES & OTHER WILDLIFE CONCERNS

The islands have multitudes of mosquitoes, roaches, ants, houseflies, and other insects. **Ants** are omnipresent here, so don't leave crumbs or dirty dishes lying around your room. A few beaches and swampy areas also have invisible **sand flies**—the dreaded *no-seeums* or *no-nos*—that bite the ankles around daybreak and dusk.

Insect repellent is widely available in most drug stores and grocery shops. The most effective contain a high percentage of "deet" (N,N-diethyl-m-toluamide).

Lather Up

The sun in these latitudes can burn your skin in a very short period of time—even on what seems like a cloudy day. Limit your exposure, especially during the first few days of your trip. Be particularly careful from 11am to 2pm. Use sunscreen with a high protection factor (SPF30 or more) and apply it liberally. If you're going snorkeling, wear a T-shirt to avoid overexposure on your back and don't forget sunscreen on the backs of your legs.

Multitudes of Animals

Don't bother complaining about the multitude of dogs, chickens, pigs, and squawking myna birds running loose out here, even in the finest restaurants. They are as much a part of life as the island-ers themselves. And don't be frightened by those little **geckos** (lizards) crawling around the rafters of even the most expensive bungalows. They're harmless to us humans, but lethal to insects.

DRINKING WATER

Tap water is safe to drink only in the city of Papeete on Tahiti and on Bora Bora. You can buy bottled spring water in any grocery store. See "Fast Facts" in the chapters that follow for particulars.

If You Get Sick

The main public hospital and two private clinics in Papeete are up to international standards. Elsewhere you can get a broken bone set and a coral scrape tended, but you may be evacuated to Tahiti for more serious ailments. Tahiti has many well-stocked drug stores (most of their products and medications are from France), and most islands have a pharmacy. Infirmaries and pharmacies are listed under the "Fast Facts" in the specific island chapters.

You may have to pay all medical costs upfront and be reimbursed later. Medicare and Medicaid do not provide coverage for medical costs outside the U.S. Before leaving home, find out what medical services your health insurance covers. To protect yourself, consider buying medical travel insurance (see "Insurance," in chapter 13).

CRIME & SAFETY

While international terrorism is a threat throughout the world, the islands are among the planet's safest destinations. Tight security procedures are in effect at Tahiti-Faaa International Airport, but once you're on the outer islands, you are unlikely to see a metal detector, nor is anyone likely to inspect your carry-on.

The islands have seen increasing property theft in recent years, however, including occasional break-ins at hotel rooms and resort bungalows. Although street crimes against tourists are still relatively rare, friends of mine who live here don't stroll off Papeete's busy boulevard Pomare after dark. For that matter, you should stay alert wherever you are after dusk.

Don't leave valuable items in your hotel room, in your rental car, or unattended anywhere. See the "Fast Facts" sections in the following chapters for specific precautions.

Women should not wander alone on deserted beaches at any time, since some Polynesian men may consider such behavior to be an invitation for instant amorous activity.

When heading outdoors, keep in mind that injuries often occur when people fail to follow instructions. Believe the experts who tell you to stay on the established trails. Hike only in designated areas, follow the marine charts if piloting your own boat, carry rain gear, and wear a life jacket when canoeing or rafting. Mountain weather can be fickle at any time. Watch out for sudden storms that can leave you drenched and send bolts of lightning your way.

The French gendarmes will come to rescue you if you get into trouble out in the wild, but believe me, they do not appreciate tourists blundering into trouble.

BE CAREFUL IN THE water

Most of French Polynesia's marine creatures are harmless to humans, but there are some to avoid. Always **seek local advice** before snorkeling or swimming in a lagoon away from the hotel beaches. Many diving operators conduct snorkeling tours. If you don't know what you're doing, go with them.

Wash and apply a good antiseptic or antibacterial ointment to all **coral cuts and scrapes** as soon as possible.

Because coral cannot grow in fresh water, the flow of rivers and streams into the lagoon creates narrow channels known as **passes** through the reef. Currents can be very strong in the passes, so stay in the protected, shallow water of the inner lagoons.

Sharks are curious beasts that are attracted by bright objects such as watches and knives, so be careful what you wear in the water. Don't swim in areas where sewage or edible wastes are dumped, and never swim alone if you have any suspicion that sharks might be present. If you do see a shark, don't splash in the water or urinate. Calmly retreat and get out of the water as quickly as you can, without creating a disturbance.

Those round things on the rocks and reefs that look like pincushions are **sea urchins,** and their calcium spikes can be more painful than needles. A sea-urchin puncture can result in burning, aching, swelling, and discoloration (black or purple) around the area where the spines entered your skin. The best thing to do is to pull any protruding spines out. The body will absorb the spines within 24 hours to 3 weeks, or the remainder of the spines will work themselves out. Contrary to popular advice, do not urinate or pour vinegar on the embedded spines—this will not help.

Jellyfish stings can hurt like the devil but are seldom life-threatening. You need to get any visible tentacles off your body right away, but not with your hands, unless you are wearing gloves. Use a stick or anything else that is handy. Then rinse the sting with saltwater or fresh water, and apply ice to prevent swelling and to help control the pain. If you can find it at an island grocery store, unseasoned meat tenderizer is a great antidote.

The **stone fish** is so named because it looks like a piece of stone or coral as it lies buried in the sand on the lagoon bottom with only its back and 13 venomous spikes sticking out. Its venom can cause paralysis and even death. You'll know by the intense pain if you're stuck. Serum is available, so get to a hospital at once. **Sea snakes, cone shells, crown-of-thorns starfish, moray eels, lionfish,** and **demon stingers** also can be painful, if not deadly. The last thing any of these creatures wants to do is to tangle with a human, so keep your hands to yourself.

SPECIALIZED TRAVEL RESOURCES

In addition to the destination-specific resources listed below, please visit Frommers.com for other specialized travel resources.

LGBT Travelers

French Polynesia is a relatively friendly destination for gay men. In the islands, many families with a shortage of female offspring rear young boys as girls, or at least relegate them to female chores around the home and village. These males-raised-as-girls are known as *mahus*. Some of them grow up to be heterosexual; others become homosexual or bisexual and, often appearing publicly in women's attire, actively seek the company of tourists. Some dance the female parts in traditional island night shows. You'll see them throughout the islands. Many of them have traveled widely and speak English fluently, making them prime candidates for jobs in hotels and restaurants.

On the other hand, women were not considered equal in this respect in ancient times, so lesbians may not find the islands quite as friendly.

Travelers with Disabilities

Most disabilities shouldn't stop anyone from traveling, even in the islands, where ramps, handles, accessible toilets, automatic opening doors, telephones at convenient heights, and other helpful aids are just beginning to appear.

Some hotels provide rooms specially equipped for people with disabilities. These improvements are ongoing; inquire when making a reservation whether such rooms are available.

A majority of hotels here consist of bungalows separated from the restaurant, bar, and other facilities, sometimes by long distances. A few upper-end resorts have golf carts or other means of transporting their guests around their properties, but most hotels do not. Anyone who has trouble walking should request accommodations near the central facilities. Make this absolutely clear when you or your travel agent make your reservations, preferably in writing. Not all hotels remember to honor such requests, so take copies of your request with you, and reiterate it when checking in.

The major international airlines make special arrangements for travelers with disabilities. Be sure to tell them of your needs when you reserve. Repeat it at the check-in counter for Air Tahiti Nui, which does not have a pre-boarding option at all airports, and whose planes often park out on the tarmac at Los Angeles International Airport, where you may ride a bus and then climb up stairs into the aircraft.

Airport security and Customs officials also will make special arrangements for travelers with disabilities, but this is not always obvious and must be requested.

Although Air Tahiti and Air Moorea, the domestic carriers, use small planes that are not equipped for passengers with disabilities, their staff members go out of their way to help everyone get in and out of the craft.

Family Travel

Some of the larger hotels are beginning to cater to families. Best are the **Four Seasons Resort Bora Bora** (p. 192) and **Le Meridien Bora Bora** (p. 194).

For the most part, however, tourism in French Polynesia is still aimed primarily at honeymooners and other couples. To be blunt, the islands are better known for sand, sea, and sex than for babysitters, nannies, and playgrounds.

That's not to say you and your offspring won't have a marvelous time doing things together here. The islanders invariably love children and are very good at babysitting. Just make sure you get one who speaks English. The hotels can take care of this for you. On the other hand, childhood does not last as long here as it does in Western societies. As soon as they are capable, children are put to work, first caring for their younger siblings and cousins and helping out with household chores, later tending the village gardens. It's only as teenagers, and then only if they leave their villages for Papeete, that they know unemployment in the Western sense. Accordingly, few towns and villages have children's facilities, such as playgrounds, outside school property.

Some resorts do not accept children at all; I point these out in the establishment listings, but you should ask to make sure. Even if they do, check whether the hotel can provide cribs, bottle warmers, and other needs, and if they have children's menus.

Disposable diapers and baby food are sold in many main-town stores, but you should take along a supply of such items as children's aspirin, a thermometer, adhesive bandages, and any special medications. Make sure your children's vaccinations are up-to-date before you leave home. If your kids are very small, perhaps you should discuss your travel plans with your family doctor.

Remember to protect youngsters with ample sunscreen. Some other tips: Certain tropical plants and animals may resemble rocks or vegetation, so teach your youngsters to avoid touching or brushing up against rocks, seaweed, and other objects. If your children are prone to swimmer's ear, use vinegar or preventive drops before swimming in freshwater streams or lakes. Have them shower soon after swimming or suffering cuts or abrasions.

Women Travelers

The islands are relatively safe for women traveling alone, but don't let the charm of warm nights and smiling faces lull you into any less caution than you would exercise at home. *Do not* wander alone on deserted beaches. In the old days, this was an invitation for sex. If that's what you want today, that's what you'll likely get. Otherwise, it could result in your being raped. And don't hitchhike alone, either.

Senior Travelers

Children are cared for communally in the islands' extended family systems, and so are seniors. Many islanders live with their families from birth to death. Consequently, the local governments don't provide as many programs and other benefits for persons of retirement age as in the United States and other Western countries. You won't find many senior discounts.

Nevertheless, mention the fact that you're a senior when you first make your travel reservations. All major airlines and many chain hotels offer discounts for seniors.

Student Travelers

Given the high costs of travel to and in French Polynesia, it's not surprising that the islands are not on the usual backpacker trail across the South Pacific. There are many pensions (boardinghouses) here, and a few dormitories and campgrounds, but they are expensive compared to the Cook Islands and Fiji, the two hot college-age destinations out here.

If you're going on to New Zealand and Australia, you'd be wise to get an **international student ID card** from the **International Student Travel Confederation (ISTC)** (www.istc.org), which offers savings on plane tickets. It also provides basic health and life insurance and a 24-hour help line. You can apply for the card online or in person at **STA Travel** (*©* **800/781-4040** in North America; www.statravel.com), the biggest student-travel agency in the world; check out the website to locate STA Travel offices worldwide.

Single Travelers

Having traveled alone through the islands for more years than I care to admit, I can tell you it's a great place to be unattached. After all, this is the land of smiles and genuine warmth toward strangers. The attitude soon infects visitors: All I've ever had to do to meet my fellow travelers is wander into a hotel bar, order a beer, and ask the persons next to me where they are from and what they have done here.

Unfortunately, the solo traveler is often forced to pay a "single supplement" charged by many resorts, cruise lines, and tours for the privilege of sleeping alone.

RESPONSIBLE TOURISM

Climate change and rising sea levels resulting from global warming are having a noticeable impact on French Polynesia and the other South Pacific islands. Some islanders I have known for more than 30 years tell me the seasons are now unpredictable (it's more likely to rain in the dry season, and vice versa), and the tides are higher than ever (in some places, the lagoons lap directly on dry land at high tide rather than on the beach). Indeed, most islanders don't want to hear any corporate-induced spin about there being no evidence of global warming and its consequences. They know it's true from firsthand experience.

French Polynesia has allowed resort developers to built hundreds of bungalows over the lagoons. In fact, manta rays reportedly have disappeared in parts of the Bora Bora lagoon because of the construction. To the islanders beyond Bora Bora, however, their lagoons are not just places where you swim around and look at beautiful corals and sea life; they are major sources of food. Protecting their lagoons and reefs is a matter of survival. Consequently, French Polynesia does have laws protecting its lagoons, reefs, and sea life. You cannot, for example, legally break off a piece of living coral to bring home (a bad idea anyway, since sea life will emit offensive odors as soon as it dies and begins to decay).

> ### 📎 Leave Fido at Home
>
> **Don't even think about bringing your pet to French Polynesia. Fido will be quarantined until you are ready to fly home.**

The high cost of doing business here has induced some hotels to turn to renewable energy. Foremost is the InterContinental Resort and Thalasso Spa Bora Bora, which gets its air-conditioning from cold seawater pumped from 2,500 feet below the surface. You likely will see solar panels and even a wind generator or two at the small pensions.

GENERAL RESOURCES FOR
responsible TRAVEL

The following websites provide valuable wide-ranging information on sustainable travel.

o **Responsible Travel** (www.responsibletravel.com) is a great source of sustainable travel ideas; the site is run by a spokesperson for ethical tourism in the travel industry. **Sustainable Travel International** (www.sustainabletravelinternational.org) promotes ethical tourism practices, and manages an extensive directory of sustainable properties and tour operators around the world.

o **Carbonfund** (www.carbonfund.org), **TerraPass** (www.terrapass.org), and **Cool Climate** (http://coolclimate.berkeley.edu) provide info on "carbon offsetting," or offsetting the greenhouse gas emitted during flights.

o **Greenhotels** (www.greenhotels.com) recommends green-rated member hotels around the world that fulfill the company's stringent environmental requirements. **Environmentally Friendly Hotels** (www.environmentallyfriendlyhotels.com) offers more green accommodation ratings.

o **Volunteer International** (www.volunteerinternational.org) has a list of questions to help you determine the intentions and the nature of a volunteer program. For general info on volunteer travel, visit **www.volunteerabroad.org** and **www.idealist.org**.

We visitors can help by practicing **responsible tourism,** which means being careful with the environments we explore and respecting the communities we visit. We can also choose to stay in properties which minimize their impact on the environment.

SPECIAL-INTEREST & ESCORTED TRIPS

Although outdoor activities take first place in the islands (see "The Active Traveler," below), you can also spend your time learning a new craft, exploring the reefs as part of a conservation project, and whale- and dolphin-watching.

Bird-watching

Avid bird-watchers are likely to see terns, boobies, herons, petrols, noddies, and many other seabirds throughout the islands. French Polynesia alone has 28 species of breeding seabirds, making memorable a visit to Motu Puarua and Motu Oeone, tiny islets out in Tikihau's lagoon, where noddies and snowy white fairy terns nest (see chapter 11).

The number and variety of land birds diminish as you go eastward. Most live in the bush away from settlements and the accompanying cats, dogs, and rats, so you will need to head into the bush for the best watching.

In French Polynesia, **Société d'Ornithologie de Polynésie** (**Ornithological Society of Polynesia;** © **50.62.09;** www.manu.pf) lists local birds on its website.

A few companies have bird-watching tours to the South Pacific, including the U.K.-based **Bird Quest** (© **44/1254 826317;** www.birdquest.co.uk) and **Bird-watching Breaks** (© **44/1381 610495;** www.birdwatchingbreaks.com).

EcoTravel Tours

The **Oceanic Society** (© **800/326-7491;** www.oceanicsociety.org), an award-winning organization based in California, has natural history and ecotourism expeditions to the islands. A marine naturalist accompanies its trips, which include village visits and bird-watching excursions.

Whale- & Dolphin-watching

Whale- and dolphin-watching are popular activities in the islands. Dolphins live here year-round, and humpback whales escape the cold of Antarctica and spend from July until October giving birth to their calves in the tropical South Pacific. They can be seen swimming off many islands.

The best dolphin-watching experiences are on Moorea in French Polynesia, where American marine biologist **Dr. Michael Poole** leads daylong excursions to visit some of the 150 spinner dolphins he has identified as regular residents. Honeymooners love to have their pictures taken while swimming with the intelligent mammals in a fenced-in area at **Moorea Dolphin Center,** at the InterContinental Resort & Spa Moorea. See chapter 6 for details.

Escorted General Interest Tours

Escorted tours are structured group tours, with a group leader (I prefer the old-fashioned term "tour guide"). The price usually includes everything from airfare to hotels, meals, tours, admission costs, and local transportation.

Escorted tours are not a big part of the business in these small islands, where it's easy to find your way around and book local tours and activities. Most of the travel agents I mention under "Knowledgeable Travel Agents," earlier in this chapter, will have someone meet and greet you at the airport upon arrival, take you to your hotel, and make sure you get on any prearranged tours and activities, but you will not have a tour guide.

Some tour companies add a short stopover in Tahiti to their escorted tours of Australia and New Zealand, but these may not include a guide for the island portion. Leaders in this add-on feature include **Tauck Tours** (© **800/788-7885;** www.tauck.com); **Qantas Vacations** (© **800/641-8772;** www.qantasvacations.com); **Australia Escorted Tours** (© **888/333-6607;** www.australia-escorted-tours.com), and **Abercrombie & Kent** (© **800/652-7986;** www.abercrombiekent.com), which adds Fiji and French Polynesia to its high-end escorted tours. Otherwise, I recommend getting a travel agent to track down an escorted tour.

Despite the fact that escorted tours require big deposits and predetermine hotels, restaurants, and itineraries, many people derive security and peace of mind from the structure they offer. Escorted tours let travelers sit back and enjoy the trip without having to drive or worry about details. They're particularly convenient for people with limited mobility and they can be a great way to make new friends.

On the downside, you'll have little opportunity for serendipitous interactions with locals. The tours can be jampacked with activities, leaving little room for individual

Special-Interest & Escorted Trips

PLANNING YOUR TRIP TO TAHITI & FRENCH POLYNESIA

sightseeing, whim, or adventure—plus they often focus on the heavily touristed sites, so you miss out on many a lesser-known gem.

CRUISING IN THE ISLANDS

Tahiti and the nearby Society Islands are ideal grounds for cruise ships, since it's barely an hour's steam from Tahiti to Moorea, half a day's voyage on to Huahine, and less than 2 hours each among Huahine, Raiatea, Tahaa, and Bora Bora. That means you spend most days and nights at anchor in lovely lagoons with plenty of time to explore the islands and play in the water. Bear in mind, however, that you'll see a lot more of the ship than you will of the islands.

Cruises could also be an affordable way to see the islands in style, since the prices usually include all meals, wine with lunch and dinner, soft drinks, and most onboard activities. You might even find a deal that includes airfare to and from Tahiti.

Adventures on the Aranui 3 ★★★

The working cargo ship *Aranui 3* (© 800/972-7268 in the U.S., or 42.36.21 in Papeete; fax 43.48.89; www.aranui.com) is the most interesting way to visit the remote Marquesas Islands, not all of which have airports. See "Exploring the Marquesas on the *Aranui 3*," p. 236.

Outfitted for up to 200 passengers, this 78m (355-ft.) freighter makes regular 13-day round-trips from Papeete to 6 of the 10 Marquesas Islands, with stops in between at Fakarava and Rangiroa in the Tuamotus. While the crew loads and unloads the ship's cargo, passengers spend their days ashore experiencing the islands and islanders. Among the activities: picnicking on beaches, snorkeling, visiting villages, and exploring archaeological sites. Experts on Polynesian history and culture accompany most voyages.

Accommodations are in 10 suites, 12 deluxe cabins, 63 standard cabins (with twin beds), and dormitories. The suites and cabins all have private bathrooms. Suites and deluxe cabins have windows and doors opening to outside decks, and their bathrooms are equipped with bathtubs as well as showers. Standard cabins lack outside doors and have portholes instead of windows. The ship has a restaurant, bar, boutique, library, video lounge, and pool.

The ship's primary job is to haul cargo, so it does not have stabilizers and other features of a luxury liner. In other words, do not expect the same level of comfort, cuisine, and service as on the other ships cruising these waters. If you only want to sit by the pool, eat prodigious quantities of fine food, and smoke cigars, the *Aranui 3* may not be your cup of tea. But for those who want to go places relatively few people visit, and learn a lot in the process, it is an excellent choice.

Fares for the complete voyage range from about US$2,079 for a dormitory bunk to US$5,445 per person for suites. All meals are included, but you have to pay your own bar bill and your airfare to and from Tahiti.

Luxury on the Paul Gauguin ★★★

Also locally owned, the 157m (513-ft.), 318-passenger *Paul Gauguin* (© 800/848-6172 or 425/440-6171 in the U.S., 54.51.00 in Papeete; www.pgcruises.com) spends most of its year making 7-day cruises through the Society Islands, but occasionally extends to the Tuamotu and Marquesas islands, and it has even ventured as far west as Cook Islands, Samoa, Tonga, Fiji, and even New Zealand. Environmentalist Jean-Michel Cousteau and other guest lecturers accompany some cruises.

All of the ship's seven suites and about half of its 152 staterooms have private verandas or balconies (the least expensive lower-deck units have windows or portholes). All are luxuriously appointed with minibars, TVs and VCRs, direct-dial phones, and marble bathrooms with full-size tubs. Most have queen-size beds, although some have two twins.

Most weeks the *Paul Gauguin* cruises from Papeete to Moorea, Raiatea, Tahaa, and Bora Bora in the Society Islands. Occasionally it adds Huahine. Fares for the 1-week Society Islands cruises start at US$2,770 per person double occupancy.

A Lot of Company on Princess Cruises

Formerly a permanent fixture here, **Princess Cruises** (© 800/774-6237; www.princesscruises.com) now sends its 670-passenger ships *Royal Princess* and *Ocean Princess* to French Polynesia for temporary stays of 3 months to 6 months. Check its website for the current schedule and fares. The *Ocean Princess* was known as the *Tahitian Princess* when it cruised here year-round.

Dining in the Lagoon with Nomade Yachting Bora Bora

From everything I could find out, the worldwide recession has been especially difficult for **Nomade Yachting Bora Bora** (© 54.45.05; fax 45.10.65; www.nomadeyachting.com), which in normal times makes 1-week cruises from Bora Bora to Huahine, Raiatea, and Tahaa. I would tread very cautiously with these cruises until the economic conditions improve.

Formerly known as Bora Bora Cruises, it owns two sleek, luxurious yachts, the *Tu Moana* and the *Tia Moana,* which are 69m (226-ft.) long and can carry up to 60 passengers in 30 staterooms spread over three decks. The boats are small enough to anchor closer to shore than the other ships here. Check the website for prices and schedules.

Fly-Fishing from the Haumana

Avid fishermen can cast lines from the *Haumana* (© 50.06.74; fax 50.06.72; www.tahiti-haumana-cruises.com). This 34m (110-ft.), 42-passenger catamaran specializes in 3-, 4-, and 7-night cruises on the calm, shallow lagoons of Rangiroa and Tikehau in the Tuamotus. Fishing is not the primary focus of the cruises (diving, surfing, and other activities are possible), but this is one of the few vessels to carry rods, reels, and other gear. It's also a much more pleasant way to visit Rangiroa's Pink Sands and Blue Lagoon than riding a speedboat an hour each way (see chapter 11). Although the *Haumana* is smaller than other ships here, its 21 air-conditioned cabins all have large windows or portholes, queen-size beds, sofas or settees, minibars, TVs, VCRs, phones, and shower-only bathrooms with hair dryers. Check the website or contact the firm for rates which usually include all meals, drinks, fishing, and kayak excursions.

THE ACTIVE TRAVELER

These islands are a dream for active travelers, especially those into diving, snorkeling, swimming, boating, and other watersports. You can also play golf and tennis, or hike into the jungle-clad mountainous interiors of the islands. Kayaking is popular everywhere, and all but a few hotels provide them for free. There's good biking along the many roads skirting colorful lagoons. You can engage in these activities everywhere, although some islands are better than others. I point out the best in the following chapters, but here's a brief rundown of my favorites.

On the Web, **Gordon's Guide** (www.gordonsguide.com) compiles adventure tours from around the world. It's a good place to search for South Pacific adventure trips in a variety of categories. Save time by searching for a specific destination.

Biking

Relatively flat roads circle most of the islands, making for easy and scenic bike riding. In fact, bicycles are one of my favorite means of getting around. It's simple and inexpensive to rent bikes on all but a few of the islands. In fact, some hotels and resorts provide bikes for their guests to use.

Diving & Snorkeling

Most of the islands have very good to great diving and snorkeling. Virtually every lagoonside resort has a dive operator on premises or nearby, and many will let snorkelers go along.

French Polynesia is famous for its bountiful sea life, from harmless tropical fish to hammerhead sharks. You'll see plenty of creatures at Moorea, Bora Bora, Huahine, and Raiatea-Tahaa, but the best diving and snorkeling is in the huge lagoons of Rangiroa, Tikehau, Manihi, and Fakarava in the Tuamotu Islands. See chapters 6, 7, 8, 9, and 11.

Most resorts offer dive packages to their guests, and the American-based **PADI Travel Network** (© **800/729-7234;** www.padi.com) puts together packages for divers of all experience levels.

Deep-Sea Fishing

Charter boats on most islands will take you in search of marlin, swordfish, tuna, mahimahi, and other game fish.

You can also cast your line while living aboard in relative luxury. In the Tuamotu Archipelago, **Haumana Cruises** (www.tahiti-haumana-cruises.com) uses a 17-cabin yacht. See "Cruising in the Islands," above.

Golf & Tennis

French Polynesia now has the **Moorea Green Pearl Golf Course of Polynesia,** an 18-hole set of links on Moorea, to complement the venerable **Olivier Breaud International Golf Course of Atimaono,** on the south coast of Tahiti. See chapters 6 and 5, respectively.

Hiking

These aren't the Rocky Mountains, nor are there blazed trails out here, but hiking in the islands is a lot of fun.

Tahiti and Moorea have several trails into the highlands, some of which run along spectacular ridges. You'll need a guide for the best hikes, but you can easily hire them on both islands. See chapters 5 and 6.

Horseback Riding

A great way to experience a South Pacific sunset (other than while sipping a cold drink) is from the back of a horse while riding along a beach. You can do just that on

Moorea and Huahine, where the ranches also have daytime rides into the mountains. See chapters 6 and 7.

Kayaking

All but a few beachfront resorts have canoes, kayaks, small sailboats, sailboards, and other toys for their guests' amusement. Since most of these properties sit beside lagoons, using these craft is not only fun, it's relatively safe. They are most fun where you can paddle or sail across the lagoon to uninhabited islets out on the reef, such as on Moorea's northwest coast. See chapter 6.

Sailing

If you are an experienced sailor, you can charter a yacht—with or without skipper and crew—and knock around some of the French Polynesian islands as the wind and your own desires dictate. The best place to start is Raiatea, which shares a lagoon with Tahaa, the only French Polynesian island that can be circumnavigated entirely within a protective reef. Depending on the wind, Bora Bora and Huahine are relatively easy blue-water trips away.

The Moorings, a respected yacht charter company based in Florida (𝄐 **888/92-8420** or 727/535-1446; www.moorings.com), operates a fleet of monohull and catamaran sailboats based at **Apooti Marina** on Raiatea's northern coast (𝄐 **66.35.93;** fax 66.20.94; moorings@mail.pf). That's a few minutes' sail to Tahaa. Prices for a 1-week bareboat cruise (that is, without skipper or crew) run about US$4,000 to US$7,000 for two people. Provisions are extra. The agency will check to make sure you and your party can handle sailboats of these sizes; otherwise, you pay extra for a skipper.

Also at Apooti Marina, **Sunsail Yacht Charters** (𝄐 **800/327-2276** in the U.S., 60.04.85 on Raiatea; www.sunsail.com) has a fleet of 11-to-15m (36–49 ft.) yachts. Check its arcane website for bareboat rates.

Tahiti Yacht Charter (𝄐 **45.04.00;** fax 45.76.00; www.tahitiyachtcharter.com) has 11-to-14m (36–45 ft.) yachts based at Papeete and Raiatea. It designs cruises throughout the territory, including lengthy voyages to the Tuamotus and Marquesas. Similar services are offered by **Archipel Croisiers** on Moorea (𝄐 **56.36.39;** fax 56.35.87; www.archipels.com).See chapters 5 and 8.

Surfing

The islands have some world-famous surfing spots such as Teahupoo on Tahiti (see chapter 5). All the best are reef breaks; that is, the surf crashes out on coral reefs instead of on sandy beaches. These are no places for beginners, since you could suffer serious injury by landing on a razor-sharp coral reef. (Or as one of my island friends puts it, "You'll become hamburger in a hurry.")

The surf pounds directly on beaches on Tahiti, where you can learn to surf with *Ecole de Surf Tura'i Mataare* (**Tahiti Surf School**) (𝄐 **41.91.37;** www.tahiti surfschool.info). See chapter 5.

STAYING CONNECTED
Mobile Phones

Known as "mobiles" (moo-*beels*) over here, cellphones are prevalent throughout the islands. No international wireless company operates in French Polynesia, however, and many American and Canadian phones won't work since French Polynesia uses the Global System for Mobiles (GSM) technology. Although GSM is a quasi-universal system, only T-Mobile and AT&T Wireless use it in the U.S., while some Rogers customers in Canada are GSM. All Europeans and most Australians use GSM. Call your wireless company to see if your phone is GSM.

You should be able to use your iPhone, Blackberry, or other GSM phone if your home provider has a roaming agreement with **Vini** (𝄐 **48.13.13;** www.vini.pf), the sole local cellphone company. Ask your wireless operator to activate "international roaming" for French Polynesia. Most carriers charge near-exorbitant fees for calling within and out of French Polynesia, so be sure to ask how much it will cost.

I can make local calls within French Polynesia on my home cellphone, but calling me requires expensive international calls for French Polynesians. In other words, their calls to my cellphone were routed to the United States and then back to French Polynesia!

I get around this since (1) my GSM phone transmits and receives on the 900mHz band; (2) it has been "unlocked" from its SIM card, the removable computer chip that stores my and my provider's information; and (3) I buy a local SIM card from Vini.

Prepaid SIM cards are available at stores displaying the VINI sign. The least expensive costs about 1,000CFP and includes 30 minutes of outgoing calls. Incoming calls are free.

The **Travel Insider** (www.thetravelinsider.info) has an excellent explanation of all this, as well as a phone-unlocking service. Click on "Road Warrior Resources" and "International Cellphone Service."

Internet & E-Mail

E-mail is as much a part of life in French Polynesia as it is anywhere else these days. Although ADSL connections are available here (ADSL is not as fast as DSL or cable access in the U.S. and other countries, but is much speedier than dial-up connections), most Internet connections are still dial-up, which will seem glacially slow if you're used to DSL or cable.

Access is also relatively expensive. **MANA** (𝄐 **50.88.88;** www.mana.pf) is the only local Internet service provider (ISP), and it charges by the minute rather than by the month. Consequently, don't expect people here to reply to your e-mail immediately. Patience definitely is a virtue when dealing with folks in French Polynesia.

Some hotels and pensions provide free Internet access, but as a general rule expect to pay from 500CFP to 1,500CFP for each hour spent online, either wired or wireless.

WITHOUT YOUR OWN COMPUTER

All but a few hotels and pensions have computers from which guests can send and receive e-mail and surf the Web.

There are **cybercafes** on several islands. I point these out under "Internet Access" in the "Fast Facts" sections in the specific island chapters.

WITH YOUR OWN COMPUTER

Most hotels and pensions also have wireless Internet connections (WiFi, pronounced *WeeFee* here), or wired high-speed dataports in their rooms. I point them out in the hotel listings in this book.

Most cybercafes have wireless connections. I mention them in the "Fast Facts" sections of each island chapter.

MANA, the local provider, has wireless **Manaspots** (© **50.88.88;** wwww. manaspot.pf) at several locations in Papeete (including the airport) and at the post offices or *mairies* (town halls) on most other islands. MANA sells prepaid access cards at its main office in Fare Tony, on boulevard Pomare between the Vaima Centre, at the post offices, and at many shops and restaurants. You can buy online using a credit card (the site is in both French and English). Hotels within range and some shops also sell Manaspot cards. They start at 660CFP for 1 hour.

You can also pay online with **Iaoranet** (© **77.24.86;** www.iaoranet.pf), whose hotspots are at the popular marinas and yacht anchorages.

Other companies within range of hotels and pensions include **Wifi Tiki** (© 56 35 67; www.wifitiki.com) and **Hotspot-WDG** (© **71.96.57**).

Note: These services use pop-up windows to clock your time online and on which you click to log out. Set your browser to not block pop-up windows; otherwise you could inadvertently remain online until all your purchased time has expired.

Newspapers & Magazines

The *Tahiti Beach Press,* an English-language weekly devoted to news of Tahiti's tourist industry, runs features of interest to tourists and advertisements for hotels, restaurants, real estate agents, car-rental firms, and other businesses that cater to tourists. Establishments that buy ads in it give away copies free. The daily newspapers, *La Dépêche de Tahiti* and *Les Nouvelles,* are in French. **Le Kiosk** in front of the Vaima Centre on boulevard Pomare in Papeete sells some international newspapers and magazines.

Telephones

All landline communications in and out of French Polynesia are handled by the Office des Postes et Télécommunications (OPT; www.opt.pf). Although relatively expensive, the system is modern and reliable.

HOW TO MAKE CALLS

To call French Polynesia: Dial the international access code (011 from the U.S.; 00 from the U.K., Ireland, or New Zealand; or 0011 from Australia), French Polynesia's country code **689,** and the local number (there are no area codes within French Polynesia).

To make international calls from within French Polynesia: First dial **00,** then the country code (U.S. or Canada 1, U.K. 44, Ireland 353, Australia 61, New Zealand 64), then the area code and phone number. Calls to the U.S., Europe, Australia, and New Zealand are 103CFP per minute, when dialed directly.

You can make them through your hotel, though with a surcharge, which can more than double the fee.

For operator assistance: Dial © **3600** if you need assistance making an overseas call. The operators speak English.

To make domestic calls within French Polynesia: No prefix or area code is required for domestic long distance calls, so dial the local number.

For directory assistance: Dial © **3612** for local directory information (*service des renseignements*). The operators speak English. You can look up local numbers online at **www.annuaireopt.pf** (it's in French).

TOLL-FREE NUMBERS

There are no toll-free numbers in French Polynesia. Calling a 1-800 number in the U.S. or Canada from French Polynesia is not toll-free. In fact, it costs the same as an overseas call.

PAY PHONES

Public pay phones are located at all post offices and are fairly numerous elsewhere on Tahiti, less so on the other islands. You must have a *télécarte* to call from public pay phones (coins won't work). The cards are sold at all post offices and by most hotel front desks and many shops in 1,500CFP, 2,000CFP, and 5,000CFP sizes. Insert the cards with the electronic chip facing up. Digital readouts on the phones tell you how many *unites* you have left on a card.

Radio & TV

French Polynesia has government-operated AM radio stations with programming in French and Tahitian. Several private AM and FM stations in Papeete play mostly American and British musical numbers in English; the announcers, however, speak French. Two government-owned television stations broadcast in French. Most hotels pick up a local satellite service, which carries CNN International in English. The government-owned radio and TV stations can be received throughout the territory via satellite.

TIPS ON ACCOMMODATIONS

French Polynesia has a wide range of accommodations, from deluxe resort hotels to mom-and-pop guesthouses and a few dormitories with bunk beds.

My favorite type of hotel accommodates its guests in individual bungalows set in a coconut grove beside a sandy beach and quiet lagoon; if that's not the quintessential definition of the South Seas, then I don't know what is! Many of these are super-romantic bungalows that actually stand on stilts out over the reef (although some of these overwater units tend to be close together and thus less private than bungalows ashore elsewhere). Others are as basic as tents. In between, they vary in size, furnishings, and comfort. In all, you get to enjoy your own place, one usually built or accented with thatch and other native materials, but containing most of the modern conveniences. An increasing number of these accommodations are air-conditioned, which is a plus during the humid summer months from December through March. All but a few bungalows have ceiling fans, which keep me comfortable during the rest of the year.

Pensions & Guesthouses

"The French don't care where they sleep as long as they can get a great meal," a local friend of mine once wisecracked. "On the other hand, you Americans don't care what you eat as long as you have a great place to sleep."

He meant that the French are willing to do without the luxuries most Americans demand—air conditioners and private bathrooms leap to mind—as long as the food is good.

It was said during a discussion of French Polynesia's many family-owned pensions and guesthouses. Such establishments are common in Europe, where a family may rent out rooms in their homes and provide breakfast to their guests. In America we call them bed-and-breakfasts. They're known as home stays in other English-speaking countries.

The big difference in French Polynesia is that you don't always rent a room in someone's home. Instead, you're more likely to have your own bungalow, perhaps in the backyard or even by the beach.

Many owners have used government-backed loans to acquire one-room guest bungalows with attached bathrooms. Although these bungalows are identical, the owners have added decorative touches (in some cases quite tasteful, in others barely so). Other more creative owners have built charming bungalows of tree limbs, thatch, and other natural materials.

With a few exceptions the units don't have air conditioners or even window screens, but they are likely to have ceiling fans and mosquito nets over their beds. And since many guests are French people on vacation from Tahiti, the owners have become adept at providing good food, usually for both breakfast and dinner. With meals included in their rates, they are among the best values here.

Tahiti Tourisme inspects the establishments and distributes lists of those it recommends (see "Visitor Information," in chapter 13). My discriminating French friend Muriel Weber and I stayed at some and visited many of them during my research trip for this edition, and she likes those I recommend in the following chapters.

Many promote themselves through an organization known as **Haere-Mai,** whose website (www.haere-mai.pf) gives the current room rates for most properties, in both French and English.

Local families operate most of them, so if you decide to go this route, an ability to speak some French may be essential.

Saving on Your Hotel Room

The rate ranges quoted in this book are known in the hotel industry as **rack rates,** or published rates—that is, the maximum a property charges for a room. These prices are becoming less meaningful as more and more hotels engage in "yield management," under which they change their rates almost daily depending on how many people are booked in for a particular night. In other words, you may not know what the price of a room is until you call the hotel or book online for a particular date. Nevertheless, rack rates remain the best way of comparing prices.

Many hotels here have been hurting for guests during the worldwide recession. Many have reduced staff, and some have even been forced to close. Those still in business have been reluctant to reduce their published rack rates, but they do offer discounts and other bargains on their websites. Regardless of how many websites I visit when searching for accommodations, I always go to the hotels' own sites before booking, since many offer their own Internet specials, often beating the big-site prices.

They also may be willing to extend their *tarifs residents* (lower rates for local residents) during the hard times. It never hurts to ask for a local rate.

Many of the American-based tour operators listed under "Getting to Tahiti & French Polynesia," earlier in this chapter, sell discounted hotel rooms as well as air tickets.

Another tactic is to check with the local **inbound tour operators.** In addition to selling tours and day trips to visitors already in the islands (that is, at hotel activities desks), these companies put together the local elements of tour packages—such as hotel rooms and airport transfers—for overseas wholesalers. They have the advantage of being on the scene and thus familiar with the properties. Some sell direct to inbound visitors as well as other tour companies.

Among more than a dozen Papeete-based companies, **Easy Tahiti.com** (www.easytahiti.com), **Islands Adventures/Air Tahiti** (www.islandsadventures.com), **Marama Tours** (www.maramatours.com), **Paradise Tours** (www.tahitiparadise.com), **Tahiti Nui Travel** (www.tahitinuitravel.com), and **Tekura Tahiti Travel** (www.tahiti-tekuratravelcom) have local packages within French Polynesia.

Always get a confirmation number and make a printout of any online booking transaction.

SUGGESTED TAHITI & FRENCH POLYNESIA ITINERARIES

4

People often ask me where they should go in Tahiti and French Polynesia. Lacking the ability to read minds, I do not have an easy answer. It depends on what you want to see and do on your own vacation. What I like is not necessarily what will interest you—but what I can do is give you the benefit of my expertise and advice so that you don't waste your valuable vacation time.

If you live in the United States, Canada, or Europe, the long flights mean you can easily burn a day getting to the islands and a day returning home. A week's worth of vacation suddenly becomes 5 days. If possible, therefore, you should spend more than just a week out here.

However you construct your own itinerary, first find out the airlines' schedules and book both your international and Air Tahiti domestic interisland flights well in advance. This is especially true of the domestic flights; do not wait until you arrive in the islands to take care of this important chore.

And remember the old travel agent's rule: Do not stay at the most luxurious property first. Anything after that will seem inferior, and you may go home disappointed. For example, most resorts on Moorea are neither as luxurious nor as picturesque as those on Bora Bora, so if you can afford to island-hop, start but don't end your visit on Moorea. And even after the luxuries of Bora Bora, you won't regret ending your trip with a bit of pampered chill time at Te Tiare Beach Resort on Huahine (p. 163) or the exquisite Le Taha'a Private Island & Spa (p. 177) on Tahaa.

THE ISLANDS IN BRIEF

French Polynesia sprawls over an area of 5.2 million sq. km (2 million sq. miles) in the eastern South Pacific. That's about the size of Europe, excluding the former Soviet Union countries, or about two-thirds the size of the continental United States. The 130 main islands, however, consist of only 3,885 sq. km (1,500 sq. miles) of dry land, an area about the size of Luxembourg, one of the smallest countries in Europe, or of Rhode Island, the smallest American state. Only about 280,000 souls inhabit these small specks.

The territory's five major island groups differ in terrain, climate, and, to a certain extent, people. With the exception of the Tuamotu Archipelago, an enormous chain of low coral atolls northeast of Tahiti, all but a few are "high" islands; that is, they are the mountainous tops of ancient volcanoes eroded into jagged peaks, deep bays, and fertile valleys. All have fringing, or barrier coral reefs, and blue lagoons worthy of postcards.

The Society Islands

The most strikingly beautiful and most frequently visited destinations are the **Society Islands,** so named by Capt. James Cook, the great English explorer, in 1769 because they lie relatively close together (see "A Look at the Past," p. 15). These include Tahiti and its nearby companion Moorea, which are also known as the Windward Islands because they sit to the east, the direction of the prevailing trade wind.

Tahiti is the most developed island in French Polynesia. Don't be surprised when you take the freeway from the airport into the noisy, bustling capital of Papeete. Chic bistros and high-rise shopping centers long ago replaced the city's stage-set wooden Chinese stores, and the glass and steel of luxury resorts out in the suburbs have supplanted its cheap waterfront hotels. If you're into cities, Papeete will be right up your alley. Even if you're not, Tahiti is well worth seeing, especially its fine museums devoted to the painter Paul Gauguin, the writer James Norman Hall, and the islanders themselves.

Most modern visitors bypass these jewels and quickly head to **Moorea,** just 20km (12 miles) west of Tahiti. The short journey is like being transported to another planet. Moorea's mountain peaks and fingerlike bays are world-renowned for their awesome beauty. Even though parts of Moorea are beginning to seem like Papeete suburbs, the island still retains more of old Polynesia than does Tahiti. It also has numerous white-sand beaches, which are in short supply on Tahiti, where most sand is of the black volcanic variety.

To the northwest lie Bora Bora, Huahine, Raiatea, Tahaa, Maupiti, and several smaller islands. Because they are downwind of Tahiti, they are also called the Leeward Islands.

One of the world's top honeymoon destinations, **Bora Bora** is French Polynesia's tourism dynamo, with more resorts than any other island. **Huahine** is almost as beautiful as Moorea and Bora Bora, but with only one resort and a handful of pensions, it retains much of its old Polynesian charm.

The administrative center of the Leeward Islands, **Raiatea** lacks beaches, but the deep lagoon it shares with Tahaa makes it the sailing capital of French Polynesia. **Tahaa** has only recently opened to tourism, with one of French Polynesia's top resorts now sitting out on a small reef islet. Virtually unscathed by tourism, but a favorite retreat of French residents of Tahiti, **Maupiti** has a few locally owned pensions. You can visit it on a day trip from Bora Bora.

The Tuamotu Archipelago

Across the approaches to Tahiti from the east, the 69 low-lying atolls of the **Tuamotu Archipelago** run for 1,159km (720 miles) on a line from northwest to southeast. The early European sailors called them the Dangerous Archipelago because of their tricky currents and because they virtually cannot be seen until a ship is almost on top of them. Even today, they are a wrecking ground for yachts and interisland trading boats. Two of them, Moruroa and Fangataufa, were used by France to test its nuclear weapons between 1966 and 1996. Others provide the bulk of Tahiti's well-known black pearls. **Rangiroa,** the world's second-largest atoll and the territory's best scuba-diving destination, is the most frequently visited. Neighboring **Tikehau,** with a much smaller and shallower lagoon, also has a modern resort hotel, as does **Manihi,** the territory's major producer of black pearls. To the south, the reef at **Fakarava** encircles the world's third-largest lagoon.

Out here you'll find marvelous snorkeling and diving in massive lagoons stocked with a vast array of sea life. The atolls may seem anticlimactic after you've seen the high islands, so I suggest visiting them before exploring the Society Islands.

The Marquesas Islands

Made famous in 2002 by the *Survivor* television series, the **Marquesas** are a group of 10 mountainous islands some 1,208km (750 miles) northeast of Tahiti. They are younger than the Society Islands, and because a cool equatorial current washes their shores, protective coral reefs have not enclosed them. As a result, the surf pounds on their shores, there are no encircling coastal plains, and the people live in a series of deep valleys that radiate out from central mountain peaks. The Marquesas have lost their once-large populations to 19th-century diseases and the 20th-century economic lure of Papeete; today, their sparsely populated, cloud-enshrouded valleys have an almost haunting air about them. Archaeological sites with their ancient tikis are prime attractions in the Marquesas.

Of the six inhabited islands, only **Nuku Hiva** and **Hiva Oa** have international standard hotels, and only they and **Ua Huka** and the incredibly beautiful **Ua Pou** have airports.

The Marquesas are best visited via *Aranui 3* cruises, which visit all the inhabited islands including **Fatu Hiva,** another dramatic beauty. (See "Cruising the Islands," p. 67.)

The Austral & Gambier Islands

With no hotels or resorts, the **Austral Islands,** south of Tahiti, are seldom visited. They are part of a chain of high islands that continue westward into the Cook Islands. The people of the more temperate Australs, which include **Rururu,**

Raivavae, and **Tubuai,** once produced some of the best art objects in the South Pacific, but these skills have passed into time.

Far on the southern end of the Tuamotu Archipelago, the **Gambier Islands** are the top of a semisubmerged, middle-aged high island similar to Bora Bora. The hilly remnants of the old volcano are scattered in a huge lagoon, which is partially enclosed by a barrier reef marking the original outline of the island before it began to sink. The largest of these remnant islands is **Mangareva.**

THE GRAND TOUR IN 2 WEEKS

This itinerary takes you to all the main spots: Tahiti, Moorea, Huahine, and Bora Bora—plus a few days in Rangiroa, the largest atoll in the Tuamotu Archipelago. I suggest going to Rangiroa first because, after seeing the awesome mountainous beauty of the Society Islands, it may seem anticlimactic to end your trip at a flat atoll. Tikehau, Manihi, or Fakarava, Rangiroa's Tuamotuan sisters, are also worthy alternatives to Rangiroa (see chapter 11).

An exceptional alternative—or a terrific add-on if you have a month to spend here—would be a cruise from Papeete to the Marquesas Islands on the *Aranui 3* (p. 67).

For the typical 10-day highlights tour (or honeymoon, as the case may be), leave off Rangiroa and forget Tahiti except while waiting for your flight home. Begin your visit on Moorea, then go to Bora Bora, and finish on Huahine (or Tahaa if you can afford to stay at Le Taha'a Private Island & Spa, p. 177).

Day 1: Circling Tahiti ★

Unless you arrive in the afternoon or early evening on one of Air Tahiti Nui's flights, you'll probably get here in the wee hours, so spend your first morning on a guided half-day **circle island tour** of Tahiti (p. 109). You won't have to drive or find your way around, so it's a good method of recovering while seeing the island. After a long French lunch, take a **walking tour** of downtown Papeete (p. 95). Even if you aren't staying in a hotel on Tahiti's west coast, head over there to watch the sunset over Moorea, one of the region's most awe-inspiring sights.

Days 2–4: Riding the Rip on Rangiroa ★★

The world's second-largest lagoon demands a full day's excursion by boat to one of its two key sites: **Les Sables Rose (Pink Sands)** or the **Blue Lagoon** (p. 214). Devote a full day to one of these trips. My choice would be the Blue Lagoon, actually a small lagoon within the large lagoon, though it's hard to pass up the Pink Sands, one of the great beaches here. On another day, don your snorkeling or scuba-diving gear and **ride the riptide** (p. 216) through the main pass into the lagoon. Be sure to watch the dolphins playing in Tiputa Pass at sunset.

The Grand Tour in 2 Weeks

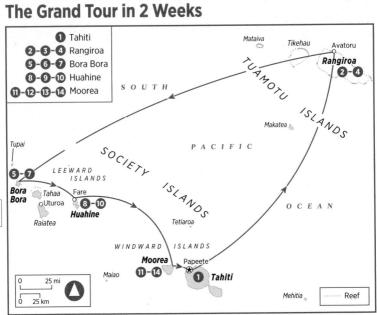

- **1** Tahiti
- **2**-**3**-**4** Rangiroa
- **5**-**6**-**7** Bora Bora
- **8**-**9**-**10** Huahine
- **11**-**12**-**13**-**14** Moorea

Mataiva · Tikehau · Avatoru · **Rangiroa** · **2**-**4**

TUAMOTU ISLANDS

SOUTH

Makatea

Tupai

SOCIETY ISLANDS

PACIFIC

LEEWARD ISLANDS

5-**7**

Bora Bora · Tahaa · Fare · **8**-**10**

Uturoa · **Huahine**

Raiatea

Tetiaroa

OCEAN

WINDWARD ISLANDS

Maiao

Moorea · Papeete

11-**14** · **1** **Tahiti**

Mehitia

0   25 mi
0   25 km

····· Reef

Days 5–7: Feeding the Sharks on Bora Bora ★★★

A change of planes in Papeete will bring you to beautiful **Bora Bora,** which many consider the world's most beautiful island. Spend part of your first day here exploring the interior by four-wheel-drive "safari expedition" (p. 188). Devote a full day to a lagoon tour by boat, the top thing to do on Bora Bora. You'll get a fish-eye view of the island's dramatic peak, snorkel while watching your guide feed a school of reef sharks, and enjoy a fresh-fish lunch on a small islet on the fringing reef (p. 188). Have dinner one night at **Bloody Mary's Restaurant & Bar** (p. 198), another night at **Villa Mahana** (p. 199).

Days 8–10: Touring Old Polynesia on Huahine ★★

After the mile-a-minute activities on Bora Bora, **Huahine** will seem like a reserved Polynesian paradise. Spend your first morning on a tour of the historic *maraes* (ancient temples) at Maeva village with Paul Atallah of **Island Eco Tours** (p. 158). The next day, tour the lagoon, swim, snorkel, or go horseback riding. I always have a sunset drink while watching the boats coming and going at **Fare,** the island's charming main town.

Days 11–14: Sightseeing on Moorea ★★★

While the lagoons are the highlights at Rangiroa and Bora Bora, the ruggedly gorgeous interior draws my eyes on **Moorea.** Whether it's via a regular guided tour, a four-wheel-drive safari excursion, or on your own, go up to the **Belvédère** overlooking **Cook's** and **Opunohu bays.** Moorea's lagoon does have its good features, especially dolphin-watching excursions led by **Dr. Michael Poole** (p. 137). And don't miss a nighttime show at **Tiki Theatre Village,** one of the region's best cultural centers (p. 137). Moorea is only 7 minutes by plane from Tahiti, which makes it a snap to connect to Papeete and your flight home.

TAHITI & MOOREA IN 1 WEEK

This itinerary outlines how you can spend your time on one of the low-end, 1-week package tours, most of which offer discounted prices for airfare and a week on Tahiti and nearby Moorea. Even if you don't buy a package, this is still the least expensive way to sample the islands, since you won't be forking out a few hundred dollars for interisland airfares and paying the relatively high prices on Bora Bora. You'll get to visit fabled Tahiti and spend a few days frolicking on Moorea. You can pick and choose from this itinerary if you have a 1- or 2-day layover on Tahiti while crossing the Pacific.

Day 1: Exploring Papeete

Get over your flight by taking it easy on the beach or around the pool this morning. Head into downtown **Papeete** in time for a long French lunch; then take a walking tour of this busy but fascinating city (p. 95). Head back to your hotel for some relaxation before watching the sunset over Moorea.

Day 2: Circling Tahiti ★★

You can either rent a vehicle or take a guided tour around Tahiti's coastal road (p. 108). Either way, stop at **James Norman Hall's Home** (p. 93), the **Gauguin Museum** (p. 95), and the **Museum of Tahiti and Her Islands** (p. 94), all of which will inform you about Tahiti's interesting history. If you drive yourself, take along a swimsuit and beach towel for a visit to **Plage de Maui (Maui Beach),** Tahiti's top sands (p. 104). At night, watch one of the dance shows at the hotels (p. 126).

Day 3: Taking a Safari Expedition into Tahiti's Interior ★★★

You may think you've seen all of Tahiti after your round-island tour, but not so. A **safari expedition** by four-wheel-drive vehicle (p. 109) will take you into the mountainous interior, which is a very different world from the coastal road. If the weather permits, these trips follow the **Papenoo Valley** into Tahiti's extinct volcanic crater. Have dinner at *les roulottes,* the carnival-like meal wagons on the Papeete waterfront.

Days 4: Sightseeing on Moorea ★★★

An early morning ferry or plane ride will get to Moorea in time to take a tour of this gorgeous island's north shore, home of the picturesque **Cook's** and **Opunohu bays** and the awesome view over them from **Le Belvédère** lookout. My favorite trip is a four-wheel-drive safari excursion (p. 136), which will take

Tahiti & Moorea in 1 Week

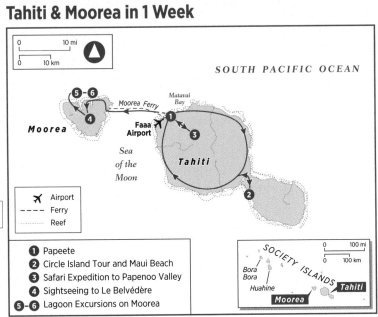

SOUTH PACIFIC OCEAN

Moorea Ferry

Matavai
Bay

Moorea

Faaa
Airport

*Sea
of the
Moon*

Tahiti

✈ Airport
- - - Ferry
.... Reef

① Papeete
② Circle Island Tour and Maui Beach
③ Safari Expedition to Papenoo Valley
④ Sightseeing to Le Belvédère
⑤-⑥ Lagoon Excursions on Moorea

SOCIETY ISLANDS

Bora
Bora

Huahine

Tahiti

Moorea

0   100 mi
0   100 km

you to the sights, along with a ride into the interior and a dip under a waterfall. After dark, take in the extraordinary dance show at **Tiki Theatre Village** (p. 137).

Day 5: Getting Wet in the Moorea Lagoon ★★★

Spending a day out on the water is a must on Moorea, and every hotel offers a half- or full-day **lagoon excursion** (p. 136). The usual route takes you across the water to a *motu* (small islet) out on the reef for some swimming, snorkeling, and a barbecue lunch that may consist of fish your crew caught on the way out.

Day 6: Dolphin-Watching on Moorea ★★★

You may have spotted dolphins playing on your Moorea lagoon excursion, but you'll learn a lot more about these friendly mammals on a trip with American marine biologist **Dr. Michael Poole** (p. 137), who has identified some 150 of them as Moorea residents.

Day 7: Finishing Up

You will need to return to Tahiti this afternoon to await your flight home, since most planes leave after dark or in the early morning hours. Enjoy your last supper while taking in the glorious view down over Papeete from **Le Belvédère** (p. 123).

The Leeward Islands in 10 Days

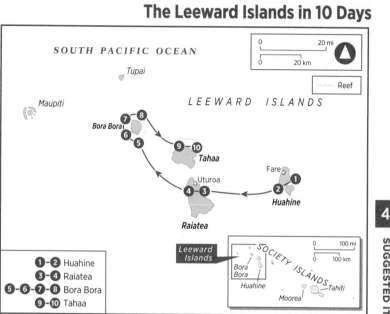

THE LEEWARD ISLANDS IN 10 DAYS

The Leeward Islands of Huahine, Raiatea, Tahaa, and Bora Bora are very different from Tahiti, or even Moorea, for that matter. With the exception of Bora Bora, which is French Polynesia's tourism magnet, all are relatively undeveloped. Except when cruise ships are in port, they will let you see what Polynesia is like without hordes of fellow visitors.

Days 1 & 2: Touring Old Polynesia on Huahine ★★

Lovely Huahine will give you a chance to relax and chill after your international flight. On your first morning, take an informative tour of the historic *maraes* (ancient temples) at Maeva village with Paul Atallah of **Island Eco Tours** (p. 158). Have lunch at **Restaurant Mauarii** on gorgeous **Avea Beach** (p. 162), one of French Polynesia's finest strands. On your second day, get out on the water with a lagoon excursion, or perhaps go horseback riding. I always have a sunset drink at **Restaurant New Temarara** (p. 166) while watching the boats coming and going at **Fare,** the island's charming main town.

Days 3 & 4: A History Lesson on Raiatea ★★★

If you can spare a day away from the beach, Raiatea will allow a glimpse of Polynesia *sans* tourists—except when cruise ships dock at **Uturoa,** the island's only town and the administrative center of the Leeward Islands. Take a morning tour to **Taputapuatea *Marae*,** the largest and most impressive ancient *marae* in French Polynesia (p. 171). You can spend your second day out on the lagoon, which Raiatea shares with Tahaa.

Days 5–8: Enjoying the Lagoon on Bora Bora ★★★

You'll spend 2 days in transit between Bora Bora and other islands, so that leaves just 2 days to experience the beauty of Bora Bora and its lagoon. Though it's barely enough time, you can make the most of the days by spending half of your first one on a four-wheel-drive safari expedition (p. 188). Devote all of the next day to a lagoon excursion, which invariably will include a shark-feeding stop, a picnic on a small islet, and time for snorkeling (p. 188). Be sure to have dinner at **Bloody Mary's Restaurant & Bar** (p. 198) one night, and at **Villa Mahana** (p. 199) the other night.

Days 9 & 10: Chilling in Luxury on Tahaa ★★★

The best way to come down after all the activities of this week is at **Le Taha'a Private Island & Spa,** on a small reef islet off Tahaa (p. 177). While you're here, take a safari excursion into the interior of Tahaa. (If Le Taha'a Private Island & Spa is too rich for your blood, finish your trip on Moorea.)

THE TUAMOTU & MARQUESAS ISLANDS IN 2 WEEKS

Your French Polynesian experience will be much richer if you really do get off the well-worn Tahiti–Moorea–Bora Bora tourist track and visit islands even less developed than Huahine, Raiatea, and Tahaa. (Although four islands in the Tuamotu Archipelago have international-class resorts, the far-flung atolls still meet this criterion.) The Marquesas Islands are even farther off the beaten path. Indeed, they are a world removed from the rest of French Polynesia, since their Polynesian residents have a different culture and even speak a different language than the Tahitians.

Since Air Tahiti has at least one flight a week between Rangiroa in the Tuamotus to Hiva Oa in the Marquesas, it's possible to combine the two groups in this itinerary. Air Tahiti doesn't fly between the Tuamotus every day, either, so your precise itinerary will hinge on its current schedule. Depending on the flights, you can start on Manihi or Tikehau instead of Fakarava (see chapter 11).

A more rewarding alternative to all this is taking a cruise through the Tuamotus and Marquesas on the *Aranui 3* (p. 67). The *Aranui 3* stops for a few hours at Fakarava on its way to the Marquesas and for a morning at Rangiroa on its return voyage. That means you can board the *Aranui 3* at Fakarava, cruise to the Marquesas, and get off at Rangiroa.

Days 1–3: Exploring a Large Lagoon & Old Village on Fakarava

An early morning flight from Papeete should put you in Fakarava in time to play in French Polynesia's second-largest lagoon. Spend your full second day here

The Tuamotu & Marquesas Islands in 2 Weeks

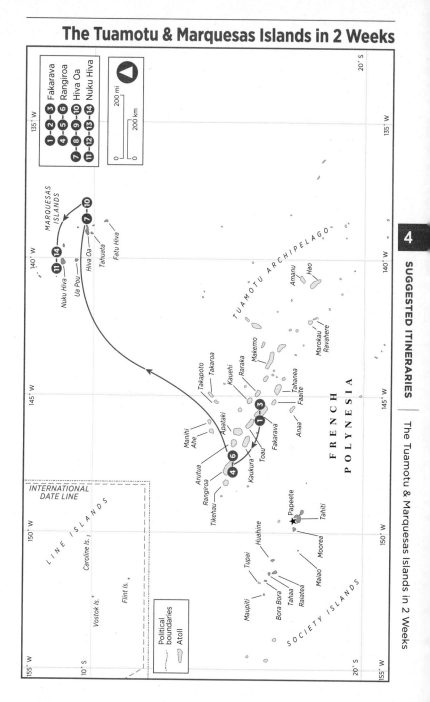

on a lagoon excursion, especially one that will take you to **Tetamanu** village (p. 228), where you'll see the ruins of an 1834-vintage Catholic church before swimming in the lagoon, riding the riptide in the adjacent pass, and enjoying a beachside picnic.

Days 4–6: Swimming with the Sharks at Rangiroa ★★★

As I noted in the Grand Tour earlier, the world's second-largest lagoon demands full-day excursions by boat to its two key sites: **Les Sables Rose (Pink Sands)** and the **Blue Lagoon** (p. 214). On your third day, don your snorkeling or scuba-diving gear and **ride the riptide** inside Avatoru Pass (p. 216). Be sure to watch the dolphins playing in Tiputa Pass at sunset. Have dinner one night at **Relais de Josephine** (p. 217).

Days 7–10: Following Paul Gauguin to Hiva Oa ★★★

The Air Tahiti flight from Rangiroa to Hiva Oa, administrative center of the Marquesas Islands, will eat up half a day, so spend your first afternoon exploring the village of **Atuona.** The French painter Paul Gauguin died in Atuona in 1903, so visit his grave and the **Tohua Papa Nui/Paul Gauguin Cultural Center,** where you will see meticulous copies of his great works (p. 257). The center shares space with **Espace Jacques Brel,** dedicated to the French singer Jacques Brel, who also expired here and is buried near Gauguin. Spend the next day on an expedition to lovely **Puamau** village (p. 257), beside a gorgeous settlement next to a half-moon beach. The snakelike road along on the northeast coast is virtually chiseled into the cliffs above the sea, so the ride out and back will occupy a full day. On another day, you can go fishing, hiking, or exploring the Atuona area on mountain bike or horseback (p. 259).

Days 11–14: "Surviving" on Nuku Hiva ★★

The *Survivor* TV series brought Nuku Hiva to the world's attention when it was taped here in 2002. However, you'll have a better chance of seeing **Taipivai Valley** if you go to see it on your own. It's where Herman Melville hid after jumping ship in the early 1800s (p. 241). Unless the local helicopter is operating, it's at least a 2-hour ride by four-wheel-drive vehicle across three mountain ranges from the airport to **Taiohae,** Nuku Hiva's only town. Spend half a day exploring the town and the **Herman Melville Memorial** beside its picturesque bay, including a visit to **Taetae Tupuna He'e Tai,** where American Rose Corser shows a fine collection of Marquesan art and sells exquisite handicrafts (p. 245). Later on, you can relax on the town's black-sand beach. Devote the next day to an excursion to the Taipivai Valley and **Hatiheu,** an enormously beautiful bay on the north coast and home to ancient *maraes* with tikis resembling the mysterious statues on Easter Island (p. 242). On your next-to-last day, you can go hiking or horseback riding (p. 244). You will need all of Day 14 for the ride back to the airport and the 3-hour Air Tahiti flight to Papeete.

TAHITI

ahiti is the modern traveler's gateway to French Polynesia, just as it was for Capt. James Cook and the other late-18th-century discoverers who used it as a base to explore the South Pacific. In later years, the capital city, **Papeete,** became a major shipping crossroads. Located on Tahiti's northwest corner, the city curves around what is still French Polynesia's busiest harbor.

There wasn't even a village here until the 1820s, when Queen Pomare set up headquarters along the shore, and merchant ships and whalers began using the harbor in preference to the less protected Matavai Bay to the east. A simple town of stores, bars, and billiards parlors sprang up quickly, and between 1825 and 1829 it was a veritable den of iniquity. It grew even more after the French made it their headquarters upon taking over Tahiti in 1842. A fire nearly destroyed the town in 1884, and waves churned up by a cyclone did severe damage in 1906. In 1914, two German warships shelled the harbor and sank the French navy's *Zélée*.

Papeete is a very different place today. Vehicles of every sort now crowd boulevard Pomare, the broad avenue along Papeete's waterfront, and the four-lane expressway linking the city to the trendy suburban districts of Punaauia and Paea on the west coast. Indeed, suburbs are creeping up the mountains overlooking the city and sprawling for miles along the coast in both directions. The island's northwestern corner is so developed and so traffic-clogged that many Tahitians commute up to 2 hours in each direction on weekdays. Many are moving to Moorea, a mere 30-minute ferry ride away.

But there is a bright side to Tahiti's development: Using money from a post-nuclear-testing economic restructuring fund, Papeete has done a remarkable job in refurbishing its waterfront, including a cruise-ship terminal and a classy park where families gather and the city celebrates its festivals. It's a real treat now to walk along the promenade fronting this storied South Seas port.

Papeete's chic shops, busy Municipal Market, and lively mix of French, Polynesian, and Chinese cultures are sure to invigorate any urbanite. If you're looking for old-time Polynesia, on the other hand, you will find it on Tahiti's rural east and south coasts and especially on its peninsula, Tahiti Iti. Its three fine museums are reason enough to spend a day or two here.

Even if you plan to leave immediately for Moorea, Bora Bora, and the other less developed islands, you'll likely have to spend at least a few hours here, since all international flights land at Faaa on the northwest coast of this legendary and still very beautiful island.

GETTING AROUND TAHITI

Except for the Route 5 expressway between Papeete and Punaauia, the island's highway system consists primarily of Route 1, a paved road running for 114km (72 miles) around Tahiti Nui, plus roads halfway down each side of Tahiti Iti. From the isthmus, a road partially lined with trees wanders up to the high, cool Plateau of Taravao, with pastures and pines more like provincial France than the South Pacific.

By Bus

Although it might appear from the number of vehicles scurrying around Papeete that everyone owns a car or scooter, many Tahitians get around by local bus. Modern buses have replaced all but a few of Tahiti's famous *le trucks,* those colorful vehicles called "trucks" because the passenger compartments are gaily painted wooden cabins mounted on the rear of flatbed trucks. The last of them operate between downtown Papeete and Centre Moana Nui, a shopping complex south of the Sofitel Tahiti Maeva Beach Resort. Elsewhere, look for modern buses.

Once upon a time, *le trucks* would stop for you almost anywhere, but today you must catch them and the buses at official stops (called *arrêt le bus* in French).

The villages or districts served by each bus are written on the sides and front of the bus. **Fares** within Papeete are 130CFP until 6pm and 200CFP thereafter. A trip to the end of the line in either direction costs about 750CFP.

BUSES GOING WEST The few remaining *le trucks* and all short-distance buses going west are painted red and white. They line up on rue du Maréchal-Foch between rue de 22 Septembre and rue Cardella (behind the blue-and-white Banque de Tahiti building) and travel along rue du Général-de-Gaulle, which becomes rue du Commandant-Destremeau and later route de-l'Ouest, the round-island road. Buses run along this route as far as the Centre Moana Nui (south of the Sofitel Tahiti Maeva Beach Resort) Monday through Friday at least every 30 minutes from 6am to 6pm, then once an hour between 6pm and midnight. Except for *le trucks* serving tourists at the hotels on the west coast, there is irregular service on Saturday, none on Sunday. Trucks and buses labeled Maeva Beach and Outumaoro will pass the airport and the InterContinental Resort Tahiti.

BUSES GOING EAST Short-distance buses going east are painted green and white. They line up in the block west of the Banque de Polynésie on boulevard Pomare, opposite the cruise-ship terminal and near the Municipal Market and rue

---

Around Tahiti by Bus

Although you had to walk across the Taravao isthmus, it was once possible to circumnavigate Tahiti by *le truck* in a single day. The long-distance buses now go into Papeete only from 6am to noon on weekdays, so it is virtually impossible to go all the way around the island in a single day. I recommend renting a vehicle or taking a guided circle island tour instead.

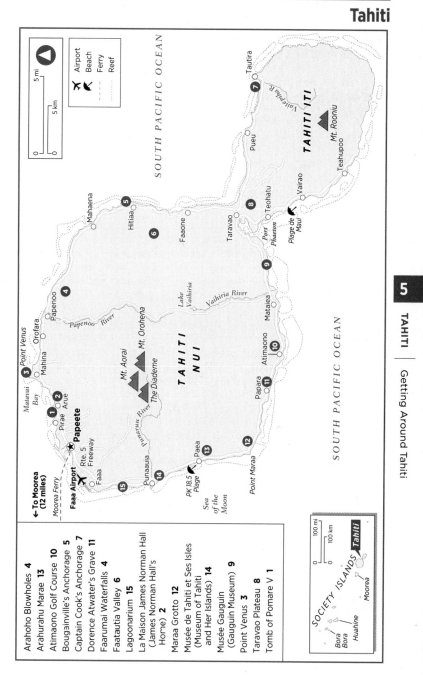

Arahoho Blowholes **4**

Arahurahu Marae **13**

Atimaono Golf Course **10**

Bougainville's Anchorage **5**

Captain Cook's Anchorage **7**

Dorence Atwater's Grave **11**

Faarumai Waterfalls **4**

Faatautia Valley **6**

Lagoonarium **15**

La Maison James Norman Hall
(James Norman Hall's
Home) **2**

Maraa Grotto **12**

Musée de Tahiti et Ses Isles
(Museum of Tahiti
and Her Islands) **14**

Musée Gauguin
(Gauguin Museum) **9**

Point Venus **3**

Taravao Plateau **8**

Tomb of Pomare V **1**

Paul Gauguin. They proceed out of town via avenue du Prince-Hinoi, passing the Radisson Plaza Resort Tahiti on their way to Pirae, Arue, and Mahina. They run frequently from 6am to 5pm as far as the Mahina. No buses run at night, so you must rent a car or take a taxi to and from the Radisson after dark and on weekends.

LONG-DISTANCE BUSES　Buses going in either direction to Tahiti's south coast and Tahiti Iti are painted orange and white. They line up next to the Tahiti Manava visitor bureau on boulevard Pomare at rue Paul Gauguin. They run on the hour from 6am to noon Monday through Friday, but there is only one afternoon trip at 4:30pm back to the villages. They do not run at night or on weekends.

By Taxi

Papeete has a large number of taxis, although they can be hard to find during the morning and evening rush hours, especially if it's raining. You can flag one down on the street or find them gathered at one of several stations. The largest gathering points are on boulevard Pomare near the market (② **42.02.92**) and at the Centre Vaima (② **42.60.77**). Most taxi drivers understand some English.

Taxi fares are set by the government and are posted on a board at the Centre Vaima taxi stand on boulevard Pomare. Few cabs have meters, so be sure that you and the driver have agreed on a fare before you get in. Note that *all fares are increased by at least 20% from 8pm to 6am.* A trip anywhere within downtown Papeete during the day starts at 1,000CFP and goes up 120CFP for every kilometer after the first one during the day, 240CFP at night. As a rule of thumb, the fare from the Papeete hotels to the airport or vice versa is about 1,700CFP during the day; from the west coast hotels to the airport, about 1,000CFP. A trip to the Gauguin Museum on the south coast costs 10,000CFP one-way. The fare for a 4-hour journey all the way around Tahiti is about 16,000CFP. Drivers may charge an extra 50CFP to 100CFP per bag of luggage.

By Rental Car

Avis (② **800/331-1212** or 41.93.93; www.avis.com), **Hertz** (② **800/654-3131** or 42.04.72; www.hertz.com), and **Europcar** (② **800/227-7368** or 45.24.24; www.europcar-tahiti.com) all have agencies on Tahiti. The best local rental company is **Daniel Location de Voitures,** in the Faaa airport terminal (② **81.96.32;** fax 85.62.64; daniel.location@mail.pf). Rates begin at 11,500CFP per day for air-conditioned models with unlimited kilometers.

DRIVING HINTS　In Papeete, priority is given to vehicles entering an intersection from the right side. This rule does not apply on the four-lane boulevard Pomare along the waterfront, but be careful everywhere else, as drivers on your right will expect you to yield the right of way at intersections where there are no stop signs or traffic signals. Be prepared to deal with numerous **traffic circles** in and near town. You must give way to traffic already in the circles.

Outside of Papeete, priority is given to vehicles that are already on the round-island road. The main round-island road is a divided highway east and west of Papeete, which means that to make a left turn, you will have to turn around at the next traffic circle and drive back to your destination.

Get Unlimited Kilometers if Driving Around Tahiti

If you rent a car, consider the unlimited kilometer rate if you intend to drive around Tahiti, since the round-island road is 114km (72 miles) long, not counting Tahiti Iti.

PARKING Parking spaces can be as scarce as chicken teeth in downtown Papeete during the day. You must pay to park in most on-street spaces from 8am to 5pm Monday to Saturday, which costs 100CFP per hour, payable by tickets sold at numerous shops and newsstands displaying signs saying **Parc Chec.** Put the *parc chec* ticket on the dashboard inside the vehicle, not outside under the windshield wiper, where it will be stolen. There are several municipal parking garages, including one under the Hotel de Ville (Town Hall); enter off rue Collette between rue Paul Gauguin and rue d'Ecole des Frères. Some large buildings, such as the Centre Vaima, have garages in their basements. Frankly, if I'm not staying downtown, I usually leave my car at the hotel and take a bus into the city during workdays.

[FastFACTS] TAHITI

The following facts apply specifically to Tahiti. For more information, see "Fast Facts: Tahiti & French Polynesia" in chapter 13.

Business Hours

Although some shops stay open over the long lunch break, most businesses are open Monday to Friday from 8 to 11:30am and 2 to 5pm, give or take 30 minutes, since "flex hours" help alleviate Tahiti's traffic problem. Saturday hours are 8 to 11:30am, although some shops in and near the Centre Vaima stay open Saturday afternoon. The Papeete

Municipal Market is a roaring beehive from 5 to 7am on Sunday, and many of the nearby general stores are open during those hours. Except for some small groceries, most other stores are closed on Sunday.

Currency Exchange

Banque de Polynésie, Banque de Tahiti, and **Banque Socredo** have at least one branch each with ATMs on boulevard Pomare and in many suburban locations where you can cash traveler's checks. See "Money & Costs" in chapter 3 for more information.

Drugstores **Pharmacie du Vaima,** on rue du Général-de-Gaulle at rue Georges La Garde behind the Centre Vaima (📞 **42.97.73**), is owned and operated by English-speaking Nguyen Ngoc-Tran, whose daughter runs Pharmacie Tran on Moorea. Pharmacies rotate night duty, so ask your hotel staff to find out which one is open after dark.

Emergencies & Police

The **central gendarmerie** is at the inland terminus of avenue Bruat (📞 **42.02.02**).

Healthcare

Both **Clinque Cardella** (📞 **42.80.10**), on rue Anne-Marie-Javouhey, and **Clinic Paofai** (📞 **43.77.00**), on boulevard Pomare, have highly trained specialists and some state-of-the-art equipment. They are open 24 hours.

Internet Access

Every hotel here has Internet access for its guests to use. **Cybernesia Tahiti,** on the second level of the Vaima Centre (📞 **85.43.67**), has both high-speed wired and wireless access for 12CFP per minute. It has English keyboards and the Skype telephone program on some of its computers, and it will burn your digital photos to CD. Open Monday to Friday 8:30am to 5:30pm, Saturday 9am to 1pm. **La Maison de la Presse,** on boulevard Pomare at Quartier du Commerce (📞 **50.93.93**), also has English keyboards. It charges 16CFP per minute.

Several wireless ManaSpots (www.mana spot.pf) are around town, including the main post office, Parc Bougainville, Tohua Toata, the Fare Tony building on boulevard Pomare, Brasserie des Remparts restaurant, and at Tahiti-Faaa International Airport.

See "Staying Connected," in chapter 3, for more information.

Laundry *Lavomatic du Pont du L'Est,* Gauguin, 64 rue Paul Gauguin (📞 **43.71.59**), at Pont de l'Est, has wash-dry-fold service for 1,900CFP a load. Open Monday to Friday 7am to 5:30pm, Saturday 7am to noon.

Libraries

The *Office Territorial D'Action Culturelle (Territorial Cultural Center)* on boulevard Pomare, west of downtown Papeete (📞 **42.88.50**; www.maisondelaculture.pf), has a small library of mostly French books on the South Pacific and other topics.

Mail

The main post office is on boulevard Pomare a block west of the Centre Vaima. Open from 7am to 6pm Monday through Friday, 8 to 11am Saturday. The branch post office at the Tahiti-Faaa International Airport terminal is open from 6 to 10:30am and noon to 2pm Monday through Friday, and from 6 to 9am on Saturday, Sunday, and holidays.

Restrooms

Both **Tahua Vaite** (the park by the cruise-ship terminal at rue Paul Gauguin) and **Tohua Toata** on the western end of downtown have free and clean public toilets.

Telephone

The main post office, the cruise-ship terminal, and Tohua Toata all have pay phones, where you can use a *télécarte* to make local and international calls. See "Staying Connected" in chapter 3 for more information about pay phones and international calls.

Visitor Information

Tahiti Tourisme's Fare Manihini visitors bureau (📞 **50.57.12**; www.tahitimanava.pf), on the waterfront on boulevard Pomare at the foot of rue Paul Gauguin, is open 7:30am to 5:30pm Monday to Friday, 8 to 4pm Saturday, 8am to 1pm on Sunday and holidays.

Water

You can drink the tap water in Papeete and its nearby suburbs, which includes all the hotels, but not out in the rural parts of Tahiti. Bottled water is available in all grocery stores.

TAHITI'S TOP ATTRACTIONS

Tahiti is shaped like a figure eight lying on its side. The "eyes" of the eight are two extinct, eroded volcanoes joined by the flat Isthmus of Taravao. The larger, western part of the island is known as Tahiti Nui ("Big Tahiti" in Tahitian), while the smaller eastern peninsula beyond the isthmus is named Tahiti Iti ("Little Tahiti"). Together they comprise about 670 sq. km (258 sq. miles), about two-thirds the size of the island of Oahu in Hawaii.

Tahiti Nui's volcano has been eroded over the eons so that now long ridges, separating deep valleys, march down from the crater's ancient rim to the coast far below. The rim itself is still intact, except on the north side, where the Papenoo River has cut its way to the sea. The highest peaks, **Mount Orohena,** 2,206m (7,353 ft.), and **Mount Aora,** 2,045m (6,817 ft.), tower above Papeete. Another peak, the toothlike Mount Te Tara O Maiao, or the **Diadème,** at 1,308m (4,360 ft.), can be seen from the eastern suburb of Pirae, but not from downtown.

Bone Up on History

A knowledge of French Polynesia's background will prove very useful as you see the sights, many of which have historical significance. I strongly recommend reading "A Look at the Past," p. 15, before setting out and referring back to it as you go.

With the exception of the east coast of Tahiti Iti, where great cliffs fall into the sea, and a few places where the ridges end abruptly at the water's edge, the island is skirted by a flat coastal plain. Tahiti's residents live on this plain, in the valleys, or on the hills adjacent to the plain.

Arahurahu Marae ★★ Arahurahu is the only *marae*—an ancient temple or meeting place—in all of Polynesia that has been fully restored, and it is maintained like a museum. Although not nearly as impressive as the great lagoonside *maraes* on Huahine and Raiatea (see chapters 7 and 8, respectively), this is Tahiti's best example of ancient Polynesian temples and meeting places, and its exhibit boards do a good job of explaining the significance of each part. For example, the stone pens near the entrance were used to keep the pigs before being sacrificed to the gods. Arahurahu is used for the reenactment of old Polynesian ceremonies during the July *Heiva Nui* celebrations.

Paea, 23km (14 miles) west of Papeete. No phone. Free admission. Daily 24 hr.

Lagoonarium de Tahiti If you won't be diving or snorkeling in the lagoons, then you will enjoy a visit to this underwater viewing room surrounded by pens containing reef sharks, sea turtles, and many colorful species of tropical fish. Also here is Captain Bligh Restaurant and Bar, best known for its Tahitian dance shows on weekends (p. 126). The view of Moorea from here is terrific.

Punaauia, 12km (7 miles) west of Papeete. ✆ **43.62.90.** Admission 500CFP adults, 300CFP children 11 and under. Daily 9am–5:30pm.

La Maison de James Norman Hall (James Norman Hall's Home) ★★★ This marvelous museum is a required stop for all of us who have ever dreamed of writing successful novels in a lovely lagoonside house. James Norman Hall was a U.S. army pilot in France during World War I, when he was shot down behind German lines and held prisoner. He met Charles Nordhoff in Paris shortly after the war, and together they wrote *The Lafayette Flying Corp,* the story of the American unit that fought for France before the U.S. entered the war. In 1920, they moved to Tahiti, where they sailed around on copra schooners and wrote *Faery Lands of the South Seas.* In 1932, they published *Mutiny on the Bounty,* the first of their three novels about the incident and its aftermath (*Men Against the Sea* and *Pitcairn's Island* are the others). It was turned into the 1935 movie starring Clark Gable and Charles

Laughton, and the 1962 remake with Marlon Brando. Hall and Nordhoff penned several more books about the islands, including *Hurricane*, which was also turned into two movies.

Hall and his wife, Sarah Teraireia Winchester Hall, lived their entire married lives here in Arue. Their family manages the house, which is an exact reproduction of their home, and has stocked it with Hall's typewriter, original manuscripts, and tons of heirlooms and memorabilia. (One of the three Oscars won by his son, the late Hollywood cinematographer Conrad L. Hall, is here.) The office is adorned with photographs of him with Zane Grey, Robert Dean Frisbee, and other men-of-the-pen when they dropped by for visits. One of Hall's grandsons still lives on the property, so you will need permission to visit his grave on the hill above the house. Staff members lead 30-minute tours and sell coffee and soft drinks. The free parking lot is across the highway beside the lagoon; if coming from Papeete, you'll have to turn around at the next traffic circle and come back to reach it.

> ### 💬 Shipwrecked
>
> While researching the novel *Pitcairn's Island*, which he coauthored with Charles Nordhoff, James Norman Hall disappeared for several months in 1933 after being shipwrecked near Mangareva, between Tahiti and Pitcairn.

Arue, 5.5km (3¼ miles) east of Papeete. ⓒ **50.01.60.** www.jamesnormanhallhome.pf. Admission 600CFP. Tues–Sat 9am–4pm. Closed public holidays.

Marché Municipale (Municipal Market) ★★★   An amazing array of fruits, vegetables, fish, meat, handicrafts, and other items are sold under the big tin pavilion of Papeete's bustling public market. Unwritten rules dictate that Tahitians sell fruits and traditional vegetables (such as taro and breadfruit), Chinese sell European and Chinese vegetables, and Chinese and Europeans serve as butchers and bakers (you may see some hogs' heads hanging in the butcher stalls). The market is busiest early in the mornings, but it's like a carnival here from 5 to 7am every Sunday, when people from the outlying areas of Tahiti, and even from the other islands, arrive to sell their produce. (**Note:** The pickings are slim by 8am.) A Tahitian string band plays during lunch at the upstairs snack bar, which purveys inexpensive island chow.

Papeete, between rue du 22 Septembre and rue François Cardella, 1 block inland from bd. Pomare. No phone. Free admission. Mon–Fri 5am–6pm; Sat 5am–1pm; Sun 4–8am.

Musée de Tahiti et Ses Isles (Museum of Tahiti and Her Islands) ★★★ Set in a lagoonside coconut grove with a gorgeous view of Moorea, this ranks as one of the best museums in the South Pacific. Exhibits show the geological history of the islands, including a terrific topographic map; their sea life, flora, and fauna; and the history and culture of their peoples. Exhibits are devoted to traditional weaving, tapa-cloth making, early tools, body ornaments, tattooing, fishing and horticultural techniques, religion and *maraes*, games and sports, warfare and arms, deaths and funerals, and writers and missionaries (note the 1938 *Tahitian Bible*). Most, but not all, of the display legends are translated into English. Start in the air-conditioned exhibit hall to the left as you enter and proceed outside. Give yourself at least 30 minutes here, preferably an hour.

Punaauia, 15km (9 miles) west of Papeete. ⓒ **58.34.76.** www.museetahiti.pf. Admission 600CFP adults, free for children. Tues–Sun 9:30am–5:30pm. Turn toward the lagoon at the Total station and follow the signs.

Musée Gauguin (Gauguin Museum) ★★★ This museum/memorial to Paul Gauguin, the French artist who lived in the Mataiea district from 1891 until 1893, owns a few of his sculptures, woodcarvings, engravings, and a ceramic vase. It has an active program to borrow his major works, however, and one might be on display during your visit. Otherwise, the exhibits are dedicated to his life in French Polynesia. It's best to see them counterclockwise, starting at the gift shop (which sells excellent prints and reproductions of his works). The originals are in the first gallery. An interesting display in the last gallery shows who owns his works today. The museum has a lagoonside restaurant, although most visitors have lunch at the nearby Restaurant du Musée Gauguin, at PK 50.5 (p. 105).

The museum is adjacent to the lush **Harrison W. Smith Jardin Botanique (Botanical Gardens),** which was started in 1919 by Harrison Smith, an American who left a career teaching physics at the Massachusetts Institute of Technology and moved to Tahiti. He died here in 1947. His gardens, which now belong to the public, are home to a plethora of tropical plants from around the world. This is the wettest part of Tahiti, so bring an umbrella.

Mataiea, 51km (32 miles) west of Papeete. © **57.10.58.** Museum admission 600CFP adults, 300CFP children 12–18. Gardens, free for children 11 and under. Daily 9am–5pm.

Point Venus ★★★ Capt. James Cook observed the transit of the planet Venus in 1769 at Point Venus, Tahiti's northernmost extremity. The low, sandy peninsula covered with ironwood (casuarina) trees is about 2km (1¼ miles) from the main road. Captains Wallis, Cook, and Bligh landed here after anchoring their ships offshore, behind the reef in Matavai Bay. Cook made his observations of the transit of Venus across the sun in 1769 from a point between the black-sand beach and the meandering river that cuts the peninsula in two. The beach and the parklike setting around the tall white lighthouse, which was completed in 1868 (notwithstanding the 1867 date over the door), are popular for picnics. There are a snack bar, a souvenir and handicrafts shop, and toilets.

Mahina, 10km (6 miles) east of Papeete. No phone. Free admission. Daily 4am–7pm. Snack bar and souvenir shop daily 8am–5pm.

WALKING TOUR: PAPEETE

START:	**Tahiti Tourisme's visitor center**
FINISH:	**Papeete Town Hall**
TIME:	**2 hours**
BEST TIME:	**Early morning or late afternoon**
WORST TIME:	**Midday, Saturday afternoon, or Sunday when most establishments are closed**

Begin at Tahiti Tourisme's visitor center in Tahua Vaiete, the park by the cruise ship dock, at the foot of rue Paul Gauguin. Stroll westward along Boulevard Pomare. Opposite the tuna boat dock stands Centre Vaima.

1 Centre Vaima

The chic shops in Papeete's first shopping mall are a mecca for Papeete's French and European residents (the Municipal Market still attracts mostly Tahitians). The infamous Quinn's Bar stood in the block east of the Centre Vaima, where the Noa Noa boutique is now. The Centre Vaima takes its name from the Vaima Restaurant, everyone's favorite eatery in those days, which it replaced.

Across the four-lane boulevard from the Vaima is the wooden boardwalk along the Quay.

2 The Quay

Cruising yachts from around the world congregate here from April to September, and resident boats are docked here all year. Beyond them, on the other side of the harbor, is **Motu Uta,** once a small natural island belonging to Queen Pomare but now home of the wharves and warehouses of Papeete's shipping port. The reef on the other side has been filled to make a breakwater and to connect Motu Uta by road to **Fare Ute,** the industrial area and French naval base to the right. The interisland boats dock alongside the filled-in reef, and their cargoes of copra (dried coconut meat) are taken to a mill at Fare Ute, where coconut oil is extracted and later shipped overseas to be used in cosmetics.

Walk west along the waterfront, past the main post office, next to which is Parc Bougainville.

3 Parc Bougainville

This shady park next to the post office is named for the French explorer who found Tahiti a little too late to get credit for its discovery. Two naval cannons flank the statue of Bougainville: The one nearest the post office was on the *Seeadler,* Count von Luckner's infamous World War I German raider, which ran aground in the Cook Islands after terrifying the British and French territories of the South Pacific. The other was on the French navy's *Zélée.* Bougainville's statue stands between the guns. There's a snack bar at the rear of the park.

Walk westward to the traffic circle at the foot of avenue Bruat.

4 Place Jacques Chirac

Few projects exemplify Papeete's vast road improvements more than the big traffic circle, under which pass the four busy lanes of boulevard Pomare, and the adjacent underground parking garage. On the harbor side, the

---

Impressions

To those who insist that all picturesque towns look like Siena or Stratford-on-Avon, Papeete will be disappointing, but to others who love the world in all its variety, the town is fascinating. My *own judgment: any town that wakes each morning to see Moorea is rich in beauty.*

—James A. Michener, *Return to Paradise,* 1951

Walking Tour: Papeete

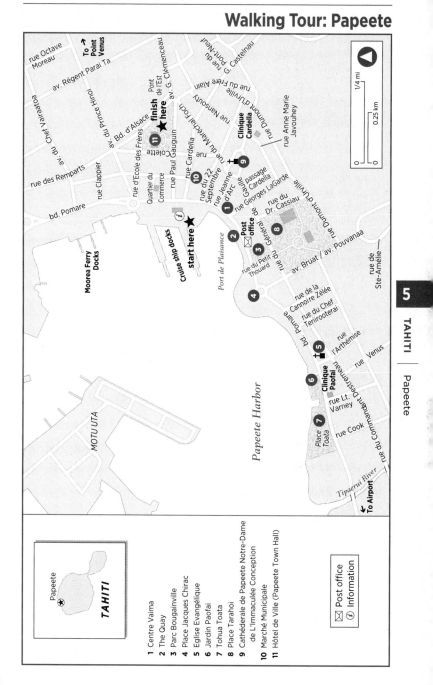

1 Centre Vaima
2 The Quay
3 Parc Bougainville
4 Place Jacques Chirac
5 Eglise Evangélique
6 Jardin Paofai
7 Tohua Toata
8 Place Tarahoi
9 Cathédrale de Papeete Notre-Dame
de L'Immaculée Conception
10 Marché Municipale
11 Hôtel de Ville (Papeete Town Hall)

⊠ Post office
ⓘ Information

semicircular-shaped park is known as Place Jacques Chirac, whose name created quite a stir because French tradition says not to name a public place after a living president. Underneath is a public parking garage. The park is the beginning of recent landfills, which have replaced a black-sand beach that used to run west of here.

Keep going west along the waterfront, to rue l'Arthémise, where you can't miss the big beige church on the mountain side of the boulevard.

5 Eglise Evangélique

An impressive steeple sits atop Eglise Evangélique, the largest Protestant church in French Polynesia. The local evangelical sect grew out of the early work by the London Missionary Society. Today, the pastors are Tahitian. Outrigger canoe racing is Tahiti's national sport, and the *va'a*—those long, sleek vessels seen cutting the harbor during lunchtime and after work—used to be kept on a black-sand beach across the boulevard from the church. Today, a section of the landfill across the boulevard is reserved for them.

Cross boulevard Pomare. On the harbor side you will enter the manicured Jardin Paofai (Paofai Gardens).

6 Jardin Paofai

Another project funded by the economic restructuring fund, this public park built on land fill features thatch-roof buildings, picnic shelters, and playgrounds for children. Black rocks, over which locals launch their colorful racing canoes, have replaced the black sand beach which lined this shore before the harbor front was expanded.

Stroll west through the gardens into Papeete's major outdoor venue.

7 Tohua Toata

Tohua Toata is a favorite gathering place for office workers during the day and families at night. They come to stroll, take in the view, and dine at inexpensive snack bars. Tohua Toata sees numerous outdoor arts and crafts festivals, and its outdoor amphitheater hosts concerts all year and the huge *Heiva Nui* festival in July. Next door, on the banks of Tipaerui River, stands the **Office Territorial d'Action Culturelle,** Tahiti's cultural center and library.

8 Take a Break 🍴

Comparable to *les roulottes* (see "Where to Dine," later in this chapter) but permanently here, Tohua Toata's open-air snack bars are great for cold drinks, ice-cream cones, or even a complete lunch. There are clean public restrooms here.

Turn around and backtrack east on boulevard Pomare to Parc Bougainville (see number 3, above), cut through the park, and proceed through the park to the spacious grounds of Place Tarahoi.

9 Place Tarahoi

Place Tarahoi, Papeete's governmental center, was royal property in the old days and site of Queen Pomare's mansion, which the French used as their headquarters after 1842. Her impressive home is long gone, but is replicated by the Papeete Town Hall (see number 10, below). As you face the grounds, the buildings on the right house the French government and include the home of the president of French Polynesia. The modern building on the left is the Territorial Assembly. You can walk around hallways of the Assembly building during business hours. In front stands a monument to Pouvanaa a Oopa (1895–1977), a Tahitian who became a hero fighting for France in World War I and then spent the rest of his life battling for independence for his homeland. During the 1960s and 1970s he spent 15 years in prison in France, but he returned home in time to see more local autonomy granted to the territory. In fact, his fellow Tahitians sent him back to Paris as a member of the French Senate.

 Avoid Rush Hour & Check on Road Work

If you drive yourself around Tahiti, avoid getting snarled in morning and evening weekday rush hours. Landslides can close the round-island road on the east coast, so ask the car-rental agent or the staff at Tourisme Tahiti's visitors information office if it is open all the way around.

Continue 2 more blocks along rue du Général-de-Gaulle, past the rear of Centre Vaima, to Cathédrale de l'Immaculée Conception.

10 Cathédrale de Papeete Notre-Dame de L'Immaculée Conception

Dating to 1875, Tahiti's oldest Catholic church houses a series of paintings of the Crucifixion. A life-size Marquesan woodcarving of the Madonna and child holding a breadfruit welcomes all to this cool, quiet, and comforting place to worship or just to contemplate.

Rue du Général-de-Gaulle becomes rue du Maréchal-Foch past the church. Follow it for a block. Bear left at rue Colette and continue until you come to Marché Municipale.

11 Marché Municipale

Take a stroll under the large tin pavilion of Papeete's Municipal Market and examine the multitude of fruits and vegetables for sale (see "Tahiti's Top Attractions," earlier in this chapter).

After sampling the market and the marvelous handicrafts stalls along its sidewalk and upstairs, walk along rue Colette for 2 more blocks, until you come to Papeete Town Hall.

12 Hotel de Ville (Papeete Town Hall)

This is a magnificent replica of Queen Pomare's mansion, which once stood at Place Tarahoi. This impressive structure, with its wraparound veranda, captures the spirit of the colonial South Pacific. This *Hôtel de Ville* or *Fare Oire* (French and Tahitian, respectively, for "town hall") was dedicated in 1990 by French President François Mitterand during an elaborate celebration. Walk up the grand entrance steps to catch a cool breeze from the broad balconies.

From here you can find your way back to Vaima Centre and some much-needed refreshment at its open-air cafes (see "Where to Dine," later in this chapter).

THE CIRCLE ISLAND TOUR ★★

A **Circle Island Tour,** or a drive around Tahiti, is the best way to see the island's outlying sights and a bit of old Polynesia away from Papeete's bustle. It can be done even if you're staying on Moorea (see "Touring Tahiti from Moorea . . . & Vice Versa," p. 109).

The road around Tahiti Nui is 114km (72 miles) long. It's 54km (32 miles) from Papeete to Taravao along the east coast and 60km (40 miles) returning along the west coast. On the land side of the road are red-topped concrete **kilometer markers** (*pointes kilomètres* in French, or **PK** for short). They tell the distance every kilometer between Papeete and the Isthmus of Taravao; that is, the distance from Papeete to Taravao in each direction, not the total number of kilometers around the island. The large numbers facing the ocean are the number of kilometers from Papeete; the numbers facing you as you drive along are the number of kilometers you have to go to Papeete or Taravao, depending on your direction. Distances between the PKs are referred to in 10ths of kilometers; for example, PK 35.6 would be 35.6km from Papeete.

The North & East Coasts of Tahiti Nui

Proceeding clockwise from Papeete, you'll leave town by turning inland off boulevard Pomare and following the broad **avenue du Prince-Hinoi,** the start of the round-island road.

FAUTAUA VALLEY, LOTI'S POOL & THE DIADEME

It's not worth the side trip, but at PK 2.5, a road goes right into the steep-walled Fautaua Valley and the **Bain Loti,** or Loti's Pool. Now part of Papeete's water-supply system, the pool is covered in concrete, but it's where Julien Viaud, the French merchant mariner who wrote under the pen name Pierre Loti, set his 19th-century novel *The Marriage of Loti,* which recounted the love of a Frenchman for a Tahitian woman. The road goes into the lower part of the valley and terminates at the beginning of a hiking trail up to the **Fautaua Waterfall,** which plunges over a cliff into a large pool 300m (985 ft.) below. The all-day hike to the head of the valley is best done with a guide (see "Golf, Hiking & Watersports," later in this chapter).

Pull off the main road into the side street opposite the big seaside park at Pirae for a look inland at the **Diadème,** a rocky outcrop protruding like a crown from the interior ridge. (I think it looks like a single worn molar sticking up from a gum.) One of Tahiti's landmarks, the Diadème can only be seen from here on the north coast and from the Punaruu Valley on the west coast.

Impressions

The air was full of that exquisite fragrance of orange blossom and gardenia which is distilled by night under the thick foliage; there was a great silence, accentuated by the bustle of insects in the grass, and that sonorous quality, peculiar to night in Tahiti, which predisposes the listener to feel the enchanting power of music.
—Pierre Loti (Julien Viaud), *The Marriage of Loti,* 1880

TOMB OF POMARE V ★★

At PK 4.7, turn left at the sign and drive a short distance to a Protestant churchyard commanding an excellent view of Matavai Bay to the right. The **tomb** with a Grecian urn on top was built in 1879 for Queen Pomare. Her remains were removed a few years later by her son, King Pomare V, who abdicated in return for a French pension and later died of too much drink. Now he is buried here, and tour guides like to say the urn is not an urn at all but a liquor bottle, which makes it a monument not to Pomare V, but to the cause of his death.

LA MAISON DE JAMES NORMAN HALL (JAMES NORMAN HALL'S HOME) ★★★

At PK 5.4, on the mountain side of the road just east of the small bridge, stands the home of **James Norman Hall,** coauthor with Charles Nordhoff of *Mutiny on the Bounty.* See "Tahiti's Top Attractions," earlier in this chapter.

> ### Impressions
>
> *Look to the Northward, stranger / Just over the hillside there / Have you in your travels seen / A land more passing fair?*
>
> —James Norman Hall (on his tombstone)

ONE TREE HILL ★★

At PK 8, past the Radisson Plaza resort, you'll come to the top of **One Tree Hill,** so named by Capt. James Cook because a single tree stood on this steep headland in the late 1700s. For many years, it was the site of a luxury hotel, now closed. Pull into the roundabout at the entrance and stop for one of Tahiti's most magnificent vistas. You'll look down on the north coast all the way from Matavai Bay to Papeete, with Moorea looming on the far horizon.

POINT VENUS ★★★

At PK 10, turn left at Super Marché Venus Star and drive to **Point Venus,** Tahiti's northernmost point, where Capt. James Cook observed the transit of the planet Venus in 1769 (see "Tahiti's Top Attractions," earlier in this chapter).

PAPENOO VALLEY

At PK 17.1, Tahiti's longest bridge crosses its longest river at the end of its largest valley at one of its largest rural villages—all named **Papenoo.** The river flows down to the sea through the only wall in Tahiti Nui's old volcanic crater. A cross-island road goes up the valley, literally through the mountains (via a tunnel), and down to Tahiti's south shore. Four-wheel-drive vehicles go into the valley on exciting excursions (see "Safari Expeditions," later in this chapter). You can drive yourself as far as **Relais de la Maroto** (✆ **57.90.29**), a small hotel and restaurant up in the valley.

ARAHOHO BLOWHOLES

At PK 22, the surf pounding against the headland at **Arahoho** has formed overhanging shelves with holes in them. As waves crash under the shelves, water and air are forced through the holes, resulting in a geyserlike phenomenon. One shoots up at the base of a cliff on the mountain side of the road, but be careful because oncoming traffic cannot see you standing there. Pull into the overlook (with free parking and toilets) west of the sharp curve. There's a local snack bar across the road, and a black-sand beach is within sight.

CASCADES DE TEFAARUMAI (FAARUMAI WATERFALLS) ★★

At PK 22.1, a sign on the right just past the blowhole marks a somewhat paved road that leads 1.5km (1 mile) up a small valley to the **Cascades de Faarumai,** Tahiti's most accessible waterfalls. The drive itself gives a glimpse of how ordinary rural Tahitians live: in simple wood houses surrounded by bananas and breadfruit. Park near the stand of bamboo trees and take a few minutes to read the signs, which explain a romantic legend. Vaimahuta falls are an easy walk; Haamaremare Iti and Haamaremarerahi falls are a 45-minute climb up a more difficult trail. Vaimahuta falls plunge straight down several hundred feet from a hanging valley into a large pool. Bring insect repellent.

MAHAENA BATTLEFIELD

At PK 32.5, the Tahitian rebellion came to a head on April 17, 1844, when 441 French troops charged several times and many poorly armed Tahitians dug in near the village of **Mahaena.** The Tahitians lost 102 men; the French lost 15.

BOUGAINVILLE'S ANCHORAGE ★

At PK 37.6, a plaque mounted on a rock on the northern end of the bridge at Hitiaa commemorates the landing of the French explorer **Bougainville,** who anchored just offshore when he arrived in Tahiti in 1768. The two small islands on the reef, Oputotara and Variararu, provided slim protection against the prevailing trade winds, and Bougainville lost six anchors in 10 days trying to keep his ships off the reef. Tahitians recovered one and gave it to the high chief of Bora Bora, who in turn gave it to Captain Cook in 1777.

FAATAUTIA VALLEY

At PK 41.8 begins a view of **Faatautia Valley,** which looks so much like those in the Marquesas that in 1957 director John Huston chose it as a location for a movie version of *Typee,* Herman Melville's novelized account of his ship-jumping adventures among the Marquesans on Nuku Hiva in the 1840s. The project was scrapped after another of Huston's Melville movies, *Moby-Dick,* bombed at the box office. The uninhabited valley surely looks much today as it did 1,000 years ago.

TARAVAO

At PK 53, after passing the small-boat marina, the road climbs up onto the **Isthmus of Taravao,** separating Tahiti Nui from Tahiti Iti. At the top are the stone walls of **Fort Taravao,** which the French built in 1844 to bottle up what was left of the rebellious islanders on the Tahiti Iti peninsula during the French-Tahitian War of 1844 to 1848. Germans stuck on Tahiti during World War II were interned here. It is now used as a French army training center. The village of **Taravao,** with its shops, suburban streets, and churches, has grown up around the military post. Its snack bars are good places for refueling stops.

The Tahiti Iti Peninsula

Tahiti Iti is much less sparsely populated and developed than its bigger twin, Tahiti Nui. Paved roads dead-end about halfway down its north and south sides. A series of cliffs plunge into the sea on Tahiti Iti's rugged east end. While the north shore holds historical interest, the south coast has Tahiti's best beach and its top surfing spot.

TARAVAO PLATEAU

If you have to choose one of three roads on Tahiti Iti, take the one by the school and stadium. It dead-ends high up into the rolling pastures of the **Taravao Plateau.** It begins at the traffic signal on the north-coast road to Tautira and runs up through cool pastures reminiscent of rural France, with huge trees lining the narrow paved road. At more than 360m (1,200 ft.) high, the plateau is blessed with a refreshing, perpetually springlike climate. Near the end of the road, you'll come to the **Taravao Plateau Overlook,** where you'll have a spectacular view of the entire isthmus and down both sides of Tahiti Nui.

THE NORTH COAST TO TAUTIRA

The road on the north coast of Tahiti Iti goes for 18km (11 miles) to the sizable village of **Tautira,** which sits on its own little peninsula. Captain Cook anchored in the bay off Tautira on his second visit to Tahiti in 1773. His ships ran aground on the reef while the crews were partying one night. He managed to get them off, but lost several anchors in the process. One of them was found in 1978 and is now on display at the Museum of Tahiti and Her Islands, which you will come to on the west side of the island.

A year after Cook landed at Tautira, a Spanish ship from Peru named the *Aguila* landed here, and its captain claimed the island for Spain. It was the third time Tahiti had been claimed for a European power. He also put ashore two Franciscan priests. The *Aguila* returned a year later, but the priests had had enough of Tahiti and sailed back to Peru.

When you enter the village, bear left and drive along the scenic coast road as far as the general store, where you can buy a cold soft drink and snack. If you can hold out longer, I usually take my break at La Plage de Maui snack bar on Tahiti Iti's south coast (see below).

THE SOUTH COAST TO TEAHUPOO

The picturesque road along the south coast of Tahiti Iti skirts the lagoon, passing through small settlements. Novelist Zane Grey had a deep-sea-fishing camp at PK 7.3, near the village of **Toahotu,** from 1928 to 1930. He caught a silver marlin that was about 4m (14 ft.) long and weighed more than 454 kilograms (1,000 lb.)—even after the sharks had had a meal on it while Grey was trying to get it aboard his boat. He wrote about his adventures in *Tales of Tahitian Waters*.

According to Tahitian legends, the demigod Maui once made a rope from his sister Hina's hair and used it to slow down the sun long enough for Tahitians to finish cooking their food in their earth ovens (a lengthy process). He accomplished this feat while standing on the reef at a point 8.5km (5 miles) along the south-coast road. Beyond Maui's alleged footprints, now under the road, the **Bay of Tapueraha** provides the widest pass and deepest natural harbor on Tahiti. It was used as a base by a large contingent of the French navy during the aboveground nuclear tests at Moruroa atoll in the 1960s and 1970s. Some of the old mooring pilings still stand just offshore.

Reminiscent of the great Matira Beach on Bora Bora, **La Plage de Maui (Maui Beach)** ★★★ borders the bay and is the best strip of white sand on Tahiti. Get out of the car and take a break at the lagoonside snack bar here (see "Take a Circle Island Break," below). A cave, known as the **Caverne de Maui,** is a short walk inland.

Near Vairao village, you'll pass the modern **IFREMER: Le Centre Océanologique du Pacifique (Pacific Oceanographic Center),** which conducts research into black-pearl oysters, shrimp farming, and other means of extracting money from seawater. The buildings were formerly used for France's nuclear testing program.

The south-coast road ends at **Teahupoo,** the famous *village de surf* (surfing village) whose beachside park overlooks the big waves curling around Havaa Pass. World-class boarders compete in the Billabong Pro tournament here every year. A footbridge crosses the Tirahi River, where a trail begins along Tahiti Iti's rugged eastern shoreline. It's a strenuous and sometimes dangerous hike done only with a guide (see "Golf, Hiking & Watersports," later in this chapter).

The South Coast of Tahiti Nui

As you leave Taravao, heading back to Papeete along Tahiti's south coast, note that the PK markers begin to decrease the nearer you get to Papeete. The road rims casuarina-ringed **Port Phaeton,** which cuts nearly halfway across the isthmus. Port Phaeton and the **Bay of Tapueraha** to the south are Tahiti's finest harbors, yet European settlement and most development have taken place on the opposite side of the island, around Papeete. The shrimp you'll order for dinner come from the aqua farms in the bay's shallow waters.

PAPEARI

At PK 52 stands Tahiti's oldest village. Apparently the island's initial residents recognized the advantages of the south coast and its deep lagoons and harbors, for word-of-mouth history says they came through the Hotumatuu Pass in the reef and settled at **Papeari** sometime between A.D. 400 and 500. Robert Keable, author of *Simon Called Peter*, a bestselling novel about a disillusioned clergyman, lived here from 1924 until he died in 1928 at the age of 40. His home, now a private residence, stands at PK 55. Today, Papeari is a thriving village whose residents often sell fruits and vegetables at stands along the road.

MUSEE GAUGUIN (GAUGUIN MUSEUM) ★★★

At PK 51.2 is the entrance to the museum/memorial to Paul Gauguin, who lived near here from 1891 until 1893 (see "Tahiti's Top Attractions," earlier in this chapter). The museum sits in the lush **Harrison W. Smith Botanical Gardens,** started in 1919 by American Harrison Smith. The museum and gardens are open daily from 9am to 5pm. There's a snack bar here, but your best bet is to continue west.

VAIHIRIA RIVER & VAIPAHI GARDENS

At PK 48, in the village of Mataiea, the main road crosses the Vaihiria River. The new cross-island road from Papenoo on the north coast terminates here. An 11km (7.3-mile) track leads to **Lake Vaihiria,** at 465m (1,550 ft.) above sea level. It is Tahiti's only lake and is noted for its freshwater eels. Cliffs up to 900m (3,000 ft.) tall drop to the lake on its north side. Also in Mataiea is the lush **Jardin Vaipehi (Vaipehi Gardens),** a cool and refreshing spot with a bubbling natural spring and an oft-photographed waterfall (it's closer to the road than any other Tahitian waterfall). The garden is lush with elephant ears, tree ferns, ground orchids, jade vines, and other tropical vegetation. Signs (in French) explain its historical importance, since ancient Tahitian nobles followed the path to the springs in order to be spiritually purified.

Take a Circle Island Break

Shoehorned between the road and the sands of Maui Beach, **La Plage de Maui Restaurant ★★** (✆ **74.71.74**) is my favorite place to stop for refreshment while taking in the gorgeous scenery. Owners Rose Wilkinson and Alain Corre, both veterans of the Sofitel Moorea Ia Ora Beach Resort, offer burgers, steaks, *poisson cru* (marinated fish), ice cream, and other temptations. Burgers cost about 900CFP, while main courses range from 1,900CFP to 2,500CFP. No credit cards accepted. Open daily 11:30am to 3pm.

The Musée Gauguin has its own restaurant, but most circle island tour buses deposit their passengers for lunch at the lagoonside **Restaurant du Musée Gauguin,** at PK 50.5 (✆ **57.13.80**), which is worth a stop just for its phenomenal view of Tahiti Iti. The lunch buffet costs about 3,100CFP per person Monday through Saturday, 3,900CFP on Sunday; sandwiches are also available. Open daily from noon to 3pm.

A less expensive option is **Beach Burger,** at PK 39 (✆ **57.41.03**), west of the golf course at Atimaono. In addition to burgers, it serves salads, steaks, Chinese fare, and pizzas. Open Sunday through Thursday from 6am to 8pm, Friday and Saturday from 6am to 9:30pm.

ATIMAONO

At PK 41 begins the largest parcel of flat land on Tahiti, site of **Olivier Breaud International Golf Course at Atimaono,** French Polynesia's only links (see "Golf, Hiking & Watersports," below). Irishman William Stewart started a cotton plantation here during the American Civil War. Nothing remains of the plantation, but it was Stewart who brought the first Chinese indentured servants to Tahiti.

The knobby *noni* fruit's reputed medicinal properties have created a new industry in the islands, where folks are growing it by the boatload. You can see how it's turned into *noni* juice and other products at **Tahitian Noni International,** at PK 42.2 (✆ **80.37.50**). Tours are given on Friday by reservation only. Like castor oil, it must be good for you if it tastes this bad!

DORENCE ATWATER'S GRAVE

At PK 36, on the lagoon side of the road in Papara village, stands a Protestant church, under whose paved yard is buried **Dorence Atwater,** American consul to Tahiti after the Civil War. Captured while serving in the Union army, Atwater was assigned to the hospital at the infamous Confederate prisoner-of-war camp at Andersonville, Georgia, where he surreptitiously recorded the names of Union soldiers who died in captivity. He later escaped and brought his lists to the federal government, thus proving that the Confederacy was keeping inaccurate records. His action made him a hero in the eyes of the Union army. He eventually moved to the south coast of Tahiti, married a daughter of a chief of the Papara district, and at one time invested in William Stewart's cotton venture.

MARAA GROTTO

At PK 28.5, on Tahiti's southwest corner, the road turns sharply around the base of a series of headlands, which drop precipitously to the lagoon. Deep into one of these

THE MOON & 21 million POUNDS

In 1891, a marginally successful Parisian painter named Paul Gauguin left behind his wife and six children and sailed to Tahiti. He wanted to devote himself to his art, free of the chains of civilization.

Instead of paradise, Gauguin found a world that suffered from some of the same maladies as the one from which he fled. Poverty, sickness, and frequent disputes with church and colonial officials marked his decade in the islands. He had syphilis, a bad heart, and an addiction to opium.

Gauguin disliked Papeete and spent his first 2 years in the rural Mataiea district, on Tahiti's south coast, where a village woman asked what he was doing there. Looking for a girl, he

replied. The woman immediately offered her 13-year-old daughter, Tehaamana, the first of Gauguin's early teenage Tahitian mistresses. One of them bore him a son in 1899.

Tehaamana and the others figured prominently in Gauguin's Impressionist masterpieces, which brought fame to Tahiti but did little for his own pocketbook. After 649 paintings and a colorful career, immortalized by W. Somerset Maugham in *The Moon and Sixpence,* Gauguin died penniless in 1903.

At the time of his death, on Hiva Oa in the Marquesas Islands, a painting by Gauguin sold for 150 French francs. In 2007, his *L'Homme à la Hache* (Man at the Axe) sold for US$40.3 million.

I was born to see sights, and no matter how many times I visit French Polynesia, I never tire of its incredible natural beauty. I always spend sunset of my first day on Tahiti's west coast, depleting my camera battery as the sun paints another glorious red-and-orange sky over Moorea's purple ridges. The InterContinental Resort Tahiti and the Restaurant Pink Coconut are my favorite places to watch (see "Where to Stay," and "Where to Dine," respectively, later in this chapter). The sun sets between 5:30 and 6:30pm here, so get there in time.

cliffs goes the **Maraa Grotto,** also called the Paroa Cave. It's actually two caves, both with water inside, and they go much deeper into the hill than they appear to at first glance. Park in the lot, not along the road, and enter at the gazebo to reach the larger of the two caves. A short trail leads from there to the smaller cave and a mini-waterfall.

The West Coast of Tahiti Nui

North of Maraa, the road runs through the Paea and Punaauia suburbs of Papeete. The west coast is the driest part of Tahiti, and it's very popular with Europeans, Americans, and others who have built homes along the lagoon and in the hills overlooking it and Moorea.

ARAHURAHU MARAE ★★

At PK 22.5, a small road on the right of Magasin Laut leads to a narrow valley, on the floor of which sits the restored **Arahurahu Marae** (see "Tahiti's Top Attractions," earlier in this chapter).

MUSEE DE TAHITI ET SES ISLES ★★★

At PK 15.1, turn left at the gas station and follow the signs through a residential area to the lagoon and the **Musée de Tahiti et Ses Isles (Museum of Tahiti and Her Islands),** one of the South Pacific's best museums (see "Tahiti's Top Attractions," earlier in this chapter).

PUNARUU VALLEY

On a cloudless day, you will have a view up the **Punaruu Valley** to the Diadème as you drive from the museum back to the main road. Tahitian rebels occupied the valley during the 1844 to 1848 war, and the French built a fort to keep them there (the site is now occupied by a television antenna). Later the valley was used to grow oranges, most of which were shipped to California. Villagers sell the now-wild fruit at roadside stands during July and August.

The Route 5 expressway goes as far south as the Punaruu River, just north of the Tahiti Museum. Instead of taking the overpass onto the expressway, stay in the right lane to the traffic circle under the overpass. The first exit off the circle will take you up into the Punaruu Valley. The second exit leads to the Route 5 expressway. The third is Route 1, the old two-lane coast road, which will take you to the Lagoonarium.

THE LAGOONARIUM

At PK 11.4, the **Captain Bligh Restaurant and Bar** has a terrific view of Moorea and is home to the **Lagoonarium de Tahiti,** an underwater viewing room (see "Tahiti's Top Attractions," earlier in this chapter).

After the Lagoonarium, Route 1 soon joins the four-lane Route 5 expressway, which passes shopping centers and marinas in Punaauia. It splits just before the Sofitel Tahiti Maeva Beach Resort. The left lanes feed into the Route 5 expressway, which roars back to Papeete. The right lanes take you along Route 1, the old road that goes past the west-coast hotels and the Tahiti-Faaa International Airport before returning to town.

Organized Tours Around the Coastal Road

Several companies offer tours along the coastal road around Tahiti Nui. They are a good way to see the island without hassling with traffic. I find them to be an especially fine way to recover from jet lag.

---

marlon's MANA

The late Marlon Brando did more than star in the remake of *Mutiny on the Bounty* when he came to Tahiti in 1960. He fell in love with his beautiful Tahitian co-star, Tarita Terepaia, the 19-year-old daughter of a Bora Bora fisherman. At first Tarita reportedly wasn't attracted to the then-dashing actor, but his good looks and charm must have won out, for she later became his wife and the mother of two of his children.

Brando also fell for **Tetiaroa**, an atoll 42km (25 miles) north of Tahiti and Moorea. In the old days, this cluster of 12 flat islets surrounding an aquamarine lagoon was the playground of Tahiti's high chiefs, who frequently were joined by the *Arioi,* traveling bands of sexually explicit entertainers and practitioners of infanticide (see "The Islanders," in chapter 2). High-ranking women would spend months doing a bit of makeover on Tetiaroa, resting in the shade to lighten their skin and gorging on starchy foods to broaden their girth. Men and women of a chiefly rank were said to possess the mystical power called *mana* by the ancient Polynesians, and the bigger the body, the more the *mana.*

For a time, a British dentist who married into the royal family owned Tetiaroa, but it was abandoned when Brando bought it in 1966. He turned one of his islets into a refuge for Tetiaroa's thousands of seabirds. He built a retreat for himself on a second islet and a small, rather rustic resort on a third.

Guests at the resort would seldom see the actor, on whose waistline Tetiaroa apparently worked its expansive magic. During the day, he would stay at home in the shade, playing with his radios and computers. At night, he would go fishing and lobstering.

A series of hurricanes almost blew his resort away in 1983, and Brando's relationship with Tahiti turned to human disaster a decade later when his son Christian—by his first wife, actress Anna Kashfi—shot and killed the boyfriend of his half-sister, Cheyenne, in Brando's Hollywood home. A year later, Cheyenne, then 25, hanged herself at Tarita's home on Tahiti. Brando did not attend her funeral; in fact, he never again returned to Tahiti.

Ex-wife Tarita operated the resort, mostly as a day-trip and weekend destination from Tahiti, until shortly before Brando's death in 2004. Richard Bailey, a long-time family friend and developer of the InterContinental Resort Tahiti and other hotels here, is building an upmarket, environmentally friendly resort on Tetiaroa.

I prefer English-speaking William Leteeg's **Adventure Eagle Tours** (℡ **77.20.03**). William takes you around in an air-conditioned van and lends his experiences growing up on the island to his commentaries. Others include **Tahiti Nui Travel** (℡ **42.40.10**; www.tahitinuitravel.com), and **Marama Tours** (℡ **50.74.74**; www.maramatours.com). They have reservations desks in several hotels. Expect to pay about 4,500CFP for a half-day tour, 5,000CFP for all day, plus entrance fees to the museums and other attractions and lunch, usually at the Restaurant du Musée Gauguin.

SAFARI EXPEDITIONS ★★★

So-called safari expeditions into Tahiti's interior allow for a very different view of the island—and some spectacular views at that. Riding in the back of open, four-wheel-drive vehicles, you follow narrow, often unpaved roads through Tahiti's central crater, usually via the breathtaking Papenoo Valley. Weather permitting, you'll reach altitudes of 1,440m (4,800 ft.) on the sides of the island's steep interior crater, and in clear conditions you may even cross the island (on the full-day versions of the trip, that is). The cool temperatures at the higher elevations are refreshing, as is a swim in a cold mountain stream.

Tahiti Safari Expedition (℡ **42.14.15**; www.tahiti-safari.com) has been around since owner Patrice Bordes pioneered the concept in 1990. He charges about 4,000CFP per person for a half-day trip, 6,500CFP for a full day. Another good operator is Arnaud Lucioni of **Natura Exploration** (℡ **43.03.83** or 79.31.21). Both Patrice and Arnaud speak French and English. They usually stop for lunch at **Relais de la Maroto** (℡ **57.90.29**), or you can bring your own picnic. Don't forget your bathing suit, a towel, hat, sunscreen, insect repellent, and camera. These are popular trips with limited space, so reserve as early as possible at any hotel activities desk.

GOLF, HIKING & WATERSPORTS

Golf

Tahiti's mountainous interior provides a spectacular backdrop to the 27-hole **Olivier Breaud International Golf Course of Atimaono,** PK 40.2 (© **57.43.41**), which sprawls over the site of William Stewart's 1860s cotton plantation. A clubhouse, pro shop, restaurant, bar, locker rooms, showers, a swimming pool, a spa pool, and a driving range are on the premises. The club is open daily from 8am until dark. Greens fees are about 5,500CFP for 18 holes. The hotel activities desks can book all-day golf outings for about 27,000CFP for one golfer, 37,000CFP for two, including greens fees, equipment, lunch, and transportation.

Hiking

Tahiti has a number of hiking trails, such as the cross-island Papenoo Valley–Lake Vaihiria route. Another ascends to the top of Mount Aorai, and another skirts the remote and wild eastern coast of Tahiti Iti. This is not the Shenandoah or some other American or New Zealand national park with well-marked trails, and the French gendarmes do not take kindly to rescuing tourists who become lost trying to scale one of Tahiti's peaks. Downpours can occur in the higher altitudes, swelling the streams that most trails follow, and the nights can become bitterly cold and damp. The side of the island that's rainy can shift from one day to the next, depending on which way the wind blows. In addition, the quick-growing tropical foliage can quickly obscure a path that was easily followed a few days before. Permits are required to use some trails that cross government land.

> ### 📎 Pick a Clear Day
>
> The safari expeditions do not go into the mountains when the weather is bad, and even if it's not raining, clouds atop the mountains can obscure what would otherwise be some fantastic views. It's best, therefore, to pick as clear a day as possible for this thrilling outing. Your best chance for that will be during the drier austral winter, June through early September.

Accordingly, always go with a guide or on organized hikes such as those offered by **Tahiti Evasion** (© **56.48.77;** www.tahitievasion.com). This Moorea-based company has all-day treks into the Fautaua valley, home of Loti's Pool; the Orofero Valley on Tahiti's south coast; and to the top of Mount Aorai, the island's third-highest peak. The treks start at 8,900CFP per person for two people and drops to 5,200CFP per person for four or more. Hikes along the wild, uninhabited east coast of Tahiti Iti take 3 days and 2 nights of camping (call for prices). All except the Mount Aorai climb are rated as easy walks. Tahiti Evasion will also organize hiking-and-watersports trips of up to 3 weeks throughout the islands.

You can also check with the **Tourisme Tahiti's visitors bureau** in Papeete (© **50.57.12**) for the names of guides and hiking clubs.

Watersports

Based at the InterContinental Resort Tahiti, **Bathy's Dive Center** (© **53.34.96;** www.bathys-diving.com) offers the most comprehensive list of watersports activities, and you don't have to be an InterContinental guest to partake in diving, sailing, snorkeling jet skiing, kayaking, and whale- and dolphin-watching. Call for reservations and prices.

SCUBA DIVING   Tahiti is not in the same diving league as the other French Polynesian islands. You can see plenty of smaller fish here, but don't expect daily encounters with sharks, rays, and other large creatures, which are plentiful around the other islands. The popular dive sites are on the west coast of Tahiti Nui, from Papeete down to Punaauia, and off the southern coast of Tahiti Nui. The **Aquarium,** near the end of the Faaa airport runway, and in clear view of Moorea, attracts both divers and snorkelers to see fish swimming around coral heads and several wrecks, including a small aircraft (it didn't crash; it was moved here in the 1990s). Nearby are another aircraft and the hulks of two cargo vessels.

For those of us who don't speak French fluently, **Bathy's Dive Center** (☏ **53.34.96;** www.bathys-diving.com), at the InterContinental Resort Tahiti (see above), is the best bet.

SNORKELING & SWIMMING   Most beaches on Tahiti have black volcanic sand, not the white variety most of us expect in the South Pacific. There is some white sand among the pebbles at the **PK 18.5 Plage de Publique (Public Beach),** on the west coast at the Punaauia-Paea border. It has a restaurant and snack bar. The best beach of all is **Plage de Maui** on Tahiti Iti (see "The Tahiti Iti Peninsula: The South Coast to Teahupoo" under "The Circle Island Tour," earlier in this chapter). It's a long haul, but its white sands, clear lagoon, and snack bar make it worth the trip.

SURFING   Tahiti is famous for world-class surfing, especially Teuhupo'o on Tahiti Iti, home of the annual Billabong Pro championships in May. The best big waves crash on jagged reefs offshore, however, so you could be turned into hamburger meat if you've never surfed before. Those new to the sport will be happy to hear that Tahiti is the only major South Pacific island where surf breaks on sandy beaches, upon which **Ecole de Surf Tura'i Mataare (Tahiti Surf School)** (☏ **41.91.37;** www.tahitisurfschool.info) teaches a half-day of surfing and bodyboarding courses for 4,800CFP (12,000CFP for a private lesson). It's a good way to find out if you have what it takes to "hang ten."

SHOPPING

There's no shortage of things to buy on Tahiti, especially in Papeete. Black pearls and handicrafts are sure to tempt you. The selection is widest here, but prices on some items may be better on Moorea.

If you just can't live without visiting a modern shopping mall, head for the **Centre Moana Nui,** on the main road in Punaauia about .5km (¼ mile) south of the Sofitel Tahiti Maeva Beach Resort. Here you'll find a huge Carrefour supermarket, several boutiques, a snack bar with excellent hamburgers, a hairdresser, a bar, banks with ATMs, and a post office (open Mon–Fri 8am–5pm, Sat 8am–noon).

Duty-free shopping is very limited, with French perfumes the best deal. **Duty Free Tahiti** (☏ **42.61.61**), on the street-level waterside of the Centre Vaima, is the largest duty-free shop. Its specialties are Seiko, Lorus, and Cartier watches and Givenchy, Yves St. Laurent, Chanel, and Guerlain perfumes. The **airport departure lounge** has two duty-free shops.

Black Pearls

Papeete has scores of *bijouteries* (jewelry shops) that carry black pearls in a variety of settings. Some stalls in Papeete's Municipal Market sell pearls, but give them a pass and buy yours from an experienced, reputable dealer. Most of these stores are in or around the Centre Vaima, along boulevard Pomare, and in the Quartier du Commerce, the narrow streets off boulevard Pomare between rue Paul Gauguin and rue d'Ecole des Frères north of the Municipal Market.

Your beginning point should be the **Musée de la Perle Robert Wan** (© **46.15.54; www.robertwan.com**), on boulevard Pomare at rue l'Arthémise, opposite Eglise Evangélique (Protestant Church). Named for Robert Wan, the man who pioneered the local industry half a century ago, this museum explains the history of pearls from antiquity, the method by which they are cultured, and the things to look for when making your selection. The museum is open Monday to Saturday from 9am to 5pm. Admission is free.

Adjoining the museum, **Robert Wan Tahiti** (© **46.15.54**) carries only excellent-quality pearls and uses only 18-karat gold for its settings, so the prices tend to be high. Robert Wan has outlets on all the main islands.

One of French Polynesia's largest dealers, **Tahia Collins,** has a small outlet on boulevard Pomare at avenue du Prince Hinoi (© **54.06.00**). Another large dealer is **Tahiti Pearl Market,** on rue Collette at rue Paul Gauguin (© **54.30.60**).

Handicrafts

Although most of the inexpensive souvenir items sold here are made in Asia, many local residents, especially on the outer islands, produce a wide range of seashell jewelry, rag dolls, needlework, and straw hats, mats, baskets, and handbags. I love the *tivaivai,* colorful appliqué quilts stitched together by Tahitian women as their great-grandmothers were shown by the early missionaries. You can also buy exquisite shell chandeliers like those adorning many hotel lobbies.

The most popular item by far is the cotton *pareu,* or wraparound sarong, which everyone wears at one time or another. They are screened, blocked, or printed by hand in the colors of the rainbow. The same material is made into other tropical clothing and various items such as bedspreads and pillowcases. *Pareus* are sold virtually everywhere a visitor might wander.

The **Papeete Municipal Market** ★★★ is the place to shop (see "Tahiti's Top Attractions," earlier in this chapter). It has stalls both upstairs and on the surrounding sidewalk, where local women's associations sell a wide selection of handicrafts at reasonable prices. The market is one of the few places where you can regularly find *pareus* for 1,000CFP, bedspreads made of the colorful tie-dyed and silk-screened *pareu* material, and *tivaivai* quilts. By and large, cloth goods are sold at the sidewalk stalls; those upstairs have a broader range of shell jewelry and other items.

For finer-quality handicrafts, such as woodcarvings from the Marquesas Islands, shell chandeliers, tapa lampshades, or mother-of-pearl shells, try **Tamara Curios,** on rue du Général-de-Gaulle in Fare Tony (© **42.54.42**).

Tropical Clothing

You've arrived in Tahiti and you notice that everyone under the sun is wearing print sundresses or flowered aloha shirts. Where do you go to get yours?

BUYING YOUR black pearl

French Polynesia is the world's largest producer of black pearls. They are cultured by implanting a small nucleus into the shell of a live *Pinctada margaritifera,* the oyster used here, which then coats it with nacre, the same lustrous substance that lines the mother-of-pearl shell. The nacre produces dark pearls known as "black" but whose actual color ranges from slightly grayer than white to black with shades of rose or green. Most range in size from 10 to 17 millimeters (slightly less than ½ to slightly less than ¾ in.).

Size, color, luster, lack of imperfections, and shape determine a pearl's value. No two are exactly alike, but the most valuable are the larger ones that are most symmetrical and have few dark blemishes, and whose color is dark with the shades of a peacock showing through a bright luster. A top-quality pearl 13 millimeters or larger will sell for 960,000CFP or more, but there are thousands to choose from in the 24,000CFP to 80,000CFP range. Some small, imperfect-but-still-lovely pearls cost much less.

Of course, the perfect pearl comes down to the eye of the beholder. Just make sure you see your dream pearl in daylight before handing over your credit card.

So many pearls were being produced a few years ago that many small pearl farms closed. Competition is still fierce among the islands' shops (or their agents—commissioned tour guides and bus and taxi drivers), some of which will bombard you with sales pitches almost from the moment you arrive. Pearls are sold at stands in the Tahiti Municipal Market (see "Tahiti's Top Attractions," earlier in this chapter), and even on the street. I would buy only at the stores I recommend in this book, which sell pearls that have been inspected and X-rayed (to determine the thickness of their nacre) by the local marine resources department.

Even at the highest-end shops, discounting is de rigueur. Despite the general rule to avoid haggling in French Polynesia, you shouldn't pay the price marked on a pearl or a piece of jewelry until you have politely asked for a discount.

With most tourists now spending minimum time on Tahiti in favor of the other islands, you might find pearl prices in Papeete to be lower than on Moorea and Bora Bora. That's not always the case, so you should look in shops like **Ron Hall's Island Fashion Black Pearls** (on Moorea) and **Matira Pearls** (on Bora Bora) before making a purchase in Papeete (see "Shopping" in chapters 6 and 9, respectively). Your salespersons in these shops are more likely to speak English fluently.

You can get a **refund** of the 16% **value added tax** (TVA) included in the price of set pearls (but not on loose pearls). The TVA is not added after the purchase like an American sales tax, so you won't see it. Don't believe them if they say you can't get a refund because they've already taken the TVA off a reduced price. Truth is, they'll have to send the government 16% of whatever price you paid. Ask your dealer how to get your money back by sending them an official form after you have left the country (you can mail it after clearing Immigration at Faaa).

Each hotel has at least one boutique carrying tropical clothing, including *pareus.* The prices there reflect the heavy tourist traffic, but they aren't much worse than at the stores in Papeete. Clothing, to put it bluntly, is dear in French Polynesia.

On boulevard Pomare, stop in **Marie Ah You** (*C* 42.03.31) and **Blue Glue** (*C* 41.37.38), both in the block west of the Vaima Centre. Their selections for women are trendy and a bit expensive. Blue Glue carries excellent pareus and clothing designed by its owner, a Tahitian who lives on Bali in Indonesia.

Maohi Art, in Fare Tony on boulevard Pomare just west of the Vaima Centre (*C* 42.97.43), specializes in block-printed traditional designs (as opposed to the swirls and swooshes with leaves and flowers popular on most *pareus*). It's the place to go if you're looking for a unique design.

WHERE TO STAY

With a few exceptions, Tahiti's accommodations are in four areas: on the west coast, where most properties enjoy at least a partial view of Moorea; in Faaa opposite the airport; in the suburbs east of Papeete, where the beaches are of black volcanic sand; and in the city of Papeete, where you can sample urban life *à la Tahitien*. Consider staying at one of the west-coast, Faaa, or Papeete city hotels if you're stopping here for just a night on your way to or from the other islands or a cruise ship. This is especially true if your connecting flight departs during the horrendous traffic of a weekday morning or evening rush hour.

A note of caution: The worldwide economic recession has especially hurt Tahiti's big hotels. The Hilton Hotel Tahiti & Spa has already closed, and some other may follow suit before you get here.

The West Coast
EXPENSIVE
InterContinental Resort Tahiti ★★★   This is the best all-around resort on Tahiti. Built in the 1960s as the Tahiti Beachcomber Travelodge (most folks here still call it "the Beachcomber"), it sits at Tataa Point on the island's northwest corner, from whence souls supposedly leapt to the ancient Polynesian homeland. Today, planes leap into the air from the nearby airport at Faaa, although the infrequent jet noise seldom penetrates the rooms here. It has a range of accommodations, including smaller rooms dating from its original Travelodge incarnation, newer and more spacious "Panoramic" rooms, and overwater bungalows with unimpeded views of Moorea. Whatever the vintage, all units now are luxuriously appointed with the likes of canopy beds and marble bathrooms, and all have private patios or balconies with views of Moorea. The original overwater units are smaller than newer models on the resort's south end, which have separate sitting areas and steps leading from their decks into the lagoon.

> ### Impressions
>
> *It's a comfort to get into a pareu when one gets back from town . . . I should strongly recommend you to adopt it. It's one of the most sensible costumes I have ever come across. It's cool, convenient, and inexpensive.*
>
> —W. Somerset Maugham, "The Fall of Edward Bernard," 1921

The resort doesn't have a natural beach, but bulkheads separate the sea from white imported sand. You can swim with the fishes in a natural aquatic reserve, or you can frolic in two pools—one in a large complex sitting lagoonside before the

Tahiti Accommodations & Dining

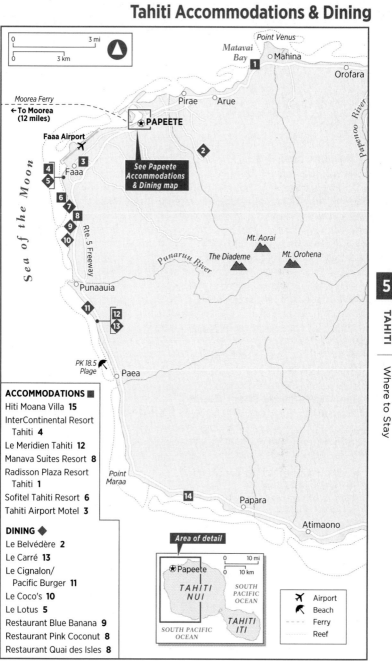

0 [____] 3 mi
0 [____] 3 km

Point Venus
Matavai Bay ○ Mahina **1**
Orofara

Moorea Ferry
← To Moorea
(12 miles)

PAPEETE
○ Pirae ○ Arue

Faaa Airport ✈

See Papeete
Accommodations
& Dining map

3
○ Faaa
4
5

6
7
8
9
10

2

S e a   o f   t h e   M o o n

Papenoo River

Rte. 5 Freeway

○ Punaauia

11
12
13

Punaruu River

Mt. Aorai ▲
The Diademe ▲   Mt. Orohena ▲▲

PK 18.5
Plage 🏖 ○ Paea

ACCOMMODATIONS ■
Hiti Moana Villa **15**
InterContinental Resort
  Tahiti **4**
Le Meridien Tahiti **12**
Manava Suites Resort **8**
Radisson Plaza Resort
  Tahiti **1**
Sofitel Tahiti Resort **6**
Tahiti Airport Motel **3**

DINING ◆
Le Belvédère **2**
Le Carré **13**
Le Cignalon/
  Pacific Burger **11**
Le Coco's **10**
Le Lotus **5**
Restaurant Blue Banana **9**
Restaurant Pink Coconut **8**
Restaurant Quai des Isles **8**

Point Maraa

14
○ Papara

○ Atimaono

Area of detail

✦ Papeete

0 [____] 10 mi
0 [____] 10 km

TAHITI NUI

SOUTH
PACIFIC
OCEAN

TAHITI ITI

SOUTH PACIFIC
OCEAN

✈ Airport
🏖 Beach
--- Ferry
─── Reef

main building, or the other smaller pool with water cascading over its horizon (and apparently into the lagoon). The latter is adjacent to the romantic **Le Lotus** restaurant (see "Where to Dine," later in this chapter). Features here include an all-night lobby bar, Tahiti's top watersports center, and free washers and dryers, a real money-saver given the exorbitant cost of laundry services (buy your soap powder before the boutique closes at 7pm).

B.P. 6014, 98702 Faaa.🕾 **800/327-0200** or 86.51.10. Fax 86.51.30. www.tahiti.interconti.com. 214 units. 32,000CFP–47,500CFP double; 60,000CFP–94,000CFP suite; 59,500CFP–86,000CFP overwater bungalow. AE, DC, MC, V. **Amenities:** 2 restaurants; 2 bars; babysitting; concierge; executive-level rooms; health club; 2 outdoor pools; room service; smoke-free rooms; spa; tennis courts; watersports equipment. *In room:* A/C, ceiling fan, TV, hair dryer, Internet (4,000CFP/day), minibar.

Le Meridien Tahiti ★★   Near the Museum of Tahiti and Her Islands, this luxury resort sits alongside one of Tahiti's few white-sand beaches. It's an excellent choice—although the usual 15-minute ride to Tahiti-Faaa International Airport can take considerably longer during the weekday morning traffic jam. A wade-in pool augments the beach and shallow lagoon. The best accommodations are 12 overwater bungalows, but note that unlike most others, they have neither glass panels in their floors for fish-watching nor steps into the lagoon from their porches. All of the luxuriously appointed guest quarters have balconies, but try to get a north-facing unit for a Moorea view. Le Meridien provides complimentary *le truck* shuttles into Papeete twice a day and on two evenings a week. **Le Carré** (p. 121) is one of the best resort dining rooms in French Polynesia. A shopping center next door has a grocery store, hairdresser, pharmacy, post office, restaurants, and a patisserie for inexpensive breakfasts.

B.P. 380595, 98718 Punaauia. 🕾 **800/225-5843** or 47.07.07. Fax 47.07.08. www.starwoodtahiti.com. 150 units. 31,000CFP–49,000CFP double; 60,000CFP–76,000CFP suite; 68,000CFP–76,000CFP overwater bungalow. AE, DC, MC, V. **Amenities:** 2 restaurants; 2 bars; babysitting; concierge; health club; Jacuzzi; outdoor pool; room service; smoke-free rooms; watersports equipment. *In room:* A/C, ceiling fan (in overwater bungalows), TV, hair dryer, minibar, Wi-Fi (1,000CFP/hour).

Sofitel Tahiti Maeva Beach Resort   This seven-story building resembling a modern version of a terraced Mayan pyramid resides beside the gray sands of Maeva Beach. The murky lagoon off the beach isn't as good for swimming and snorkeling as it is for anchoring numerous yachts, whose masts slice the beach's view of Moorea. Equipped with modern European-style amenities (the bright, lime-green bathrooms nearly blinded me), the smallish rooms open to balconies. Odd-numbered rooms on the upper floors on the north (or "beach") side have views of Moorea, while those on the garden side look south along Tahiti's west coast. Don't

---

📎 **It Pays to Shop for Room Rates**

Like many big hotels these days, those in French Polynesia adjust their room rates according to such factors as the season and how many guests they expect to have on a given day, and many offer Internet specials on their websites. Accordingly, their published "rack rates" are nearly meaningless, except as a means by which to compare relative rates at different hotels. Be sure to check the hotel websites for discounts and other specials. See also "Tips on Accommodations" (p. 73).

expect the same amount of space, luxuries, or amenities as at the InterContinental Resort Tahiti or Le Meridien Tahiti.

B.P. 6008, 98702 Faaa. ⓒ **800/763-4835** or 86.66.00. Fax 41.05.05. www.sofitel.com. 230 units. 27,000CFP–29,000CFP double; 36,000CFP suite. AE, DC, MC, V. **Amenities:** 2 restaurants; 2 bars; babysitting; Jacuzzi; outdoor pool; room service; smoke-free rooms; tennis courts; watersports equipment. *In room:* A/C, TV, hair dryer, minibar, Wi-Fi (850CFP/hour).

MODERATE

Manava Suites Resort ★★ 🐟   Opened in 2009, this modernistic, high-tech property sits lagoonside in Punaauia, just south of where the main highway splits from the old coastal road. It lacks a beach but boasts Tahiti's largest horizon-edge outdoor pool, from which you can see Moorea across the Sea of the Moon. You can also wade into the lagoon. In two three-story buildings, most units are suites with full kitchens and patios or balconies. Some have separate bedrooms, but beware: many units here have twin beds, so ask for a queen or king if that matters. You'll pay more for a unit with a view of Moorea. A dozen hotel rooms lack the kitchens and balconies but are good value for quick layovers. Opening to a courtyard, the restaurant offers both a French *carte* and an inexpensive bistro menu. The resort sends a shuttle to downtown Papeete twice a day (600CFP per rider each way).

B.P. 2851, 98703 Punaauia. ⓒ **800/657-3275** or 47.31.30. Fax 47.31.01. www.spmhotels.com. 121 units. 15,000CFP double; 18,500CFP–45,000CFP suite. Rates include full breakfast. AE, MC, V. **Amenities:** Restaurant; 2 bars; babysitting; health club; Jacuzzi; outdoor pool; room service; smoke-free rooms; spa; watersports equipment; Wi-Fi (free). *In room:* A/C, ceiling fan, TV/DVD, hair dryer, Internet (free), kitchen (109 units), minibar.

INEXPENSIVE

Hiti Moana Villa ★★ 🐟   Beside the lagoon in Papara, on the south coast 32km (19 miles) from Papeete, this is one of Tahiti's better pensions. The English-speaking Brothersen family keeps everything running smoothly, and son Steve will take you fishing and on guided tours of the island. Half the units here are standard government-issue bungalows with one room for living and sleeping, an attached bathroom to the rear, and a front porch. One of these faces the lagoon, as do two other Mediterranean-style "villa" units with separate bedrooms and their own kitchens. These villas open to a lagoonside swimming pool, which makes up for the lack of a beach. A pier extends over the lagoon. Guests here get free use of kayaks. Breakfast is available.

B.P. 20055, 98718 Papara. ⓒ **57.93.93.** Fax 57.94.44. www.hitimoanavilla.com. 8 units. 10,000CFP–14,500CFP double. Discounts for 2 nights or more. AE, MC, V. **Amenities:** Outdoor pool; watersports equipment. *In room:* Ceiling fan, TV, fridge, kitchen (4 units), no phone, Wi-Fi (660CFP/hour).

In Faaa

Tahiti Airport Motel   Carved into a hill directly across Route 1 from the airport terminal, this three-story, walk-up hotel has simply furnished but reasonably comfortable rooms. A communal balcony across the front overlooks the airport and Moorea on the horizon. Although lacking in facilities, this is a convenient and relatively cost-conscious place to sleep off your overnight flight after you arrive, or to wait for a late-night or early-morning departure. The hotel supplies free coffee round-the-clock and sells continental breakfast packs, but it does not provide airport transfers, so you'll have to rent a car, take a taxi, or make the steep climb uphill. The vehicular entry is off route St. Hillare, the road linking the airport to the Route 5 freeway. Restaurants and shops are nearby.

B.P. 2407, 98713 Papeete. ☎ **50.40.00.** Fax 50.40.01. www.tahitiairportmotel.com. 42 units. 13,400CFP–21,600CFP double. AE, MC, V. *In room:* A/C, TV, fridge, Wi-Fi (660CFP/hour).

East of Papeete

It was getting toward the end of its days during my recent visit, but if it's still open, the **Hotel Le Royal Tahitien,** in Pirae about 4km (2½ miles) east of downtown (☎ **50.40.40,** fax 50.40.41; www.hotelroyaltahitien.com), will be one of the better values here. Built in the 1960s, it's essentially an aging American motel set in beautiful gardens beside a beach of black sand. While the rooms may lack charm, the same cannot be said of its fine, moderately priced restaurant, which occupies a 1937-vintage building with a thatched ceiling.

Radisson Plaza Resort Tahiti ★   This modern resort resides beside the deep black sands of Lafayette Beach on Matavai Bay, where the 18th-century explorers dropped anchor. A huge, turtle-shaped thatched roof covers most of the central complex, which holds two restaurants, a bar, an arts-and-crafts center, and a full-service spa. Outside is a horizon-edge pool beside the beach. Currents create an undertow here, so heed the DANGEROUS SEA signs when swimming in the lagoon. Seven hotel buildings hold the accommodations, which include standard rooms, two-story town house–style "duplexes" (their upstairs bedrooms have their own balconies), suites, and—my favorites—rooms with hot tubs romantically placed behind louvers on their balconies. Furnishings and decor are tropical with a European flair. The Radisson sends a shuttle to downtown Papeete each morning and afternoon, but public buses do not run out here after 5pm, meaning you will need to rent a car or take a taxi to get to and from downtown after dark. As at Le Meridien Tahiti, rush-hour traffic can make for a long trek to the airport from here. This Radisson is a smoke-free hotel.

B.P. 14170, 98701 Arue (on Matavai Bay, 7km/4¼ miles east of downtown). ☎ **800/333-3333** or 48.88.88. Fax 43.88.89. www.radisson.com/aruefrp. 165 units. 19,000CFP–23,000CFP double; 26,000CFP suite. AE, DC, MC, V. **Amenities:** 2 restaurants; 2 bars; health club; Jacuzzi; outdoor pool; room service; smoke-free rooms; spa; watersports equipment. *In room:* A/C, TV, hair dryer, minibar, Wi-Fi (free).

In Papeete
MODERATE

Hotel Le Mandarin   Attractive primarily to business travelers and cost-conscious tourists heading to the cruise ships, this Chinese-accented hotel is a bit shopworn, but is in a somewhat quieter downtown location—on rue Collette opposite the Town Hall—than is the Hotel Tiare Tahiti Noa Noa (see below). Most rooms are rather smallish, but many have narrow balconies with mountain views. I would not stay here on Friday, however, since dancers can spill from the noisy nightclub onto the street. There's a coffee shop in the hotel, and **Le Mandarin** dining room next door is one of the city's better Chinese restaurants.

B.P. 302, 98713 Papeete. ☎ **50.33.50.** Fax 42.16.32. 37 units. 15,500CFP–17,500CFP double. AE, MC, V. **Amenities:** 3 restaurants; 3 bars. *In room:* A/C, TV, fridge, Wi-Fi (900CFP/hour).

Hotel Tahiti Nui ★ ✦   The best downtown hotel, this sleek facility opened in 2009 on Avenue Prince Hinoi 3 blocks from the waterfront. The 6-story building encloses a small courtyard garden. Facing outside, every unit has a balcony with a

Papeete Accommodations & Dining

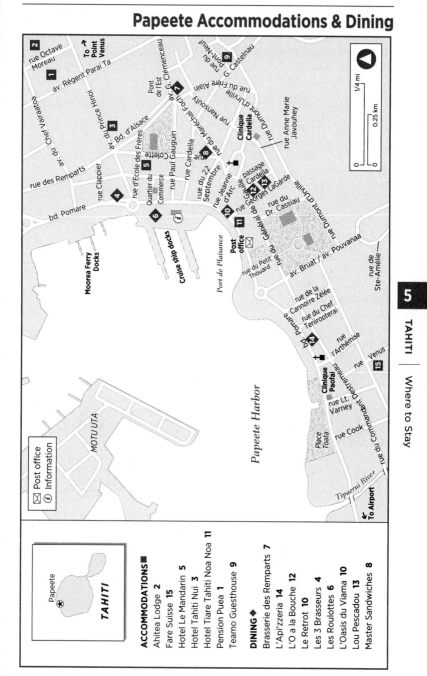

ACCOMMODATIONS ■
Ahitea Lodge **2**
Fare Suisse **15**
Hotel Le Mandarin **5**
Hotel Tahiti Nui **3**
Hotel Tiare Tahiti Noa Noa **11**
Pension Puea **1**
Teamo Guesthouse **9**

DINING ◆
Brasserie des Remparts **7**
L'Api'zzeria **14**
L'O a la Bouche **12**
Le Retrot **10**
Les 3 Brasseurs **4**
Les Roulottes **6**
L'Oasis du Viama **10**
Lou Pescadou **13**
Master Sandwiches **8**

view of the city. About half of the units are standard hotel rooms, while the rest are divided between junior and executive suites. With two bedrooms and cooking facilities, the executive suites see double duty as family units. The decor is modern with few Polynesian influences, including the chic French restaurant and its mezzanine bar.

B.P. 302, 98713 Papeete. ☏ **46.38.99.** Fax 85.12.99. www.hoteltahitinui.com. 91 units. 16,000CFP double; 18,500CFP–32,500CFP suite. AE, MC, V. **Amenities:** Restaurant; bar; health club; outdoor pool; smoke-free rooms; spa. *In room:* A/C, TV, hair dryer, Internet (free), kitchen (in executive suites), minibar.

Hotel Tiare Tahiti Noa Noa This upstairs, five-story facility, on boulevard Pomare a block west of the Centre Vaima, is simple but clean. Amenities are scarce, but the friendly front-desk staffers speak English and are adept at helping you arrange tours and other activities. Many overseas guests here are on low-budget package tours or are heading to one of the cruise ships. The rooms are minimally furnished and can be noisy, since most face directly onto the busy boulevard. Be sure to request a unit on the upper floors, which are quieter and have better views from their slim, unfurnished balconies. Continental breakfast is available in an open-air room on the second floor.

B.P. 2359, 98713 Papeete. ☏ **50.01.00.** Fax 43.68.47. hoteltiarietahiti@mail.pf. 38 units. 13,500CFP–15,000CFP double. AE, MC, V. **Amenities:** Restaurant (breakfast only). *In room:* A/C, TV, Wi-Fi (660CFP/hour).

INEXPENSIVE

Ahitea Lodge This bed-and-breakfast provides an oasis in the midst of a closely packed Tahitian neighborhood with the usual collection of roosters and dogs. A high fence surrounds the lush yard with an outdoor pool and a pond stocked with tropical fish. The least expensive units are in an attached building, but these all share toilets and showers, and they have small fresh-air vents instead of windows. Preferable are bedrooms in the main house, especially those upstairs opening to a balcony overlooking the pool and pond. Best of these is a corner unit with TV, fridge, private bathroom, and air-conditioning (it is the only air-conditioned unit here). The hosts provide a tropical breakfast in the communal kitchen each morning. Staying here will expose you to modern urban life as lived by middle- and working-class Tahitians.

Av. Chef Vairaatoa, 98713 Papeete. ☏ **53.13.53.** Fax 42.09.35. www.ahitea-lodge.com. 13 units (9 with bathroom). 8,500CFP–13,500CFP. Rates include tropical breakfast. MC, V. **Amenities:** Outdoor pool. *In room:* A/C (1 unit), fan, TV (2 units), fridge (1 unit), no phone, Wi-Fi (660CFP/hour).

Fare Suisse ★★ ✦ Beni Huber moved to Tahiti from Switzerland and opened this spotlessly clean guest house uphill on rue Venus, a side street in the Paofai neighborhood and just 3 blocks inland from Tohua Toata and the waterfront. Sea breezes usually cool the light, airy rooms. One has over-and-under (bunk) double beds and a convertible sofa; it sees double duty as a dormitory. An apartment downstairs has its own kitchen and two bedrooms, one of which can be rented separately. The dorm and one of the rooms share a bathroom; the other units have their own private facilities. Breakfast is available at this home away from home. Beni speaks German, English, and French.

B.P. 20355, 98713 Faaa (rue Venus, south of rue des Poilus Tahitiens). ☏/fax **42.00.30.** www.fare-suisse.com. 4 units (3 with bathroom), 2 dorm beds. 9,500CFP–15,000CFP double; 4,700CFP dorm bed. AE, MC, V. **Amenities:** Free airport transfers. *In room:* Kitchen (1 unit), no phone, Wi-Fi (free).

Pension Puea   About a block from Ahitea Lodge (see above), this simple but friendly pension appeals to backpackers and other cost-conscious travelers who need no frills. Guests swap yarns in the lounge and communal kitchen under a lean-to roof (breakfast is served here daily). The bright, well-ventilated rooms are all upstairs. Largest and best are the three air-conditioned family units with either two double beds or a double and a single. One of these also has a private bathroom (the other units share two toilets and two showers). It lacks the convenience and in-room amenities of Teamo Guest House (see below).

B.P. 5597, 98716 Pirae (87 rue Pasteur Octave Moreau, Papeete). ☏ **85.43.43.** Fax 42.09.35. www. pensionpuea.com. 6 units (5 with shared bathroom). 6,500CFP–8,500CFP. Rates include tropical breakfast. AE, MC, V. *In room:* A/C (3 units), fan, no phone.

Teamo Guest House   Although it has been around for more than 2 decades, this guesthouse-cum-hostel is much improved now that friendly, English-speaking owners Gerald and Kay Teriierooiterai have added TVs, fridges, and air conditioners to all the rooms. In a primarily residential neighborhood 6 blocks from the waterfront, it occupies a wood-frame house built around 1880. Rooms were small in those days, so don't expect them to be spacious today. Some upstairs units have balconies. Two downstairs rooms have six bunk beds each and are used for male and female dorms. There's a comfy lounge at the front of the house and a communal kitchen on a covered patio out back.

B.P. 2407, 98713 Papeete (rue du Pont-Neuf off rue du Général Castelnau, Faaa). ☏ **42.47.26** or 42.00.35. Fax 43.56.95. www.teamoguesthouse.com. 11 units (all with bathrooms), 18 dorm beds. 5,800CFP–7,500CFP double; 2,500CFP dorm bed. Rates include continental breakfast. MC, V. **Amenities:** Internet (1,000CFP/hour). *In room:* A/C, fan, TV, fridge.

WHERE TO DINE

Tahiti has a plethora of excellent French, Italian, and Chinese restaurants. Those I recommend below are but a few of many; don't hesitate to strike out on your own.

Downtown Papeete has a **McDonald's** at the corner of rue du Général-de-Gaulle and rue du Dr. Cassiau behind Centre Vaima, and there's a second on the main road in Punaauia. For Tahiti's version of fast food, see "Don't Miss *Les Roulottes,*" p. 125. If you want to make your own meals or a picnic, the downtown **Champion** supermarket is on rue du Général-de-Gaulle in the block west of the Eglise Evangélique. On the west coast, head for the huge **Carrefour** supermarket in the Centre Moana Nui, south of the Sofitel Tahiti Maeva Beach Resort.

The West Coast
EXPENSIVE

Le Carré ★★ 🍴 FRENCH   Although not as spectacular a setting as Le Lotus at the InterContinental Resort Tahiti (see below), Le Meridien Tahiti's fine-dining outlet has tables under a round thatched roof and romantically posited on the deck beside the beach and the resort's wade-in swimming pool—but no view of Moorea here. Although basically French, the cuisine has numerous island influences, and the chef frequently offers two different methods of preparing the same dish.

At Le Meridien Tahiti, PK 15, Punaauia. ☏ **47.07.07.** Reservations recommended. Main courses 3,000CFP–5,000CFP. AE, DC, MC, V. Daily noon–2:30pm and 7–10pm.

Le Coco's ★★★ FRENCH   Along with Le Lotus (see below), this lagoonside restaurant shares top rank as Tahiti's finest and most romantic place to dine, especially the tables out on the lawn, where you will have a gorgeous look at Moorea (moonlit nights are awesome). Other tables shaded by a thatched cabana also share the view. The cuisine is French but with island ingredients and influences. The fixed-price, 7-course menu is a gastronomic adventure. Arrive early enough to sip a drink and watch the sun set over Moorea. The efficient waiters here are experienced and knowledgeable; if in doubt, take their advice.

PK 13.2, Punaauia. ⓒ **58.21.08.** Reservations recommended. Main courses 4,550CFP; 7-course tasting menu 14,900CFP. AE, MC, V. Tues–Sat 11:45am–1:30pm and 7–9:30pm; Sun 11:45am–1:30pm.

Le Lotus ★★★ FRENCH/CONTINENTAL   With two round, thatched-roof dining rooms extending over the lagoon and enjoying an uninterrupted view of Moorea, Le Lotus has a setting rivaled only by Le Coco's. The widely spaced tables are all at the water's edge (a spotlight between the two dining rooms shines into the lagoon, attracting fish in search of a handout). The gourmet French fare and attentive but unobtrusive service more than live up to this romantic scene. The resort often invites some of Europe's top master chefs to take working vacations here. Whomever is in residence, you're in for a gastronomic delight.

In InterContinental Resort Tahiti, Faaa (7km/4 miles west of Papeete). ⓒ **86.51.10,** ext. 5512. Reservations highly recommended. Main courses 2,100CFP–3,900CFP. AE, DC, MC, V. Daily noon–2:30pm and 6:30–9pm.

MODERATE

Restaurant Blue Banana ☺ FRENCH/ITALIAN   Opened in 2007 by Steven Baker, son of an American father and Chinese-Tahitian mother, this casual, family-oriented restaurant has an unimpeded view of Moorea. A play area to keeps kids busy while their parents choose from a menu including very big burgers, Italian fare such as spaghetti, lasagna, and pizzas from a wood-fired oven, and traditional French steaks and fish. Be sure to reserve a table out on the pier with a Moorea view. This is one of the few restaurants on Tahiti that caters to children.

PK 11.2, Punaauia. ⓒ **42.22.24.** www.bluebanana-tahiti.com. Reservations recommended. Burgers 1,650CFP–1,850CFP; pizza and pasta 1,250CFP–2,900CFP; main courses 2,200CFP–3,600CFP. AE, MC, V. Tues–Sat 11:30am–2:30pm and 6:30–10pm; Sun 11:30am–2:30pm.

Restaurant Pink Coconut ★★ INTERNATIONAL   This open-air restaurant commands a view of Moorea through the masts of yachts moored at Marina Taina. Most tables are under a roof, but unless it's raining or too hot, I opt for one outside on the terrace. The bill of fare ranges the globe. My delicious shrimp in curry and coconut cream was spicier than the usual local versions, and it was accompanied by terrific puréed squash. The seafood pasta with shrimp, salmon, scallops, and tuna was excellent. Reduced priced drinks from 5 to 6pm make this a great place to watch the sunset over Moorea. The Pink Coconut and the adjacent Restaurant Quai des Isles (see below) often have live music on weekend nights.

PK 9, Punaauia, at Marina Taina. ⓒ **42.22.23.** www.pinkcoconuttahiti.com. Reservations recommended. Main courses 2,350CFP–3,450CFP. AE, MC, V. Restaurant Mon–Sat 11:30am–2pm and 7–10pm. Bar Mon–Sat 5–11pm. Heading south, turn right into marina after first traffic circle and follow the signs.

Restaurant Quai des Isles ★★ FRENCH/CREOLE   In the same building as the Pink Coconut (see above) but with a better view of Moorea, this restaurant specializes in Caribbean Creole cuisine from Martinique and Guadeloupe. It is most famous in Tahiti, however, for its healthy *panier vapeus*—steamed salmon, shrimp, scallops, and vegetables. On a recent visit I opted for a Creole sampler plate which included Indian-style samosas, spicy chicken wings, and both blood and pork sausage (I preferred the latter, served with red beans in a tomato sauce). The Creole items are also available as tapas, which go well with a drink while watching the sunset over Moorea.

PK 9, Punaauia, at Marina Taina. ✆ **81.02.38.** Reservations recommended on weekends. Main courses 2,350CFP–3,600CFP. AE, MC, V. Tues–Sun 11:30am–2pm and 7–10pm.

INEXPENSIVE

Le Cignalon/Pacific Burger ✦ PIZZA/SNACK BAR   Cost-conscious guests at Le Meridien Tahiti resort walk next door to Pacific Burger, the open-air snack bar side operated by Le Cignalon (an Italian restaurant) for good, reasonably priced salads, *poisson cru*, sashimi, burgers (beef, chicken, or fish), grilled rib-eye steaks, fish with or without sauce, and very good two-person pizzas from a wood-fired oven. A big tarp covers plastic patio tables and chairs in front of the fast-food-style counter. The menu is in French and English. The Tahiti museum is a few blocks away, so this is a good place to stop for refreshment on your round-island tour.

PK 15, Punaauia. ✆ **42.40.84.** Burgers 450CFP–850CFP; pizza and pasta 1,400CFP–2,000CFP; main courses 2,000CFP–2,700CFP. MC, V. Tues–Thurs 10am–3pm and 5:30–9pm; Fri–Sun 10am–3pm and 5:30–9:30pm.

In Papeete
EXPENSIVE

L'O a la Bouche ★★★ FRENCH   One of the top restaurants in all of French Polynesia, this charming bistro's sophisticated, muted ambience would make it at home in the wine countries of Napa or Baroosa—except for the vintage labels pictured on the walls, which are all French. Although the chef offers several traditional French dishes, this is anything but a typical French restaurant. His talent soars with

---

🏷 DINING WITH A belle VIEW

I like to spend my last evening on Tahiti up at **Le Belvédère** (✆ 42.73.44). This innlike establishment has a spectacular view of the city and Moorea from its perch 600m (2,000 ft.) up in the Fare Ape Valley above Papeete. The restaurant provides round-trip transportation from your hotel up the narrow, one-lane, winding, switchback road that leads to it (I don't encourage anyone to attempt this drive in a rental car). Take the 5pm pickup so you'll reach the restaurant in time for a sunset cocktail. They'll drop you back at the airport if you're leaving that night. The specialty of the house is fondue Bourguignonne served with six sauces. The 5,900CFP fixed price includes three courses, wine, and transportation, so it is a reasonably good value. The quality of the cuisine doesn't match the view, however, so treat the evening as a sightseeing excursion, not as a fine-dining experience. Reservations are required; American Express, MasterCard, and Visa are accepted. Closed Wednesdays.

creations such as a moon fish steak under passion-fruit and ginger sauce (the ginger perfectly tempered the fruit's sweetness). I preceded that with a smoked salmon and shrimp salad with *pamplemousse* (local grapefruit), which was delightfully refreshing after a day of tramping around Papeete. Next time, I'm going with scallops marinated with red peppers, or perhaps scorched tuna with a light curry sauce. The list of French wines is short but excellent. The menu is in both French and English here.

Passage Cardella (btw. rue du Général-de-Gaulle and rue Anne-Marie Javouhey). ℭ **45.29.76.** Reservations recommended, especially on weekends. Main courses 3,350CFP–3,950CFP. AE, MC, V. Mon–Fri 11:30am–2:30pm and 7:15–10pm; Sat 7:15–10pm.

MODERATE

Brasserie des Remparts FRENCH   The blues cascade from speakers at this American-style, brass-and-dark-wood pub, whose food is much better than at the otherwise comparable Les 3 Brasseurs (see below). Despite the 5¢-PAY-TOILET sign and other American memorabilia hanging on the walls, the chow is definitely French, with the likes of andouille sausage in mustard sauce, mahimahi meunière, an Alsatian-style casserole, Moroccan couscous, and rib-eye steaks with Roquefort, pepper, or béarnaise sauces. The plate-size salads make healthy meals unto themselves. Try for a sidewalk table.

Av. Georges Clemenceau, at Rond Pont de L'Est traffic circle. ℭ **42.80.00.** Reservations accepted. Main courses 1,950CFP–2,300CFP. AE, MC, V. Mon–Fri 7am–3pm and 6:30–11pm.

L'Api'zzeria ★★ 🍴 ITALIAN   On par with Lou Pescadou (see below) but with a garden setting, this restaurant in a grove of trees across from the waterfront has been serving very good pizza and pasta since 1968. I prefer a table outside under the trees rather than inside, where the dining room resembles an Elizabethan waterfront tavern accented with nautical relics. The food, on the other hand, is definitely Italian. Both pizzas and tender steaks are cooked in a wood-fired oven. The menu also features spaghetti, fettuccine, lasagna, steak Milanese, veal in white or Marsala wine sauce, and grilled homemade Italian sausage.

Bd. Pomare, between rue du Chef Teriirooterai and rue l'Arthémise. ℭ **42.98.30.** Reservations not accepted. Pizza and pasta 520CFP–2,080CFP; meat courses 1,870CFP–2,850CFP. MC, V. Mon–Sat 11:30am–10pm.

Les 3 Brasseurs FRENCH   The quality of its food tends to be up and down, but this sidewalk microbrewery is the nearest thing Papeete has to an American-style bar-and-grill. The sidewalk tables are fine for a cold one while waiting for the Moorea ferry at the docks across the boulevard. The tabloid menu is all in French, but those on the waitstaff speak enough English to explain the dishes. Choose from sandwiches, salads, roast chicken served hot or cold, and grilled steaks, mahimahi, and tuna plain or with optional sauces. The best deal here is a *croque brasseur,* a ham sandwich served under melted Gruyère cheese and accompanied by a glass of beer and a green salad with excellent vinaigrette dressing, all for 900CFP. There's live music here on weekends.

Bd. Pomare, between rue Prince Hinoi and rue Clappier, opposite Moorea ferry docks. ℭ **50.60.25.** www.3brasseurs-pacific.com. Sandwiches and salads 600CFP–950CFP; main courses 1,600CFP–2,800CFP. MC, V. Daily 9am–1am.

Lou Pescadou 🍴 ITALIAN   A lively young professional clientele usually packs this quintessential Italian trattoria (red-and-white-checked tablecloths, dripping

DON'T MISS les roulottes

Although prices in some hotel dining rooms and restaurants here can be shocking, you don't need to spend a fortune to eat reasonably well in French Polynesia. In fact, the best food bargains in Papeete literally roll out after dark on the cruise-ship docks: portable meal wagons known as *les roulottes.*

Some owners set up charcoal grills behind their trucks and small electric generators in front to provide plenty of light for the diners, who sit on stools along either side of the vehicles. A few operate during the daytime, but most begin arriving about 6pm. The entire waterfront soon takes on a carnival atmosphere, especially on Friday and Saturday nights. So many cruise-ship passengers and other tourists eat here that most truck owners speak some English.

The traditional menu includes char-broiled steaks or chicken with french fries (known, respectively, as *steak frites* and *poulet frites*), familiar Cantonese

dishes, *poisson cru,* and *salade russe* (Russian-style potato salad, tinted red by beet-root juice) for 900CFP to 1,700CFP per plate. Glassed-in display cases along the sides of some trucks hold actual examples of what's offered at each (not exactly the most appetizing exhibits, but you can just point to what you want rather than fumbling in French). You'll find just as many trucks specializing in crepes, pizzas, couscous, and waffles *(gaufres).* Even if you don't order an entire meal at *les roulottes,* stop for a crepe or waffle and enjoy the scene.

Although they now have permanent homes, the open-air restaurants at **Tohua Toata,** on the western end of the waterfront, were born as roulottes, and they still offer some of the same fare if not the same prices as their mobile siblings. They're open for lunch Monday through Saturday, for dinner Friday and Saturday.

candles on each table, Ruffino bottles hanging from every nook and cranny). They come for good, fresh, and tasty Italian fare at reasonable prices (be prepared to wait for a table). The individual-size pizzas are cooked in a wood-fired oven; the excellent pasta dishes include lasagna, spaghetti, and fettuccine under tomato, carbonara, and Roquefort sauces.

Rue Anne-Marie Javouhey at passage Cardella. ☎ **43.74.26.** Pizza and pasta 1,000CFP–1,950CFP; meat courses 1,850CFP–2,750CFP. MC, V. Mon–Sat 11:30am–2pm and 6:30–11pm. Take the narrow passage Cardella, a 1-block street that looks like an alley, directly behind Centre Vaima.

INEXPENSIVE

Le Retrot FRENCH/ITALIAN/SNACKS You'll find better food elsewhere, but this Parisian-style sidewalk cafe is Papeete's best place to rendezvous or to grab a quick bite, a drink, or an ice cream while watching the world pass along the quay. A selection of salads, sandwiches, and burgers gets attention from the cafe crowd.

Bd. Pomare, front of Centre Vaima, on waterfront. ☎ **42.86.83.** Salads, sandwiches, and burgers 300CFP–1,250CFP; main courses 1,750CFP–2,150CFP. AE, MC, V. Daily 6am–midnight.

L'Oasis du Vaima SNACK BAR You'll find me having a breakfast of a small quiche or a tasty pastry with strong French coffee at this kiosklike building on the southwest corner of Centre Vaima. In addition to dishing out ice cream and milkshakes to passersby at a sidewalk counter, it serves up a variety of goodies, from crispy *casse-croûtes* (sandwiches) to two substantial *plats du jour* selections each day, on a covered dining terrace and in an air-conditioned dining room upstairs.

Rue du Général-de-Gaulle at rue Jeanne d'Arc (at the corner of Centre Vaima, opposite Cathédrale de l'Immaculée Conception). © **45.45.01.** Sandwiches, quiches, omelets, small pizzas 400CFP–1,000CFP; meals 1,500CFP–2,100CFP. No credit cards. Mon–Sat 5am–5pm.

Master Sandwiches ★ 🎁 SNACK BAR   There's no place to sit at this cafeteria-style carryout, but the sandwiches, salads, and other items are so fresh and reasonably priced that patrons often mob the sidewalk at lunch, and crispy French baguette sandwiches fly out of here by the hundreds. Also available are daily hot lunches such as chow mien, pastas, couscous, paella, and Tahitian-style poisson cru. This is the best place in town to grab a ready-made sandwich or salad to eat in a shady park or beside the harbor.

Rue du Maréchal Foch at Rue Collette and re du 22 Septembre. © **43.03.43.** Most items 200CFP–850CFP. No credit cards. Mon–Fri 5am–5pm, Sat 6am–4pm.

ISLAND NIGHTS ON TAHITI

A 19th-century European merchant wrote of the Tahitians, "Their existence was in never-ending merrymaking." In many respects this is still true, for after the sun goes down, Tahitians like to make merry as much today as they did in the 1820s, and Papeete has lots of good choices for visitors who want to join in the fun.

Tahitian Dance Shows ★★★

Traditional Tahitian dancing isn't as indecent as it was in Captain Cook's day (see "A Most Indecent Song & Dance," p. 36), but seeing at least one show should be on your agenda. You'll have plenty of chances, since nightlife on the outer islands consists almost exclusively of dance shows at the resorts, usually in conjunction with a feast of Tahitian food.

Each of Tahiti's big resort hotels has shows at least 1 night a week. Not to be missed is the **Grande Danse de Tahiti ★★★** troupe, which usually performs at the InterContinental Resort Tahiti (© **86.51.10**) on Wednesday, Friday, and Saturday evenings (the Sat show is a reenactment of the dance that seduced the crew of HMS *Bounty*). Call the resort to confirm the schedule. Another good place to catch a show is the **Captain Bligh Restaurant and Bar,** at the Lagoonarium de Tahiti in Punaauia (© **43.62.90;** see "Tahiti's Top Attractions," earlier in this chapter), which usually has them on Friday and Saturday at 8:30pm. Expect to pay

---

Impressions

They have several negative comments on the beachcombing life in Tahiti: Not much cultural life. No intellectual stimulus. No decent library. Restaurant food is disgraceful . . . But I noticed that Saturday after Saturday they turned up at Quinn's *with the most dazzling beauties on the island. When I reminded them of this they said, "Well that does compensate for the poor library."*

—James A. Michener, *Return to Paradise,* 1951

from 5,000CFP for the show and dinner at the Captain Bligh to 9,800CFP at the big resorts.

Pub-Crawling

Papeete has a nightclub or watering hole to fit anyone's taste, from upscale private (*privé*) discothèques to down-and-dirty bars and dance halls where Tahitians strum on guitars while sipping on large bottles of Hinano beer (and sometimes engage in fisticuffs after midnight). If you look like a tourist, you'll be allowed into the private clubs. Generally, everything gets to full throttle after 9pm (except on Sun, when most pubs are closed). None of the clubs are inexpensive. Expect to pay a cover of at least 1,000CFP, which will include your first drink. After that, beers cost at least 500CFP, with most mixed drinks in the range of 1,000CFP to 1,500CFP.

The narrow rue des Ecoles is the heart of Papeete's *mahu* district, where male transvestites hang out. The **Piano Bar** (*℃* **42.88.24**) is the most popular of the "sexy clubs" along this street, especially for its late-night strip shows featuring female impersonators. It's open daily from 3pm to 3am. The multistory **Mana Rock Cafe,** at boulevard Pomare and rue des Ecoles (*℃* **48.36.36**), draws a more mixed crowd to its bars and discothèque (you can check your e-mail between sips here).

MOOREA

Like most visitors to French Polynesia, I soon grab the ferry to Moorea, just 20km (12 miles) west of Tahiti. James Michener may have thought Bora Bora was the world's most beautiful island, but Moorea is my choice. In fact, it's so stunningly gorgeous that I have trouble keeping my eyes on the road here. Hollywood often uses stock shots of Moorea's jagged mountains, deep bays, and emerald lagoons to create a South Seas setting for movies that don't even take place in French Polynesia.

Geologists attribute Moorea's rugged, otherworldly beauty to a great volcano, the northern half of which either fell into the sea or was blown away in a cataclysmic explosion, leaving the heart-shaped island we see today. In other words, Moorea is only half of its old self. The remaining rim of the crater has eroded into the jagged peaks and spires that give the island its haunting, dinosaurlike profile. Cathedral-like Mount Mouaroa—Moorea's trademark "Shark's Tooth" or "Bali Hai Mountain"—shows up on innumerable postcards and on the 100CFP coin.

Mount Rotui stands alone in the center of the ancient crater, its black cliffs and stovepipe buttresses dropping dramatically to the sides of Cook's Bay and Opunohu Bay, two dark blue fingers that cut deep into Moorea's interior. These mountain-shrouded bays are certainly among the world's most photographed bodies of water.

Perched high up on the crater's wall, the Belvédère overlooks both bays, Mount Rotui, and the jagged old crater rim curving off to left and right. Do not miss the Belvédère, for it is one of the South Pacific's most awesome panoramas.

With traffic choking Tahiti, and Moorea only a 30-minute ferry ride away from Papeete, the island is already a bedroom community for its big sister. Still, it has maintained its Polynesian charm to a large extent. Its hotels and resorts are spread out enough so that you don't feel like you're in a tourist trap, and the locals don't feel inundated by us. They still have time to stop and talk with visitors.

Most of Moorea's 20,000 or so residents live on the coastal plain fringing the island, many of them in small settlements where lush valleys meet a lagoon enclosed by an offshore coral reef. This calm blue lagoon makes Moorea ideal for swimming, boating, snorkeling, and diving. Unlike the black sands of Tahiti, white beaches stretch for miles on Moorea.

GETTING AROUND MOOREA

All ferries from Papeete land at Vaiare on Moorea's east coast 5km (3 miles) south of **Temae Airport** (see "Getting Around Tahiti & French Polynesia," in chapter 3).

By Bus

The only scheduled buses on Moorea are those that carry passengers from and to the morning and afternoon ferries at Vaiare. Tell the drivers where you're going; they will show you which vehicle is going to your hotel. The trip from Vaiare to the end of the line at the old Club Med site takes about 1 hour. The buses also return from the Petite Village shopping center in Haapiti to Vaiare, leaving the shopping center about 1 hour prior to each ferry departure. They go by the hotels, so ask the front-desk staff when you can expect the next bus to pass. Or you can flag them down along the road elsewhere. The one-way fare is 600CFP, regardless of direction or length of ride.

By Taxi

Unless you catch a ferry bus or rent a vehicle, you're at the expensive mercy of Moorea's taxi owners, who don't run around looking for customers. The only **taxi stand** is at the airport (✆ **56.10.18**). It's staffed daily from 6am to 6pm. Your hotel desk can call one for you, or else phone **Pero Taxis** (✆ **56.14.93**), **Albert Tours** (✆ **55.21.10**), or **Justine Taxi** (✆ **77.48.26**). Make advance reservations for service between 6pm and 6am.

Fares are 800CFP during the day, 1,700CFP at night, plus 110CFP per kilometer. They double from 8pm to 6am. Expect to pay about 2,000CFP one-way from the ferry or airport to the Cook's Bay area, about 4,000CFP one-way from the airport or Cook's Bay to the Haapiti area, less for stops along the way. Be sure that you understand what the fare will be before you get in.

> ### Impressions
>
> *From Tahiti, Moorea seems to have about 40 separate summits: fat thumbs of basalt, spires tipped at impossible angles, brooding domes compelling to the eye. But the peaks which can never be forgotten are the jagged saw-edges that look like the spines of some forgotten dinosaur.*
>
> —James A. Michener, *Return to Paradise*, 1951

By Rental Car & Scooter

Avis (✆ **800/331-1212** or 56.32.68; www.avis.com) and **Europcar** (✆ **800/ 227-7368** or 56.34.00; www.europcartahiti.com) both have booths at the Vaiare ferry wharf and at several hotels. Although I usually rent from Avis, Europcar is the more widespread and slightly less expensive of the two, with unlimited-kilometer rates starting at 9,300CFP a day. The local firm **Albert Rent-a-Car** (✆ **56.19.28**; www.albert-transport.net) is the least expensive, with unlimited-kilometer rates starting at 8,500CFP for a day.

[FastFACTS] MOOREA

The following facts apply specifically to Moorea. For more information, see "Fast Facts: Tahiti & French Polynesia," in chapter 13.

Currency Exchange Banque Socredo, Banque de Tahiti, and **Banque de Polynésie** have offices and ATMs in or near the Maharepa shopping center. Banque de Polynésie's office in Le Petit Village shopping center in Haapiti has an ATM and a currency-exchange machine. Banks are open Monday through Friday from 8am to noon and 1:30 to 4:30pm.

Drugstores Pharmacie Moorea (𝄐 **56.10.51**) in Maharepa is open Monday to Friday from 7:30am to noon and 2 to 6pm, Saturday from 8am to noon and 3:30 to 6pm, and Sunday and holidays from 8 to

10am. The owner speaks both French and English.

Emergencies & Police The **emergency police** phone number is 𝄐 **17.** The phone number for the **gendarmerie** in Cook's Bay is 𝄐 **56.13.44.** Local police have offices at Pao Pao (𝄐 **56.13.63**) and at Haapiti (𝄐 **56.10.84**), near Club Med.

Healthcare The island's **infirmary,** which has an ambulance, is at Afareaitu on the southwest coast (𝄐 **56.24.24**). Several doctors are in private practice; ask your hotel staff for a recommendation.

Mail Moorea's main post office is in the Maharepa shopping center. It's open Monday through Thursday from 7:30am to noon and 1:30 to 4pm, Friday from 7:30am to noon and 1:30

to 3pm, and Saturday from 7:30 to 9:30am. A post office in Papetoai village is open Monday through Thursday from 7:30am to noon and 1:30 to 4pm, Friday from 7:30am to noon and 1:30 to 3pm, and Saturday from 8 to 10am.

Safety There have been thefts on Moorea's public beaches, so keep an eye on your valuables and never leave them unattended.

Taxes Moorea's municipal government adds 100CFP to 150CFP per night to your hotel bill. Don't complain: The money helps keep the island litter-free.

Water Tap water on Moorea is not safe to drink, so buy bottled water at any grocery store. Some hotels filter their water; ask if it's safe before drinking from the tap.

In addition to automobiles, Europcar also rents little "Bugsters" (noisy contraptions with two seats and no top) for about 8,800CFP for 8 hours. They are fun to drive on sunny days. So are scooters, which Albert rents starting at 5,000CFP for 4 hours and 6,000CFP for 24 hours, including full insurance, and unlimited kilometers.

Making reservations for cars and scooters is a very good idea, especially on weekends, when many Tahiti residents come to Moorea.

By Bicycle

The 60km (36-mile) road around Moorea is relatively flat. The two major hills are on the west side of Cook's Bay and just behind the Sofitel Moorea Ia Ora Beach Resort (the latter is worth the climb, as it has a stupendous view of Tahiti). Some resorts have bikes for their guests to use, and **Europcar** (see above) rents mountain bikes for about 1,600CFP for 8 hours, 2,000CFP all day.

EXPLORING MOOREA: THE CIRCLE ISLAND TOUR ★★★

Most of the island's accommodations, along with activities and attractions, are found along Moorea's north coast, between the ferry wharf at **Vaiare** and the area known as **Haapiti** on the island's northwestern corner. A large Club Med dominated Haapiti until it closed in 2002, and many locals still say "Club Med" when referring to this area.

The sights of Moorea may lack great historical significance, but the physical beauty of the island makes a tour—at least of Cook's and Opunohu bays and up to the Belvédère lookout—a highlight of any visit here. There are few places on earth this gorgeous.

As on Tahiti, Moorea's round-island road—about 60km (36 miles) long—is marked every kilometer with a PK post. Distances are measured between the intersection of the airport road with the main round-island coastal road and the village of Haapiti on Moorea's opposite side. In other words, the distances indicated on the PKs increase from the airport in each direction, reaching 30km near Haapiti. They then decrease as you head back to the airport.

The hotel activities desks offer tours around Moorea and up to the Belvédère lookout in the interior. **Albert Tours** (*©* **55.21.10**) and **Moorea Explorer** (*©* **56.12.86**) have half-day circle island tours, including the Belvédère, for about 3,500CFP per person. The tour buses all stop at one black-pearl shop or another (guess who gets a commission when you buy the orb of your dreams?). See "Buying Your Black Pearl" (p. 113) and "Shopping," later in this chapter, before making a purchase.

Temae & Maharepa

Begin at Moorea's northeast corner. The airstrip is on the island's only sizable area of flat land. At one time it was a *motu,* or small island, sitting on the reef by itself. Humans and nature have since filled the lagoon except for Lake Temae, which you can see from the air if you fly to Moorea.

Head west from the junction of the round-island road and airport road. **Temae,** 1km (½ mile) from the junction, supplied the dancers for the Pomare dynasty's court in the 19th century and is still known for the quality of its performers. Herman Melville spent some time here in 1842 and saw the famous, erotic *upaupa,* which he called the "lory-lory," performed clandestinely, out of sight of the missionaries. Today, Moorea's golf course is here (see "Fishing, Golf, Watersports & Other Outdoor Activities," later in this chapter).

The relatively dry north shore between the airport and the entrance to Cook's Bay is **Maharepa,** the island's commercial center. The road skirts the lagoon and passes the Moorea Pearl Resort & Spa and soon reaches the island's main shopping center.

> **Pai's Spear**
>
> Tahitian lore says the legendary hero Pai made the hole in the top of Mount Tohiea when the god of thieves attempted to steal Mount Rotui in the middle of the night. Pai threw his spear from Tahiti and pierced Mount Tohiea. The noise woke up Moorea's roosters, whose commotion alerted the citizenry to put a stop to the dastardly plan.

Cook's Bay ★★★

As the road curves to the left, you enter **Cook's Bay,** the fingerlike body of water virtually surrounded on three sides by the jagged peaks lining the semicircular "wall" of Moorea. The tall thumb with a small hole in its top is **Mount Tohiea.** Coming into view as you drive farther along the bay is **Mount Mauaroa,** Moorea's trademark cathedral-like "Shark's Tooth" mountain buttressed on its right by a serrated ridge.

Huddled along the curving beach at the head of the bay, the village of **Pao Pao** is the site of Moorea's public schools. The *Cooperatif de Pêche Moorea* (**Moorea Fish Market**) is open Monday through Saturday from 5am to 5pm and Sunday from 5 to 8am. The paved road that seems to run through the school next to the bridge cuts through the valley between Cook's Bay and Opunohu Bay. It intersects with the main road between Opunohu Bay and the Belvédère lookout.

The small **St. Joseph's Catholic Church** sits on the shore on the west side of Cook's Bay, at PK 10 from the airport (it's the small one, to the left as you face the bay). Inside is a large mural that artist Peter Heyman painted in 1946 and an altar decorated with mother-of-pearl. From the church, the road climbs up the side of the hill, allowing for some fine views, and then descends back to the lagoon's edge.

Watch on the left for the road leading inland to **Jus de Fruits de Moorea** (**Moorea Fruit Juices;** ✆ **56.22.33**), a factory and distillery that turns the island's produce into the Rotui juices and the potently alcoholic Tahiti Drink you will see in every grocery store. I like to refresh here by tasting the yummy fruit liqueurs. Many souvenirs are for sale, too. Hours are Monday through Friday from 8:30am to 4:30pm, Friday and Saturday from 8:30am to 12:30pm.

Opunohu Bay ★★★

Towering over you is jagged **Mount Rotui,** the huge green-and-black rock separating Moorea's two great bays. Unlike Cook's Bay, Opunohu is virtually devoid of development, a testament to efforts by local residents to maintain the natural beauty of their island (they have ardently resisted efforts to build a luxury resort and golf course here).

As soon as the road levels out, you can look through the trees to yachts anchored in **Robinson's Cove,** one of the world's most photographed yacht anchorages. Stop here and put your camera to work.

The road soon curves right along a black-sand beach backed by shade trees and the Opunohu Valley at the head of the bay. The beach was turned into Matavai Bay on Tahiti for the 1983 production of *The Bounty,* starring Mel Gibson and Anthony Hopkins.

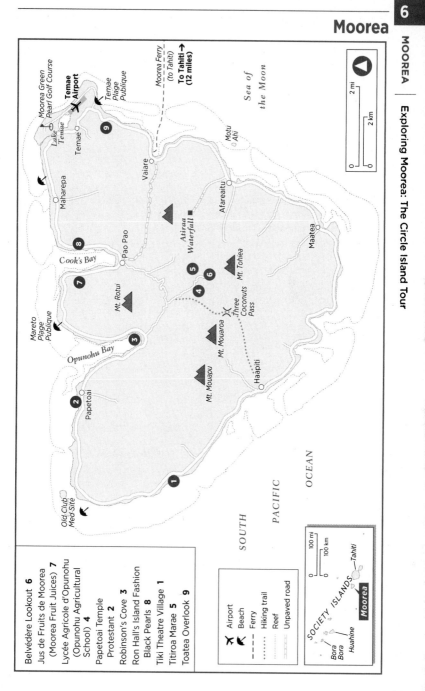

Belvédère Lookout **6**

Jus de Fruits de Moorea (Moorea Fruit Juices) **7**

Lycée Agricole d'Opunohu (Opunohu Agricultural School) **4**

Papetoai Temple Protestant **2**

Robinson's Cove **3**

Ron Hall's Island Fashion Black Pearls **8**

Tiki Theatre Village **1**

Titiroa Marae **5**

Toatea Overlook **9**

✕ Airport
↙ Beach
– – – Ferry
· · · · · Hiking trail
░░░ Reef
▒▒▒ Unpaved road

SOCIETY ISLANDS

Huahine
Bora Bora
Moorea — Tahiti

0   100 mi
0   100 km

Belvedere Lookout ★★★

After the bridge by the beach, a paved road runs up Moorea's central valley through pastureland, across which Warren Beatty and Annette Bening strolled in their flop movie *Love Affair* (the scenes with Katharine Hepburn were filmed in the white house on the hill to your right). You can stop at **Lycée Agricole d'Opunohu (Opunohu Agricultural School),** on the main road (*©* **56.11.34**), to see plantations for vanilla and other crops. It's open Monday through Friday from 8am to 4:30pm, Saturday from 9am to 12:30pm.

> ### Impressions
>
> *Seen for the first time by European Eyes, this coast is like nothing else on our workaday planet; a landscape, rather, of some fantastic dream.*
> —Charles Nordhoff and James Norman Hall, *Mutiny on the Bounty,* 1933

At the head of the valley, the road climbs steeply up the old crater wall to the restored **Titiroa Marae,** which was part of a concentration of *maraes* and other structures. Higher up, you'll pass an archery platform used for competition (archery was a sport reserved for high-ranking chiefs and was never used in warfare in Polynesia). A display in the main *marae* parking lot explains the history of this area. You can walk among the remains of the temples, now shaded by towering Tahitian chestnut trees that have grown up through the cobblestone-like courtyards.

The narrow road then ascends to **Belvédère Lookout,** whose awesome panorama of the valley and the bays on either side of Mount Rotui is unmatched in the South Pacific. You won't want to be without film or camera batteries here.

Papetoai

Back on the coastal road, the sizable village of **Papetoai** was the retreat of the Pomare dynasty in the 1800s and the base from which Pomare I launched his successful drive to take over all of Tahiti and Moorea. It was also headquarters for the London Missionary Society's work throughout the South Pacific. The road to the right, past the new post office, leads to the octagonal **Papetoai Temple Protestant,** built on the site of a *marae* dedicated to Oro, son of the supreme Taaroa and the god of war. The original church was constructed in the 1820s, and although advertised as the oldest European building still in use in the South Pacific, the present structure dates from the late 1880s.

Haapiti

From Papetoai, the road runs through the Haapiti hotel district at Pointe Hauru, Moorea's northwestern corner. A long stretch of white-sand beach wraps around the point and conspires with two islets out on the reef's edge and great sunset views to make the Haapiti area popular with tourists. Beginning in the 1970s, a 300-bungalow Club Med generated much business here, including Le Petit Village shopping center across the road. Although it closed in 2002, many locals still refer to the Club Med when giving directions. The area has been depressed since the club closed, and the worldwide recession hasn't helped (some restaurants here are open only on weekends). Still, this is your last chance to stop for refreshment before the sparsely populated southern half of Moorea. There are several choices here (see "Where to Dine," later in this chapter).

About 4km (2½ miles) beyond Le Petit Village, look for the **Tiki Theatre Village ★★★**, a cultural center consisting of thatched huts on the coastal side of the road. It's the only place to see what a Tahitian village looked like when Captain Cook arrived, so pull in. See "Tiki Theatre Village," below, for details.

When the first Europeans arrived, the lovely, mountain-backed village of **Haapiti** was home to the powerful Marama clan, which was allied with the Pomares. It became a center of Catholic missionary work after the French took over the territory, and it is one of the few villages with a Catholic church as large as its Protestant counterpart. Stop here and look up behind the village for a view of Mount Mouaroa from a unique perspective.

The Southeast Coast

South of Haapiti, just as the road curves sharply around a headland, is a nice view of a small bay with the mountains towering overhead (there's no place to park on the headland, so stop and walk up for the view). In contrast to the more touristy north shore, the southeast and southwest coasts have retained an atmosphere of old Polynesia. There's a reason for this, of course: There are no beaches.

The village of **Afareaitu,** on the southeast coast, is the administrative center of Moorea, and the building that looks like a charming hotel across from the village church actually is the island's *mairie,* or town hall.

About half a kilometer (¼ mile) beyond the town hall, opposite an A-frame house on the shore, an unpaved road runs straight between several houses and then continues uphill to the **Atiraa Waterfall ★★**. Often called Afareaitu Waterfall, it plunges more than 32m (100 ft.) down a cliff, into a small pool. You can drive partway to the falls and then walk 20 minutes up a steep, slippery, and muddy trail. Wear shoes or sandals that have good traction if you make this trek, for in places the slippery trail is hacked into a steep hill; if you slip, it's a long way down to the rocks below. Villagers will be waiting at the beginning of the footpath to extract a small fee.

Beyond Afareaitu, the small bay of **Vaiare** is a beehive of activity when the ferries pull in from Papeete. On workdays, commuters park their vehicles at least 1km (½ mile) in either direction from the wharf.

Toatea Overlook & Temae Plage Publique ★★★

Atop the hill north of the Sofitel Moorea Ia Ora Beach Resort is the **Toatea Overlook ★★★**. Here you'll have a magnificent view of the hotel, the green lagoon flecked with brown coral heads, the white line of the surf breaking on the reef, the deep blue of the Sea of the Moon, and all of Tahiti rising magnificently from the

---

○ The View from Belvédère Lookout

If the view from Le Belvédère restaurant on Tahiti doesn't thrill me enough, the scene from the Moorea lookout of the same name certainly does. I never tire of standing at the base of that cliff and watching dramatic Mount Rotui separate the deep-blue fingers of Cook's and Opunohu bays.

horizon. There's a parking area at the overlook. A monument remembers the 20 people killed when a small Air Moorea plane crashed into the sea in 2007.

The unpaved road to the right at the bottom of the hill leads to the **Temae Plage Publique (Temae Public Beach),** Moorea's finest stretch of public beach. Follow the left fork through the coconut grove to the lagoon. This is a continuation of the Sofitel Moorea Ia Ora Beach Resort's beach, except that here you don't have a staff to rake the leaves and coral gravel from the sand. Locals often sell snacks and souvenirs, especially on weekends. Bring insect repellent, and never leave your valuables unattended.

SAFARI EXPEDITIONS, LAGOON EXCURSIONS & DOLPHIN-WATCHING

The activities mentioned below tend to be specific in what they do. More general is **Tahiti Expeditions ★★** (© **28.37.22;** www.tahitiexpeditions.com), a Moorea-based company led by Frank Murphy, an American biologist who arrived on Moorea in the early 1990s as manager of the University of California's Gump Research Station. The expeditions range from one-day coral reef excursions off Moorea to extended sailing trips to the Tuamotu Archipelago. Emphasis is on the ecology and history of the islands.

Safari Expeditions ★★

You can see the sights and learn a lot about the island on a four-wheel-drive excursion through Moorea's mountainous interior. Every hotel activities desk will book you on one of these adventures. **Albert Tours** (© **55.21.10;** www.albert-transport. net) and **Moorea Explorer** (© **56.12.86**) both have them. I've been with Alex and Gheslaine Haamatearii's **Inner Island Safari Tours** (© **56.20.09;** intersaf@mail. pf), which will take you through the valleys, up to Belvédère Lookout, and then down to a vanilla plantation in Opunohu Valley. They explain the island's flora and fauna along the way. The best trips end with a drive around Moorea's south coast and a hike up to Atiraa Waterfall for a refreshing swim (see "The Southeast Coast" under "Exploring Moorea: The Circle Island Tour," earlier in this chapter). Expect to visit a black pearl shop and Jus de Fruits de Moorea (see "Shopping" below). These half-day trips cost about 5,000CFP per person.

> ### Tahiti in All Its Glory
>
> My neck strains every time I cross the hill behind Moorea's Sofitel Moorea Ia Ora Beach Resort, for there, across the Sea of the Moon, sits Tahiti in all its green glory. What amazement the early explorers must have felt when those mountains appeared over the horizon!

In a variation on this theme, both Albert Tours and **Mahana ATV Tours** (© **56.20.44**) take you on all-terrain vehicles into the Opunohu Valley.

Lagoon Excursions ★★★

The lagoon around Moorea is not as beautiful or diverse as Bora Bora's, but it's worth a day's outing. Most hotel activities desks will book you on a lagoon excursion, the

TIKI THEATRE village ★★★

The best cultural experience in French Polynesia is at **Tiki Theatre Village,** at PK 31, or 2km (1¼ miles) south of old Club Med (ⓒ **55.02.50;** www.tikivillage.pf). Founded by Olivier Briac, a Frenchman whom the local Tahitians call *Le Sauvage Blanc* (White Savage), it's built in the fashion of ancient Tahitian villages. This cultural center has old-style *fares* (houses) in which the staff demonstrates traditional tattooing, tapa-cloth making and painting, wood and stone carving, weaving, cooking, and making costumes, musical instruments, and flower crowns. There's even a "royal" house floating out on the lagoon, where you can learn about the modern art of growing black pearls.

Tiki Theatre Village will even arrange a traditional beachside wedding. The bride is prepared with flowery *monoi* oil like a Tahitian princess, and the groom is tattooed (with a wash-off pen). Both wear traditional costumes.

The village is open Tuesday to Saturday from 11am to 3pm. Admission and a guided tour cost 1,500CFP.

Not to be missed is the authentic Tahitian feast and dance show here on Tuesday, Wednesday, Friday, and Saturday nights. They pick you up from your hotel and deposit you on the beach for a rum punch and sunset. After the staff uncovers the earth oven, they take you on a tour of the village. A buffet of both Tahitian and Western foods is followed by an energetic 1½-hour dance show with some of the most elaborate yet traditional costumes to be seen in French Polynesia. The dinner and show cost 8,000CFP per person, or you can come just for the 9pm show for 4,000CFP. Kids 3 to 12 pay half-price. Add 1,150CFP for round-trip transportation.

best way to experience the magnificent setting. The full-day version of these excursions invariably includes a "*motu* picnic"—a lunch of grilled fresh fish, *poisson cru,* and salads served on a *motu* (little islet) out on the reef. Quite often, the fresh fish is caught on the way. You'll have an opportunity to snorkel in the lagoon and learn how to husk a coconut. Some tours also include shark- and ray-feeding, one of the most interesting and exciting things to do in the water here. Wear shoes that you don't mind getting wet. The cost is about 7,000CFP per person.

Dolphin & Whale-Watching ★★★

Watching and swimming with dolphins is as much a part of the Moorea experience as is swimming with the sharks on Bora Bora (see chapter 9). You also stand a good chance of seeing humpback whales offshore from July until October, when they migrate from Antarctica to calve.

The best way to observe the animals in their natural habitat is on a dolphin- and whale-watching excursion led by American marine biologist **Dr. Michael Poole** (ⓒ **56.23.22** or 77.50.07; www.drmichaelpoole.com). An expert on sea mammals and a leader in the effort to have French Polynesian waters declared a whale sanctuary, Dr. Poole will take you out beyond the reef to meet some of the 150 acrobatic spinner dolphins he has identified as regular Moorea residents. In calm conditions, and if the animals are agreeable, you can don snorkeling gear and swim with them.

You'll also be on the lookout for pilot whales that swim past year-round and giant humpback whales that frequent these waters from July to October. The half-day excursions cost about 7,500CFP for adults, half-price for kids, including pickup at most hotel docks. Make reservations in advance, and be prepared not to go if the sea isn't calm.

Among the many activities at the InterContinental Resort and Spa Moorea (see "Watersports," below) and by far the most popular is the **Moorea Dolphin Center ★★** (© **55.19.48;** www.mooreadolphincenter.com). The intelligent sea mammals are sure to excite young and old alike—and many honeymooners love to have their photos taken face-to-face with "smiling" dolphins. The dolphins live in a fenced area, although the center professes to be dedicated to their care and conservation. Kids 16 and older can join adults in snorkeling with the mammals in deeper water (all must be good swimmers) for 24,900CFP per person. Both parents and children ages 5–11 can "Meet and Greet A Dolphin," a 30-minute encounter which costs 15,500CFP per person, and kids 3 to 5 can go on family programs (55,400CFP per family). They'll even take honeymooners on their own private encounter.

FISHING, GOLF, WATERSPORTS & OTHER OUTDOOR ACTIVITIES

Most hotels have active watersports programs for their guests, such as glass-bottom-boat cruises and snorkeling in, or sailing on, Moorea's beautiful lagoon. Moorea has no public tennis courts, so pick a hotel that has them if tennis is important to you.

Fishing

Chris Lilley, an American who has won several sport-fishing contests, takes guests onto the ocean in search of big-game catch on his *Tea Nui* (© **55.19.19,** ext. 1903, or 56.15.08 at home; teanuiservices@mail.pf). In keeping with South Pacific custom, you can keep the little fish you catch; Chris sells the big ones. Contact Chris for rates and reservations.

Golf

Encompassing Lake Temae west of the airport, the **Moorea Green Pearl Golf Course** (© **56.27.32;** www.mooreagolf-resort.com) has 18 holes designed by Jack Nicklaus. The par-70 course measures 6,002m (6,596 yards). Greens fees are 10,000CFP for 9 holes, 18,000CFP for 18 holes. Carts and equipment are available. The course is open daily from 7:30am to 5pm. You can practice by driving balls into the lake. The club house has a restaurant and bar. Plans call for a resort hotel to be built here.

Hiking

You won't need a guide to hike from the coast road up the Opunohu Valley to Belvédère Lookout. Up and down will take most of a day. It's a level, but hot walk along the valley floor and gets steep approaching the lookout. Bring lots of water.

Several unmarked hiking trails lead into the mountains, including one beginning in Cook's Bay and ending on the east coast near the Vaiare ferry dock, another from the southwest coast near Haapiti village across Three Coconuts Pass and into Opunohu

Valley. Go with a guide on longer hikes up in the mountains. Moorea-based **Tahiti Evasion** (✆ **56.48.77;** www.tahitievasion.com) has half-day treks to the archaeological sites in the Opunohu Valley, across Three Coconuts Pass between the Belvédère and the south coast, and to the Afareaitu waterfall and the pierced Mount Tohiea. Prices range from 4,500CFP to 8,000CFP per person.

Horseback Riding

Landlubbers can go horseback riding along the beach and into the interior with **Ranch Opunohu Valley** (✆ **56.28.55**). Rates are about 6,000CFP for a 1½-hour ride. Advance reservations are essential.

Watersports

The most extensive array of sporting activities is at the **InterContinental Resort and Spa Moorea** (✆ **55.19.19**), and its facilities can be used by both guests and visitors who are willing to pay. Options include scuba diving, parasailing (magnificent views of the bays, mountains, and reefs), water-skiing, wake-boarding, scooting about the lagoon and Opunohu Bay on jet skis, viewing coral and fish from Aquascope boats, walking on the lagoon bottom while wearing diving helmets, line fishing, and speedboat rentals. Nonguests can also pay to use the pool, snorkeling gear, and tennis courts, and to be taken over to a small islet. Call the hotel for prices, schedules, and reservations, which are required.

SCUBA DIVING

Although Moorea's lagoon is not in the same league with those at Rangiroa, Fakarava, or even Bora Bora, its outer reef has some decent sites for viewing sea life, and especially the whitetip and blacktip reef sharks. Since the northern side of Moorea fell away from the rest of the island eons ago, the reef slopes away gently here, as opposed to the precipitous drop-offs found on Tahiti and most other South Pacific islands. The shallow lagoon has mostly dead coral, so you must dive to deeper depths in order to see the colors of the living reef.

Most sites are within short boat rides of the northwest-coast resorts and require dives of 10 to 20m (33–70 ft.). The **Tiki,** off the island's northwestern point, is popular thanks to the shark-feeding (as on Bora Bora, many dives feature shark-feeding, although not all of Moorea's operators engage in this practice). Even novice divers can pet the friendly rays at **Stingray World,** just off the InterContinental Resort and Spa Moorea. **Opunohu Canyons,** off the mouth of the bay, is another favorite shark-feeding site. You can drift dive through **Taotoi Pass,** to the west of Opunohu Bay. Experienced divers can see a huge expanse of flat montipora coral at the **Roses,** at a depth of 30 to 40m (100–130 ft.) halfway between Opunohu and Cook's bays. Inside the lagoon, the **Wreck** is an old ship that was sunk to provide an artificial reef home to a multitude of fish.

The island's best diving operator is **Bathy's Diving** (✆ **55.19.19,** ext. 1139; www.bathys.net), at the InterContinental Resort and Spa Moorea, and **Scubapiti Moorea** (✆ **56.20.38;** www.scubapiti.com), at Hotel Les Tipaniers. All charge about 6,500CFP for a one-tank dive, including equipment (gauges are metric).

SNORKELING & SWIMMING

Sharing the lagoon with the Sofitel Moorea Ia Ora Beach Resort, the gorgeous **Temae Plage Publique (Temae Public Beach)** has some of the island's best snorkeling, and it's relatively safe (p. 136). Also good is the lagoon around the islets off Haapiti, but watch out for strong currents coming in and out of the nearby reef passes.

Another favorite with locals for sunning and swimming is **Mareto Plage Publique (Mareto Public Beach),** in a coconut grove west of the Sheraton Moorea between the two bays. Go around the barbed-wire fence on the eastern end.

There's good snorkeling over coral gardens off **Pianapo (Pineapple) Beach** (✆ 74.96.96; www.painapo.com), on the Haapiti coast. This picturesque little playground charges a one-time 2,000CFP for a day pass, including use of snorkeling gear. I love to fill up on Sunday at the restaurant here (see "A Sunday Tahitian Feast" under "Where to Dine," later in this chapter).

The lagoon off Moorea's northwest corner is blessed with offshore *motus,* small islets where you can sunbathe, swim, and snorkel (but beware of strong currents). You can rent a boat to get over there from **Moorea Locaboat** (✆ 78.13.39), based next to Hotel Les Tipaniers, or take a transfer from **Tip Nautic** next door (✆ 73.76.73) for 700CFP round-trip. Tip Nautic also rents snorkel gear for 500CFP for a half-day and kayaks starting at 500CFP per hour, and it has water-skiing and dolphin-watching trips as well.

SHOPPING

The Shopping Scene

The island's primary commercial center is at **Maharepa,** where you'll find black-pearl shops, banks, grocery stores, hairdressers, the main post office, and other services. The neocolonial buildings of **Le Petit Village** shopping center anchor the northwestern corner, where numerous stores sell *pareus,* T-shirts, and souvenirs. **Supersonics** (✆ 56.29.73) carries film, camera batteries, stamps, magazines, and other items. There's also a grocery store.

Boutiques and art galleries are numerous on Moorea, but they come and go as frequently as their owners arrive from France and then decide to go home. The shops below should still be here when you arrive. One of the most reliable places to look for *pareus,* tropical dresses, aloha shirts, bathing suits, T-shirts, shell jewelry, and handicrafts is **La Maison Blanche (White House),** in Maharepa near the Moorea Pearl Resort & Spa (✆ 56.13.26). It's housed in a whitewashed vanilla planter's house with a railing enclosing a magnificent veranda, which alone makes it worth a stop. Open daily from 8:30am to 5pm.

Art

Boutique d'Art Marquisien (Marquesan Art Boutique)　Tahia Vaatete, who hails from Ua Huka in the Marquesas Islands, runs this attractive shop, where she sells exquisite art and handicrafts from her native archipelago. Woodcarvings top the list, including intricately carved tables that will cost a fortune to ship home. More manageable are war clubs, paintings, stone work, masks, tikis, and carved coconut shells. Open Monday through Saturday from 8am to 5:30pm. Cook's Bay, in Cooks Bay Center shops. ✆ 29.34.91.

Galerie van der Heyde ★★　Dutch artist Aad van der Heyde has lived and worked on Moorea since 1964. One of his bold Impressionist paintings of a Tahitian woman was selected for French Polynesia's 100CFP postage stamp in 1975, and his landscape of Bora Bora appeared on a 2004 stamp. Aad will sell you an autographed lithograph of the paintings. Some of his works are displayed on the gallery's garden wall. He has also produced excellent videos of the islands and will gladly sell you a copy on DVD. In addition, you'll see a small collection of pearls, woodcarvings, tapa cloth, shell and coral jewelry, and primitive art from Papua New Guinea. Open Monday through Saturday from 8am to 5pm. East side of Cook's Bay. ✆**56.14.22.**

Black Pearls

Moorea has more pearl shops than you can visit on a normal vacation. In fact, many of the stores will come looking for you, with offers of free transportation to and from your hotel or the cruise-ship landing in Opunohu Bay, and tour operators are likely to deposit you at the shop offering the highest commission at the end of your excursion. But Moorea also has small, family-owned shops that carry quality pearls that cost less, since the shops don't have high overheads and promotion expenses. Always shop around—and read "Buying Your Black Pearl" (p. 113) before making your purchase.

Among several stores near the old Club Med site in Haapiti is **Tahia Collins** (✆ **55.05.00;** www.tahiacollins.com). Owner and chief designer Tahia Collins was a Miss Moorea and is a scion of the Albert Haring family (you will see the Albert name all over the island). Her husband, Marc Collins, was born in Hawaii of an American father and Tahitian mother. Theirs is the most aggressive pearl dealership on Moorea. Others worth visiting in this area are **Herman Perles** (✆ **56.42.79**) and **Pai Moana Pearls** (✆ **56.25.25;** www.paimoanapearls.net).

My favorites are the lower-key shops on the other side of the island, to wit:

Ann Simon Boutique   The French owner of this shop, Ann Simon, specializes in darker pearls—those with rich blue and green hues—set in 18-karat gold. That combination makes them anything but inexpensive, but this is a good place to see what high-quality black pearls look like. Some of Ann's designs are unique. Open Monday through Saturday from 8am to 7pm. Maharepa, west of the post office. ✆**56.44.55.** www.annsimonblackpearl.com.

Eva Perles   Eva Frachon, the French gemologist who owns this little shop, graduated from the University of Wisconsin at Oshkosh with a bachelor's degree in photography and art metals; thus, she does her own creative settings, and speaks American-style English. She carries high-quality orbs in all price ranges. Open Monday through Saturday from 9:30am to 5:30pm. Maharepa, opposite the post office. ✆ **56.10.10.** www.evaperles.com.

Ron Hall's Island Fashion Black Pearls ★★★ 🐚   Ron Hall sailed from Hawaii to Tahiti with the actor Peter Fonda in 1974. Peter went home; Ron didn't. Now Ron and his son, Heimata, run this air-conditioned Moorea retail outlet. It's worth a stop to see the antiques and old photos, including one of the infamous Quinn's Bar and a William Leeteg painting of a Tahitian *vahine* (Ron's wife and Heimata's mother, Josée, was herself a championship Tahitian dancer). In 15 minutes of "pearl school," you will learn the basics of picking a pearl. They will have your selection set in a mounting of your choice, their prices are fair, and they donate 10% of every pearl purchase to Dr. Michael Poole's dolphin and whale research (see "Dolphin- & Whale-Watching," above). They also carry one of Moorea's best selections of bathing suits, aloha shirts, and T-shirts, and are the only Cook's Bay dealers who can legally send a courtesy shuttle to pick you up.. Open Monday through Saturday from 9am to 6pm. East side of Cook's Bay. 📞 **56.11.06.**

WHERE TO STAY

Most of Moorea's hotels and restaurants are grouped in or near Cook's Bay, between Cook's and Opunohu bays, or in the Haapiti district on the northwest corner of the island around the old Club Med site. With the exception of the Sofitel Moorea Ia Ora Beach Resort, those in or near Cook's Bay do not have the best beaches on the island, but the snorkeling is excellent and most have unsurpassed views of the mountains. The establishments between the two bays have beaches, but they are a bit inconvenient to the facilities at both Cook's Bay and Haapiti. Those on the northwest corner have generally fine beaches, lagoons like giant swimming pools, and unobstructed views of the sunset, but not of Moorea's famous mountains. The areas are relatively far apart, so you might spend most of your time near your hotel unless you rent a vehicle or otherwise make a point to see the sights. An alternative is to split your stay between the areas.

The Cook's Bay Area
EXPENSIVE
Moorea Pearl Resort & Spa ★★   You can easily walk from this multifaceted resort to Maharepa's shops and restaurants. The resort faces the open ocean, but unfortunately its overwater bungalows block most of the sea view. On the other hand, snorkeling is excellent here, especially from the decks of the 20 deluxe, overwater bungalows perched out on the edge of the clifflike reef. They and 18 beach bungalows with private pools in their courtyards are the pick of a mixed litter of accommodations. Some of the garden bungalows are stand-alone, while others are in less private duplex units. Sporting private backyards with plunge pools, the bungalows are identical inside, with tasteful native wood accents. The least expensive units are 30 spacious hotel rooms in two-story blocks at the rear of the property. They all have king-size beds and balconies or patios, and eight family rooms add two single beds. Big thatched roofs cover a large dining room and pool-level bar, which hosts Tahitian dance shows twice a week. The smallish beach and big infinity swimming pool serve as centers for numerous outdoor activities.

B.P. 3410, 98728 Maharepa, Moorea. 📞 **800/657-3275** or 55.17.50. Fax 55.17.51. www.spmhotels.com. 95 units. 29,000CFP–38,000CFP double; 36,000CFP–77,000CFP bungalow. AE, DC, MC, V. **Amenities:** 2 restaurants; 2 bars; babysitting; bikes; Jacuzzi; outdoor pool; room service; smoke-free rooms; spa; watersports equipment. *In room:* A/C, ceiling fan, TV, fridge, hair dryer, Wi-Fi (500CFP/hour).

Sofitel Moorea Ia Ora Beach Resort ★★★   Dating to the 1960s but completely overhauled in recent years, this sprawling resort sits beside Moorea's best lagoon and beach (it's known as Temae Public Beach north of the resort). The Sofitel is the only resort here with a view of Tahiti, whose green, cloud-topped mountains seem to climb out of the horizon beyond the reef. Most overwater units face the lagoon rather than Tahiti, however, so try to get bungalow no. 117, 119, 120, 122, or 215 through 218. Ashore, the best views are from three deluxe bungalows on the south end of the property; these are the most private units here, although the

Moorea Accommodations

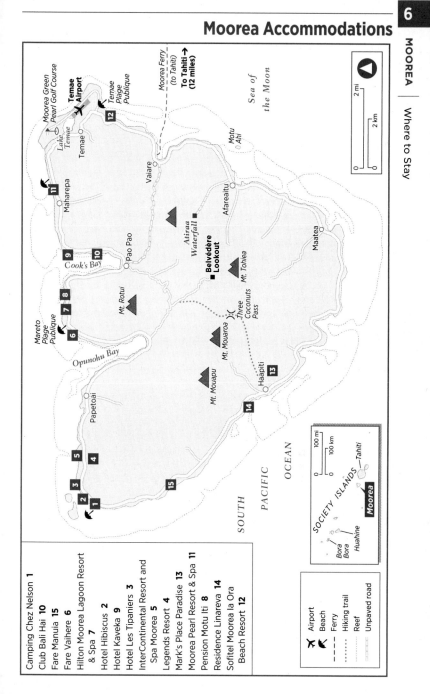

Camping Chez Nelson **1**
Club Bali Hai **10**
Fare Manuia **15**
Fare Vaihere **6**
Hilton Moorea Lagoon Resort & Spa **7**
Hotel Hibiscus **2**
Hotel Kaveka **9**
Hotel Les Tipaniers **3**
InterContinental Resort and Spa Moorea **5**
Legends Resort **4**
Mark's Place Paradise **13**
Moorea Pearl Resort & Spa **11**
Pension Motu Iti **8**
Residence Linareva **14**
Sofitel Moorea Ia Ora Beach Resort **12**

✕✈ Airport
✈ Beach
--- Ferry
······· Hiking trail
░░░ Reef
▭▭▭ Unpaved road

SOCIETY ISLANDS — Tahiti
Bora Bora
Huahine
Moorea

beach is much better on the north side. Least expensive are the garden bungalows whose views are squeezed through the beachfront units. I've had terrific lunches at **Pure,** the resort's open-air casual restaurant. At dinner the thatched-roof, sand-floor **Restaurant K** is both extremely romantic and reasonably priced (reservations are required).

B.P. 28, Maharepa, Moorea (Temae, on the northeast coast facing Tahiti). © **800/763-4835,** 55.03.55, or 41.04.04 in Papeete. Fax 41.05.05. www.accorhotels.com. 119 units. 43,000CFP–83,000CFP double. AE, DC, MC, V. **Amenities:** 2 restaurants; 2 bars; babysitting; bikes; health club; outdoor pool; room service; sauna; smoke-free rooms; spa; 2 tennis courts; watersports equipment. *In room:* A/C, ceiling fan, TV, hair dryer, minibar, MP3 docking station (over-water units only), Wi-Fi (900CFP/hour).

MODERATE

Club Bali Hai 🏝 The last property operated by Moorea's two surviving Bali Hai Boys (see the "The Bali Hai Boys" box, below), this basic hotel has an incredible view of Moorea's ragged mountains across Cook's Bay, a scene epitomizing the South Pacific. Under a bayside thatched roof, **Snack l'Ananas Bleu (Blue Pineapple;** p. 152) serves breakfast and lunch. It also is the scene for Muk McCallum's bring-your-own happy hours from 5:30 to 7pm Thursday to Tuesday, when he "talks story" about the good old days on Moorea (see "Sunsets with Muk at Club Bali Hai," at the end of this chapter). It's worth stopping by the club's Wednesday-night Tahitian dance shows, too. A swimming pool with a rock waterfall augments the man-made beach here. Half of the guest units are part of a timeshare operation, but that means they come equipped with cooking facilities, a plus for budget-minded travelers. The overwater bungalows are the least expensive in French Polynesia, while the beachfront bungalows have huge bathrooms with gardens growing in them, another trademark

THE BALI HAI boys

Californians Jay Carlisle, Don "Muk" McCallum, and the late Hugh Kelley gave up their budding business careers as stockbroker, lawyer, and sporting-goods salesman, respectively, and in 1960 bought an old vanilla plantation on Moorea. Instead of planting, they refurbished a beachfront hotel that stood on their property (now occupied by the Moorea Pearl Resort & Spa). Taking a page from James A. Michener's *Tales of the South Pacific,* they renamed it the Bali Hai and opened for business in 1961. With construction of Tahiti-Faaa International Airport across the Sea of the Moon, their timing couldn't have been better. With Jay managing the money, Hugh building the resort, and Muk entertaining their guests, they quickly

had a success on their hands. Travel writers soon dubbed them the "Bali Hai Boys."

Supplies and fresh produce weren't easy to come by in those days, so they put the old vanilla plantation to work producing chickens, eggs, and milk. It was the first successful poultry and dairy operation on the island.

Thank Jay, Muk, and Hugh for overwater bungalows—those cabins sitting on pilings over the lagoon, with glass panels in their floors so that we can watch the fish swim below. They built the world's first in 1968 on Raiatea. A novelty at the time, their romantic invention is now a staple at resorts well beyond French Polynesia.

of the Bali Hai Boys. Most other units are in one- or two-story, motel-style buildings. All are simply but comfortably furnished. This is good value if you don't need a phone in your room or other such luxuries, and the view is worth a million bucks.

B.P. 8, 98728 Maharepa, Moorea. ⓒ **877/426-7262** or 56.13.68. Fax 56.13.27. www.clubbalihai.com. 39 units. US$150 double; US$210–US$320 bungalow. AE, DC, MC, V. **Amenities:** Restaurant (breakfast and lunch); bikes; outdoor pool; watersports equipment; Wi-Fi (1,000CFP/hour). *In room:* A/C, ceiling fan (some units), fridge, hair dryer, kitchen, no phone.

Hotel Kaveka ⚐ Another modest property with a marvelous view, Greg Hardee's compact, all-bungalow hotel sits behind a rock wall along the road, but its other side opens to Cook's Bay. Noted for its fish burgers, the hotel's overwater **Kaveka Restaurant** (p. 149) enjoys a view rivaled only by Snack l'Ananas Bleu (Blue Pineapple) at the Club Bali Hai. The white-sand beach here is small (a breakwater fronts most of the property), but snorkeling is very good, especially off the hotel's long pier. The bungalows are made of timber with shingle roofs covering pandanus ceilings. Most have attractive mat walls, single and king-size platform beds, and shower-only bathrooms. The windows and front doors of the newest unit, added in 2009, are one-way mirrors so you can see out but people outside can't see in. The least expensive lanai units lack porches and air conditioners. All units have ceiling fans, but none have window screens. The few-frills Kaveka often is the least expensive hotel offered in package trips to French Polynesia.

B.P. 373, 98728 Maharepa, Moorea. ⓒ **877/354-5902** or 56.50.50. Fax 56.52.63. www.hotelkaveka.com. 30 units. 13,500CFP–26,500CFP double. AE, MC, V. **Amenities:** Restaurant; bar; bikes; watersports equipment. *In room:* A/C, ceiling fan, TV, TV/DVD, TV/VCR, movie library, fax, fridge, hair dryer, Internet, kitchen, minibar, MP3 docking station, no phone, Wi-Fi (1,000CFP/hour).

Between Cook's & Opunohu Bays

EXPENSIVE

Hilton Moorea Lagoon Resort & Spa ★★ Until recently a Sheraton hotel, this luxury resort is not particularly convenient to restaurants and activities, but it does provide shuttles to the Tiki Village Theatre and the Vaiare ferry dock. Two stunning, conical thatched roofs cover the reception area and a French restaurant overlooking a white-sand beach. Steps lead down to a beachside pool with its own sunken bar. All the guest bungalows are identical except for their location. A Y-shaped pier leads to half of them out over the lagoon. These all have glass floor panels for fish-viewing and decks with steps down into the clear, 4-foot-deep water. The others are situated in a coconut grove by the beach; they have plunge pools in their wrap-around decks. Every unit is equipped with niceties such as CD players, complimentary snorkeling gear, plush robes, and claw-foot bathtubs.

B.P. 1005, 98279 Papetoai, Moorea. ⓒ **800/325-3535** or 55.11.11 in Moorea. Fax 86.48.40. www.hilton.com. 106 units. 45,500CFP–86,000CFP bungalow. AE, DC, MC, V. **Amenities:** 2 restaurants; 3 bars; babysitting; bikes; concierge; health club; Jacuzzi; outdoor pool; room service; smoke-free rooms; spa; watersports equipment; Wi-Fi (500CFP/hour). *In room:* A/C, ceiling fan, TV, hair dryer, minibar.

MODERATE

Fare Vaihere ★ On the eastern shore of Opunohu Bay, Philippe and Corinne Guery's bed-and-breakfast has four small bungalows in its tropical gardens beside the beach and lagoon. Although the buildings all have tin roofs, they sport Polynesian decor inside. Each is equipped with a both a queen-size and a twin bed and has a front porch. Everyone gets a complimentary tropical breakfast in a lagoon-front lounge building. You can explore the lagoon with kayaks and snorkeling gear. Philippe, who speaks English as well as French, is a dive instructor and may have his own operation here by the time you arrive. Corinne will cook dinner for guests on request.

B.P. 1806, 98729 Papetoai, Moorea. ⓒ **56.19.19** or 29.07.19. www.farevaihere.com. 4 units. 17,800CFP double. Rates include continental breakfast. MC, V. **Amenities:** Bikes; watersports equipment. *In room:* Ceiling fan, fridge, no phone, Wi-Fi (free).

Pension Motu Iti   Auguste and Dora Ienfa's little pension sits beside the lagoon west of the Sheraton Moorea Lagoon Resort & Spa. They have no beach, only a bulkhead along the shore, but a pier goes to an overwater cabana for relaxing. Their five government-issue bungalows are clean, comfortable, and reasonably spacious. Three of them directly face the lagoon. There's also a small dormitory over the main building. The dining room serves breakfast, lunch, and dinner daily, although the food at **Restaurant Aito** (p. 153) next-door is much more interesting.

B.P. 189, 98728 Maharepa, Moorea. ⓒ **55.05.20.** Fax 55.05.21. www.pensionmotuiti.com. 5 units. 10,500CFP–12,000CFP bungalow; 1,650CFP dorm bed. AE, MC, V. **Amenities:** Restaurant; bar; Internet (500CFP/hour); watersports equipment. *In room:* TV, no phone.

The Northwest Coast
EXPENSIVE

InterContinental Resort and Spa Moorea ★★★   Moorea's busiest resort is famous as home to the Moorea Dolphin Center (see "Safari Expeditions, Lagoon Excursions & Dolphin-Watching," earlier in this chapter). The beach and sometimes murky lagoon here aren't the island's best, but the resort has the widest range of watersports activities on the island—all of them available both to guests and to nonguests who are willing to pay (see "Fishing, Golf, Watersports & Other Outdoor Activities," earlier in this chapter). The airy central building with a shingle roof opens to a large pool area. Most of the guest bungalows extend partially over the water from man-made islands. Those ashore have plunge pools in their gardens. Although the construction style is European, mat walls and rattan furnishings lend tropical ambience. A curving two-story building holds 52 spacious hotel rooms; they all have patios or balconies facing the beach. The Tahitian dance show on the beach is one of Moorea's most colorful.

B.P. 1019, 98729 Papetoai, Moorea. ⓒ **800/327-0200** or 55.19.19. Fax 55.19.55. www.interconti.com. 52 rooms, 102 bungalows. 33,800CFP–39,700CFP double; 46,500CFP–94,600CFP bungalow. AE, DC, MC, V. **Amenities:** Restaurant; bar; babysitting; bikes; concierge; health club; Jacuzzi; outdoor pool; room service; smoke-free rooms; spa; tennis court; watersports equipment. *In room:* A/C, ceiling fan, TV, hair dryer, Internet (1,350CFP/hr), minibar, Wi-Fi.

Legends Resort   Opened in 2008, this property consists of 46 luxury-laden villas on a hillside opposite the InterContinental Resort and Spa Moorea. Ranging from one to three bedrooms, the thatched-roof houses have full kitchens, two bathrooms, washers and dryers, and Jacuzzi-equipped sun decks with either sea or mountain views. The Balinese-style tropical decor is identical throughout. Serving as a clubhouse for guests, a central building houses a restaurant and gourmet deli; it opens to an infinity-edge swimming pool overlooking the sea. Complimentary shuttles take guests around the property, to a beach across the road, and to a small private island, which has a daytime snack restaurant and bar. Legends is a good bet for families and get-away-from-it-all couples, but it is more like a suburban housing development and is definitely not a beachside resort.

B.P. 4546, 98713, Papeete. (℡) **55.15.15.** Fax 55.15.01. www.legendsresortvillas.com. 46 units. 31,500CFP–88,000CFP per villa. AE, MC, V. **Amenities:** Restaurant; bar; babysitting; health club; Jacuzzi; outdoor pool; smoke-free rooms; spa; tennis court; Wi-Fi (1,000CFP/hour). *In room:* A/C (in bedrooms), ceiling fan, TV/DVD, movie library, hair dryer, kitchen.

MODERATE

Fare Manuia ★ Beside a beach of spectacularly white sand on Moorea's south-western coast, Jeanne Salmon's pension consists of seven thatched-roof bungalows flanking a large, palm-accented lawn. Choice among them is unit no. 1, whose large porch overlooks the beach. It has a bedroom with a queen-size bed, and there are two single beds in the living room. Other units are larger and can accommodate up to six persons. The bungalows are Tahitian-style, with unscreened, push-out windows, but they all have kitchens, electric fans, and hot-water showers. This is a good choice for families, although I recommend ample use of insect repellent. The location is a bit remote, so unless you want to be away from it all, consider renting a car.

PK 30, 98729 Papetoai, Moorea. (℡) **56.26.17.** Fax 56.10.30. www.tahitiguide.com. kinarei@hotmail.com. 7 units. 15,000CFP–18,000CFP. No credit cards. *In room:* TV, kitchen, no phone.

Hotel Hibiscus Occupying a lagoonside coconut grove in the Haapiti restaurant-and-shopping district, this hotel has been around for years. Although its 29 bunga-lows are showing their age a tad, they still have traditional island charms, such as natural thatched roofs extending over front porches. They also have kitchenettes, making the Hibiscus attractive for longer-term stays. Next to the pool, a newer build-ing holds 12 less charming, but air-conditioned hotel-style rooms. The beach is minimal, but a section of the lagoon has been walled off to make a safe swimming hole for children. The beachside **Sunset Restaurant** serves decent pizzas and pastas, and it's a fine place to sip a cocktail at sunset.

B.P. 1009, 98279 Papetoai, Moorea (in Haapiti, east of old Club Med site). (℡) **56.12.12.** Fax 56.20.69. www.hotel-hibiscus.pf. 41 units. 14,000CFP double; 16,400CFP–27,000CFP bungalow. AE, MC, V. **Ame-nities:** Restaurant; bar; outdoor pool; watersports equipment. *In room:* A/C (hotel rooms only), kitchen, Wi-Fi (660CFP/hour).

Hotel Les Tipaniers ★★ 🍴 One of Moorea's best values, this friendly, French-owned establishment sits in a coconut grove beside the sandy beach wrapping around the island's northwestern corner. The widely spaced bungalows stand back in the trees, which gives the small complex an open, airy atmosphere. They also are far enough from the road to be quiet. The "standard superior" bungalows have L-shaped settees facing sliding glass doors to covered porches. Behind the settee, a raised sleeping area supports a queen-size bed, and behind that, a fully tiled bath-room has a sizable shower and vanity space. To the rear of the property, other bun-galows are equipped with kitchens and can sleep up to five persons. Also out back, a building houses four small, hotel-style rooms equipped with twin beds (you can push them together), reading lights, and ample tiled bathrooms with showers. Okay for couples, these rooms are the least expensive yet comfortable place to stay on

Moorea. Unlike the others, however, they do not have phones, fridges, or safes. All units here have ceiling fans but not air conditioners.

Les Tipaniers Restaurant de la Plage (**Restaurant by the Beach;** p. 154), with a deck over the white sands, is open during the day, while the hotel's very good **Restaurant Les Tipaniers** (p. 154) serves Italian and French cuisine at dinner. Guests can make free use of canoes and bicycles, or pay Tip Nautic for kayaking, water-skiing, *motu* trips, and diving with Scubapiti, which is based here.

If you'd like to have a bungalow without the hotel accouterments, consider **Les Tapaniers Iti,** a five-unit annex near Papetoai village. A shuttle will bring you to the main hotel, where you can make use of its facilities. Rates at the annex are lower than at the main property, and discounts are given for longer stays.

B.P. 1002, 98729 Papetoai, Moorea (in Haapiti, east of old Club Med). *©* **56.12.67.** Fax 56.29.25. www. lestipaniers.com. 22 units. 7,600CFP double; 14,200CFP bungalow. AE, MC, V. **Amenities:** 2 restaurants; 2 bars; babysitting; bikes; watersports equipment; Wi-Fi (in reception; 900CFP/hour). *In room:* Ceiling fan, fridge, kitchen (13 units).

Residence Linareva   This pension has accommodations of varying size beside a beach on Moorea's southwest coast. All are tropically attired with thatched ceilings, split bamboo walls, and bright fabrics, and all have porches and cooking facilities. They range from the least expensive duplex garden studios, which can sleep two persons, to an air-conditioned beachside bungalow, which can sleep up to six. Breakfast and dinner are available.

B.P. 1H, 98729 Papetoai, Moorea (PK 34.5, on the southwest coast). *©* **55.05.65.** Fax 55.05.67. www. linareva.com. 8 units. 14,500CFP–26,000CFP bungalow. MC, V. *In room:* A/C (some units), TV, kitchen, no phone.

INEXPENSIVE

Camping Chez Nelson   All guests share toilets, cold-water showers, and communal kitchen facilities at this campground and hostel in a beachside coconut grove about 183m (600 ft.) west of the former Club Med. In addition to camping space on a shadeless lawn, basic accommodations here include tiny bungalows for couples (just enough room for a double bed), four blocks of small rooms (two beds each), and four other thatched-roof hostel bungalows down the road (and still on the beach).

B.P. 1309, 98279 Papetoai, Moorea (in Haapiti, west of old Club Med). *©*/fax **56.15.18.** www.camping-nelson.pf. 4 bungalows, 15 rooms, 20 dorm beds. 1,400CFP–1,500CFP per camper; 1,800CFP–2,200CFP dorm bed; 4,500CFP–6,300CFP double; 4,900CFP–5,400CFP bungalow. Lower rates for stays of more than 1 night. AE, DC, MC, V. *In room:* No phone.

Mark's Place Paradise   A cabinetmaker from Idaho, Mark Walker moved to French Polynesia in 1980 and has put his skills to work on the creatively rustic units at this retreat in the Haapiti Valley. No two alike, his units range in size from a honeymoon unit that has a TV with DVD player to one large enough for groups or use as a dormitory. Bungalows have TVs, kitchens, and private bathrooms. Although it isn't on the beach, this is a good place for backpackers and other adventurous souls.

B.P. 41, 98279 Papetoai, Moorea (at PK 23.5 in Haapiti valley). *©* **56.43.02** or 78.93.65. www. marksplacemoorea.com. 9 bungalows (all with bathroom), 6 dorm beds. 8,000CFP bungalow; 2,500CFP dorm bed. MC, V. Minimum 2-night stay required. **Amenities:** Bikes; watersports equipment. *In room:* Fan, TV, kitchen, no phone, Wi-Fi (1,000CFP/hour).

WHERE TO DINE

The restaurant scene changes quickly on Moorea, so I can only hope the ones I recommend below are still in business—or haven't been sold to another chef—when you get here. As on Tahiti, you can save by eating at snack bars for breakfast, lunch, or an early dinner.

The Cook's Bay Area
EXPENSIVE

Restaurant Honu Iti (Chez Roger) ★ FRENCH   This bayside restaurant is the domain of owner-chef Roger Iqual, who once won the *Concours National de la Poêle d'Or* (Golden Pot Contest) in Cannes for a sea-bass concoction. The scenic setting beside Cook's Bay is terrific. Roger devotes much of his time now to painting (his works hang on the walls here), but oversees his and wife Sui-Lane's two sons back in the kitchen. They specialize in fresh seafood prepared in the classic French fashion. Be sure to order the delicate mahimahi mousse. Sting rays gather here for a snack after 8pm.

Pao Pao, north of Municipal Market. ☎ **56.19.84.** www.restaurant-te-honu-iti.com. Reservations recommended. Main courses 2,900CFP–3,800CFP; tourist menu 5,000CFP. AE, MC, V. Mon 6:30–9pm; Tues–Sat 11:30am–2pm and 6:30–9pm.

MODERATE

Kaveka Restaurant FRENCH/CHINESE/ITALIAN   Even if I'm not staying at Hotel Kaveka, I come in for Moorea's best mahimahi burger and the terrific view of Cook's Bay from its overwater restaurant. Pizzas, pastas, Chinese stir-fries, and French steaks and chicken are inferior to the fish burgers, but they are good value nonetheless, especially considering the view. A portable bar rolls out on the hotel's pier, making it a great place to watch the sunset (from this vantage, it disappears into the sea, but also paints the mountains surrounding Cook's Bay with a phenomenal array of colors). A Tahitian string band usually performs here during dinner on Friday and Saturday.

> **Call for Transportation**
>
> Most Moorea restaurants will either come get you or pay half, if not all, of your taxi fare if you make reservations for dinner. Although they restrict this service to nearby guests, depending on the size of your group, it pays to call ahead and ask.

Cook's Bay, in Hotel Kaveka. ☎ **56.50.50.** www.hotelkaveka.com. Reservations recommended for dinner. Burgers and sandwiches 850CFP–1,950CFP; pizza and pasta 1,650CFP–1,800CFP; main courses 1,100CFP–2,850CFP. AE, MC, V. Daily 6:30–9:30am, 11:30am–2pm, and 6:30–9pm.

Le Cocotier FRENCH   Popular with the local gendarmes, Le Cocotier has widely spaced tables under a natural thatched roof, which helps make it one of the island's more romantic places to dine. The chef specializes in mahimahi steamed in paper with basil sauce, tuna steak in a green-pepper sauce, and other seafood prepared the traditional French way. For a change of pace, I enjoyed his homemade ham (like the sugar-cured version we get in Virginia) in a port-wine sauce. For dessert, don't miss the bananas roasted in coconut cream and served with vanilla ice cream.

Maharepa. ☎ **56.12.10.** Reservations recommended. Main courses 2,400CFP–3,600CFP. MC, V. Mon and Wed–Fri 9:30am–2pm and 6–10pm; Sat–Sun 6–10pm.

Le Mahogany ★ 🍴 FRENCH/CHINESE   French chef François Courtien spent 30 years cooking at the former Hotel Bali Hai before joining Tahitian Blondine Agnia at her pleasant little dining spot next to the local gym. It's a favorite with local expatriates who appreciate value and friendly service. Polished mahogany tables, art-adorned walls, and a window opening to a garden provide tropical ambience. A rich avocado-and-shrimp cocktail is a good way to start. Consistently good are Moorea-grown shrimp with curry or Provençal sauce, and shrimp and scallops in a puff pastry with a light cream sauce. The Cantonese main courses are better than those at any Chinese restaurant here. Or you can opt for the special tourist menu of a salad, mahimahi grilled or with meunière sauce, and ice cream for dessert. Otherwise, end with a *tarte tatin*, a caramelized apple pie served with vanilla ice cream.

Maharepa. ☎ **56.39.73.** Reservations recommended. Main courses 1,650CFP–3,450CFP; tourist menu 4,650CFP. MC, V. Thurs–Tues 11am–2:30pm and 6–9:30pm.

Le Miki Miki Bar-Restaurant ★ FRENCH   In the clubhouse at Moorea Green Pearl Golf Course, this restaurant is a fine place for lunch, when you can look out over the links and Lake Temae. Unfortunately this view is not available at night, but the same fine food is. An accomplished young chef was employed here during my recent visit. Among his French fare were some "exotic" offerings such as mahimahi in rich and tasty coconut and pineapple sauce. His shrimp salad was an excellent choice for lunch or a substantial dinner appetizer.

Temae, at Moorea Green Pearl Golf Course. ☎ **56.26.70.** Reservations recommended. Main courses 1,450CFP–2,600CFP. MC, V. Tues–Sat noon–3pm and 6:30–9pm.

Le Sud ★ FRENCH   For a pleasant change of French pace, head to this little white house in the Maharepa shopping district for paella, Provençal-style fish dishes, and seafood pastas from *le sud* (the south) of France. The *plats du jour* are very good value, especially at lunch. Torches contribute to romantic nighttime dining on the patio.

Maharepa. ☎ **56.42.95.** Reservations recommended. Main courses 2,800CFP–3,500CFP. MC, V. Tues–Sat 11am–2pm and 6–9pm; Mon 6–9pm.

Rudy's ★ FRENCH/STEAKS   This hacienda-style steakhouse is the latest creation of Tahiti-born Syd Pollack, who has started several restaurants and other projects both here and in Hawaii. This one is named for his son Rudy, who oversees the kitchen here. In addition to tender New Zealand steaks, there is fresh local seafood. I always check the specials board for the likes of parrotfish grilled and stuffed with crab, or beef in a red-wine sauce, but with island influences.

Maharepa, west of post office. ☎ **56.58.00.** Reservations recommended. Main courses 2,200CFP–3,200CFP. MC, V. Daily 5:30–10pm.

INEXPENSIVE

Allo Pizza 🍴 PIZZA/STEAKS   Nicely spiced pies come from the wood-fired oven at this hole-in-the-wall pizzeria. I say hole-in-the-wall because that's pretty much what it is—a long wooden counter with stools in front of the kitchen, plus two picnic tables to one side. Some of the pizzas are unusual, such as the delightful Basque-style pie with bacon cooked next to the coals, from which also cometh excellent

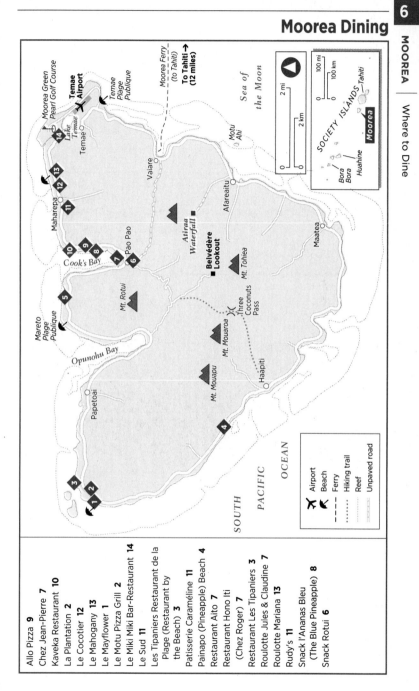

Allo Pizza **9**

Chez Jean-Pierre **7**

Kaveka Restaurant **10**

La Plantation **2**

Le Cocotier **12**

Le Mahogany **13**

Le Mayflower **1**

Le Motu Pizza Grill **2**

Le Miki Miki Bar-Restaurant **14**

Le Sud **11**

Les Tipaniers Restaurant de la
Plage (Restaurant by
the Beach) **3**

Patisserie Caraméline **11**

Painapo (Pineapple) Beach **4**

Restaurant Aito **7**

Restaurant Hono Iti
(Chez Roger) **7**

Restaurant Les Tipaniers **3**

Roulotte Jules & Claudine **7**

Roulotte Mariana **13**

Rudy's **11**

Snack l'Ananas Bleu
(The Blue Pineapple) **8**

Snack Rotui **6**

steaks (served with au gratin potatoes and a salad). Delivery to nearby hotels is available. The staff speaks English as well as French.

Cook's Bay, opposite gendarmerie. (C) **56.18.22.** Pizzas 1,300CFP–1,900CFP; steaks 1,950CFP. No credit cards. Mon 5–9pm, Tues–Sat 11am–2pm and 6–9pm.

Chez Jean-Pierre CANTONESE   When my body tells me to eat my vegetables, I get off the tourist track and join the locals at this plain but clean Chinese family restaurant beside Cook's Bay. You can try very good Chinese-style *poisson cru* (it's spicy) or chicken with sweet Moorea pineapple. Everything's fresh and tasty here.

Pao Pao, near Municipal Market. (C) **56.18.51.** Main courses 1,650CFP–2,450CFP. MC, V. Mon 11:15am–2:30pm; Tues and Thurs–Sat 11:15am–2:30pm; Thurs–Tues 6:15–9:30pm.

Patisserie Caraméline PATISSERIE/SNACKS   A good choice for a cooked breakfast, this patisserie also offers a selection of pastries, crepes, pizzas, salads, omelets, quiches, burgers, sandwiches, *poisson cru*, shrimp in coconut curry sauce, grilled tuna and mahimahi, fruit plates, ice cream, sundaes, and other goodies. The patio tables here are a relaxing spot to write a postcard.

Maharepa, next to the post office. (C) **56.15.88.** Breakfasts 750CFP–1,750CFP; snacks and light meals 500CFP–2,100CFP. MC, V. Daily 7am–5pm.

Snack l'Ananas Bleu (Blue Pineapple) BREAKFAST/SNACKS   Matahi Hunter's "snack" occupies what was once the sunken bayside bar at the Club Bali Hai, where a stupendous view of Cook's Bay accompanies the cooked or continental breakfasts and the lunches of big juicy beef, fish, or teriyaki burgers and french fries. Ice cream and fruit drinks provide relief from the midday heat. There's a seafood barbecue on Wednesday night following the hotel's Tahitian dance show.

Pao Pao, in Club Bali Hai. (C) **56.12.06.** Breakfast 600CFP–1,900CFP; burgers and sandwiches 800CFP–1,650CFP; main courses 1,500CFP–2,400CFP. MC, V. Daily 7am–3pm.

Snack Rotui SNACK BAR   On the shore of Cook's Bay, this walk-up "snack" is run by a Chinese family, and for about 600CFP you can get a sandwich, a soft drink, and a slice of delicious homemade cake. The owners prepare Chinese plate lunches across the road and bike them over here. A few tables under a roof beside the beach

Check Out Moorea's *Roulottes*

As on Tahiti, your best bet for inexpensive nighttime meals is the local *roulottes* (see "Don't Miss *Les Roulottes*," p. 125). The best of these Moorea meal wagons is **Roulotte Mariana** ((C) **77.49.56**), in front of Magasin Chez Remy and just west of Le Mahogany restaurant in Maharepa. Unlike most of these roadside stands, this one has a kitchen complete with dishwasher, and since it's part of the grocery store it seldom runs out of supplies. Open Wednesday through Sunday from 6 to 9pm. At the fish market in Pao Pao, **Roulotte Jules & Claudine** ((C) **56.25.31**), the best item is local shrimp in a tasty coconut-curry sauce. Open Monday through Saturday from 6:30 to 8:30pm. Prices at both range from 1,000CFP to 1,800CFP. Neither accepts credit cards. You'll find other *roulottes* near the bridge in Pao Pao and at Le Petite Village shopping center in Haapiti.

A Sunday Tahitian Feast

Locals love to partake of huge *ma'a Tahiti* feasts on Sunday afternoon, and I join them at Ron Sage's **Painapo (Pineapple) Beach** (℘ 55.07.90; www.painapo.com), on the southwestern coast. It's a lovely setting with tables under a natural thatched-roof restaurant (with sand floor) as well as outside under the shade of a sprawling beachside tree. Ron's all-you-can-eat Sunday buffet of traditional Tahitian foods costs 3,500CFP, a steal in these expensive islands. He also serves an a la carte menu of fresh grilled fish for 2,000CFP to 2,500CFP Monday to Thursday, when Pineapple Beach is open from 9am to 3pm. Bring cash, for Ron does not accept credit cards. See "Eating & Drinking" (p. 37) for more information about Tahitian chow.

catch the breezes off the bay; for more than 20 years, I've taken in this splendid view while munching a *casse-croûte* sandwich.

Pao Pao, west of the bridge at the head of Cook's Bay. ℘ **56.18.16.** Sandwiches 200CFP–400CFP. No credit cards. Tues–Sun 7am–6pm.

Between Cook's & Opunohu Bays

Restaurant Aito ★ FRENCH/CORSICAN   Extending out over the lagoon, this open-air cafe preserves the old South Seas ambience better than any other restaurant on Moorea. Adding to the charm are big *aito* (ironwood) trees growing through the deck and thatched roof (hence the restaurant's name). Owner Jean-Baptiste Cipriani grew up in Marseilles eating the cooking of his Corsican ancestors, and he repeats some of those dishes here, including a luscious tomato sauce that requires 10 hours to prepare. You can dip your bread into some *very* spicy Corsican peppers while waiting. When they are available, Aito is one of the few restaurants serving coconut crab, a land-dwelling crustacean with one huge claw capable of cracking open a coconut. This isn't the cleanest place on Moorea, but it's a terrific spot for a lagoonside meal, as many celebrity visits attest.

PK 13.1, west of Sheraton Moorea btw. Cook's and Opunohu bays. ℘ **56.45.52.** www.aitomoorea.com. Reservations recommended. Main courses 2,100CFP–5,000CFP. MC, V. Wed–Mon 11am–2:30pm and 6–9pm.

The Northwest Coast
EXPENSIVE

La Plantation ★★ FRENCH/CAJUN   It's not exactly New Orleans quality, but Nathalie Richard and Bertrand Jardon do a fine imitation of Louisiana fare at this large restaurant with tables inside or on a plantation-like veranda. Spicy gazpacho, jambalaya, and whole crab Cajun-style offer relief from the French sauces that rule elsewhere. Nathalie and Bertrand turn down the lights at night, creating romantic ambience.

Haapiti (opposite old Club Med). ℘ **54.45.10.** www.laplantationmoorea.com. Reservations recommended. Main courses 2,600CFP–4,500CFP. MC, V. Wed 6:30–9:30pm; Thurs–Mon 11am–9:30pm.

MODERATE

Le Mayflower ★★ 🍴 CASUAL FRENCH   This roadside restaurant draws mostly local residents, who rightly proclaim it to be Moorea's best for both food and

---

Sunsets with Muk at Club Bali Hai

If I'm on Moorea, you'll find me beside Cook's Bay at the **Club Bali Hai** (✆ **56.13.68**) swapping yarns with Muk McCallum, one of the original Bali Hai Boys. His bring-your-own happy hours run Thursday through Tuesday between 5:30 and 7pm (the club has no bar and the restaurant closes at 3pm, so you'll have to bring whatever you want to drink and munch). This is one of the great vistas in the South Pacific; you'll want to become a modern Paul Gauguin in order to capture the changing colors of the bay, sky, and jagged mountains.

---

value. The sauces are lighter than you will experience elsewhere, and there is always a vegetarian selection. I like to start with a salad of warm local shrimp over cool, fresh greens. The house special—lobster ravioli in a cream sauce—is a worthy main choice, as are seafood pasta under pesto or the reliable shrimp in coconut curry. Mahimahi in a lobster sauce highlights a special tourist menu here.

Haapiti, west of old Club Med site. ✆ **56.53.59.** www.restaurantmayflower.com. Reservations recommended. Main courses 1,650CFP–2,650CFP. AE, MC, V. Tues–Sun 11:30am–2pm and 6:30–10:30pm.

Restaurant Les Tipaniers ★ 🍴 ITALIAN/FRENCH   This romantic, thatched-roof restaurant is popular with visitors and Moorea's permanent residents, who come here for delicious pizzas with a variety of toppings and homemade spaghetti, lasagna, tagliatelle, and gnocchi served with Bolognese, carbonara, or seafood sauce. French dishes include pepper steak and filets of mahimahi in butter or vanilla sauce. Discounted transportation is available for Haapiti-area hotel guests.

Haapiti, at Hotel Les Tipaniers, east of old Club Med. ✆ **56.12.67.** www.lestipaniers.com. Reservations recommended. Pasta and pizza 1,000CFP–1,480CFP; main courses 1,850CFP–3,250CFP. AE, DC, MC, V. Daily 6:30–9:15pm.

INEXPENSIVE

Le Motu SNACK BAR   You can get grilled steak or fish with french fries at this open-air restaurant, but it's best for pizzas, sandwiches, and large hamburgers. Light fare includes salads, crepes, and soft ice cream, and a selection of soft drinks, beer, and wine.

Haapiti, opposite old Club Med. ✆ **56.16.70.** Burgers, sandwiches, and salads 500CFP–900CFP; pizza 900CFP–1,000CFP; main courses 1,200CFP–1,800CFP. MC, V (2,000CFP minimum). Tues–Sat 11am–2:15pm and 5–8pm.

Les Tipaniers Restaurant de la Plage (Restaurant by the Beach) ★ ITALIAN/ SNACK BAR   Under a soaring thatched roof and opening to the lagoon, this is the best place in Haapiti for a lagoonside lunch or sunset cocktail. It offers a good selection of salads (some with fruit) and a big juicy burger. Or you can select one of the pastas that make the hotel's nighttime restaurant popular (see above). Breakfast is also served here.

Haapiti, at Hotel Les Tipaniers, east of old Club Med. ✆ **56.19.19.** Salads, sandwiches, burgers 900CFP–1,680CFP; pastas 900CFP–1,580CFP; main courses 1,850CFP–2,300CFP. AE, DC, MC, V. Daily 6:30–9:30am and noon–2:15pm. Bar daily 6:30am–7pm.

ISLAND NIGHTS ON MOOREA

The one required nighttime activity here is an authentic feast and dance show at **Tiki Theatre Village** in Haapiti (© **55.02.50**). For details, see p. 137.

Moorea's major resorts also have Tahitian feasts and dance shows at least once a week. The most elaborate is the Saturday-evening lagoonside show at the InterContinental Resort and Spa Moorea. Most charge 8,000CFP to 9,500CFP per person for the dinner and dance show.

One notable exception is a free show at the **Club Bali Hai** (© **56.13.68**) every Wednesday at 6pm. It's followed by an a la carte seafood barbecue at Snack l'Ananas Bleu (Blue Pineapple). Meals range from 1,800CFP to 3,900CFP. Reservations are required for the barbecue.

Among the restaurants, **Le Sud** (© **56.42.95**), **Restaurant Aito** (© **56.45.52**), and **Kaveka Restaurant** (© **56.50.50**) have live music on weekends. See "Where to Dine," earlier in this chapter.

HUAHINE

Pronounced Wa-*ee*-nee by the French (who never sound an "h") and *Who*-a-hee-nay by the Tahitians (who always do), Huahine ranks with Easter Island and Raiatea (see chapter 8) as the three most important Polynesian archaeological sites. Here, the ancient chiefs built a series of *maraes* on the shores of **Lake Fauna Nui,** which separates the north shore from a long, *motu*-like peninsula, and on Matairea Hill above the lakeside village of **Maeva.** These have been restored, and informational markers explain their history and purposes.

Many honeymooners and other visitors make Huahine their last vacation stop, drawn by its relaxed ambience, lovely beaches, and friendly people. **Baie Avea (Avea Bay),** on the far southwestern coast of Huahine Iti, is fringed by one of French Polynesia's most glorious beaches. Another is right in the small hamlet of **Fare,** one of the region's best examples of what the South Seas were like in the days of trading schooners and copra planters.

Personally, I think Huahine is the third most beautiful of the Society Islands (behind Moorea and Bora Bora). Geographically, it is actually two rugged islands—**Huahine Nui** and **Huahine Iti** (Big Huahine and Little Huahine, respectively)—enclosed by the same reef and joined by a short bridge, which, in turn, separates two picturesque bays, Maroe and Bourayne. With basaltic thumbs reaching from jagged mountains on either side of the bays, this vista reminds me of Moorea.

France did not annex Huahine until 1897, more than 50 years after it took over Tahiti, and its 5,500 residents are still independent in spirit. When the first Europeans arrived, Huahine was governed as a single chiefdom and not divided into warring tribes as were the other islands, and this spirit of unity is still strong. Pouvanaa a Oopa, the founder of modern French Polynesia's independence movement, hailed from here. Unrushed by hordes of tourists, the friendly people of Huahine still say *"Ia orana"* to us visitors.

GETTING AROUND HUAHINE

Huahine's airport is on the flat peninsula paralleling the north side of the island, 3km (2 miles) from Fare. Unless you have previously reserved a rental car or are willing to walk into Fare, take your hotel minibus. At other times, **Enite's Taxi** (✆ **68.82.37**) will carry you around. Fares are about 600CFP from the airport into Fare, and about 2,500CFP to the southern end of Huahine Iti.

Avis (✆ **800/230-4898** or 68.73.34; www.avis.com), **Europcar** (✆ **800/227-7368** or 68.82.59; www.europcar-tahiti.com), and **Hertz** (✆ **800/654-3131** or 68.76.85; www.hertz.com) have agents in Fare. Europcar's vehicles start at 11,500CFP a day for air-conditioned models. Europcar rents scooters for 6,200CFP a day, bicycles for 2,000CFP a day. **Huahine Lagoon,** on the Fare waterfront (✆ **68.70.00**), has bicycles for 1,500CFP for 8 hours. On Huahine Iti, **Moana Turquoise** (✆ **68.85.57**), at Pension Mauarii, rents scooters for 6,500CFP a day and bicycles for 2,500CFP a day.

Each district has local **buses,** which run into Fare at least once a day, but the schedules are highly irregular. If you take one from Fare to Parea, for example, you might not be able to get back on the same day.

[FastFACTS] HUAHINE

The following facts apply specifically to Huahine. For more information, see "Fast Facts: Tahiti & French Polynesia," in chapter 13.

Currency Exchange
Banque Socredo is in Fare, on the road that parallels the main street and bypasses the waterfront. **Banque de Tahiti** is on Fare's waterfront. Both have ATMs.

Drugstore The pharmacist at the drugstore, on the main road between Fare and the airport, speaks English (✆ **68.80.90**). Open Monday to Friday 7:30am to noon and 2:30 to 5pm, Saturday 8am to noon,

Sunday and holidays 8 to 9am.

Emergencies & Police
The emergency **police** telephone number is ✆ **17.** The phone number of the **gendarmerie** in Fare is ✆ **68.82.61.**

Healthcare The **government infirmary** is in Fare (✆ **68.82.48**). Ask your hotel for the names of doctors and dentists in private practice.

Internet Access
AO Api New World (✆ **68.70.99**), on the Fare waterfront, has both wired and wireless Internet connections. Open Monday to Friday 8:30am to 6:30pm.

Access costs 15CFP a minute.

Mail The colonial-style post office is in Fare, on the bypass road north of the waterfront area. Hours are Monday to Thursday 7:30am to 3pm, Friday 7am to 2pm.

Visitor Information
The **Manava Huahine Visitors Bureau** (✆/fax **68.78.81**) was relocating during my recent visit; it should be at the north end of the Fare waterfront.

Water Don't drink the tap water on Huahine. Bottled water is available at all grocery stores.

EXPLORING HUAHINE
Visiting the Maraes & Fare Potee ★★★

The village of **Maeva,** beside the pass where Lake Fauna Nui flows toward the sea, was a major cultural and religious center before Europeans arrived in the islands. All of Huahine's chiefly families lived here. More than 200 stone structures have been discovered between the lakeshore and **Matairea Hill,** which looms over Maeva, including some 40 *maraes* (the others were houses, paddocks, and agricultural terraces).

To see the *maraes* on your own, start west of Maeva village at the big reed-sided building known as **Fare Potee,** which houses an excellent museum (*©* **24.16.63**). Flanked by *maraes* and extending out over Lake Fauna Nui, Fare Potee is modeled after a large meetinghouse that stood here in 1925, but was later destroyed by a hurricane. Take time to read the historical markers outside, which expertly explain the history and use of the *maraes*. Inside, you'll observe *adzes* (stone axes), fishhooks, and other artifacts uncovered during restoration work by Dr. Yoshiko H. Sinoto, the chairman of the anthropology department of the Bernice P. Bishop Museum in Honolulu. He restored this and many other *maraes* throughout Polynesia. Fare Potee is open Monday through Friday 9am to noon and 2 to 4pm, Saturday 9am to noon. Admission is 200CFP per person.

Ask at Fare Potee for directions to six *maraes* and other structures (some were built as fortifications during the 1844 to 1848 French-Tahitian war) on Matairea Hill. The track up the hill can be muddy and slippery during wet weather, and the steep climb is best done in early morning or late afternoon. Better yet, take a tour (see below).

Easier to reach, the large **Manunu Marae** stands on the beach about 1km (½ mile) across the bridge on the east end of Maeva. Follow the left fork in the road after crossing the bridge. The setting is impressive.

From the bridge, you will see several stone **fish traps.** Restored by Dr. Sinoto, they work as well today as they did in the 16th century, trapping fish as the tide ebbs and flows in and out of the narrow passage separating the lake from the sea.

Historical Tours

The most informative way to see the historical sites—and much of Huahine, for that matter—is with Paul Atallah of **Island Eco Tours ★★★** (*©* **68.79.67;** www. island-eco-tours.com). Paul is an American who graduated from the University of Hawaii with a major in anthropology and a minor in Polynesian Island archaeology. He has lived in French Polynesia for more than a decade. His is more than a typical safari expedition, for he gives in-depth commentary about the Maeva *maraes* and other historical sites. He charges 5,000CFP for either morning or afternoon trips from Monday through Friday. The 3½- to 4-hour trips depart daily at 8am and 1pm. He will pick you up at your hotel. Paul can also guide you to the *maraes* on Matairea Hill by special arrangement.

Touring the Island

You can rent a vehicle and tour both parts of Huahine in half a day. The main roads around both islands are about 32km (20 miles) long and are paved. Be careful on the

Huahine

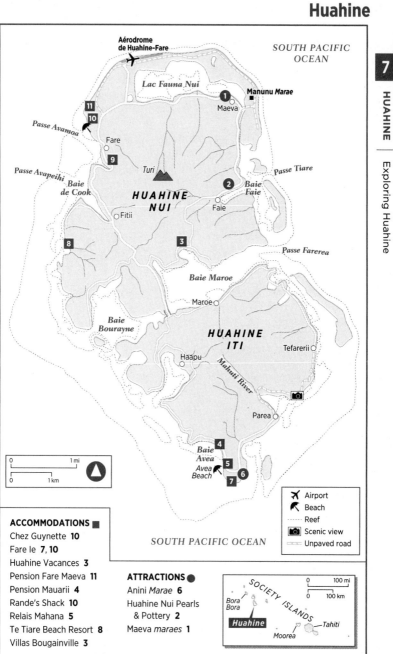

Aérodrome de Huahine-Fare

SOUTH PACIFIC OCEAN

Lac Fauna Nui

1 Maeva ■ **Manunu** *Marae*

11

10 *Passe Avamoa*

Fare **9**

Turi

Passe Avapeihi

Baie de Cook

HUAHINE NUI

2 *Baie Faie*

Faie

Passe Tiare

Fitii

3

8

Passe Farerea

Baie Maroe

Maroe

Baie Bourayne

HUAHINE ITI

Tefarerii

Haapu

Mahuti River

Parea

4 *Baie Avea*

5 *Avea Beach*

6

7

SOUTH PACIFIC OCEAN

0 ____ 1 mi
0 ____ 1 km

✈	Airport
🏄	Beach
⋯⋯	Reef
📷	Scenic view
⋮⋮⋮	Unpaved road

ACCOMMODATIONS ■

Chez Guynette **10**
Fare Ie **7, 10**
Huahine Vacances **3**
Pension Fare Maeva **11**
Pension Mauarii **4**
Rande's Shack **10**
Relais Mahana **5**
Te Tiare Beach Resort **8**
Villas Bougainville **3**

ATTRACTIONS ●

Anini *Marae* **6**
Huahine Nui Pearls & Pottery **2**
Maeva *maraes* **1**

SOCIETY ISLANDS

Bora Bora

Huahine

Moorea

Tahiti

0 ____ 100 mi
0 ____ 100 km

steep *traversière* (cross-island road) that traverses the mountains from Maroe Bay to Faie Bay on the east coast. (I would not ride a scooter or bicycle over this road.) Heading clockwise from **Fare,** you skirt the shores of Lake Fauna Nui and come to the *maraes* outside Maeva village (see "Visiting the *Maraes* & Fare Potee," above).

From Maeva, the road heads south until it turns into picturesque Faie Bay. Here you'll pass the landing for **Huahine Nui Pearls & Pottery ★ (℅ 78.30.20),** a pearl farm and pottery studio (p. 162). Once you're past Faie village at the head of the bay, the road starts uphill across the *traversière* (see above). At the top, you'll be rewarded with a view down across Moorea-esque **Maroe Bay,** which splits Huahine into two islands.

Turn right at the dead-end by the bay and drive west to the main west-coast road. Turn left and follow it across the bridge over the narrow pass separating Huahine Nui from Huahine Iti. A right turn past the bridge will take you along the winding west-coast road to **Avea Bay,** where Relais Mahana (p. 164) and Pension Mauarii (p. 165) sit beside one of the South Pacific's greatest beaches. Either is an excellent place to stop for refreshment.

Sitting at the end of the peninsula at the south end of Huahine Iti, **Anini Marae** presents a glorious view of the island's southern coast. Nearby on the grounds of Fare Ie (see "Where to Stay," below), another small *marae* bears the **Taiharuru Petroglyphs. Parea** is one of Huahine's largest villages. From there, you'll skirt the shoreline until you come to the village of **Tefarerii** on the east coast. In between is a pull-off with a marvelous view over the reefs and sea. From here, it's an easy drive to Maroe Bay. The large cruise ships land their passengers at Maroe village on the south side of the bay.

Revisiting the Old South Seas in Fare

The main village of **Fare ★★★** (*Fah*-ray) is hardly more than a row of Chinese stores and a wharf opposite the main pass in the reef on the northwest shore, but it takes us back to the days when trading schooners were the only way to get around the islands. Even today, trucks and buses arrive from all over Huahine with passengers and cargo when the interisland boats put in from Papeete. The rest of the time, Fare lives a lazy, slow pace, as people amble down its tree-lined main street and browse through the stores facing the town wharf. A monument on the waterfront designates it as **Place Hawaiki,** the starting point for October's big outrigger canoe race to Raiatea and Bora Bora.

Beginning at the Restaurant New Temarara (p. 166), a pebbly promenade leads north along the waterfront to a sandy swimming beach.

LAGOON EXCURSIONS & SAFARI EXPEDITIONS

Lagoon Excursions

As on Moorea and Bora Bora, one of the most enjoyable ways to see the island is on a lagoon excursion that includes snorkeling and a picnic on an islet out on the reef. The biggest difference here is that with relatively few tourists around, you and your companions are likely to have the islet all to yourselves.

The all-day excursion with **Huahine Nautique** (© 68.83.15; www.huahine-nautique.com) takes you by outrigger canoe through Maroe Bay and around Huahine Iti. You'll stop for snorkeling and a picnic featuring freshly made *poisson cru,* and you will observe shark-feeding before returning to Fare. Huahine Nautique's canoes have shade canopies, and the guides speak English as well as French. Don't be surprised if you visit Huahine Nui Pearls & Pottery (p. 162). The excursions cost about 8,500CFP per person.

Safari Expeditions

As on most of the Society Islands, you can make four-wheel-drive expeditions into the mountains here. You will see a bit of the interior of Huahine Nui with Paul Atallah on his **Island Eco Tours** (see "Historical Tours," above), which I would take first. You will repeat seeing the Maeva *maraes,* but either **Huahine Land** (© 68.89.21), which is owned by American expatriate Joel House, or **Huahine Explorer** (© 68.87.33), will also take you to Huahine Iti on its half-day expeditions. Both charge about 5,500CFP per person.

WATERSPORTS & OTHER OUTDOOR ACTIVITIES

Fishing

For lagoon or deep-sea fishing, contact **Huahine Marine Transports** (© 68.84.02; hua.mar.trans@mail.pf), owned by American expatriate Rich Shamel, who has lived on Huahine for many years and who runs the transfer boats for Te Tiare Beach Resort (p. 163). Rich charges about 65,000CFP for a half-day fishing on his 11m (36-ft.) Hatteras sport-fishing boat. He lives and works at the resort's transfer base, just across the bridge on the south side of Fare.

Horseback Riding

One of the best horseback-riding operations in French Polynesia is **La Petite Ferme** (**Little Farm;** © 68.82.98), on the main road north of Fare, just before the airport turnoff. It has Marquesas-bred horses that can be ridden with English or Western saddles along the beach and around Lake Fauna Nui. Prices range from about 5,500CFP for 2 hours to 11,000CFP for an all-day trail ride. The farm also has accommodations, from a dormitory to bungalows.

Sailing

You can go for a half- or full-day cruise with Claude and Martine Bordier of **Sailing Huahine Voile** (✆/fax **68.72.49;** www.sailing-huahine.com) on their *Eden Martin,* a 15m (50-ft.) yacht, which they sailed from France in 1999. A half-day of sailing costs about 7,500CFP per person; a whole day, 13,000CFP. They also have sunset cruises for 7,000CFP per person. That's assuming Claude and Martine are on Huahine and not on a 1- or 2-week charter cruise in the Leeward or Tuamotu islands.

Scuba Diving

Huahine's lagoon and fringing reef have several dive sites with a multitude of sea life, and you don't have to be an experienced diver to see much of it. You'll need a boat to get to it, but even snorkelers will enjoy the **Seafari Aquarium,** inside the barrier reef off Avea Beach on Huahine Iti. Tropical fish congregate around the colorful coral heads that dot the lagoon here, and rays troll the sandy bottom. The aquarium is only 2 to 3m (7–10 ft.) deep. Novice divers can also explore the canyons beyond **Tiare Pass,** off Faie Bay on the eastern side of Huahine-Nui. You will need intermediate skills to explore Huahine's most famous site, **Avapehi Pass,** the entry through the reef off Cook's Bay and a short boat ride from Fare. Conditions in the pass draw feeding schools of barracuda and other fish, which in turn get the attention of gray reef sharks.

Pacific Blue Adventure (✆ **68.87.21;** fax 68.80.71; www.divehuahine.com) and **Mahana Dive** (✆ **73.07.17;** www.mahanadive.com) have offices on the Fare wharf. Both charge about 6,500CFP for a one-tank dive.

Snorkeling & Swimming

You don't have to leave Fare to find a fine little swimming and snorkeling beach; just follow the seaside promenade north past Restaurant New Temarara. Huahine's best, however, is the magnificent crescent of sand at **Avea Beach,** skirting Baie Avea on Huahine Iti. A hilly peninsula blocks the brunt of the southeast trade winds, so the speckled lagoon here is usually as smooth as glass. **Moana Turquoise** (✆ 68.85.57), at Pension Mauarii (see "Where to Stay," below), rents snorkeling gear. It also has powerboats for rent.

SHOPPING

You are not as likely to be pestered to buy black pearls on Huahine as on Tahiti, Moorea, and Bora Bora—another of Huahine's appealing attributes, in my opinion. One stop you should make is **Huahine Nui Pearls & Pottery ★** (✆ **78.30.20**), a pearl farm and pottery studio operated by American expatriate Peter Owen on a *motu* off Baie Faie (see "Touring the Island," above). Peter offers free tours daily from 10am to 4pm, with the boat leaving Faie Bay every 15 minutes. If you aren't going to the Tuamotus, this is a good place to see how black pearls are grown.

Be sure to look in the small art galleries and other shops along the Fare waterfront, especially the wood carvings and paintings by local artists in **Pacific Art** (✆ **68.70.09**), owned by American expatriate Joe Perrone and his French wife, Frédérique.

WHERE TO STAY

Expensive

Te Tiare Beach Resort ★★★ Rudy Markmiller made a fortune in the overnight courier business in California and then spent more than a decade—and a sizable chunk of his loot—building this luxury resort, one of French Polynesia's finest. Although it's on the main island, guests are ferried here from Fare, which makes this seem like a remote offshore resort (never fear: a shuttle boat makes the 10-min. run to and from Fare about every hour from 5:30am–11pm). You will land at a thatched-roof, overwater structure housing a reception area, lounge, bar, and dining room serving excellent international cuisine. A long pier connects this central complex to a westward-facing, white-sand beach with gorgeous sunsets over Raiatea and Tahaa out on the horizon. The lagoon is not deep here, but it's still good for swimming and snorkeling over coral heads close to shore. You can use canoes, paddleboats, and kayaks, or cool off in a beachside swimming pool equipped with its own terrific bar serving libations and snacks all afternoon. Diving, sailing, fishing, picnicking on a *motu,* horseback riding, and touring the *maraes* cost extra. Jet skis and water-skiing are available, though not in front of the resort.

> ### The Swimsuit Models Were Here
>
> Those extraordinarily beautiful women seen briefly—in both time and clothing—at Te Tiare Beach Resort were here to model for the 2006 swimsuit issue of *Sports Illustrated* magazine.

The 41 spacious bungalows are not as luxuriously appointed as the newer, high-luxe models on Bora Bora, but they don't cost as much, either, which makes Te Tiare very good value. You won't have a fish-viewing glass panel in the floor, but you can step out to a huge L-shaped deck, half of it under the shade of a thatched roof. The decks also have privacy screens so your neighbors can't see you dining in the nude, or whatever. Steps lead into the lagoon from the decks of the 11 "deep overwater" bungalows that have spa tubs as well as showers in their bathrooms (all other units, including five "shallow overwater" models, have large showers). Six bungalows sit beside the beach, but the garden units (the least expensive here) don't have unimpeded views of the lagoon. One bungalow is reserved for massages.

B.P. 36, 98731 Fare, Huahine (in Fitii District, 10 min. by boat from Fare). © **888/600-8455** or 60.60.50. Fax 60.60.51. www.tetiarebeach.com. 40 units. 36,500CFP–70,000CFP double. AE, DC, MC, V. **Amenities:** 2 restaurants; 2 bars; babysitting; bikes; outdoor pool; room service; smoke-free rooms; watersports equipment. *In room:* A/C, ceiling fan, TV, hair dryer, minibar, Wi-Fi (500CFP/hour).

Moderate

Fare Ie Instead of a bungalow, you'll have your own safari tent at this establishment's two locations. One is north of Fare and within walking distance of town. The other is on the outskirts of Paea village, near Huahine Iti's southernmost point. The Paea location is remote, but the beach is very good, and it's actually on the grounds of an ancient *marae* bearing the Taiharuru Petroglyphs. The tents are all screened and have electric fans, two beds, and their own bathrooms. Two larger tents at Paea also have kitchens just outside under thatched roofs. Guests share communal kitchens at both locations.

B.P. 746, 98331 Fare, Huahine (north of Fare and in Paea village, Huahine Iti). ℂ/fax **60.63.77**. www. tahitisafari.com. 6 units. 16,500CFP–27,000CFP per tent. No credit cards. **Amenities:** Bikes; watersports equipment. *In room:* No phone.

Relais Mahana 🍴   This hotel has one of the South Pacific's best beach-lagoon combinations. Half of it sits beside Avea Beach, with white sand stretching along the peninsula on Huahine's south end. A pier from the main building runs out over a giant coral head, around which fish and guests swim. Just climb down off the pier and swim with the fishes. Choice guest quarters are the thatch-topped deluxe models beside the beach. Although a bit smaller than at other resorts, they have king-size beds and their showers open to private rear gardens. Other units here are somewhat larger, but they're north of the central building where the beach has been eroded. All in all, Relais Mahana is good value.

B.P. 30, 98731 Fare, Huahine (Avea Bay, Huahine Iti). ℂ **60.60.40**. Fax 68.85.08. www.relaismahana. com. 32 units. 25,000CFP–30,000CFP. AE, MC, V. **Amenities:** Restaurant; bar; babysitting; bikes; outdoor pool; watersports equipment. *In room:* Ceiling fan, TV, fridge, hair dryer, Wi-Fi (free).

Inexpensive

Chez Guynette 🍴   This basic but friendly hotel stands across the main street from the Fare waterfront. A corridor runs down the center of the building to the kitchen and lounge at the rear. The simple but clean rooms and dorms flank the hallway on either side. The units have screens, ceiling fans, and their own bathrooms with hot-water showers. The dorms also have ceiling fans; they share two toilets and showers. Owners Olivier and Lawrence Lebrun serve breakfast and lunch (sandwiches, burgers, salads, and *poisson cru*, plus wine and beer) on the street-side patio. It's the best place in Fare to slake your thirst and get into a good conversation.

B.P. 87, 98731 Fare, Huahine (opposite the town wharf). ℂ **68.83.75**. www.pension-guynette-huahine. com. 7 units (all with bathroom), 8 bunks. 1,750CFP–2,000CFP dorm bed; 5,900CFP–6,200CFP double (higher rates apply to 1-night stays). MC, V. **Amenities:** Restaurant (breakfast and lunch); bar. *In room:* Ceiling fan, no phone, Wi-Fi (900CFP/hour).

Pension Fare Maeva   Located between Fare and the airport, this pension has some features that make it seem more like a cost-conscious resort. It overlooks a white-sand beach, although the lagoon here is so rocky and shallow that you cannot wade in for a swim. You can take a dip in the pool, though, which resides in a beachside lawn in front of the restaurant. You can order a cold one at the bar and escape the midday sun under the tin roof of a *fare potee*, or outdoor lounge, beside the pool. The 20 units here are evenly divided between bungalows and hotel-style rooms, all in lush tropical gardens rather than on the beach. The bungalows are more expensive, but come with kitchens and separate bedrooms. Accommodations are rather spartan, but tin roofs, tile floors, porches, and simple bathrooms with hot-water showers are common to all units. You'll get a fan, but not window screens.

B.P. 675, 98731 Fare, Huahine (2.5km/1½ miles north of Fare). ℂ **68.75.53**. Fax 68.70.68. www.fare-maeva.com. 20 units (all with bathroom). 7,000CFP double; 12,100CFP bungalow. MC, V. **Amenities:** Restaurant; bar; outdoor pool. *In room:* Fan, kitchen (bungalows only), no phone, Wi-Fi (660CFP/hour).

Pension Mauarii ★★ Beside Avea Beach, this little pension may not have all the comforts of home, but it is one of the most charming in French Polynesia. Its buildings are constructed of thatch, bamboo, tree trunks, and other natural materials. Although cleverly designed, they seem to be slapped together, which adds to the rustic ambience. Most units are in the tropical gardens, but the rooms open to a long porch right on the beach, as does the one over-the-beach bungalow—my favorite here. All units have ceiling fans, but not all have bathrooms, and their windows aren't screened. The pension provides a host of waterborne activities. The restaurant also is the most charming on the island (see "Where to Dine," below).

B.P. 473, 98731 Fare, Huahine (Baie Avera, Huahine-Iti). © **68.86.49.** Fax 60.60.96. www.mauarii.com. 5 bungalows (all with bathroom), 4 rooms (2 with bathroom). 9,500CFP double; 11,500CFP–20,000CFP bungalow. AE, MC, V. **Amenities:** Restaurant; bar; bikes; watersports equipment. *In room:* Fan, no phone, Wi-Fi (500CFP/hour).

House Rentals with Cars & Boats

American Rande Vetterli has two clean, well-equipped houses for rent at **Rande's Shack,** on the shore north of Fare (© **68.86.27;** www.haere-mai.pf; randeshack@mail.pf). Both have TVs, fans, and kitchens. One house has two bedrooms and can sleep five people; a one-bedroom model can sleep three people. Rates are 15,000CFP and 10,000CFP, respectively.

Two lodgings, both on the north shore of Maroe Bay, throw in the use of a car and motorboat in their rates.

Huahine Vacances (© **68.73.63;** www.huahinevacance.pf) is owned by Bordeaux native Michel Sorin, who learned to speak English while living in Canada before relocating to the islands in the early 1980s and marrying his Tahitian wife, Jacqueline. Although their modern villas could be at home in most suburbs, the tin roofs and fretwork around the eaves add an old-plantation touch. Two have three bedrooms and two bathrooms, while the third has two bedrooms and a single bathroom. Both are good choices for groups or families. You'll have a fully equipped kitchen (including a microwave), a large front porch from which to observe the bay, window screens, and your own bathroom with hot-water shower. Jacqueline will babysit the kids while you drive your car into Fare for dinner. The Sorins provide linens, but you do the housework.

Within hailing distance is **Villas Bougainville** (© **60.60.30** or 79.70.59; www.villas-bougainville.com), where the three houses are a bit larger, as are the surrounding tropical gardens. The two- and three-bedroom villas have wraparound verandas, modern kitchens, and bathrooms with hot-water showers. The bedrooms are somewhat spartan, but all have ceiling fans and some have air conditioners (for which you must pay extra). Cribs and babysitting are available, but not housekeeping.

Both Huahine Vacances and Villas Bougainville charge 20,500CFP per night for two people.

WHERE TO DINE

You'll meet the locals having breakfast or lunch while watching the passing scene from the patio at **Chez Guynette** in Fare (p. 164). You can also enjoy the fine dining room at **Te Tiare Beach Resort** (p. 163), though you will need to make reservations and pay 500CFP per person for the boat ride there and back.

You'll find Huahine's *roulottes* on the Fare wharf. They're open for both lunch and dinner. See "Don't Miss *Les Roulottes*" (p. 125) for details.

Restaurant Mauarii FRENCH/TAHITIAN   This restaurant sits almost over the sand with a great view southward along Avea Beach. It's a charmer, with a thatch-lined ceiling and tables hewn from tree trunks. Lunchtime sandwiches include a "Killer" baguette loaded with grilled fish and french fries (yes, in the sandwich) under your choice of vanilla or other sauces. For my money, this is a good place to sample Tahitian treats such as *fafa ru* (chicken with taro leaves in coconut cream), or try different dishes on a Polynesian platter. Ask for a menu in English if the friendly staff doesn't figure you out first.

Avea Beach, Huahine Iti (at Pension Mauarii). ℂ **68.86.49.** Reservations recommended for dinner. Sandwiches and burgers 600CFP–1,600CFP; main courses 1,600CFP–3,500CFP. AE, MC, V. Daily noon–2pm and 6–8pm.

Restaurant New Temarara ★ FRENCH   Facing due west beside the lagoon at the north end of Fare's wharf, this is my favorite place for a sundown cocktail or cold Hinano beer during half-price happy hour from 5:30 to 6:30pm. The *poisson cru* is outstanding, as is the coconut-crumbed mahi-mahi, a spicy version of breaded fish. If offered, you might also try the parrotfish with lemon butter. You can get a good beef or fish burger here, as well as steaks and fish with French sauces.

Fare, north end of wharf. ℂ **68.89.31.** Reservations accepted. Burgers 800CFP–900CFP; main courses 1,800CFP–2,800CFP. MC, V. Daily 11:30am–9pm. Bar open all day, to 11pm Fri–Sat.

RAIATEA & TAHAA

he mountainous clump of land you can see on the horizon from Huahine or Bora Bora may appear to be one island, but it actually is two, Raiatea and Tahaa, which are enclosed by a single barrier reef. Cruising yachts can circumnavigate Tahaa without leaving the lagoon, and Huahine and Bora Bora are relatively easy hauls from here. Accordingly, this is French Polynesia's yacht-chartering center. There are no white-sand beaches on either Raiatea or Tahaa other than a few on islets out on the reef, and except for sailing and cruise-ship visits, tourism is not an important part of their economies, which are based on agricultural produce and, in the case of Raiatea, government salaries.

Raiatea, the largest of the Leeward Islands, is by far more important than Tahaa, both in terms of the past and the present. In the old days, it was the religious center of all the Society Islands, including Tahiti. Polynesian mythology has it that Oro, the god of war and fertility, was born in **Mount Temehani,** the extinct flat-top volcano towering over the northern part of Raiatea. **Taputapuatea,** on its southeast coast, was at one time the most important *marae* in the islands. Legend also has it that the great Polynesian voyagers who discovered and colonized Hawaii and New Zealand left from there. Archaeological discoveries have substantiated the link with Hawaii.

Today, Raiatea (pop. 10,000) is still important as the economic and administrative center of the Leeward Islands. Next to Papeete, the town of **Uturoa** (pop. 4,500) is the largest settlement and is one of the most important transportation hubs in French Polynesia. A modern cruise-ship terminal and welcome center dominate Uturoa's waterfront and make it the only island port other than Papeete where the cruise ships spend their nights tied up to a wharf.

Tahaa (pronounced *Tah*-ah-ah) is much smaller than Raiatea in terms of land area, population (about 2,000), and the height of its terrain. It's a lovely island, with a few very small villages sitting deep in bays that cut into its hills. Tahaa has a few family-operated pensions, but other than sailors and guests at three fine resorts out on its reef islets, few visitors see it, and most of those who do, see it on day tours from Raiatea.

GETTING AROUND RAIATEA & TAHAA

The Raiatea airstrip, 3km (2 miles) north of Uturoa, serves both islands. You have to rent a vehicle or take a taxi, for there is no regular public transportation system on either Raiatea or Tahaa.

Europcar (© 800/227-7368 or 66.34.06; www.europcar-tahiti.com) and **Hertz** (© 800/654-3131 or 66.44.88; www.hertz.com) have rental-car offices here. Europcar's prices start at 10,700CFP a day for air-conditioned models, including insurance and unlimited kilometers. It also rents scooters, bicycles, and open-air "Bugster" vehicles. **L'Hibiscus,** a pension on Tahaa (© 65.61.06; www.hibiscus tahaa.com), rents cars.

Trucky Tour (© 78.23.36) provides transfers from the airport to the hotels and to Apooiti Marina for 500CFP to 700CFP per person. There is a taxi stand near the cruise-ship terminal in Uturoa, or you can contact **René Guilloux** (© 66.31.40), **Marona Teanini** (© 66.34.62), or **Apia Tehope** (© 66.36.41). Fares are about 600CFP from the airport to town and 1,200CFP to the Hawaiki Nui Hotel.

The passenger ferry *Tamarii Tahaa* (© 65.67.10) docks in front of the Champion store on Uturoa's waterfront and runs from there to Patio on Tahaa's northern coast. It departs from Uturoa Monday to Friday, but its schedules vary greatly depending on school days and schedules. Check with Tourisme Tahiti's information office in the Gare Maritime for the latest (see "Fast Facts Raiatea & Tahaa," below). The one-way fare is 700CFP. **Dave's Tours** (© 65.62.42) also runs a shuttle from Uturoa to Tahaa, departing Monday to Saturday at 9am, returning at 4:30pm. Fares are 1,500CFP one-way, 2,500CFP round-trip. Reservations are required. **Water-taxi** service is available at the waterfront (© 65.66.64); rides cost about 2,000CFP.

[FastFACTS] RAIATEA & TAHAA

The following facts apply specifically to Raiatea and Tahaa. For more information, see "Fast Facts: Tahiti & French Polynesia," in chapter 13.

Currency Exchange
French Polynesia's three banks have offices with ATMs on Uturoa's main street. There is no bank on Tahaa.

Drugstores **Pharmacie de Raiatea** (© 66.34.44) in Uturoa carries French products. Open Monday to Friday 7:30am to noon and 1:30 to 5:30pm; Saturday 7:30am to noon; Sunday 9:30 to 10:30am.

Emergencies & Police
The emergency police telephone number is © 17.

The telephone number of the **Uturoa gendarmerie** is © 66.31.07. The **Tahaa gendarmerie** is at Patio, the administrative center, on the north coast (© 65.64.07).

Healthcare Opposite the post office, the **hospital** at Uturoa (© 66.32.92) serves all the Leeward Islands. Tahaa has an

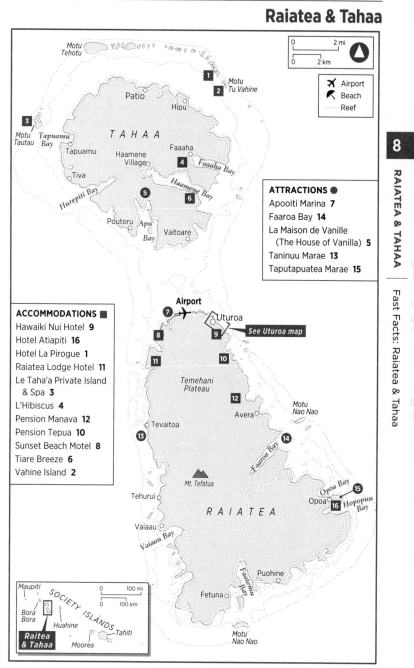

Raiatea & Tahaa

Motu Tehotu

1

Motu Tu Vahine

2

Patio

Hipu

3

Motu Tautau

Tapuamu Bay

T A H A A

Tapuamu

Haamene Village

Faaaha

4

Faaaha Bay

Tiva

Haamene Bay

5

6

Hurepiti Bay

Poutoru

Apu Bay

Vaitoare

| 0 | 2 mi |
| 0 | 2 km |

✈ Airport
🏖 Beach
⋯⋯ Reef

ATTRACTIONS ●
Apooiti Marina **7**
Faaroa Bay **14**
La Maison de Vanille
  (The House of Vanilla) **5**
Taninuu Marae **13**
Taputapuatea Marae **15**

Airport

7 ✈

8

Uturoa

9 *See Uturoa map*

11

10

Temehani Plateau

12

Avera

Motu Nao Nao

ACCOMMODATIONS ■
Hawaiki Nui Hotel **9**
Hotel Atiapiti **16**
Hotel La Pirogue **1**
Raiatea Lodge Hotel **11**
Le Taha'a Private Island
  & Spa **3**
L'Hibiscus **4**
Pension Manava **12**
Pension Tepua **10**
Sunset Beach Motel **8**
Tiare Breeze **6**
Vahine Island **2**

Tevaitoa

13

14

Faaroa Bay

Mt. Tefatua

R A I A T E A

Tehurui

Opoa Bay

15

Opoa **16** Hopopuu Bay

Vaiaau

Vaiaau Bay

Puohine

Faatemu Bay

Fetuna

Motu Nao Nao

Maupiti

SOCIETY ISLANDS

| 0 | 100 mi |
| 0 | 100 km |

Bora Bora

Huahine

Raiatea & Tahaa

Moorea

Tahiti

infirmary at Patio
(📞 **65.63.31**).

Internet Access
ITS/Escace.com, in the Gare Maritime on the Uturoa waterfront (📞 **60.25.25**), has computers with Internet access for 500CFP for 30 minutes. Open Monday to Friday 8am to noon and 1:30 to 5pm, Saturday 8 to 11:30am. It will burn your digital photos to CDs. There is ManaSpot Wi-Fi in the Gare Maritime and at Apooiti Marina (see "Staying Connected," in chapter 3).

Post Office
The post and telecommunications office is in a modern building north of Uturoa on the main road (as opposed to a new road that runs along the shore of reclaimed land on the north side of town). It is open Monday to Thursday 7:30am to 3pm, Friday 7am to 2pm, and Saturday 8 to 10am. There's a small branch upstairs in the Gare Maritime on the waterfront.

Restrooms The Gare Maritime on the waterfront has clean restrooms.

Visitor Information
Tourisme Tahiti
(📞 **60.07.77**; www.tahiti-tourisme.pf) has a visitor information office in the Gare Maritime on the waterfront. Open Monday through Friday 8am to 4pm and on Saturdays and Sundays when cruise ships are in port.

Water Don't drink the tap water on either Raiatea or Tahaa.

EXPLORING RAIATEA & TAHAA

Highlights of your time here will include visits to the ancient *maraes*, day trips to and around Tahaa, picnics on small islands on the outer reef, and four-wheel-drive excursions into the mountains.

A paved road runs for 150km (92 miles) around the shoreline of rugged **Raiatea,** the second-largest island in French Polynesia, behind only Tahiti. Its tallest peak, **Mount Tefatoaiti,** at 1,017m (3,337 ft.), occupies the triangular-shaped island's southern end. To the north, the flat top of sacred **Mount Temehani** soars to 792m (2,598 ft.). Much of Mount Temehani is a high plateau, where the five-petal *tiare apetahi* flower grows (see "Delicate Petals," below). Polynesians in ancient times believed that when they died, their souls ascended to the plateau, where they faced a fork in the road. If they were told to go right, they went to Paradise. If they went left, it was into the crater and their version of Purgatory.

The western side of Mount Temehani is a huge cliff. Coupled with a view of Bora Bora on the horizon, it makes that side of Raiatea especially scenic.

Adding to Raiatea's scenic beauty are several rivers which carve steep valleys on their way from the highlands to six bays indenting the coast. One of them, the **Faaroa River,** is the only navigable waterway in French Polynesia. It empties into mountain-sided **Faaroa Bay,** which provides a protected anchorage for yachts and other small craft. Most charter-boat operators, however, are based at the more convenient **Apooiti Marina** on the north shore beside the strait separating Raiatea and Tahaa.

With 88 sq. km (34 sq. miles), **Tahaa** is about one-third the size of Raiatea, but it is still French Polynesia's fourth-largest island. Its main villages are **Tapuamu** on the west coast, **Patio** on the north side, and **Haamene** in the center. Tahaa is a rugged island, with its tallest peak, **Mount Ohiri,** reaching to 598m (1,975 ft.). The island's inhabitants live along a narrow coastal plain and at the head of four narrow

> ### Delicate Petals
>
> Found nowhere else except in Raiatea's mountains, the *tiare apetahi* is a one-sided white flower of the gardenia family. Legend says that its five delicate petals are the fingers of a beautiful Polynesian girl who fell in love with a prince but couldn't marry him because of her low birth. Just before she died, heartbroken, in her lover's arms, she promised to give him her hand to caress each day throughout eternity. At daybreak each morning, accordingly, the *tiare apetahi* opens its five petals.

bays, two of which—**Haamene** and **Harepiti**—almost cut Tahaa into two. Completely surrounded by a deepwater lagoon, and with the sheltered bays providing fine anchorages, Tahaa is a sailor's heaven.

Visiting the Marae

Raiatea is known as the "Sacred Island" because of its religious importance in pre-European times. On the outskirts of **Opoa** village, 29km (18 miles) south of Uturoa, the **Taputapuatea Marae ★★★** is the second-most-significant archaeological site in all of Polynesia, behind only Easter Island. Legend says that Te Ava Moa Pass offshore was the departure point for the discovery and settlement of both Hawaii and New Zealand. The large *marae* on the site was actually built centuries later by the Tamatoa family of chiefs. Vying for supremacy, the Tamatoas mingled religion with politics by creating Oro, the ferocious god of war and fertility supposedly born on Mount Temehani, and by spreading his cult. It took almost 200 years, but Oro eventually became the most important god in the region. Likewise, the Tamatoas became the most powerful chiefs. They were on the verge of conquering all of the Society Islands when the missionaries arrived in 1797. With the Christians' help, Pomare I became king of Tahiti, and the great *marae* the Tamatoas built for Oro was soon left to ruin, replaced by the lovely Protestant church in nearby Opoa village.

The *marae* was restored in the 1960s and, more recently, Tahiti Museum archaeologists discovered human bones under some of the structures, apparently the remains of sacrifices to Oro. The *marae's* huge *ahu,* or raised altar of stones for the gods, is more than 45m (150 ft.) long, 9m (30 ft.) wide, and 3.3m (11 ft.) tall. Flat rocks, used as backrests for the chiefs and priests, still stand in the courtyard in front of the ahu. The entire complex is in a coconut grove on the shore of the lagoon, opposite Te Ava Moa Pass, and legend says that bonfires on the *marae* guided canoes through the pass at night.

Taputapuatea is worth a visit not only for the *marae* itself, but also for the scenery here and along the way. The road skirts the southeast coast and follows Faaroa Bay to the mouth of the river, and then back out to the lagoon.

On the west coast, 15km (9 miles) from Uturoa, **Taninuu Marae** was also dedicated to Oro. Stones bordering the foundation of the ancient chief's home bear petroglyphs of turtles. This is a place of Christian history, too, since the lovely white Eglise Siloama is one of the oldest churches in French Polynesia.

> ### 🗨 Omai Scores a Hit in London
>
> Capt. James Cook discovered Raiatea during his first expedition to the islands in 1769. On his second voyage, in 1773, he took home with him a young Raiatean named Mai, or Omai to the English, who was living on Huahine at the time. Like Ahutoru, a Tahitian brought to Paris by the French explorer Antoine de Bougainville 2 years earlier, Omai was seen as living proof of philosopher Jean-Jacques Rousseau's theory of humans as "noble savages." The first Polynesian to visit England, Omai became an instant hit with London society and even met King George III and Queen Charlotte, who apparently were impressed with his grace and good manners. Great artists painted him, and writers spun many words about him (including some pornography). High society soon lost interest, however, and Cook brought Omai home in 1777 on his third and last great voyage of discovery.

Walking Around Uturoa

There was not even a village at Uturoa before the Rev. John Williams, who proselytized throughout the South Pacific, set up a London Missionary Society headquarters here in the 1820s. The settlement later became the Leeward Islands' administrative center and major trading post. A number of Chinese-owned stores still line Rue Centrale, Uturoa's main street, but the center of activity is the glistening **Gare Maritime,** a cruise-ship terminal built with money from France's economic restructuring fund. You can't miss this big Mediterranean-style building that houses restaurants, shops, the island's visitor information office, and public restrooms. Needless to say, the waterfront is busiest when a cruise ship arrives, and local women sell handicrafts and souvenirs in small thatch buildings next door known as *fares des mamas* (mamas' houses). Across the street is the **Marché Municipale (Municipal Market),** the local produce market. As in Papeete's market, stalls upstairs sell handicrafts.

You can make a walking tour of Uturoa by following the four-lane road northward from the town docks along the shore, past a park built on landfill to the public yacht marina on the northern edge of town. From the traffic circle, follow Rue Centrale back through the business district. Although Rue Centrale was once along the shoreline, landfill has left the street a block inland from the waterfront. Behind it on the mountain side, an expressway speeds vehicles past downtown (there's a traffic circle on each end).

SAFARI EXPEDITIONS & LAGOON EXCURSIONS

Safari Expeditions

Raiatea 4×4 (✆ **66.24.16**) will take you via four-wheel-drive jeep into Raiatea's interior, including a ride up to the plateau and into the ancient crater of Mount Temehani. The tour stops at Taputapuatea Marae before heading back to Uturoa.

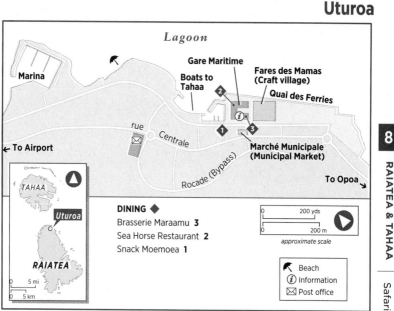

Uturoa

Lagoon

Marina

Gare Maritime

Boats to Tahaa

Fares des Mamas (Craft village)

Quai des Ferries

← To Airport

rue Centrale

Marché Municipale (Municipal Market)

Rocade (Bypass)

To Opoa →

TAHAA

Uturoa

RAIATEA

5 mi
5 km

DINING ◆
Brasserie Maraamu **3**
Sea Horse Restaurant **2**
Snack Moemoea **1**

0 ____ 200 yds
0 ____ 200 m
approximate scale

↖ Beach
ⓘ Information
✉ Post office

These expeditions are less thrill ride and more oriented to history and culture than those on Bora Bora. They cost 4,500CFP per person and reservations are required.

The mountains of Tahaa have much less dramatic scenery than on Raiatea, and the island lacks the historical importance of its big sister. Consequently, safari expeditions here include visits to **La Maison de Vanille** (**House of Vanilla**; ℂ **57.61.92**), where visitors are informed about the cultivation and uses of vanilla (Tahaa's major product), and to a black-pearl farm. Most tours follow a four-wheel-drive trail through the mountains from Patio, on the north coast, to Haamene, in the center of the island. These invariably include a refreshment stop high on a ridge with a view over Haamene Bay. I thoroughly enjoyed my expedition with **Dave's Tours** (ℂ **65.62.42**), which will pick you up at Uturoa.

Lagoon Excursions

An all-day excursion by boat is the best way to see firsthand the Raiatea-Tahaa lagoon, one of the most beautiful in French Polynesia. All trips include snorkeling, and most include picnics on the *motus* (tiny islets) sitting on the outer reef; unlike the mainland of Raiatea and Tahaa, they have beautiful white-sand beaches.

Marie and Tony Tucker (she's French; he's South African) of **West Coast Charters** (ℂ **66.45.39**) offer a complete tour around Tahaa with swimming, guided snorkeling over the magnificent coral gardens next to Le Taha'a Private Island & Spa, a shark-feeding stint, a pearl-farm visit, and lunch for 8,500CFP a person. Both Marie and Tony speak fluent English as well as French.

8

RAIATEA & TAHAA

Safari Expeditions & Lagoon Excursions

A Tahitian couple named Edwin and Jacqueline of **Tahaa Tours Excursions** (© **65.62.18** or 79.27.56) also speak English and French. They stop for lunch at the family homestead and charge 6,500CFP per person.

Andrew Brotherson of **Manava Excursions** (©/fax **66.28.26;** maraud@mail.pf) charges 7,800CFP per person for his all-day trips to Tahaa. They include visits to a vanilla plantation and pearl farm, a picnic on a *motu,* and snorkeling over the coral gardens. He also takes a boat trip up the Faaroa River and on to the Taputapuatea Marae, priced at 4,900CFP per person.

Another option is Bruno Fabre's **L'Excursion Bleue** (© **66.10.90;** www.tahaa. net), whose full-day trip around Tahaa costs 9,500CFP per person.

HIKING, SAILING & WATERSPORTS

Hiking

Just north of downtown Uturoa, the street to the left as you face the gendarmerie leads to a four-wheel-drive track ascending to the television towers atop 291m (970-ft.) **Papioi Hill.** (Be sure to close the gates, which keep the cows out of the station.) From the top, you can see Uturoa, the reef, and the islands Tahaa, Bora Bora, and Huahine.

Serious hikers can take another trail leading to the plateau atop Mount Temehani. The route begins with a four-wheel-drive track about 183m (600 ft.) south of the bridge at the head of Pufau Bay on the northwest coast. It is not marked, so a guide is advisable. The best here is Eric Pellé of **Raiatea Randonée** (© **66.49.54;** ktiki@mail.pf). Eric charges 5,000CFP for a half-day hike to three waterfalls or 7,800CFP for a full-day trek up Mount Temehani.

Sailing ★★★

As noted in "Sailing" under "The Active Traveler" (p. 68), **The Moorings** (© **800/535-7289** or 727/535-1446; www.moorings.com), **Sunsail Yacht Charters** (© **800/327-2276** or 207/253-5400 in the U.S., or 60.04.85 on Raiatea; www. sunsail.com), and **Tahiti Yacht Charter** (© **45.04.00;** www.tahitiyachtcharter. com) have bases at Apooiti Marina. All charter sailboats with or without crew. If a boat is available, it can be chartered on a daily basis. Arrangements for longer charters ordinarily should be made before leaving home.

Scuba Diving & Snorkeling

Raiatea may not have beaches, but the reef and large, clear lagoon are excellent for scuba diving and snorkeling.

SCUBA DIVING The best wreck dive site in all of French Polynesia is a descent of 15 to 27m (50–90 ft.) above the **S.S. *Norby,*** a three-masted Danish schooner that sunk off Uturoa in 1900. Its main deck has collapsed, so even novice divers can explore its topside. Intermediate divers can swim through the 150-foot-long hull and see a multitude of sea life, including black coral. Although the lagoon can be murky here, the *Norby* makes for good night diving. Nearby, novices can drift dive at Teavapiti Pass, where a coral wall just outside the reef attracts fish, rays, and gray, whitetip, and blacktip sharks. Other sites here, such as the **Little Caves** and the **Mounts of Céran,** both off Tahaa's eastern coast, are known for spectacular underwater scenery.

With bases at the Hawaiki Nui Hotel and at Apooiti Marina, Hubert Clot's **Hémisphère Sub Raiatea** (℗ **66.12.49;** www.raiatea-diving.com) takes divers on one-tank excursions for 6,500CFP.

SNORKELING You'll have to take a lagoon excursion (see above) to experience the best snorkeling near the offshore islands, especially over the coral gardens off Le Taha'a Private Island & Spa on Tahaa's northwestern coast. Or you can don mask, snorkel, and fins at the Hawaiki Nui Hotel (below), where the overwater bungalows are perched atop a clifflike reef face.

SHOPPING

The Gare Maritime on the waterfront has several black-pearl and other shops. The best is **My Flower** (℗ **66.19.19**), where owner Flora Hart carries not just floral arrangements, but also excellent tapa drawings and woodcarvings—some from the Marquesas Islands, others done in *hue papaa* wood, a specialty of Raiatea's own carvers.

Local vendors sell handicrafts on the second level of Uturoa's *Marché Municipale* **(Municipal Market),** opposite the Gare Maritime.

Other shops line Rue Centrale, the main street. In addition to black pearls and fine jewelry, **La Palme d'Or** (℗ **66.23.79**) carries vanilla extract, vanilla powder, and even vanilla soup prepared by Jeanne Chane—Raiatea's *préparatrice de vanilla.*

Roselyne Brotherson at Pension Manava (℗ **66.28.26;** see "Where to Stay," below) hand-paints colorful pareus. Stop in as you're driving south of Uturoa.

WHERE TO STAY

On Raiatea
EXPENSIVE

Hawaiki Nui Hotel ★ ✦ This hotel is of historical importance in its own right, for it was here in 1968 that Jay Carlisle, Don "Muk" McCallum, and the late Hugh Kelley built the world's first overwater bungalows (see "The Bali Hai Boys," p. 144). It was their way of compensating for the lack of a beach here. The hotel has changed names since its days as the Hotel Bali Hai Raiatea, but those bungalows still stand out on the edge of the reef; from them, you can climb right into the water and get the sensation of flying as you snorkel along the clifflike face. They are a bit small compared to newer models elsewhere, but they are among the least expensive overwater units in French Polynesia. The land-based bungalows, some of which have two units under their thatched roofs, are either along the seawall or in the gardens beyond. The least expensive units are hotel rooms, which have the same amenities as the bungalows and are air-conditioned. Opening to the pool and lagoon, and serving French fare and libations, the hotel's restaurant and bar are favorite local haunts. A Friday night Tahitian dance show and live music on Saturday evenings are pretty much Raiatea's nightlife. This is still Raiatea's best hotel and its only resort. The friendly and helpful staffers speak English as well as French.

B.P. 43, 98735 Uturoa, Raiatea (2km/1¼ miles south of town). ℂ **66.20.23.** Fax 66.20.20. www.
hawaikinuihotel.com. 32 units. 13,400CFP double; 15,000CFP–23,600CFP bungalow. AE, MC, V. **Amenities:** Restaurant; bar; babysitting; outdoor pool; watersports equipment; Wi-Fi (in central building;
1,800CFP/day). *In room:* A/C (except overwater bungalows), ceiling fan, TV, fridge, hair dryer.

MODERATE

Hotel Atiapiti   Virtually next-door to Taputapuatea Marae, this remote but pleasant little hotel sits beside the lagoon facing Te Ava Moa Pass and Huahine. There is
no natural beach here, but a row of coconut palms and sand behind a bulkhead
makes it seem like a beach resort. Five of the six bungalows directly face this vista.
All have stucco sides and wood-shingled roofs extending over front porches, some
strung with hammocks. Each beachfront unit has a separate bedroom with a king-
size bed, while each garden unit has a double bed and two singles in its main room,
plus a small second room with a single bed. Owner Marie-Claude Rajaud, who
speaks several languages including English, applies her cooking skills to fresh seafood in the French country–style restaurant. It's an excellent stop for lunch while
you're visiting the *marae,* but call ahead for reservations if you're not a guest here.
This is a relaxing place to stay if you don't mind being a long way from everything
except the *marae.*

B.P. 884, 98735 Uturoa, Raiatea (east coast, 30km/18 miles south of Uturoa). ℂ/fax **66.16.65.** www.
atiapiti.com. 7 units. 14,500CFP double. MC, V. **Amenities:** Restaurant; bar; bikes; watersports equipment. *In room:* Fan, TV, kitchen, no phone, Wi-Fi (free).

Raiatea Lodge Hotel   This plantation-style hotel sits in a large lawn across the
main road from the lagoon on the west coast. The restaurant and bar in the middle
of the two-story clapboard building open onto the swimming pool out in the front
yard. The rooms and one suite extend to each side. The medium-size units are identical, with pine floors, tables, desks, balconies with a view of the lagoon, and bathrooms with open, French-style showers. The suite adds two bedrooms. A pier gives
access to the lagoon for boating and swimming. The location is a bit remote, but the
setting is so peaceful that you can hear the birds singing outside your room.

B.P. 1147, 98735 Uturoa, Raiatea (west coast, 8km/5 miles from town). ℂ **60.20.00.** Fax 66.20.02. www.
raiateahotel.com. 16 units. 17,000CFP double; 31,600CFP suite. AE, DC, MC, V. **Amenities:** Restaurant;
bar; bikes; outdoor pool; smoke-free rooms. *In room:* A/C, TV, fridge, hair dryer, Wi-Fi (some rooms;
500CFP/hour).

INEXPENSIVE

Pension Manava   Roselyne and Andrew Brotherson rent two rooms in their
house and have four bungalows in their gardens, across the road from the lagoon.
The two rooms share a bathroom and the Brothersons' kitchen. The bungalows have
corrugated tin roofs, screened louvered windows, double and single beds, and large
bathrooms with hot-water showers. Two of them also have kitchens. Roselyne will
cook breakfast and provide free dinner transportation to town on request.

B.P. 559, 98735 Uturoa, Raiatea (6km/3½ miles south of town). ℂ **66.28.26.** www.manavapension.com.
6 units. 5,000CFP rooms; 8,500CFP bungalow. MC, V. *In room:* Ceiling fans, kitchen (in bungalows), no
phone, Wi-Fi (free).

Pension Tepua   There's a lot packed into this small parcel of land next to the
lagoon south of Uturoa, including a swimming pool and Raiatea's only dormitory,
making this pension a good choice for backpackers. Despite being shoehorned into

the property, the buildings are tropically attractive, with split bamboo siding and shingle roofs. The choice bungalow sits right beside the lagoon, with a view of Hotel Hawaiki Nui across a small bay. It's the only unit here with a television. Three other bungalows stand away from the lagoon near the pool. Another building houses four hotel-style rooms and the dormitory. The restaurant provides breakfast and lunch to guests and is open to the public at dinner. Dorm residents share toilets and showers, but all other units have private bathrooms with hot-water showers.

B.P. 1298, 98735 Uturoa, Raiatea (2.7km/1½ miles south of Uturoa). ⓒ **66.33.00.** Fax 66.32.00. www. pension-tepua.com. 8 units, 12 dormitory beds (shared bathrooms). 5,000CFP–7,500CFP double; 10,000CFP–13,000CFP bungalow; 2,500CFP dormitory bed. MC, V. **Amenities:** Restaurant; bar; outdoor pool. *In room:* TV (1 unit), no phone, Wi-Fi (500CFP/hour).

Sunset Beach Motel ★ 🍴   One of the best values in French Polynesia, this is not a motel, but rather a collection of cottages set in a coconut plantation on a peninsula sticking out west of the airport. The cottages sit in a row just off a palm-draped beach, the only one on Raiatea. The lagoon here is very shallow, but the beach enjoys a gorgeous westward view toward Bora Bora, and a long pier stretches to deep water (guests can paddle free kayaks from it). Of European construction rather than Polynesian, the bungalows are spacious, comfortably furnished, and have fully equipped kitchens and large covered verandas facing the sea. Part of the grove is set aside for campers, who have their own building with toilets, showers, and kitchen (bring your own tent). Manager Steve "Moana" Boubée speaks English. There is no restaurant here, but you can order breakfast in your bungalow.

B.P. 397, 98735 Uturoa, Raiatea (in Apooiti, 5km/3 miles northwest of Uturoa). ⓒ **66.33.47.** Fax 66.33.08. www.sunset-raiatea.pf. 22 units. 12,000CFP double bungalow; 1,100CFP per person camping. MC, V. **Amenities:** Bikes; watersports equipment; Wi-Fi (500CFP/hour). *In room:* Ceiling fan, TV, kitchen, no phone.

On Tahaa
EXPENSIVE

Hotel La Pirogue ★★   Beside a white-sand beach and shallow lagoon on Motu Porou, a small reef islet off Hipu village on Tahaa's northeastern coast, this is the domain of chef Giuliano Tognetti and his wife, Séverine, who hail from the Italian side of Switzerland. Consequently, the food is first-rate, including thin-crust pizzas for lunch. All of the buildings have natural thatched roofs. Four of the guest bungalows, including a suite, sit beside the beach and have platforms extending out over the sand, where you can sit and take in the sunsets behind Tahaa and Bora Bora off in the distance. Each unit also has a mosquito net over its king-size bed, and its front porch is furnished with chaise loungers. Separate buildings hold the main dining room and a tappanyaki-style Japanese restaurant. Giuliano and Séverine speak French, English, and Italian.

B.P. 668, 98735 Uturoa, Raiatea (on Motu Porou). ⓒ **60.81.45.** Fax 60.81.46. www.hotel-la-pirogue. com. 8 units. 26,000CFP–42,000CFP bungalow. AE, MC, V. **Amenities:** 2 restaurants; bar; watersports equipment. *In room:* Ceiling fan, TV, hair dryer, minibar, Wi-Fi (1,600CFP/stay).

Le Taha'a Private Island & Spa ★★★   When I was traveling by yacht back in the 1970s, we anchored near Motu Tautau, an islet on the reef off Tahaa's west coast, and went ashore to get an unsurpassed view of Bora Bora from its outer edge. There was nothing on Tautau then except palm trees, a brackish lake, and several million mosquitoes. Since 2002 the "mossies" have mostly resided on the sea side of the *motu*, while one of French Polynesia's most luxurious and architecturally creative resorts has occupied the lagoon shoreline. A 40-minute boat ride from the Raiatea airport, or 15 minutes by helicopter from Bora Bora, this Relais & Châteaux–affiliated hotel sports some of French Polynesia's most tastefully decorated bungalows. Most stand out over the hip-deep lagoon, where their large decks have privacy fences screening covered sitting areas under thatched roofs. Most face hilly Tahaa, but a few have views of Bora Bora through a shallow reef pass between Tautau and its neighboring *motu*. Ashore beside the brilliant white-sand beach, 10 villa suites are even larger and more private. The villas all have living rooms, bedrooms, and courtyards with plunge pools hidden behind high rock walls. Two Royal Villas enlarge on them by adding a separate bungalow within their compounds, 24-hour butler service, and private shows and barbecues on the beach.

At the center of it all is a stunning, two-story central building, where stairs built in a tree lead up to the main bar and casual gourmet restaurant with both indoor and outdoor tables, all with a view. The most romantic tables sit by themselves on extensions from the terrace. Or you can retire to the air-conditioned, fine-dining restaurant. The resort's infinity pool, a lunchtime restaurant and bar, full-service spa, and air-conditioned gym are on one end of the property, thus removing most daytime activities from the vicinity of the bungalows. There's much to do here, from snorkeling to safari expeditions on Tahaa. This is a marvelous place to chill after the rigors of Bora Bora.

B.P. 67, 98733 Patio, Tahaa (on Motu Tautau). ⓒ **800/657-3275** or 60.84.00. Fax 60.84.01. www. letahaa.com. 60 units. 70,000CFP–290,000CFP bungalow. AE, DC, MC, V. **Amenities:** 2 restaurants; 2 bars; babysitting; concierge; health club; Jacuzzi; outdoor pool; room service; sauna; smoke-free rooms; spa; tennis court; watersports equipment. *In room:* A/C, ceiling fan, TV, hair dryer, minibar, Wi-Fi (500CFP/hour).

Tiare Breeze ★★ This hillside bungalow offers the luxuries and privacy that attract star couples like Goldie Hawn and Kurt Russell, who recently got away from it all here. Built of native materials and topped with thatch, the bungalow opens to a large deck with a terrific view of Haamene Bay. There is no restaurant here but fruit and freshly baked pastries are delivered each morning, and the bungalow has a fully equipped kitchen. Guests can swim and snorkel from The Pontoon, a thatch-roof lounge sitting over the lagoon at the end of a long pier. Hosts Tama and Virginie Castagnoli make sure all their guests, rich and famous or not, feel at home.

B.P. 178, 98734 Haamene, Tahaa. ⓒ **65.62.26** or 73.83.97. www.tiarebreeze.com. 1 unit. 39,500CFP–43,500CFP bungalow. Rates include breakfast. AE, MC, V. **Amenities:** Bikes; watersports equipment. *In room:* Ceiling fan, TV (on request), hair dryer, kitchen, no phone, Wi-Fi (free).

Vahine Island In a coconut grove on flat Motu Tuuvahine, off Tahaa's northeastern coast, this intimate little hotel offers bungalows both beside a brilliant white-sand beach and built out over a shallow lagoon beautifully speckled with coral heads. The three thatched-roof overwater units are the pick, since they are larger and more private than the beachside units—and they have a stunning view of Bora Bora on the far horizon. The bungalows ashore have shingle roofs, but all are decorated in traditional Polynesian style, with native lumber and bamboo trim. Each sports a porch in front and a shower-only bathroom to the rear. The dining room serves good

French fare with island touches. There's a guest lounge with a collection of books and videos in both English and French.

B.P. 510, 98735 Uturoa, Raiatea (on Motu Tuuvahine). *Ⓒ* **65.67.38.** Fax 65.67.70. www.vahine-island.com. 9 units. 46,000CFP–65,000CFP double. AE, DC, MC, V. **Amenities:** Restaurant; bar; watersports equipment. *In room:* Ceiling fan, TV/DVD (overwater units only), hair dryer, minibar, Wi-Fi (500CFP/hour).

INEXPENSIVE

L'Hibiscus   This lively little pension beside Haamene Bay is the domain of Léo Morou, a bearded Frenchman who settled here more than 30 years ago, and his charming Tahitian wife, Lolita. I stayed here in the early 1990s when they had three simple bungalows sharing communal showers and toilets. The Morous have added four government-issued bungalows, each with its own bathroom as well as front porch. The bungalows climb a hill across the road from a 200-seat waterside restaurant and bar, a long pier, and moorings out in the bay, which attract dozens of yachties for a bit of libation and a meal. Parties, music, and Tahitian dance shows have been known to extend well into the night. The lagoon is a protected breeding area for sea turtles, thanks to Léo's non-profit **Foundation Hibiscus Tahaa.**

B.P. 184, 98734 Haamene, Tahaa (north shore of Haamene Bay). *Ⓒ* **65.61.06.** Fax 65.65.65. www.hibiscustahaa.com. 7 units (all with bathroom). 10,500CFP double. MC, V. **Amenities:** Restaurant; bar; Internet (free); watersports equipment. *In room:* Ceiling fan, TV, fridge, no phone.

WHERE TO DINE

On Raiatea

Les roulottes, Raiatea's inexpensive meal wagons, congregate after dark near the Gare Maritime in the middle of Uturoa's business district, and in the seaside park north of the business district. They stay open past midnight on Friday and Saturday. See "Don't Miss *Les Roulottes*" (p. 125) for details.

An inexpensive daytime option is **Snack Hai Ling** (*Ⓒ* **66.10.11**), a walk-up snack bar in the public square opposite the Gare Maritime. It has the usual *roulotte* menu of sandwiches, burgers, steaks, and Chinese dishes.

Brasserie Maraamu *✦* CHINESE/TAHITIAN   Before it moved into the Gare Maritime, this restaurant occupied a waterfront shack and was widely known for its simple but good Chinese dishes, *poisson cru,* and fried chicken and steaks served with french fries. The chow is still good, as witnessed by the number of local office workers who head here for lunch. Local business types like to hang out here over strong cups of morning coffee served French-style in soup bowls (the better to dunk your baguette).

In Gare Maritime, Uturoa waterfront. *Ⓒ* **66.46.64.** Breakfast 800CFP–1,200CFP; main courses 900CFP–1,750CFP. MC, V. Mon–Fri 7am–2pm and 6:30–9pm; Sat 10am–2pm.

Le Voile d'Or Bar Restaurant ★ FRENCH   Behind the Raiatea Yacht Club at Apooiti Marina, this little restaurant enjoys a spectacular view of Tahaa and Bora Bora, making it a terrific place for a sunset drink. It's owned by Pascal and Carole Hauteville-Longet, who moved from France and took it over in 2003. Pascal waits the tables while Carole does the cooking. Most of her dishes are traditional French but she also grills fresh fish plainly, making this one of Raiatea's healthiest places to dine. Carole speaks English, Pascal does not.

At Apooiti Marina. ✆ **66.12.97.** www.la-voile-d-or.com. Reservations accepted. Main courses 1,850CFP– 2,250CFP. MC, V. Daily 7am–8pm.

Restaurant Club House FRENCH   Under a large, Polynesian-style shingle roof, this restaurant at the entry to Apooiti Marina is as close to a fine-dining setting as you will find on Raiatea. You can also have a drink or dine at outdoor tables near the multitude of yachts moored here. The limited menu features seafood and steaks, both with and without French sauces. I enjoyed "tuna in the middle"—a slice of tuna delicately cooked in paper-thin crust with lemon sauce. You can also order hamburgers and cheeseburgers here.

At Apooiti Marina. ✆ **66.11.66.** Reservations accepted. Burgers 1,200CFP–1,300CFP; main courses 1,790CFP–2,900CFP. MC, V. Tues–Sun 10am–2pm and 5:30–9pm (bar later).

Sea Horse Restaurant CHINESE   Proprietor Alphonse Léogite, scion of a major Raiatea family, lived in the United States for 15 years before returning home and opening this excellent establishment in the Gare Maritime. You can dine outside on the plaza or inside, where tropical furniture, potted plants, and linen tablecloths set a refined but relaxed ambience for very good Chinese cuisine. Most items on the menu will be familiar, such as sautéed beef with peanut sauce. Check the specials board for the day's fish selections.

In Gare Maritime, Uturoa waterfront. ✆ **66.16.34.** Reservations recommended on weekend evenings. Main courses 900CFP–2,100CFP. MC, V. Mon–Fri 9:30am–2pm and 5:30–10pm; Sat 9:30am–2:30pm and 6–10pm.

Snack Moemoea 🐟 SNACKS/FRENCH/CHINESE   Predating the Gare Maritime by many years, this old corner storefront has tables both outside on the sidewalk and inside on the ground floor or on a mezzanine platform. It's another good place for breakfast, from croissants to omelets. The crepes are very good anytime. The lunch menu includes *casse-croûte* sandwiches, fine hamburgers, grilled fish and steaks, and Raiatea's best *poisson cru*. I love to slake my thirst here with an ice-cold coconut.

Waterfront, Uturoa (in Toporo Building). ✆ **66.39.84.** Breakfast 400CFP–1,050CFP; burgers and sandwiches 300CFP–1,200CFP; main courses 1,450CFP–1,800CFP. MC, V (2,000CFP minimum). Mon–Fri 6am–5pm; Sat 6am–2pm.

On Tahaa

Chez Louise TAHITIAN   This local restaurant beside the lagoon in Tiva village, on Tahaa's west coast, is a popular stop for cruise-ship passengers, and it's close enough to Le Taha'a Private Island & Spa that its guests come here for lunch or dinner, too (call for dinner pickup at Tapuamu wharf). The *ma'a Tahiti* fare is first-rate, as are lobster and other fresh seafood items. There's a gorgeous view of Bora Bora from here, so come in time for a sunset drink.

Tiva village, lagoonside. ✆ **71.23.06.** Reservations required. Full meals 3,500CFP–5,000CFP. MC, V. Daily 8am–10pm.

Restaurant Tahaa Maitai ★ FRENCH   Chef Bruno François cooks excellent French fare at his restaurant on the waterfront in Haamene village, at the head of the bay. He also serves salads and burgers, making this the best stop for lunch on a tour of Tahaa. The crab salad is excellent, as is Bruno's mahi-mahi in vanilla sauce. His fixed-priced tourist menu includes a cocktail and three courses. The nighttime clientele is mostly local, but yachties often tie their dinghies to the dock out front.

Haamene village, on the waterfront. 🕿**65.70.85.** Reservations recommended. Burgers 1,350CFP; main courses 1,750CFP–2,470CFP; tourist menu 4,150CFP. MC, V. Tues–Fri 11:30am–2:30pm and 6:45–10pm; Sat 6:45–10pm; Sun 11:30am–2:30pm.

BORA BORA

ecause of its fame and extraordinary beauty, little Bora Bora is a playground for the well-to-do, occasionally the famous, and honeymooners blowing a wad. As French Polynesia's tourist magnet, it has more overwater bungalows per capita than any other island, their piers reaching out like tentacles into its gorgeous lagoon.

Most of the bungalows were built in the past dozen years or so, the result of the local government's decision to rapidly expand the territory's tourism infrastructure to offset the loss of income from France's defunct nuclear weapons program. The tax advantages were so great that developers could construct a new resort virtually for free, provided they operated it for 5 years. But along with the rest of the world, Bora Bora saw its economic bottom begin to fall out in 2008. Three of the island's stalwart resorts—Hotel Bora Bora, Bora Bora Lagoon Resort, and the Club Med—are now closed. Others may follow.

The building boom also saw Bora Bora's population rapidly expand. With income from construction and hotel jobs, the locals built houses, often in tightly-packed beachside neighborhoods, and bought luxury items such as pleasure boats. The big metal wheels of boat lifts standing in the lagoon mar the vista at **Matira Beach,** one of French Polynesia's most magnificent. Now that many of those jobs have disappeared, some neighborhoods are beginning to look rundown, including the hotel district on the island's southern end.

On the other hand, the recent developments have not taken away Bora Bora's awesome beauty. Some of us who remember it in a more pristine time often bemoan that development has ruined it. But I suspect you will be blown away by Bora Bora just as I was when I spent a week camping here in the 1970s.

Lying 230km (143 miles) northwest of Tahiti, Bora Bora is a middle-aged island consisting of a high center completely surrounded by a lagoon enclosed by coral reef. It has a gorgeous combination of sand-fringed *motus* (small islets) sitting on the outer reef enclosing the multi-hued lagoon, which cuts deep bays into the high central island. Towering over it all is Bora Bora's trademark, the basaltic tombstone known as **Mount Otemanu** (725m/2,379 ft.). Next to it is the more normally rounded **Mount Pahia** (660m/2,165 ft.).

Bora Bora is so small that the road around it covers only 32km (19 miles) from start to finish.

GETTING AROUND BORA BORA

There is no regularly scheduled public transportation system on Bora Bora. Buses do take passengers from Vaitape to the Matira hotel district on cruise-ship days, though, and anyone can catch a ride for 500CFP.

Some hotels on the main island shuttle their guests to Vaitape and back once or twice a day, but the frequency can vary depending on how many guests they have.

Arriving & Getting to Your Hotel

Bora Bora's airport is on **Motu Mute,** the long, flat island on the northwestern edge of the barrier reef. U.S. marines built the airstrip during World War II when Bora Bora was a major refueling stop on the America-to-Australia supply line.

You will see the lagoon close up soon after landing because all passengers are ferried across it from the airport. Some resorts send boats to pick up their guests (be sure to tell them your flight number when making your reservations). The major resorts have welcome desks in the terminal to greet you and steer you to the correct boat. It can be a tad confusing out on the dock, where baggage is unloaded. You do not want to end up on the wrong *motu,* so pay attention, and ask someone if you are not sure which boat is yours.

If your hotel does not send a boat, you will take Air Tahiti's launch to **Vaitape,** the only village and the center of most commerce. Buses will take you from Vaitape to your hotel. Get in the bus displaying the name of your hotel, or ask the driver if you are not sure. Bus fare from Vaitape to the Matira Point hotel district is 500CFP.

See "Getting to Tahiti & French Polynesia" and "Getting Around Tahiti & French Polynesia," in chapter 3, for more information.

By Rental Car, Scooter & Bicycle

Avis (© **800/331-1212** or 41.93.93; www.avis.com) is the only international firm here. It has an office at Vaitape wharf. Rates start at 13,500CFP a day for the smallest air-conditioned models, including unlimited kilometers and insurance. Avis also rents open-air Bugsters for about 14,000CFP for 4 hours. Bicycles cost about 1,800CFP for half a day.

The 32km (19 miles) of road around Bora Bora are paved, but always drive or ride slowly and carefully, and be on the lookout for pigs, chickens, pedestrians, and especially dogs.

Impressions

I saw it first from an airplane. On the horizon there was a speck that became a tall, blunt mountain with cliffs dropping sheer into the sea. And about the base of the mountain, narrow fingers of land shot out, forming magnificent bays, while about the whole was thrown a *coral ring of absolute perfection. . . . That was Bora Bora from aloft. When you stepped upon it the dream expanded.*

—James A. Michener, *Return to Paradise,* 1951

By Taxi

No taxis patrol Bora Bora looking for passengers, but several firms have transport licenses, which means they can come get you if someone calls. The hotel desks and restaurants will do that for you, or you can phone **Taxi Simplet** (© 79.19.31), **Léon** (© 70.69.16), **Otemanu Tours** (© 67.70.49), **Jacques Isnard** (© 67.72.25), or **Dino's Land & Water Taxi** (© 79.29.65). Fares between Vaitape and the Matira Point hotel district are at least 1,500CFP from 6am to 7pm and 3,000CFP from 7pm to 6am. A ride between Vaitape and Anau village costs 3,000CFP during the day, 5,000CFP at night. (Add up your expected fares; it may be more economical to rent a vehicle.) The taxis aren't metered, so make sure you and the driver agree on a fare before setting out.

If you're staying at a resort on an islet and don't want to wait for the next boat shuttle, you can call **Dino's Land & Water Taxi** (© 79.29.65), **Manu Taxiboat** (© 79.11.62 or 67.72.04), or **Taxi Motu** (© 67.60.61). The ride to the main island costs about 3,000CFP.

[FastFACTS] BORA BORA

The following facts apply specifically to Bora Bora. For more information, see "Fast Facts: Tahiti & French Polynesia," in chapter 13.

Currency Exchange Banque de Tahiti, Banque Socredo, and **Banque de Polynésie** have branches with ATMs in Vaitape.

Drugstores Pharmacie de Bora Bora, north of the small boat harbor in Vaitape (© 67.70.30), is open Monday through Saturday from 8am to 6pm, Sunday and holidays from 9 to 11am.

Emergencies & Police The **emergency police** phone number is © **17.** The **gendarmerie** (© 67.70.58) is opposite the Vaitape harbor.

Healthcare The island's **infirmary** is in Vaitape (© 67.70.77), as is **Dr. Azad Roussanaly** (© 67.77.95).

Internet Access Aloe Cafe, in the Centre Commercial Le Pahia just north of the Vaitape wharf (© 67.78.88), has Wi-Fi and computer terminals with Skype, either of which costs 500CFP for 20 minutes of online time. See "Where to Dine," later in this chapter. The post office has ManaSpot Wi-Fi.

Mail The Vaitape post office is open Monday through Thursday from 7:15am to 3:15pm, Friday from 7:15am to 2:15pm, and Saturday from 8 to 10am.

Taxes Bora Bora's municipal government adds 100CFP to 150CFP per night to your hotel bill.

Visitor Information The **Bora Bora Comité du Tourisme,** B.P. 144, Vaitape, Bora Bora (© **73.54.22;** www.borabora-tourisme. com), has a visitor center in Fare Manihini, the octagon-shaped building on the Vaitape wharf. Open Monday to Friday from 9am to noon and 1 to 4pm, Saturday from 9am to noon, and on cruise-ship days from 8am to 4pm.

Water Bora Bora has a huge desalinization plant, so the tap water is safe to drink. Most local residents still drink bottled water, available at all groceries.

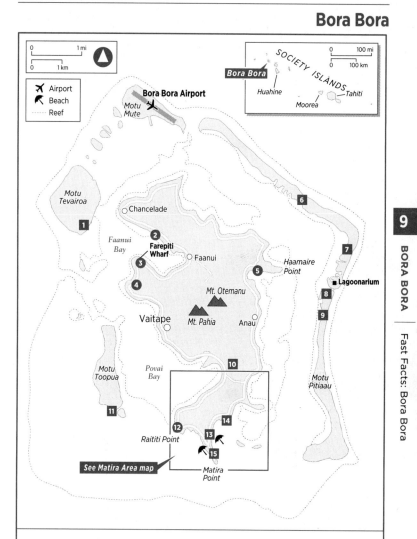

ACCOMMODATIONS ■

Chez Nono **15**

Bora Bora Pearl Beach Resort **1**

Four Seasons Resort Bora Bora **6**

Hilton Bora Bora Nui Resort & Spa **11**

Hotel Matira **15**

InterContinental Le Moana Resort **15**

InterContinental Resort and Thalasso
Spa Bora Bora **9**

Le Maitai Polynesia
Bora Bora **13**

Le Meridien Bora Bora **8**

Pension Robert et Tina **15**

Rohutu Fare Lodge **10**

Sofitel Bora Bora Marara Beach
Resort and Private Island **14**

St. Regis Resort Bora Bora **7**

Village Temanuata **13**

ATTRACTIONS ●

Aehautai Marae **5**

Marotetini Marae **3**

Old Hotel Bora Bora
Site **12**

U.S. guns **4**

U.S. wharf **2**

EXPLORING BORA BORA: THE CIRCLE ISLAND TOUR

Most of Bora Bora's residents live on the coastal strip ringing the island. The paved round-island road skirts the shoreline and runs in and out of the bays. Except for three hills on the east coast, it is flat all the way around. Because the road is only 32km (19 miles) long, many visitors see it by bicycle (give yourself a full day), scooter, or car.

Some of the sights mentioned below may not be easy to find, however, so consider taking a guided tour around the island. **Otemanu Tours** (✆ **67.70.49;** otemanu. tours@mail.pf) still uses one of the traditional, open-air *le truck* vehicles, which adds an extra dimension to its trips, but be sure your tour is in *le truck* and not an air-conditioned bus. The cost is about 4,000CFP per person; you can book at any hotel activities desk.

Vaitape

Either driving or biking, you should begin at the small boat harbor in **Vaitape,** Bora Bora's only town and its administrative center. The harbor is the center of attention in Vaitape, as Air Tahiti, the cruise ships, and the shuttle boats from the resorts on Motu Toopua (the large islet offshore) land their passengers here. The island's visitor information center and women's handicrafts center are in the large building beside the harbor. Vaitape's only street is lined with boutiques, black-pearl shops, and other establishments designed to wrench money from your pockets. The post office is to the right as you face the mountains, but most business activity takes place north of the harbor, especially at the modern Centre Commercial La Pahia.

In the parking lot, opposite the gendarmerie, is a monument to famed French socialite, author, and yachtsman **Alain Gerbault,** who single-handedly skippered his boat *Firecrest* around the world between 1923 and 1929, stopping for an extended period in French Polynesia. Gerbault returned to French Polynesia in 1933 and championed the cause of the islanders against the colonial bureaucracy. He also introduced soccer to the locals. Gerbault was interned on Moorea at the outbreak of World War II in Europe because he favored the pro-Nazi Vichy government in Paris, while French Polynesians sided with Gen. Charles de Gaulle and the Free French. He was released on the condition he leave the territory. He sailed to Indonesia, where he died on Timor in 1941. Six years later, the French navy returned his ashes to Bora Bora, his favorite island.

From the harbor, walk northward through Vaitape, taking in its large Christian church, which stands at the base of soaring Mount Pahia. When you've seen enough of this Polynesian village, turn south and head counterclockwise around the island.

Matira Beach ★★★

After following the shore of semicircular Povai Bay, the road climbs the small head-land, where a huge banyan tree marks the entrance to the former Hotel Bora Bora on **Raititi Point,** and then follows curving **Matira Beach,** one of French Polynesia's finest. Some of the island's best snorkeling is in the shallow, sand-bottom lagoon off these powdery white sands. People have homes on both sides of the road, and the metal boat lifts they have placed in the lagoon mar this otherwise extraordinary scene.

The road follows the beach and then curves sharply to the left at the south end of the island. Watch here for a narrow paved road to the right. This leads to **Matira Point,** the sandy, coconut-studded, heavily populated peninsula extending from Bora Bora's south end. Down this track about 46m (150 ft.) is a **public beach** on the west side of the peninsula, opposite the InterContinental Le Moana Resort. The lagoon is shallow all the way out to the reef at this point, but the bottom is smooth and sandy. When I first came to Bora Bora in 1977, I camped for a week on Matira Point; the InterContinental Le Moana Resort is now just one of many structures in what was then a virtually deserted coconut grove completely surrounded by unspoiled beach.

The East Coast

After rounding the point, you'll pass through the island's busy hotel-and-restaurant district. This has become another densely populated area, and in the absence of zoning or planning laws, you see everything from fine homes to a junk yard along the beach.

The road continues north and climbs a hill above the former Club Med, on Faaopore Bay. A steep trail begins at a set of steps on the mountain side of the road and goes up to a lookout over the bay. Another trail cuts off to the right on the north side of the hill and goes to the **Aehautai Marae,** one of several old temples on Bora Bora. This particular one has a great view of Mount Otemanu and the blue outlines of Raiatea and Tahaa islands beyond the *motu* on the reef.

You will go through a long stretch of more homes and coconut plantations before entering **Anau,** a Polynesian village with a large church, a general store, and tin-roof houses crouched along the road. Anau is the landing point for boats going to and from Le Meridien Bora Bora and the Inter-Continental Resort and Thalasso Spa Bora Bora, whose overwater bungalows you will see out on Motu Pitiaau. (Also on the *motus,* the St. Regis Resort Bora Bora and the Four Seasons Resort Bora Bora take their guests directly to Vaitape.)

The road goes over two hills at Point Haamaire, the main island's easternmost extremity, about 4km (2½ miles) north of Anau village. Between the two hills on the lagoon side of the road stands **Aehautai Marae,** a restored temple. Out on the point is **Taharuu Marae,** which has a great view of the lagoon. The Americans installed naval guns in the hills above the point during World War II.

The North & West Coasts

On the deserted northeast coast, you will ride through several miles of coconut plantations pockmarked by thousands of holes made by *tupas* (land crabs). Across the lagoon are Motu Mute and the airport.

> ### A Killer View
>
> The round-island road curves along the shore of **Povai Bay,** where Mount Otemanu and Mount Pahia tower over you. Take your time along this bay; the views here are the best on Bora Bora. When you reach **Bloody Mary's Restaurant & Bar,** go out on the pier for a killer view back across the water at Mount Otemanu.

On the west coast, **Faanui Bay** was used during World War II as an Allied naval base. It's not marked, but the U.S. Navy's Seabees built the concrete wharf on the north shore as a seaplane ramp. Just beyond Farepiti Wharf, the main cargo shipping dock at the point on the southern entrance to Faanui Bay, is the restored **Marotetini Marae,** which in pre-European days was dedicated to navigators. In his novel *Hawaii,* James Michener had his fictional Polynesians leave this point to discover and settle the Hawaiian Islands. Nearby are tombs in which members of Bora Bora's former royal family are buried. If you look offshore at this point, you'll see the only pass into the lagoon. The remains of two **U.S. guns** that guarded it stand on the hill above, but are best visited on a safari tour (see "Safari Expeditions," below).

Entering Vaitape, **Magasin Chin Lee** is a major gathering place for local residents. It's a good place to soak up some island culture while quenching your thirst with a cold bottle of Eau Royale.

SAFARI EXPEDITIONS & LAGOON EXCURSIONS

Safari Expeditions ★

The regular tours stick to the shoreline, but safari expeditions venture into the hills in four-wheel-drive vehicles for panoramic views and visits to the old U.S. Navy gun sites. Compared to safari expeditions on Moorea, Huahine, and Tahaa, which emphasize local culture as well as scenery, here they are more like scenic thrill rides. The journey can be rough, so I do not recommend it for children, the elderly, or anyone prone to carsickness. The mountain roads are mere ruts in places, so you could become stuck if it has been raining.

The most comfortable choice is **Vavau Adventures** (℡ **72.01.21;** temana689@ mail.pf), which has morning and afternoon expeditions around the island and up into the mountains in an air-conditioned Land Rover. These tours also emphasize Bora Bora's history, culture, flora, and fauna, and they stop at the World War II guns and at a fish farm, where you will see tropical species being raised to restock the magnificent lagoon. They cost 7,600CFP per person.

The largest operator is the Levard family's **Tupuna Four-Wheel-Drive Expeditions** (℡ **67.75.06**), which uses open-air vehicles. On this tour, your last stop will be at the Farm, the Levards' black-pearl operation (see "Shopping," below).

Lagoon Excursions & Shark-Feeding ★★★

Bora Bora has one of the world's most beautiful lagoons, and getting out on it, snorkeling and swimming in it, and visiting the islands on its outer edge are absolute musts. Although it's a widespread activity now, this is where **shark-feeding** began. That is, your guide feeds reef sharks while you watch from a reasonably safe distance. Some conservationists have criticized shark-feeding, but it is guaranteed to leave an indelible imprint on your memory.

Any hotel activities desk can book you on an all-day excursion with one of several operators. My longtime favorite is Nono Levard's **Teremoana Tours** (℡ **67.71.38**), which everyone here calls Nono's Tours. **Moana Adventure Tours** (℡ **67.62.41;** www.moanatours.com) is another long-time operator. You spend the day going around the lagoon in a speedy outrigger canoe. Depending on the weather, you'll go

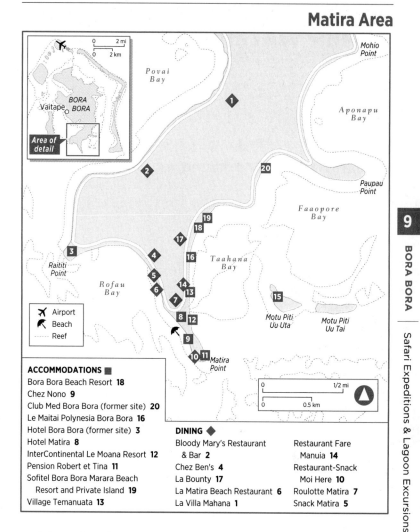

ACCOMMODATIONS ■

Bora Bora Beach Resort **18**
Chez Nono **9**
Club Med Bora Bora (former site) **20**
Le Maitai Polynesia Bora Bora **16**
Hotel Bora Bora (former site) **3**
Hotel Matira **8**
InterContinental Le Moana Resort **12**
Pension Robert et Tina **11**
Sofitel Bora Bora Marara Beach
  Resort and Private Island **19**
Village Temanuata **13**

DINING ◆

Bloody Mary's Restaurant
  & Bar **2**
Chez Ben's **4**
La Bounty **17**
La Matira Beach Restaurant **6**
La Villa Mahana **1**

Restaurant Fare
  Manuia **14**
Restaurant-Snack
  Moi Here **10**
Roulotte Matira **7**
Snack Matira **5**

snorkeling and watch a shark-feeding demonstration in the morning. You'll stop on a *motu* for swimming and a picnic lunch, and then pet stingrays on your way home in the afternoon. Expect to pay about 9,000CFP for a full-day outing.

Even if your all-day excursion doesn't feature it, you can still visit the **Bora Bora Lagoonarium** (✆ **67.71.34**), a fenced-in underwater area near Le Meridien Bora Bora. Here you can swim with (and maybe even ride) manta rays and observe sharks (which are on the other side of the fence here). The Lagoonarium has its own morning tour with shark-feeding and lunch on the *motu*, plus an afternoon excursion with fish-watching. The morning excursion costs about 8,000CFP, the afternoon tour is 6,600CFP, or you can do both for 12,000CFP.

SCUBA DIVING, SNORKELING & OTHER WATERSPORTS

Every hotel has some water toys for its guests to use, and hotel activities desks can arrange fishing, diving, and other watersports. You can go water-skiing, sail on Hobie Cats, paddle canoes, and get a bird's-eye view of the lagoon while hanging below a parasail.

Matira Jet Tours (② **77.63.63**) offers lagoon excursions by jet ski as well as inland tours via all-terrain vehicles. Many of the people you'll see riding above the lagoon are with **Bora Bora Parasail** (② **78.27.10**).

Scuba Diving & Snorkeling ★★

While snorkeling off the reef face at the Hotel Bora Bora late one afternoon, I was startled to see a large manta ray gliding by virtually overhead, seemingly just a few feet away. It's one of my most indelible Bora Bora moments. You may have one, too, for both divers and snorkelers can swim among the manta rays, eagle rays, sharks, and some 1,000 species of colorful tropical fish in the lagoon here.

One of the most popular snorkeling sites is over the coral gardens in and near the **Bora Bora Lagoonarium** (see "Lagoon Excursions & Shark-Feeding," above). Even novice divers can explore the site known as Anau, in the lagoon between there and Point Haamaire, where manta rays frequently hang out. Divers and snorkelers also share the lagoon off the eastern side of Motu Toopua and the islet next to it, Motu Toopua Iti.

The most easily accessible dive site outside the reef is off Motu Tapu, the islet just south of Teavanui Pass. Two others—the White Valley, off the airport, and Tupitipiti, on the reef's southeastern corner—both require lengthy boat rides and can experience strong currents.

Among the best snorkeling spots are the aptly named "Aquarium," off the southern end of Motu Pitiaau, and around Motu Piti Uuuta, home of the Sofitel Motu. These require boat transportation, but you can walk to the outer reef from the southern tip of Point Matira, thus increasing your chances of seeing more fish than if you snorkel off Matira Beach south of the Hotel Bora Bora. Best of all, in my opinion, are the reef faces, above which sit the Hotel Bora Bora's overwater bungalows.

Every resort has snorkeling gear for its guests as well as a scuba-diving program. They all charge about 6,500CFP for 30-minute introductory courses or a one-tank lagoon dive. Open-water and night dives cost about 9,000CFP.

The island's largest dive operator is **Nemo World Bora Diving** (② **67.71.84** or **67.77.85**; www.boradiving.com), which has two bases: Nemo World Bora Bora near

---

◉ Like Flying Underwater

Shining with every hue on the blue end of the color spectrum, Bora Bora's watery playground is one of my favorite snorkeling spots. Hotel Bora Bora has bungalows sitting right on the edge of a reef that drops precipitously to dark depths. I experience the exhilaration of flying when I drift out over that underwater cliff. If you're lucky, a manta ray will gracefully glide by.

the Sofitel Bora Bora Marara Resort, and Bora Bora Diving Cener near the former Hotel Bora Bora. Two-tank dives cost about 14,000CFP. Nondivers can walk on the bottom while wearing a diving helmet with Nemo's Aqua Safari (© **67.71.84**).

SHOPPING

Most shopping here is in Vaitape, where you'll find several souvenir shops and upscale black-pearl dealers. Other boutiques and shops are scattered along the main road, especially in the Matira hotel district.

Bora Bora I Te Fanau Tahi   Local artisans display their wares in the large hall at the wharf. It's the least expensive place to shop for straw hats, *pareus*, and other handicrafts items. Open Monday to Friday 8:30am to 4pm, and on the weekend when cruise ships are in port. Vaitape, at the small boat landing. No phone.

Boutique Bora Bora   Catering to the cruise ship crowd, this store has more T-shirts and *pareus* than most others, plus it sells woodcarvings, books, curios, calendars, and a few black pearls. It's a good place to stock up on Hinano beer glasses. Open daily from 9am to 5:30pm. Vaitape, opposite the ferry wharf. © 67.79.72.

Boutique Gauguin   In a white house 1.5km (1 mile) north of Hotel Bora Bora, Boutique Gauguin is one of the larger stores here, offering a selection of handicrafts, clothing, black pearls, and curios. This is the best place on Bora Bora to shop for prints of Paul Gauguin's paintings. Some of the *pareus* here are particularly artistic. Open daily from 8am to 5:30pm. Povai Bay. © 67.76.67.

The Farm   You need to know about the Farm, since it's owned by the Levard family and thus you are likely to be deposited here after going on one of their safari excursions. They will show you how pearls are grown, harvested, graded, and turned into jewelry. The final products are for sale in the **Bora Pearl Company,** the showroom here. It's worth a visit here to see how it's all done. Open daily from 9am to 6pm. Raititi Point, near Hotel Bora Bora. © 70.06.65.

Gallerie d'Art Pakalola   This fine art gallery is the creation of Isabelle Kerrien, who displays paintings, wood and bone carvings, and other fine objects created by French Polynesian artists and artisans. Isabelle speaks English fluently. Open Monday to Saturday from 9am to 5pm. Vaitape, upstairs next to the post office. © 70.75.60.

Matira Pearls ★★★ ✒   You will have ample opportunities to shop for black pearls here (Vaitape village alone has a dozen outlets), but this is my favorite. It's owned by Steve Fearon, whose family once had a piece of the Hotel Bora Bora. Steve's chief assistants are his son, Heirama, who graduated from Pepperdine University in California, and daughter-in-law Tehani, herself educated in Los Angeles (Heirama and Tehani met there, not here). Unlike some other stores, their customized settings emphasize the pearl, not the gold. Set and loose pearls start at 10,000CFP. Open Monday through Saturday from 9am to 5:30pm, and Sunday, 10am to 5pm. East side of Matira Point. © 67.79.14.

Mom's Boutique   Erina Gould, wife of Bloody Mary's Restaurant & Bar maitre d' Gregg Gould (see "Where to Dine," later in this chapter), sells only traditional aloha shirts, dresses, *pareus*, straw hats, and handicrafts at her little shop. In other words, the designs are like those prevalent when I first came here in the 1970s. Open Monday through Saturday from 9am to 5:30pm. Vaitape, behind Fashion Bora Bora. © 67.69.29.

WHERE TO STAY

As I noted earlier, the worldwide recession has been especially brutal to Bora Bora. A mainstay on the island since 1961, the luxurious Hotel Bora Bora closed in October 2008 ostensibly for a complete rebuilding in time for its 50th anniversary in 2011. It is still closed as I write, and I would not place a bet on the chances of its reopening. Also gone permanently from the scene are the Bora Bora Lagoon Resort & Spa and the Club Med Bora Bora.

Expensive

Bora Bora Pearl Beach Resort ★★★ Covered by interconnected conical thatched roofs, the open-air restaurant, main bar, and library of this resort stand on a manmade hill, which enhances their views over a large swimming pool to the lagoon and the main island. With natural bamboo furniture and pandanus mat accents, the bungalows ooze Polynesian charm. The 15 premium overwater units enjoy unimpeded views of Bora Bora. For more privacy, consider one of the garden bungalows, which have wall-enclosed courtyards with sun decks and splash pools. Beachside bungalows with separate bedrooms are good for families. Although it lacks a sea view, the gorgeous spa is on an islet surrounded by lily ponds (among other treatments, you can get a tattoo). The resort's shuttle boats land at Chancelade on Bora Bora's northwestern corner, an expensive taxi ride if you don't catch one of the infrequent shuttle buses to Vaitape.

> ### Be Prepared for Mosquitoes & *No-Nos*
>
> Keep in mind that mosquitoes and *no-nos* (sand flies) love to feast on guests on Bora Bora's *motus,* so you'll want a good supply of insect repellent if you opt to stay at one of the offshore resorts.

B.P. 169, 98730 Vaitape, Bora Bora (on Motu Tevairoa). ℂ **800/657-3275** or 60.52.00. Fax 60.52.22. www.spmhotels.com. 80 units. 60,000CFP–80,000CFP bungalow. AE, DC, MC, V. **Amenities:** 3 restaurants; 2 bars; babysitting; concierge; health club; Jacuzzi; outdoor pool; room service; smoke-free rooms; spa; tennis court; watersports equipment; Wi-Fi (in main bldg. and some overwater bungalows; 500CFP/hour). *In room:* A/C, ceiling fan, TV, hair dryer, minibar.

Four Seasons Resort Bora Bora ★★★ ☺ Opened in 2008, Bora Bora's newest resort is in many ways its most luxurious. You realize that immediately when the *Leana,* a lovingly restored 1920s shuttle boat from New York City, awaits you at the airport for the 20-minute ride to Motu Omee, the long reef island on the northeastern side of the lagoon. This location affords a view of Mt. Otemanu's flat tombstone, which no other resort on the eastern islets can claim. Accommodations are in 100 overwater bungalows, all identical indoors. They each have a living room and a bedroom separated by a spacious bath, in which a large tub seemingly sits outdoors. Those at the ends of the piers have the best views and also sport plunge pools in their overwater decks. Ashore, seven villas also have pools as well as private beaches. With separate suites for parents and kids, they are excellent for families. So are the state-of-the-art children and teen centers, which have a marine biologist on hand to instruct the youngsters during school holiday periods. French Polynesia's first legal tourist wedding was performed in the resort's chapel, which has a view of Mount Otemanu.

B.P. 547, 98730 Vaitape, Bora Bora (on Motu Omee). ⓒ **800/819-5053** or 60.31.70. Fax 60.31.71. www.fourseasons.com/borabora. 107 units. 85,000CFP–600,000CFP. AE, MC, V. **Amenities:** 3 restaurant; 4 bars; babysitting; bikes; children's center; concierge; health club; Jacuzzi; outdoor pool; room service; smoke-free rooms; spa; 2 tennis courts (with pro); watersports equipment. *In room:* A/C, ceiling fan, TV/DVD, movie library, hair dryer, minibar, MP3 docking station, Wi-Fi (2,000CFP/day).

Hilton Bora Bora Nui Resort & Spa ★★★ This sprawling resort occupies the southern end of hilly Motu Toopua, a 15-minute boat ride off Vaitape. It faces west toward the sea, thus depriving its public areas and all but a handful of its bungalows of the typical Bora Bora view. A beachside, two-level infinity swimming pool serves as the focal point of activities. It's backed by two public buildings, one with a fine-dining outlet, an air-conditioned library, and a fascinating photo collection of U.S. marines building the airstrip on Motu Mute during World War II. The overwater bungalows have separate bedrooms, huge bathrooms with both tubs and walk-in showers, and big decks with privacy screens. Two three-bedroom, two-story overwater bungalows with swimming pools in their decks are tops here. Housed in a hillside hotel-style building, the "lagoon-view suites" are the least expensive units, and they interconnect to accommodate families. Top-of-the-line are the huge royal suites.

B.P. 502, 98730 Vaitape, Bora Bora (on Motu Toopua). ⓒ **800/HILTONS** [445-8667] or 60.32.00. Fax 60.32.01. www.boraboranui.com. 122 units. 61,000CFP double; 82,000CFP–290,000CFP bungalow; 62,000CFP–68,500CFP suite. AE, DC, MC, V. **Amenities:** 3 restaurants; 2 bars; babysitting; bikes; children's programs; concierge; health club; Jacuzzi; outdoor pool; room service; smoke-free rooms; spa; tennis courts; watersports equipment. *In room:* A/C, ceiling fan, TV, hair dryer, minibar, Wi-Fi (free).

InterContinental Le Moana Resort Bora Bora ★★★ On the eastern side of the Matira peninsula, this is one of the older resorts here, although much improved over the years. Its bungalows, most of them overwater, aren't the largest but they are some of the most charmingly designed here. They were the first in which you could remove the tops of the glass coffee tables and actually feed the fish swimming in the turquoise lagoon below. Ashore, 11 beachside bungalows are less enchanting, but like the overwater units, they have Raiatea and Tahaa in their lagoon views. Two bungalows—one overwater, one ashore—have kitchenettes, making them suitable for families. Also beside the beach, a circular thatched-roof building houses the reception area, a lounge, and the restaurant and bar, both with outdoor seating. Guests can take a shuttle boat to the InterContinental Resort and Thalasso Spa Bora Bora (see below) and use the facilities there. I am fond of this resort because its charming bungalows are just a short walk from the hotel district restaurants.

B.P. 156, 98730 Vaitape, Bora Bora. ⓒ **888/424-6835** or 60.49.00. Fax 60.49.99. www.interconti.com. 64 units. 74,500CFP–137,000CFP bungalow. AE, DC, MC, V. **Amenities:** Restaurant; bar; babysitting; bikes; concierge; Jacuzzi; outdoor pool; room service; smoke-free rooms; watersports equipment; Wi-Fi (in lobby; 1,800CFP/hour). *In room:* A/C, ceiling fan, TV, hair dryer, kitchen (2 units), minibar.

InterContinental Resort and Thalasso Spa Bora Bora ★★★ This luxury resort shares the blazing white sands of Motu Piti Aau—an atoll-like island stretching 10km (6 miles) along the southeastern side of the outer reef—with Le Meridien Bora Bora (see below). It has won environmental awards as the world's first resort to be air-conditioned using seawater pumped from 2,500 feet down in the ocean. The 13°C (55°F) seawater also is used by the Thalasso Spa—officially the Deep Ocean Spa by Algotherm, the French company that uses deep seawater in its beauty products and treatments. The spa is the real star here, especially its three treatment

9

rooms extending over the shallow, sand-bottom lagoon (yes, you can watch fish swimming below while getting a massage). You'll also feel like you're floating on air as you go down the glass-floor aisle of the overwater wedding chapel. Extending from two pincer-shaped piers, the 80 suite-size guest bungalows are identical except for three two-bedroom, two-bathroom "villa suites" that have kitchens and are thus good choices for well-heeled families. The thatched-roof bungalows and central building are furnished in chic, Balinese tropical style, so the resort lacks Polynesian flair. A boat shuttles between here and the InterContinental Le Moana Resort (see above), so getting to restaurants and activities on the main island is easy.

B.P. 156, 98730 Vaitape, Bora Bora (on Motu Piti Aau). (© 800/327-0200 or 60.49.00. Fax 60.76.99. www.boraboraspa.intercontinental.com. 80 units. 95,000CFP–160,500CFP. AE, DC, MC, V. **Amenities:** 2 restaurants; 2 bars; babysitting; children's program; concierge; health club; Jacuzzi; outdoor pool; room service; smoke-free rooms; spa; watersports equipment; Wi-Fi (in central bldg.; 2,000CFP/hour). *In room:* A/C, ceiling fan, TV, hair dryer, Internet, kitchen (3 units), minibar.

Le Meridien Bora Bora ★★★ ☺

Located on the northern tip of Motu Piti Aau, this is one of the best family resorts in French Polynesia. Its Melanesian architecture is reminiscent of its sister property on Tahiti (see Le Meridien Tahiti, p. 116). The architects also created a seawater-fed, lakelike lagoon, in which you can swim with endangered sea turtles, bred there as part of the resort's award-winning preservation program. Children love it. Of the 98 guest units, 85 are built overwater. Only a few of these have views of Mount Otemanu's skinny side. Standing over waist-deep water, they are notable for their huge glass floors, which make it seem as if you're walking on air (maids cover the glass with carpets at evening turndown). The overwater units here are smaller than those at Bora Bora's other resorts. Ten "beach" bungalows actually sit beside the man-made lagoon, but most of them have fine views of Bora Bora. Four of these are villas with bedrooms and baths flanking a central living area. Since the shallow man-made lagoon is safe for swimming, they are excellent for families with small children. The hotel's launch shuttles to Anau village. Plans were in the works to build a full-service spa on its own islet; in the meantime, one bungalow is devoted to massages.

B.P. 190, 98730 Vaitape, Bora Bora (on Motu Pitiaau). (© 800/225-5843 or 60.51.51. Fax 60.51.10. www. lemeridien-borabora.com. 98 units. 63,000CFP–182,000CFP. AE, DC, MC, V. **Amenities:** 3 restaurants; 2 bars; babysitting; children's programs; concierge; health club; Jacuzzi; 2 outdoor pools; room service; smoke-free rooms; watersports equipment. *In room:* A/C, ceiling fan, TV, hair dryer, minibar, Wi-Fi (4,000CFP/day).

St. Regis Resort Bora Bora ★★★

Nicole Kidman and Keith Urban were among the first to honeymoon at this superluxurious resort when it opened in 2007. They took the 1,208-sq.-m (13,000-sq.-ft.) Royal Estate, a walled-off compound with its own pool. Apparently the chef even came over and prepared their meals, for no guest ever caught a glimpse of the celebrity duo. The Royal Estate sits on land beside its own beach. If I were a quazillionaire, however, I would have opted for one of the Royal Over Water Villas, which have their own swimming pools with terrific views of Bora Bora. I am not pulling your leg: They have swimming pools built into their overwater decks. The guest quarters come in eight categories, from land-based villas with pools to stripped-down overwater bungalows. Stripped down, that is, in that they do not have pools or even Jacuzzis. Shame on you if you have to settle for one of those luxurious hovels! Butlers are on call for all units.

B.P. 506, 98730 Vaitape, Bora Bora (on Motu Omee). © **800/787-3447** or 60.78.88. Fax 60.78.56. www.stregis.com/borabora. 100 units. 98,000CFP–1,500,000CFP. AE, DC, MC, V. **Amenities:** 3 restaurants; 3 bars; babysitting; children's center; concierge; health club; Jacuzzi; outdoor pool; room service; smoke-free rooms; spa; tennis court; watersports equipment. *In room:* A/C, ceiling fan, TV, TV/DVD, TV/VCR, movie library, fax, fridge, hair dryer, Internet, kitchen, minibar, MP3 docking station, no phone, Wi-Fi (3,000CFP/day).

Sofitel Bora Bora Marara Beach and Private Island ★   This resort is the recent consolidation of the **Sofitel Bora Bora Marara Resort** and the **Sofitel Bora Bora Motu Private Island.** The latter occupies rocky, one-hill Motu Piti Uu Uta, a 3-minute shuttle-boat ride from the older, Marara part of the property. Italian movie producer Dino De Laurentis built the Marara in 1977 to house star Mia Farrow and the crew working on his box-office bomb *Hurricane.* It underwent an extensive rejuvenation in 2006. A beehive-shaped building houses its restaurant; it and an attractive bar open to a walk-in swimming pool. The Marara's overwater bungalows have some of Bora Bora's largest decks, but be sure to ask for a unit away from the nearby round-island road or you will wonder if you're sleeping over the lagoon. Overwater units nos. 48 to 51, 62, and 63 are the most private and have the best views. Unlike most Bora Bora resorts, the private island has a gorgeous, picture-postcard view of Mount Otemanu's tombstone face. Most but not all overwater bungalows out there enjoy the view, so ask for one that does. Often-steep stone pathways lead up and downhill to the guest bungalows on the *motu;* for this reason, I don't recommend it to travelers with disabilities or anyone who has trouble walking. Several small beaches on the *motu* offer hammocks and easy chairs, and one has a shower mounted on a tree.

B.P. 6, 98730 Vaitape, Bora Bora. © **800/763-4835** or 41.04.04 in Papeete, or 60.55.00 on Bora Bora. Fax 41.05.05 or 67.74.03. www.sofitel.com. 70 units. 38,000CFP–90,000CFP. AE, DC, MC, V. **Amenities:** 2 restaurants; 2 bars; babysitting; bikes; concierge; Jacuzzi; outdoor pool; room service; smoke-free rooms; spa; watersports equipment. *In room:* A/C, ceiling fan, TV, hair dryer, minibar, Wi-Fi (1,500CFP/hour).

Moderate

Hotel Matira   This is not so much a hotel as a collection of bungalows on and near the beach at the northern end of the Matira peninsula. Imported from Indonesia, the teak units have thatched roofs, porches on one corner, shower-only bathrooms, and pairs of double beds. You'll get a ceiling fan, fridge, and coffeemaker, but forget amenities like TVs, phones, and hair dryers. What you get here is an essentially unscreened cottage, so keep your insect repellent handy. The choicest and most expensive models rest beside Matira Beach, while the others are back in the garden. Ask for a discount if you book directly.

B.P. 31, 98730 Vaitape, Bora Bora. © **67.70.51.** Fax 67.77.02. www.hotel-matira.com. 14 units. 21,000CFP–35,500CFP. MC, V. *In room:* Ceiling fan, fridge, no phone.

Le Maitai Polynesia Bora Bora ★★ 🍴   One of the best hotel values on Bora Bora, this resort straddles the round-island road on the eastern side of Matira Beach. The thatched-roof main building and blocks of hotel rooms are on the mountain side of the road. The upper floor rooms have spectacular lagoon views. On the lagoon side of the road, a high wall of black volcanic rock shields the beachside and overwater bungalows, which are among the more reasonably priced in French

Polynesia—provided you don't pay the rack rates, which few guests do since Le Maitai is featured in many discount package deals. The bungalows are smaller than those at the more expensive resorts, but they are packed with Polynesian decor. Those over water have glass-topped coffee tables for fish-viewing. Of the two restaurants here, one sits beachside.

B.P. 505, 98730 Vaitape, Bora Bora. ⓒ **60.30.00.** Fax 67.66.03. www.hotelmaitai.com. 74 units. 16,700CFP–32,300CFP double; 39,000CFP–53,300CFP bungalow. Rates include full breakfast. AE, MC, V. **Amenities:** 2 restaurants; 2 bars; babysitting; bikes; smoke-free rooms; watersports equipment. *In room:* A/C, ceiling fan, TV, hair dryer, minibar, Wi-Fi (1,400CFP/hour).

Inexpensive

The modest but attractive **Bora Bora Beach Resort** (ⓒ **60.59.50**) had just switched from being the Novotel Bora Bora Beach Resort when I was here recently. I would stay elsewhere until the dust has settled.

Rohutu Fare Lodge ★★ 🌊 Virtually hidden in lush botanical gardens on the mountainside overlooking Povai Bay, this little lodge is the creation of Nir Shalev, an Israeli expatriate whom I met shortly after he first arrived on Bora Bora wearing a backpack in 1989. With teak floors and natural thatched roofs, his cleverly designed bungalows are for lovers, definitely not puritans. In addition to suggestive paintings, statues, and other paraphernalia in the sleeping quarters, faucets in the outdoor bathrooms pour water from certain unmentionable parts of nude statues. (After a night here, you may not be up to the 15-min. bike ride to Matira Beach!) Nir's two lagoon-view bungalows are more charming and have better vistas than his family unit. They all have decks with lounge furniture, and four-poster beds with mosquito nets. You will not have to leave here to enjoy a view of Mount Otemanu's tombstone face, but should you decide to leave, Nir will give you a lift in his four-wheel drive vehicle.

B.P. 400, 98730 Vaitape, Bora Bora. ⓒ **70.77.99.** www.boraboralodge.com. 3 units. 18,900CFP bungalow. MC, V. **Amenities:** Free airport transfers; bikes. *In room:* Ceiling fan, kitchen, Wi-Fi (free).

Village Temanuata 🌊 On a small part of Matira Beach in the hotel district, this few-frills establishment has 11 thatched-roof bungalows ranging from one-room to family-size units with kitchens. All have private bathrooms with hot water showers but few other amenities. Choice are the two units directly facing the beach. Matira's restaurants and shops are either next door or an easy walk away. You can stay 3 nights for the price of 2 in January, February and November, 2 nights for the price of 1 in May and June.

B.P. 544, 98730 Vaitape, Bora Bora. ⓒ **67.75.61.** Fax 67.78.17. www.temanuata.com. 11 units. 15,000CFP–17,000CFP bungalow. MC, V. **Amenities:** Bikes. *In room:* Fan, kitchen (6 units), no phone.

Pensions

Chez Nono Sitting on the western side of the Point Matira peninsula, this pension is the domain of Noël (Nono) Levard—of *the* Bora Bora Levards, who operate lagoon excursions, safari expeditions, and the Farm black-pearl operation. Since guests here can step from their accommodations right out onto the powdery sands of Matira Beach, this is the most popular beachside pension with French residents of Tahiti (book early). The least expensive units are six simple bedrooms in Nono's house; these all share toilets, hot-water showers, and a kitchen. Two beachside bungalows can accommodate two persons each, while two family-size bungalows are notable for their thatched roofs. All four bungalows have their own bathrooms with hot-water showers. With all of Nono's activities going on, this is a very busy place.

B.P. 282, 93730 Vaitape, Bora Bora. ℂ **67.71.38.** Fax 67.74.27. nono.levard@mail.pf. 10 units (6 with shared bathroom). 7,450CFP double; 13,000CFP bungalow. MC, V. *In room:* Fan, no phone.

Pension Robert et Tina This quiet, family-run pension consists of three two-story houses right on the southern extremity of Matira Point. One house has six rooms, while the others have three each. You'll share each house's kitchen, toilets, and cold-water showers. If you have a family or group, and don't mind shivering in the shower, Robert and Tina will reduce the rates if you rent an entire house for a week or more. The beach is minimal here, but you can walk across the shallow lagoon to excellent snorkeling near the outer reef. The trade winds can make the point quite breezy and cool during the winter months from June through August.

93730 Vaitape, Bora Bora. ℂ **67.63.55** or 79.22.73. Fax 67.72.92. pensionrobertettina@mail.pf. 15 units (13 with shared bathrooms). 7,700CFP–9,000CFP double. MC, V. *In room:* No phone.

WHERE TO DINE

Restaurants here primarily are in Matira, on the island's southern end; Povai Bay, on the southwest coast; and in Vaitape village. That's how I have organized them below.

Matira

Chez Ben's SNACK BAR/PIZZA Honeymooners from the nearby Hotel Bora Bora frequently wander to this lean-to across the road from a shady portion of Matira Beach, where Bora Bora–born Ben Teraitepo and his Oklahoma-born wife, Robin, have been serving American-style cooked breakfasts, lunches, and afternoon pick-me-ups since 1988. Ben's fresh tuna-salad sandwiches, pizzas and pastas, unusually spicy *poisson cru,* tacos, and fajitas are homemade and substantial, although Ben's and Robin's company is the main reason to hang out here. They will shoo the dogs and cats away if they bother you.

Matira Beach. ℂ **67.74.54.** Most items 800CFP–1,900CFP. No credit cards. Daily 8am–5pm.

La Bounty ★ 🍴 FRENCH/ITALIAN This casual restaurant under a thatched roof provides some of the island's best pizza and other reasonably priced Italian (and French) fare. A pie makes an ample meal for one person or can be shared as an appetizer. The spaghetti and tagliatelle are tasty, too, with either smoked salmon, carbonara, Alfredo, Neapolitan, blue cheese, or seafood sauce. Steaks and fish are served under French sauces such as mustard or creamy vanilla. Pizzas are dished up quickly here, but everything else is prepared to order and takes longer. Whatever you choose, it will be excellent quality for the price.

Matira. ℂ **67.70.43.** Reservations recommended. Pizza and pasta 1,000CFP–2,250CFP; main courses 1,800CFP–2,900CFP. MC, V. Tues–Sun 11:30am–2pm and 6:30–9pm.

La Matira Beach Restaurant FRENCH Literally hanging over the beach, this casual, bistro-style restaurant is an excellent place to have a lagoonside lunch, perhaps a salad under a slice of grilled tuna. Burgers, grilled fish, and pastas also appear at midday. Dinner switches to a fine if somewhat pricey French menu with local twists, such as roast pork with bananas. It's a beautiful spot on a moonlit night; otherwise, I do lunch here.

Matira. ⓒ **67.53.79.** Reservations recommended at dinner. Lunch 1,500CFP–1,950CFP; main courses 3,850CFP–3,950CFP. MC, V. Fri–Wed 7–10am, 11am–2pm, and 6–9pm.

Restaurant Fare Manuia ★ FRENCH A thatched roof lends charm to this French restaurant known for large servings, such as huge slabs of prime rib served plain or with a choice of French sauces. The tender beef comes from New Zealand, as do the freshly ground hamburgers served at lunch and fine rack of lamb at night. Other dinner main courses include mahimahi served on a wood plank with vanilla sauce, rare tuna with wasabi, and a hearty soup with mussels, shrimp, scallops, and fish. Breakfast here is strictly continental.

Matira. ⓒ **67.68.08.** Reservations recommended. Breakfast 500CFP–1,600CFP; burgers 1,400CFP–2,200CFP; main courses 1,900CFP–4,900CFP. MC, V. Daily 7–10am, 11:30am–2pm, and 7–10pm.

Restaurant-Snack Moi Here REGIONAL Tree limbs hold up the thatched roof covering this little Tahitian-owned restaurant, which almost hangs over Matira Beach. It's less restaurant than permanent *roulotte* (food wagon) with a view. The menu offers local plain fare such as grilled steaks and fish (served with french fries), hamburgers, sashimi, chow mein, and *poisson cru*. My steak was tough, so I always order fish here. Breakfast is continental, while lunch turns to burgers, sandwiches, and omelets. The view is the best thing about this place.

Matira. ⓒ **67.56.46.** Reservations accepted. Most items 500CFP–2,000CFP. No credit cards. Daily 6am–9pm.

> ### Call for a Ride
>
> Most restaurants provide free transportation for their dinner guests; always ask when making your reservations.

Roulotte Matira (Chez Sam) ★ 🌶 REGIONAL This is one of the best *roulottes* in French Polynesia, especially when owner Samuel Rouver cooks beef masala from a recipe handed down by his East Indian father. Otherwise, he works at the gas grill to produce steaks and fish, both served with french fries. Anything with legumes will be a so-so Chinese-style stir-fry. You can get a continental breakfast here. Grab a white plastic table; there's waiter service.

Matira. No phone. Sandwiches and burgers 600CFP–700CFP; main courses 1,600CFP–2,000CFP. No credit cards. Daily 7:30am–2pm and 6–10pm.

Snack Matira SNACK BAR Beside Matira Beach and within hailing distance of Chez Ben's, this open-air snack bar is a favorite lunch and afternoon retreat of Bora Bora's French-speaking expatriates. It offers a *roulotte*-style menu of pizzas, salads, omelets, grilled steaks and fish, juicy burgers, and *casse-croûte* sandwiches, plus ice cream and milkshakes. The lagoon view is superb.

Matira Beach. ⓒ **67.77.32.** Reservations not accepted. Most items 500CFP–2,000CFP. No credit cards. Tues–Sun 10am–4pm.

Povai Bay

Bloody Mary's Restaurant & Bar ★★★ SEAFOOD/STEAKS Having a few drinks and a slab of barbecued fish at this extraordinarily charming structure is as much a part of the Bora Bora experience as taking a lagoon excursion. Ceiling fans, colored spotlights, and stalks of dried bamboo dangle from a large thatched roof over a floor of fine white sand (stash your sandals in a foot locker and dine in your bare feet). The butcher-block tables are made of coconut-palm lumber, and the seats are sections of palm trunks cut into stools. Bloody Mary's is essentially an American-style barbecued fish and steak joint—a welcome relief after a diet of lard-laden French sauces. You'll be shown the seafood and beef laid out on a bed of ice. (If it's offered, choose the mouthwatering teriyaki-style wahoo.) The chef will charbroil your selection to order and serve it with a salad, vegetables, and your choice of sauce on the side. Open all day, the cozy bar is cut from a beautifully polished litchi tree and is one of my favorite watering holes. The lunch menu consists of the same bar menu served at dinner. Bloody Mary's American owner, Dexter Hewitt, shares the profits with the staff; consequently, the service here is some of the best in French Polynesia. You will have an evening of fun, as have the many famous names posted on a board out by the road.

Povai Bay. © **67.72.86.** www.bloodymarys.com. Reservations strongly recommended. Lunch 800CFP–1,500CFP, dinner main courses 2,800CFP–3,500CFP. AE, MC, V. Restaurant Mon–Wed and cruise-ship days 11am–3pm; Mon–Sat 6–9pm. Bar Mon–Sat 9:30am–11pm. Closed Dec.

La Villa Mahana ★★★ INTERNATIONAL   You will need one night for fun at Bloody Mary's, another for a romantic dinner at this fine little restaurant, the best in all of French Polynesia. Owner Damien Rinaldi Dovio, an accomplished young Corsican-born chef, started my friends and me with tuna *tartare exotique,* a luscious version of *poisson cru* with a sharp wasabi-accented sauce. My friends went on to mahimahi perfectly cooked with a subtle version of coconut curry sauce, while I opted for filet mignon with vanilla cream gnocchi. Both were outstanding. The fixed-price menus for four or five courses will save money. The walls of this Mediterranean-style villa are adorned with the works of noted French Polynesian artist Garrick Yrondi, but Damien has only six tables, so consider calling or e-mailing for a reservation well before you get here.

Povai Bay, behind Boutique Gauguin, 1.5km (1 mile) north of Hotel Bora Bora. © **67.50.63.** www.villa mahana.com. Reservations required. Main courses 5,000CFP–11,000CFP; fixed-price dinners 10,500CFP–15,000CFP. AE, MC, V. Wed–Thurs 6–8pm.

Vaitape

Inexpensive *roulottes* roll out near the Vaitape small-boat harbor, some during the day when cruise ships are in port. See "Don't Miss *Les Roulottes*" (p. 125) for details on these inexpensive food wagons.

Aloe Cafe ★ 🍴 FRENCH/PASTRIES   I often have breakfast here, for this patisserie bakes very good croissants, tarts, and quiches to go with the strong French coffee. Also on the lunch menu: sandwiches, burgers, pastas, kebabs, and a *plat du jour*. You can use the computer terminals or the Wi-Fi network here to check your e-mail (see "Fast Facts: Bora Bora," earlier in this chapter).

North of the Vaitape wharf, in Centre Commercial le Pahia. ☎ **67.78.88.** Most items 300CFP–2,500CFP. MC, V. June–Oct Mon–Sat 6am–9pm, Nov–May Mon–Sat 6am–6pm.

Restaurant Le St. James 🍴 FRENCH   Overlooking the lagoon from the Helen's Bay shopping center, north of the small boat harbor, this restaurant provides a picturesque setting for sandwiches, burgers, pasta, and seafood. French residents I know consider the fare here to be very good value. Have a pre-dinner drink at the thatch-covered bar down by the lagoon.

Vaitape, in Centre Helen's Bay. ☎ **67.64.62.** Reservations recommended at dinner. Sandwiches and burgers 1,400CFP–1,700CFP; main courses 1,200CFP–2,950CFP. AE, MC, V. Mon–Sat 11:30am–2pm and 6–9pm.

ISLAND NIGHTS ON BORA BORA

As on all the outer islands, things are really quiet on Bora Bora after dark (this is, after all, one of the world's most romantic honeymoon hideaways, not a place to practice your dance steps). You might want to listen to a Tahitian band playing at sunset or watch the furious hips in a Tahitian dance show, which all the resorts have at least 1 night a week. The schedules change, so call ahead.

The island's sole nightclub is **Le Récife Discothèque,** about 1km (½ mile) north of Vaitape (☎ **67.73.87**), which opens only on Fridays and Saturdays at 11pm (that's right, 11pm) and closes at 3am (or later) the following morning. The young local patrons have been known to throw a few fists at that late hour.

MAUPITI

A favorite pastime throughout the Pacific islands is comparing one place to how another place used to be. Locals like to say that Tahiti is like Hawaii used to be, for example, and that Huahine is like Moorea used to be. In the case of French Polynesia's last westward outpost, Maupiti is like Bora Bora used to be.

Just 40km (25 miles) west of Bora Bora, this little jewel even resembles its larger neighbor, in that it consists of an outer barrier reef topped by a ring of sand-edged *motus* enclosing a clear lagoon around a high central island. Here, there is more dry land out on the fringing *motus* than on the main island, which has an area of just 14 sq. km (5¼ sq. miles). The road around the main island is just 9.6km (5¾ miles) long.

Unlike Bora Bora, Maupiti has not a hint of modern tourism. Many of the visitors who come here are French residents of Tahiti, who like to spend their weekends relaxing at one of several small pensions, Maupiti's only choice of accommodations. Indeed, Maupiti is definitely a throwback to old Polynesia, when, among other things, very few locals spoke English.

Maupiti reminds me of the Bora Bora of more than 30 years ago, when I camped on a nearly deserted Pointe Matira, now a key part of Bora Bora's tourism infrastructure. **Plage Tereia (Tereia Beach),** a gorgeous strip of white-and-pink sand wrapping around a peninsula on the western side of Maupiti's central island, especially reminds me of those bygone days. Although local residents are building homes next to Plage Tereia, they flatly rejected a proposed resort at this lovely location.

Just as Mount Otemanu's tombstone face is Bora Bora's trademark, Maupiti's distinguishing landmark is **Mount Hotu Parata,** a black-basaltic cliff dramatically rising 165m (540 ft.) above **Vaiea,** the island's main village. The cliff is pockmarked with caves that attract throngs of nesting seabirds.

Despite its small size, Maupiti was an important island in pre-European days. Archaeologists have uncovered both *maraes* and petroglyphs on the main island. They have also discovered human remains and other items out on **Motu Paeao,** a small islet separating two shallow passes on Maupiti's north side. Stone axes, whale teeth, and fishhooks have been dated to about A.D. 850, making it one of the oldest settlements in the Society Islands.

Whether you stay on Maupiti or see it as a day trip from Bora Bora, you are in for an authentic old Polynesian treat.

[FastFACTS] MAUPITI

The following facts apply specifically to Maupiti. For more information, see "Fast Facts: Tahiti & French Polynesia," in chapter 13.

Currency Exchange Maupiti does not have a bank, which explains why most pensions here do not accept credit cards. Bring enough cash or traveler's checks to cover your anticipated expenses.

Emergencies & Police The **emergency police** telephone number is ☎ **17.** Maupiti does not have its own gendarmerie (the nearest is on Bora Bora), so ask your pension staff for assistance in case of emergency.

Healthcare The **government infirmary** (☎ **67.80.18**) is in the *mairie* (town hall) complex in Vaiea village.

Internet Access The island's *mairie* (town hall) has ManaSpot wireless connection, but there is no cybercafe on the island. Ask if your pension has, or can arrange, access if you can't live without e-mail or surfing the Web while here.

Post Office The post office is in the *mairie* (town hall) complex in Vaiea village. Hours are Monday through Thursday from 7:30am to 3pm, Friday from 7am to 2pm.

Visitor Information There is no visitor information office on Maupiti, so be sure to pick up an island map before you get here.

Water Don't drink the tap water on Maupiti. Bottled water is available at the grocery stores.

GETTING AROUND MAUPITI

Air Tahiti flies to Maupiti from Raiatea about four times a week. Its flights are geared toward Friday-to-Sunday weekend travelers.

The airstrip is on **Motu Tuanai,** the long islet off the northeastern side of the central island. The pensions send boats to pick up guests who have reservations, or you can take the Air Tahiti launch to Vaiea.

The fast *Maupiti Express* ferry arrives from Bora Bora three times a week (see "Maupiti as a Day Trip from Bora Bora," below). It docks at the island's only wharf, in Vaiea on the southeastern point of the main island. It and all other vessels must negotiate **Onoiau Pass,** the only navigable entry into the lagoon. Subject to strong currents and breaking surf, the narrow pass can be treacherous in rough weather. On infrequent occasions the *Maupiti Express* and other boats cannot get into or out of the lagoon.

There is no local transportation system on Maupiti. Since the island is so small, most visitors rent bicycles. The round-island road is flat and follows the coastline except when it climbs over a steep ridge between Plage Tereia and the south coast. When the *Maupiti Express* docks, local residents will be waiting at the wharf to rent bikes for 1,000CFP a day. At other times, you can contact the **Total** service station at the wharf (☎ **67.83.46**), **Puanere Locations** (☎ **67.81.68;** fax 67.80.85), or **Loana** (☎ **78.94.38**).

EXPLORING MAUPITI
Touring the Island

The narrow coastal plain on the east coast is occupied by **Vaiea, Petei,** and **Fararuu,** three villages resting at the base of the Mount Hotu Parata cliff. The great majority of

Maupiti

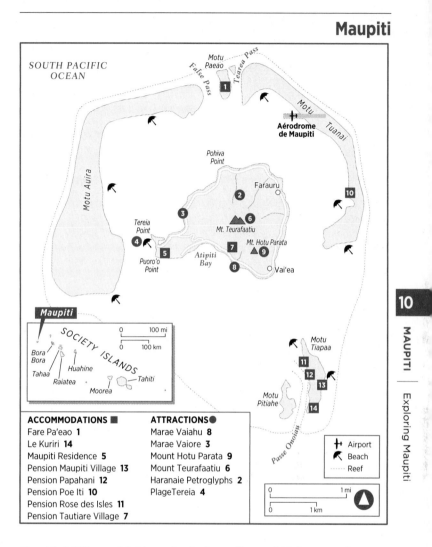

SOUTH PACIFIC
OCEAN

Motu
Paeao

False Pass

Tearea Pass

Aérodrome
de Maupiti

Motu Tuanai

Pohiva
Point

Farauru

Motu Auira

Tereia
Point

Mt. Teurafaatiu

Mt. Hotu Parata

Puoro'o
Point

Atipiti
Bay

Vai'ea

Maupiti

SOCIETY ISLANDS

Bora
Bora

Tahaa

Huahine

Raiatea

Moorea

Tahiti

0   100 mi
0   100 km

Motu
Tiapaa

Motu
Pitiahe

Passe Onoiau

ACCOMMODATIONS ■	ATTRACTIONS●
Fare Pa'eao **1**	Marae Vaiahu **8**
Le Kuriri **14**	Marae Vaiore **3**
Maupiti Residence **5**	Mount Hotu Parata **9**
Pension Maupiti Village **13**	Mount Teurafaatiu **6**
Pension Papahani **12**	Haranaie Petroglyphs **2**
Pension Poe Iti **10**	PlageTereia **4**
Pension Rose des Isles **11**	
Pension Tautiare Village **7**	

＋ Airport
🗸 Beach
----- Reef

0   1 mi
0   1 km

Maupiti's 1,200 or so inhabitants live in these villages, which have its only grocery stores and other facilities. They run together, so you won't know when you've left one and entered another, especially when strolling along the picturesque **lagoonside promenade** from the wharf to the island's school. You will see very few older homes here, since a devastating 1997 hurricane destroyed most of Maupiti's houses.

The north coast is notable for the **Haranaie Valley,** site of several **petroglyphs,** including one of a turtle. The petroglyphs are not easy to find, so I recommend a guided tour (see below). From the road, you'll have fine views of the three *motus* enclosing the north side of the lagoon. The road rounds the base of Mount Hotu, at the northwestern corner, and then follows the west coast, where you'll pass several ancient *maraes*, including **Marae Vaiorie.** This ancient stone structure was built in two parts with a freshwater stream in between.

Go straight when you come to the road junction and follow the sign to the magnificent white-and-pink sands of **Plage Tereia ★★★**. Situated in a coconut grove and facing a shallow lagoon, this is one of French Polynesia's best beaches. Locals are building more and more homes here (the warning sign at the path to the beach means keep off of their homesteads, not the beach). There may be a snack bar open on weekends, but there are no changing rooms, water fountains, or other facilities. At low tide, you can wade across the waist-deep "Baby Sharks Crossing" to **Motu Auira.** (Yes, you may see small black tip reef sharks in the shallow lagoon.) Motu Auira, the largest of Maupiti's islets, has melon plantations and a wind-generating facility.

From the beach, you will have to backtrack to the road junction, where the *traversière* (cross-island road) heads up the ridge between the west and south coasts. Push your bike up the hill for a fine view of the west coast and the lagoon from the top.

Be careful riding down the steep descent, which will take you down to the populated south coast. On the shore about two-thirds of the way back to Vaiea, you'll come to **Marae Vaiahu,** the most important temple on the island. Maupiti's royalty lived in this area during the olden days, and chiefs from Bora Bora and the other islands often joined them at gatherings at Marae Vaiahu. It's notable for its stone fish box, apparently used in ceremonies to bless the fishing fleet.

HIKING, LAGOON EXCURSIONS & SNORKELING

Hiking

Maupiti has two mountain trails that will test your endurance, but reward you with fantastic views. One track begins opposite Snack Tarona (p. 208) and goes to the top of **Mount Teurafaatiu** (also known as Mount Nuupure), Maupiti's tallest peak at 380m (1,247 ft.). It's a hike of about 1½ hours to the top. The trail is easy to follow going up, but be very careful on the way back down or you can easily lose your way.

Another very steep climb ascends **Mount Hotu Parata,** the cliff looming above Vaiea village. This track is very steep in places, and since the volcanic rock at the top is unstable, you cannot go to the cliff's edge. In places, this trail is more like mountain climbing than hiking. Ask your pension to arrange a guide for the Mount Hotu Parata trail.

Lagoon Excursions

Although Maupiti's lagoon is not as large or deep as Bora Bora's, getting out on it is an essential ingredient of a visit here. (Getting under it is another matter, since no scuba-diving operator has set up shop on Maupiti.) The excursions pretty much follow the usual script: a boat ride, snorkeling and swimming off a white-sand beach, a stop to see the ancient ruins on Motu Paeao, and a picnic on a *motu*. Every pension will arrange an all-day lagoon excursion. These usually cost about 3,000CFP per person without lunch, 4,000CFP if a picnic is included.

Snorkeling, Diving, Whale- & Dolphin-watching

There is very good snorkeling in the lagoon around Motu Paeao, between the two shallow entries into the lagoon: **Tearea (Hiro's) Pass** and **False Pass.** The latter is called False Pass because from the sea, it looks likes a navigable pass, while in reality it is only a few feet deep. You'll find more good snorkeling in the south on the lagoonside Motu Tipaa, but be careful of the strong currents into and out of nearby Onoiau Pass.

Maupiti Nautique (© **67.83.80;** www.maupiti-nautique.com) has both snorkeling and scuba diving expeditions. Both snorkelers and divers can follow an underwater Marine Discovery Trail marked with explanatory boards suspended from the bottom. And there's a good chance of seeing humpback whales and manta rays during the austral winter from June through August. Maupiti Nautique charges 6,500CFP per person for one-tank dives or whale-watching excursions, 3,500CFP for snorkeling with manta rays or exploring the Marine Discover Trail, and 5,000CFP for dolphin-watching excursions. Reservations are required with as much advance notice as possible.

WHERE TO STAY

As mentioned in the introduction to this chapter, Maupiti's residents have rejected proposals to build luxury resorts here. The result: Your choice will be one of the island's small, family-run establishments. A few are on the main island, but the most appealing are out on the skinny islets surrounding the lagoon. Those on the ocean side of the *motus* are cooled by the prevailing southeast trade winds.

A Whaler's Tale

In 1842, a new American whaling ship named the *Charles W. Morgan* put into Maupiti to refresh its crew. One of them was so refreshed by the daughter of a local chief that he stayed behind and founded a large family. The *Charles*

W. Morgan kept on working until 1921. The last 19th-century whaling ship still afloat, it's now berthed at Mystic Seaport in Mystic, Connecticut (www. mysticseaport.org).

As on Bora Bora, dogs are part of life here, so don't be surprised to find a few sharing your pension.

On Motu Paeao

Fare Pa'eao (Chez Janine)   Jeanine Tavaerii's pension sits by itself on Motu Paeao, the flat islet between the two shallow passes at the northern end of the lagoon. She has six of the one-room, government-backed bungalows seen so often in French Polynesia; each has a front porch, a ceiling fan, and a bathroom with cold-water shower. There is very good snorkeling in this part of the lagoon, and Jeanine provides free kayaks with which to explore.

B.P. 33, 98732 Vaiea, Maupiti. ℂ **67.81.01**. www.maupitilodge.com. 6 units. 23,120CFP double. Rates include breakfast and dinner. MC, V. **Amenities:** Restaurant; bar; watersports equipment. *In room:* No phone.

On Motu Tiapaa

Le Kuriri ★★★   Beside a white-sand beach on the ocean side of Motu Tiapaa, the sophisticated and charming Le Kuriri is more small hotel than pension. Kindred spirits of mine, Anne-Marie and Camille Marjorel deserted the corporate life in France to sail around the world, after which they settled on Maupiti and took over this pension. They have added some very nice touches, such as a huge daybed beside the beach, and an open-air dining room/guest lounge with a crushed-coral floor and library shelves stocked with books left by guests who came here from many countries spanning the globe. Usually featuring fresh seafood, excellent dinners are served dinner party–style in this comfortable setting. Guests enjoy breakfast under a beach-side pavilion. The spacious bungalows have lots of Polynesian accents, including thatched roofs and split-bamboo matting on the walls. They all have fans, furnished porches, and outdoor bathrooms with hot-water showers. The push-out windows are not screened—true of all Maupiti pensions—but mosquito nets hang over the beds. Anne-Marie and Camille speak English as well as French.

B.P. 23, 98732 Maupiti. ℂ **74.54.54**. Fax 67.82.23. www.maupiti-kuriri.com. 4 units (all with bathroom). 12,500CFP per person. Rates include breakfast and dinner. MC, V. **Amenities:** Restaurant; bar; free airport transfers; watersports equipment; Wi-Fi (free; e-mail only). *In room:* Fan, no phone.

Pension Maupiti Village   Also on the ocean side of Motu Tiapaa, this no-frills pension is one of Maupiti's most basic. The buildings consist simply of plywood sides and tin roofs—pretty much what you got before the advent of the more modern government-issued bungalows. The largest quarters here is a modern two-bedroom

---

✎ Staying Near a Deserted Beach

I prefer to stay on **Motu Tiapaa**, beside the Onoiau Pass, since it has excellent beaches on both its lagoon and ocean sides. There are four pensions on the island, so if I tire of eating at mine, I can walk over and make a reservation at another. If one side of the *motu* gets too hot, a sea breeze usually cools the other. Skinny-dipping has been known to occur at a deserted beach wrapping around the northern end of the island. The lagoon is very shallow at this gorgeous spot, but the view of the main island is terrific.

villa with its own kitchen. Two other units are individual bungalows with two double beds, front porches, and their own bathrooms with hot-water showers. Two very small and basic rooms and a dormitory all share outside toilets and cold-water showers. A white-sand beach fronts the property, but the lagoon between here and the fringing reef is too shallow for serious swimming. Hard-working owner Audine Colomes prepares meals of fresh seafood and occasionally duck, which guests eat at a long table in a beachside building. She treats her guests to a complimentary picnic on a *motu* once a week. Audine speaks scant English but her daughter, Raipoe, speaks English as well as French.

98732 Vaiea, Maupiti. ✆/fax **67.80.09.** maupiti.village@mail.pf. 6 units (3 with shared bathroom), 6 dorm beds (shared bathrooms). 12,000CFP per person in bungalow; 7,000CFP per person in rooms; 6,000 per person in dormitory. Rates include all meals. No credit cards. **Amenities:** Restaurant; bar; watersports equipment. *In room:* No phone.

Pension Papahani   Friendly Tahitians Denis and Vilna Tuheiava own this pension beside a lovely white-sand beach on the lagoon side of Motu Tiapaa. They have three newer, reasonably spacious "family" bungalows; one of these has a front porch directly facing the beach. Two older bungalows in the garden are smaller and less comfortable. Except for mosquito nets over their double beds, all are rather sparsely furnished, especially the older units. Each has a private bathroom with hot-water shower. Vilna serves good French and Tahitian fare in an open-air, sand-floor building by the beach. The lagoon next to the pension is shallow, but you can wade out to deeper snorkeling water. Denis and Vilna don't speak much English, but you can converse in English with their children.

B.P. 1, 98732 Vaiea, Maupiti. ✆ **60.15.35.** Fax 60.15.36. pensionpapahani@hotmail.fr. 5 units. 10,000CFP–13,000CFP per person. Rates include all meals. No credit cards. **Amenities:** Restaurant; bar. *In room:* No phone.

Pension Rose des Isles   Sharing the same beach as Pension Papahani (see above), Rose des Isles is the charming creation of Juliette and Areti Tiauaroa. Juliette moved here from Brittany in the late 1970s and later married Areti, then a rower on Tahiti's championship canoe racing team. Areti built their two rustic bungalows and the roofs over their outdoor kitchen and lounge entirely of tree limbs and thatch. Juliette decorated the bungalows with traditional Tahitian designs, shells, carvings and other handcrafts. The Tiauaroas say they intend to buy regular beds; meantime, the mattresses are on the floor Japanese-style. Guests in the bungalows and two campsites share toilets and showers, one of which is outdoors behind a mat wall. Juliette often cooks crepes and other dishes from Brittany, and she speaks French, English, and Italian.

B.P. 55, 98732 Vaiea, Maupiti. ✆ **70.50.70.** Fax 67.82.47. www.pension-rose-des-iles.com. 2 units (both with shared bathroom), 4 tent sites. 10,000CFP–12,000CFP per person room or bungalow (including breakfast and dinner); 2,000CFP per person camping (no meals). No credit cards. **Amenities:** Restaurant; bar; watersports equipment. *In room:* No phone.

On Motu Tuanai

Poe Iti Guest House ★★   Facing the main island across a white-sand beach, this excellent pension is operated by Gerard and Josephine Sachet, who also own the *Maupiti Express*. Although they're located in the gardens rather than beside the beach, their four modern bungalows have air conditioners, refrigerators, and satellite-fed TVs, all rarities among French Polynesian pensions. The equipment is powered by both solar panels and two windmill generators, which stand incongruously above the flat island. Josephine serves family-style meals in a beachside pavilion. Morning and afternoon transfers to the main island are complimentary. Gerard speaks excellent English as well as French, but it will help if you know some *Français* when he's not around. Note that meals are not included in the rates here. Breakfast costs 1,000CFP; lunch and dinner, 2,500CFP each.

B.P. 39, 98732 Vaiea, Maupiti (on Motu Tuanai). ✆/fax **67.83.14** or 76.58.76. www.maupitipoeiti.com. 4 units. 9,000CFP double. No credit cards. **Amenities:** Restaurant; bar; watersports equipment. *In room:* A/C, TV, fridge, no phone.

On the Main Island

Maupiti Residence   These identical rentals are two of the new houses recently built beside Plage Tereia. Standing side by side, each has a large front porch from which steps lead down to the brilliant white sand. Inside is a living room with satellite TV, two bedrooms with private bathrooms, and a fully equipped kitchen. Breakfast is available at extra cost, and meals can be ordered for delivery from Snack Tarona (see "Where to Dine," below). Use of bikes, snorkeling gear, kayaks, Windsurfers, and a Hobe Cat are included in the rates, but air-conditioning in the bedrooms costs an extra 500CFP per day. The lower rates below are for stays of more than 2 nights.

B.P. 51, 98732 Vaiea, Maupiti. ✆/fax **67.82.61.** maupiti.residence@mail.pf. 2 units. 10,800CFP–12,000CFP double. MC, V. **Amenities:** Bikes; watersports equipment. *In-room:* A/C, fan, TV/DVD, kitchen, no phone.

Pension Tautiare Village   On the southern shore of the main island, this pension consists of one modern house with four bedrooms, each with its own hot-water bathroom. This a good place to see island life firsthand. The coast here does not have a beach, but the pension is about halfway between the village and Plage Tereia. The hosts will give you a free lift to either.

B.P. 16, 98732 Vaiea, Maupiti. ✆ **60.15.90.** Fax 60.15.91. pension-tautiare@mail.pf. 5 units (1 with shared bathroom). 7,500CFP per person. Rates include breakfast and dinner. No credit cards. **Amenities:** Bikes; watersports equipment. *In room:* Ceiling fan, no phone.

WHERE TO DINE

If meals aren't already included in the room rates, I strongly advise purchasing at least a *demi pension* meal plan (that is, half-board, or breakfast and dinner). This is especially important if you stay out on a *motu*, since you will not be able to go into the village after dark.

Snack Tarona FRENCH/TAHITIAN   This snack bar is Maupiti's chief gathering place for both food and libations. The picnic-style tables and chairs sit on a floor of coral gravel under a thatched-roof pavilion and usually catch the prevailing southeast trade winds, making this a refreshingly breezy location to recover from a bicycle ride around the island. The fare is the typical Polynesian potpourri of grilled steaks with french fries, shrimp with coconut-curry sauce, chow mein, and chicken and shrimp sautéed with vegetables. The *poisson cru,* made with freshly caught fish and tomatoes, cucumbers, and beans straight from the garden, is among the best I've had anywhere.

Farauru (lagoonside in the village). *©* **67.82.46.** Reservations not accepted. Main courses 800CFP–1,400CFP. No credit cards. Mon–Sat 11am–1:30pm and 6–8pm.

11 | THE TUAMOTU ARCHIPELAGO

W hen Paul Woodard and I sailed our 12.5m (41-ft.) yacht *Felicity* from the U.S. East Coast to Tahiti, our voyage was a relative piece of cake—until we came to the great line of atolls known as the Tuamotu Archipelago. Like a fence stretching for 1,159km (720 miles), the Tuamotu islands block the northeastern approaches to Tahiti. They are so low—never more than 3m (10 ft.) above sea level, not including the height of the coconut palms growing all over them—that hundreds of yachts and ships have been wrecked on these reefs, either unable to see them until it was too late or dragged ashore by tricky currents swarming between the islands and ripping through the passes into their lagoons. Those of us who go down to the sea in yachts well understand why the Tuamotus were once known as the Dangerous Archipelago.

Needless to say, Paul and I had to be on our toes when navigating these waters. While he signaled me from the bow, where he could more easily see coral heads in the water, I steered *Felicity* through narrow Tiputa Pass and into the lagoon at **Rangiroa.** Once safely inside, the calm water made it seem as if we had sailed into a monstrous lake in the middle of the South Pacific Ocean.

Like all atolls, those of the Tuamotus are necklaces of perfectly flat islets enclosing crystal-clear lagoons. Consequently, they offer a very different kind of experience than French Polynesia's high, mountainous islands. You will find many black-pearl farms (most of the country's orbs are produced here) and small villages with whitewashed churches, but there is much less to be seen aboveground than there is underwater—sharks, rays, and more than 400 species of colorful tropical fish inhabit these lagoons, making for French Polynesia's finest snorkeling and scuba diving.

There are a few gorgeous beaches in the Tuamotus, but most shorelines consist not of fine white sand but of gravel-like crushed coral, which can be brutal to bare feet. Bring and wear protection for you feet such as aqua socks, reef sandals, or old athletic shoes.

Of the 76 atolls, only **Rangiroa, Tikehau, Manihi,** and **Fakarava** have accommodations up to international standards; accordingly, they are the most visited. Only yachties and a few other intrepid travelers go elsewhere.

You will find drier and hotter climes than in the Society Islands, and sand so brilliantly white that it alone requires sunglasses in the midday sun. So grab your hat, your snorkeling gear, and your fins. Those of us who love the water are in for a treat up here in the Dangerous Archipelago.

RANGIROA ★★

The largest and most often visited of the Tuamotu atolls, Rangiroa lies 312km (194 miles) northeast of Tahiti. Its ring of low, skinny islets encloses one of the world's largest lagoons. At more than 70km (43 miles) long and 26km (16 miles) wide, it's big enough so that when you stand on one side, you cannot see the other. It's easy to see why it's named Rangiroa, which means "long sky" in the local language. In fact, the entire island of Tahiti could be placed in it, with room to spare.

In the early morning and late afternoon, schools of dolphins usually play in **Avatoru Pass** and **Tiputa Pass,** the two navigable passes into Rangiroa's interior lagoon, both on its north side. Currents of up to 6 knots race through the passes as the tides first fill the lagoon and then empty it during their never-ending cycle.

> ### Impressions
>
> *At Rangiroa you pick up a hundred natives with pigs, guitars, breadfruit and babies. They sleep on deck, right outside your bunk, and some of them sing all night.*
> —James A. Michener, *Return to Paradise*, 1951

Most visitors come to Rangiroa primarily for French Polynesia's best scuba diving, snorkeling, and fishing. Others venture across the lagoon to Rangiroa's islets, where they can relax on a pink-sand beach or frolic in a small lagoon within the big lagoon.

Rangiroa's airstrip and its accommodations are on a perfectly flat, 11km-long (7-mile) stretch of sand and palm trees running between Avatoru and Tiputa passes on the northern side of the lagoon. This main island does not have a name, as it actually consists of seven islets separated by narrow and very shallow reef passes, known in local parlance as *hoa.* On the western end, **Avatoru** village is the commercial and governmental center for the northern Tuamotu islands. On the eastern end, Tiputa Pass separates the main island from **Tiputa** village. All but a handful of Rangiroa's 2,500 residents live in Avatoru and Tiputa villages.

Rangiroa's tourism mainstay for more than 3 decades was the luxurious **Hotel Kia Ora,** which closed in 2009 ostensibly for renovations. I saw no signs of it reopening any time soon. Without it pumping cash into the local economy, the island's top boutique and its two best restaurants had gone out of business.

Getting Around Rangiroa

Rangiroa's airstrip is on the main island, about equidistant between Avatoru and Tiputa passes. The hotel and pensions send buses or vans to meet their guests. Otherwise, you are on your own, since there is no public transportation on the island.

I usually rent a bicycle, scooter, or car for a day to explore the main island. Its only road crosses six bridges, none of them with guardrails and some of them only one lane wide. The pavement is uneven, adding to the need for constant caution when driving here.

Rangi Rent a Car is the local agent for **Europcar** (✆ **800/227-7368** or 96.02.28; www.europcar-tahiti.com). Cars rent for 12,000CFP a day. Scooters and open-air "Bugsters" (the most you'll need here) cost about 6,000CFP for 8 hours (which is longer than you'll need to see the islet). Bicycles rent for 900CFP for a half-day, 1,500CFP for a full day.

Arehahio Locations (✆ **96.82.45** or 73.92.84) in Avatoru rents cars for 8,400CFP per day, scooters for 5,200CFP a day, and bicycles for 1,600CFP a day.

For a cab call **Taxi Rangiroa Men** (✆ **26.67.26**).

You can cross Tiputa Pass to Tiputa village via **Maurice Navette** (✆ **96.67.09** or 78.13.25), which operates water taxis daily from 6am to 5pm. Call or check with your hotel staff for schedules and fares.

[Fast FACTS] RANGIROA

The following facts apply specifically to Rangiroa. For more information, see "Fast Facts: Tahiti & French Polynesia," in chapter 13.

Currency Exchange
Banque Socredo has an agency with an ATM in Avatoru post. It's open Wednesday and Friday from 8am to noon; Monday and Thursday from 1:30 to 4:30pm.
Banque de Tahiti also has a branch in Avatoru. It's open Monday, Tuesday, Thursday, and Friday 8 to 11am and 1 to 4pm.

Drugstore Pharmacie de Rangiroa, in Avatoru

(✆ **93.12.35**), is open Monday to Friday 8am to 12:30pm and 3 to 6:30pm, Saturday from 8am to 12:30pm and 4:30 to 6:30pm, Sunday and holidays 10 to 11:30am.

Emergencies & Police
The emergency **police** telephone number is ✆ **17.** The phone number of the **gendarmerie** on Rangiroa is ✆ **96.03.61.**

Healthcare There are **infirmaries** at Avatoru (✆ **96.03.75**) and across the pass at Tiputa (✆ **96.03.96**).

Internet Access The hotels and pensions have wireless Internet access for their guests, and the post offices in Avatoru and Tiputa both have ManaSpot Wi-Fi. See "Staying Connected" on p. 70 for more information about ManaSpots.

Mail The post office in Avatoru is open Monday to Thursday from 7am to 3pm, Friday 7am to 2pm.

Water Except at the hotels, the tap water is brackish. Don't drink it.

Northern Tuamotu Archipelago

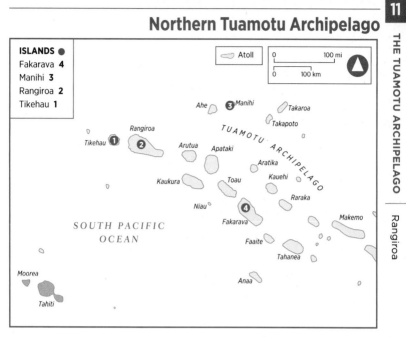

ISLANDS ●
Fakarava **4**
Manihi **3**
Rangiroa **2**
Tikehau **1**

Exploring Rangiroa
THE VILLAGES

Avatoru and Tiputa are typical Tuamotuan villages. I consider **Avatoru** to be the more interesting of the two. Not only is it on the main island (you will need to ride a boat across the pass to Tiputa; see "Getting Around Rangiroa," above), but it is also larger and has a bit more to see. When you get into town, follow the main road straight ahead until it makes a right turn at the picturesque Protestant church beside Avatoru Pass. Along the way, you'll see the *mairie* (town hall), post office, banks, and three general stores. The whitewashed stone wall along this part of the road is typical of Tuamotuan villages. You can make a loop by following the main street beyond the church; it circles a large public park before returning to the main road.

Come Up Here First

There isn't a lot to do in the Tuamotu Islands except snorkeling and scuba diving, which makes them great for resting and recovering from your long flight before tackling Tahiti, Moorea, Bora Bora, and the other Society Islands. I recommend coming here first for a little R & R, then visiting the more developed mountainous islands and their incredible scenery. In its infinite and not always perfectly guided wisdom, Air Tahiti has non-stop flights from Bora Bora to Rangiroa and Tikihau but not in the other direction.

💬 **The Exile Islands**

Although the archipelago is now known as the Tuamotu ("many islands"), the chain was once called Puamotu, meaning subservient islands. In the old days, chiefs on Tahiti who did bad things were exiled to the atolls. The indigenous peoples up here refer to the archipelago as Puamotu, its name in those days, and they still speak a distinct Polynesian dialect known in English as Puamotuan.

LAGOON EXCURSIONS ★★★

Plan to explore this fantastic lagoon. If you're not diving, the best way is on a full-day excursion. The two main attractions are on the eastern and western ends of the lagoon, each at least a 1½-hour boat ride away from the main island each way. That means you will spend at least 3 hours going and coming, so you will need a full day for each attraction—and a good set of sea legs if a strong wind kicks up choppy waves on the lagoon. The tours do not operate in bad weather or really rough seas, which are more likely to occur during the austral summer months from December through March. In other words, don't be disappointed if the weather washes out your planned excursion.

Don't forget to bring aqua socks, reef sandals, or old athletic shoes to protect your feet from jagged-edge coral.

Most interesting to me is *Lagon Bleu* (**Blue Lagoon**), on the western edge of the big lagoon. Literally a lagoon within a lagoon, this shallow pool is full of colorful corals and plentiful sea life. The area is a breeding ground for black-tip reef sharks, as you will discover when scores of the youngsters gather around your boat as it anchors about 200 meters (200 yards) from the inner lagoon. They will swim near your feet as you trudge across the shallow reef to the nearest islet—don't worry, they're harmless to humans. Your Polynesian hosts will throw them the left-over scraps from your *motu* picnic, which encourages them to stick around.

Thousands of seabirds nest nearby on aptly named *Ile aux Oiseaux* (**Bird Island**).

Les Sables Rose (**Pink Sands**), on the eastern end, is one of French Polynesia's most picturesque beaches, and to call it deserted is an understatement. There is no shade at the beach, however, so take extra precautions to avoid sunburn.

A third day here can be spent at *Ile aux Récifs* (**Reef Island**), on the south side, where erosion has created razor-sharp coral formations. Two bordering islets create a good swimming lagoon fringed by a fine beach.

Plan on paying about 8,500CFP to 12,000CFP per person for a full day's outing, including lunch, soft drinks, and use of snorkeling gear. Ask your hotel or pension to make the arrangements. The excursions don't go every day, so give them as much notice as possible.

A shorter alternative if you don't have that much time—or that much spare change—is a **glass-bottom boat ride** over the coral heads inside the passes. You'll see lots of fish and, if you're lucky, a shark or two. Most accommodations can arrange these excursions for about 3,000CFP per person.

While most of its lagoon shoreline consists of pebbly coral, and waves crash directly on the reef over on the ocean side, the main island does have a decent beach

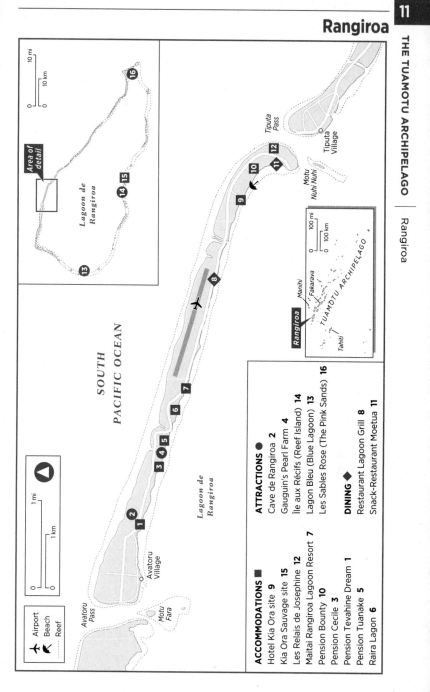

SOUTH
PACIFIC OCEAN

Lagoon de
Rangiroa

Avatoru
Village

Avatoru
Pass

Motu
Fara

Airport
Beach
Reef

0 — 1 mi
0 — 1 km

Area of
detail

Lagoon de
Rangiroa

0 — 10 mi
0 — 10 km

Tiputa
Pass

Tiputa
Village

Motu
Nuhi Nuhi

Rangiroa

Manihi
Fakarava

TUAMOTU ARCHIPELAGO

Tahiti

0 — 100 mi
0 — 100 km

ACCOMMODATIONS ■
Hotel Kia Ora site **9**
Kia Ora Sauvage site **15**
Les Relais de Josephine **12**
Maitai Rangiroa Lagoon Resort **7**
Pension Bounty **10**
Pension Cecile **3**
Pension Tevahine Dream **1**
Pension Tuanake **5**
Raira Lagon **6**

ATTRACTIONS ●
Cave de Rangiroa **2**
Gauguin's Pearl Farm **4**
Île aux Récifs (Reef Island) **14**
Lagon Bleu (Blue Lagoon) **13**
Les Sables Rose (The Pink Sands) **16**

DINING ◆
Restaurant Lagoon Grill **8**
Snack-Restaurant Moetua **11**

Dolphin-Watching

All of Rangiroa's hotels and pensions can arrange dolphin-watching cruises, usually for about 3,000CFP per person, but you can ride or walk to the public park at the western side of Tiputa Pass and watch them play for free. The best time is late afternoon, when the playful animals frolic in the pass, often leaping high above the waves churned by the strong currents.

where the island makes a hook on its eastern end—that is, from the Hotel Kia Ora eastward to Tiputa Pass.

SCUBA DIVING & SNORKELING ★★★

Rangiroa is one of the world's top diving destinations, with an extraordinary array of sea life. Hurricanes have damaged the coral here, so come to see fish, rays, and especially sharks rather than colorful reefs.

Tiputa Pass and **Avatoru Pass** are the two top dive sites in French Polynesia. You can see graytip and blacktip sharks all year, but the best time is from December to March, when huge hammerhead sharks gather just outside the passes for their mating season. Another good (and less scary) time is between July and October, when harmless manta rays look for mates. Diving in and out of the pass is for intermediate and advanced divers only, since it is both deep and subject to strong currents. Novices can dive inside the reef near Avatoru Pass and around the small islets sitting just inside both passes. Most other dives here are deep and long compared to American standards, so bring a buddy and be prepared to stretch the limits of the dive tables in order to see the magnificent sea life. Divers must be certified in advance and bring their medical certificates.

Scuba divers can **"ride the rip"** tide through Tiputa Pass, one of the most exhilarating waterborne experiences in French Polynesia. You are dropped off just outside the reef and literally drift with the incoming current through the pass, which looks like an underwater valley.

Snorkelers can get a similar thrill by drifting on the current past Motu Fara, just inside Avatoru Pass. Since everyone merely drifts with the current, and the guide boats are always nearby, anyone who can snorkel can go. The drift snorkeling trips cost about 5,000CFP and are well worth it. Book at your hotel activities desk.

Any of the hotels or pensions can arrange scuba dives. The best operators are **TOP-dive Rangiroa** (© 72.39.55; www.topdive.com). Other outfitters include **The Six Passengers** (© 96.02.60; www.the6passengers.com), which allows only six divers on its boat at any one time; **Raie Manta Club** (© 96.04.80; http://raiemantaclub. free.fr); and **Rangiroa Paradive** (© 96.05.55; http://paradive.chez.com). One-tank day dives cost about 6,500CFP. Night dives are more expensive.

SHOPPING

Rangiroa does not produce black pearls in the same quantity as Manihi, but you can visit **Gauguin's Pearl Farm,** west of the airport (© 93.11.30; www.gauguinspearl. com), and see how it's done. You can buy loose pearls in the shop, which is open Monday to Friday 8am to 5:30pm (with demonstrations Mon–Fri at 8:30am, 10:30am, and 2pm), weekends 9am to noon and 3 to 5pm.

Cave de Rangiroa, near Avarotu, is the display room for Vin de Tahiti (Tahiti Wines; (© **96.04.70;** www.vindetahiti.pf), French Polynesia's only vineyard and winery. The Carignan, muscat de Hambourg, and Italia varieties were first planted in a coconut grove out on the *motu* west of the main islet in 1999. Call to see if the cave is open and if vineyard tours are being offered.

Where to Stay

As I noted in the introduction to this section, the luxurious **Hotel Kia Ora** (© **96.02.22;** www.hotelkiaora.com) was Rangiroa's premier hotel for more than 30 years. It closed in 2009, ostensibly to undergo a thorough renovation. It had not reopened during my recent visit, and locals were betting on its remaining closed until worldwide economic conditions improve.

The same was true of its subsidiary, the **Kia Ora Sauvage,** a rustic, Robinson Crusoe experience on the southern side of Rangiroa's lagoon.

Check the website to see if they have reopened.

EXPENSIVE

Maitai Rangiroa Lagoon Resort In the absence of the Hotel Kia Ora, this modest but attractive resort is the only international-standard hotel here. Formerly a Novotel resort, it sits beside a rocky stretch of lagoon shoreline. Brilliant white sand has been brought in to form a sunbathing strip along the property, and you can swim off a pier extending over the lagoon. The 38 bungalows and main building (with French restaurant and bar) are tightly packed on limited land. The attractive units come either as individual bungalows or as duplex rooms that are narrower than the much more spacious bungalows. Both are tastefully decorated with tropical furniture and fabrics; they also have adequate bathrooms and front porches.

B.P. 17, 98775 Avatoru, Rangiroa. © **93.13.50.** Fax 93.13.51. booking@rangiroa.hotelmaitai.com. 38 units. 19,200CFP–29,300CFP bungalow. AE, MC, V. **Amenities:** Restaurant; bar; bikes. *In room:* A/C, ceiling fan, TV, fridge, hair dryer, Wi-Fi (500CFP/hour).

MODERATE

Les Relais de Josephine ★ 🍴 You can watch the dolphins frolic in Tiputa Pass from this comfortable inn, the creation of the charming Denise Caroggio, an English-speaking Frenchwoman who is the grande dame of Rangiroa. Her spacious bungalows flank a Mediterranean-style villa with an expansive veranda overlooking the pass. Guests can relax there or in a lounge equipped with a TV, VCR, and CD player. At night, the veranda turns into Le Dolphin Gourmand restaurant, serving excellent three-course French and Mediterranean meals. Furnished with reproductions of French colonial antiques, the bungalows have thatched roofs over solid white walls. Sliding doors open to the porches, outfitted with high-quality wooden patio furniture. Neither the doors nor the prop-up windows are screened, but the queen-size beds are covered by mosquito nets. The substantial bathrooms have double sinks and walk-in showers. Do anything possible to get one of the three units beside the pass.

B.P. 140, 98775 Avatoru, Rangiroa. ©/fax **96.02.00.** http://relaisjosephine.free.fr. 6 units. 15,200CFP per person, double occupancy. Rates include breakfast and dinner. AE, MC, V. **Amenities:** Restaurant; bar; bikes. *In room:* Ceiling fan, no phone, Wi-Fi (700CFP/day).

INEXPENSIVE

Pension Bounty   Although it's not directly beside the lagoon, a sandy path leads from this pension to the main island's best beach. Rooms are in a modern, motel-style building of red cedar and local *kohu* hardwood. Breakfast is included here, but each unit has a kitchen to go along with its ceiling fan, double bed, and private bathroom with hot-water shower. All of the windows are screened, as are the sliding doors to each unit's large porch. Dinner is available on request. The French hosts also speak English and Italian.

B.P. 296, 98775 Avatoru, Rangiroa. ℂ/fax **96.05.22.** www.pension-bounty.com. 4 units. 7,500CFP per person. Rates include breakfast. AE, MC, V. **Amenities:** Restaurant; bar. *In room:* Ceiling fan, kitchen, no phone, Wi-Fi (free).

Pension Cecile   The bungalows at this lagoonside pension are of the government-issue, plywood-and-shingle variety, each with a front porch and rear bathroom (with cool water showers). Seven of them face the lagoon, which is fronted here by a rock bulkhead. Plans were in the works to replace the ramshackle but charming open-air dining room with a modern building. Steps lead over the wall and into the lagoon, and a there's a pier. Some family members speak English as well as French.

B.P. 98, 98775 Avatoru, Rangiroa. ℂ **93.12.65.** Fax 93.12.66. pensioncecile@mail.pf. 9 units. 7,500CFP–8,500CFP per person. Rates include breakfast and dinner. MC, V. **Amenities:** Restaurant; bar; free airport transfers; bikes; watersports equipment. *In room:* Fan, no phone, Wi-Fi (free).

Pension Tevahine Dream   The most up-market of Rangiroa's pensions, Tevahine Dream was still a work in progress during my recent visit, as owners Norbert and Tilda Lau were upgrading to offer more of a hotel experience. Two of their spacious bungalows are built of thatch, pandanus mats, and other natural materials, including crushed coral floors in their large, garden-style bathrooms. The other unit is constructed of knotty pine planks and paneling. The largest has an outdoor kitchen. None has insect screens on windows and doors. Meals are prepared in another outdoor kitchen surrounded by a spacious wooden deck, into which a cabin-cruiser boat has apparently "sunk." Snorkeling trips, dolphin-watching excursions, and visits to Avatoru village are included in the rates here.

c/o Poste Restante, 98775 Avatoru, Rangiroa. ℂ/fax **93.12.75.** 3 units. 12,500CFP per person. Rates include breakfast and dinner. No credit cards. **Amenities:** Restaurant; bar; free airport transfers; bikes; watersports equipment. *In room:* Ceiling fan, kitchen (1 unit), fridge, no phone, Wi-Fi (free).

Pension Tuanake   This little lagoonside pension sits in a coconut grove on a point of land fringed by pebbly beaches on two sides. Friendly owner Roger Terorotua has six bungalows, all with plywood sides, thatched roofs covered with tin, front porches, mat-lined walls, screened windows, fans, and bathrooms with hot-water showers. They range in size from small units equipped with two single beds to a family-size affair with double and single beds both downstairs and in a loft, which can be entered via its own outdoor stairway. A former leader of Haere Mai, French Polynesia's organization of pensions and small family-run hotels (see "Pensions & Guesthouses," p. 74), Roger and his family speak enough English to make non–French speakers feel welcome here. His is a down-to-earth Tahitian place, with chickens and dogs running free around the property.

B.P. 21, 98775 Avatoru, Rangiroa. ℂ/fax **96.03.52.** www.pensiontuanake.pf. 6 units. 10,185CFP–19,215CFP double. Rates include breakfast. MC, V. **Amenities:** Restaurant; bar; free airport transfers; bikes, watersports equipment. *In room:* Ceiling fan, no phone, Wi-Fi (free).

Raira Lagon ★ Virtually next-door to the Maitai Rangiroa Lagoon Resort, Raira Lagon sits beside a rocky beach equipped with chairs under shade trees. French owners Jean-Frederic and Sandrine Ott, who also speak English, took it over in 2007 and upgraded the entire property, including the addition of air conditioners, sliding windows, and warm-water bathrooms to all of the thatched-roof bungalows. The lagoonside restaurant serves good French fare to both guests and outsiders, although you are likely to have little choice of main courses.

B.P. 87, 98775 Avatoru, Rangiroa. ✆ **99.12.30.** Fax 99.12.31. www.raira-lagon.pf. 10 units. 10,500CFP–14,000CFP per person. Rates include breakfast and dinner. AE, MC, V. **Amenities:** Restaurant; bar; bikes, watersports equipment. *In room:* A/C, ceiling fan, no phone Wi-Fi (500CFP/hour).

Where to Dine

Nonguests are welcome at Les Relais de Josephine's (see above) **Le Dolphin Gourmand** restaurant, where the three-course meals cost 4,750CFP per person. Make your reservations before 10am. Outsiders are also welcome in the dining rooms of the **Maitai Rangiroa Lagoon Resort** and the **Raira Lagon.**

The local *roulottes* set up shop after dark at the Tiputa Pass wharf and in Avatoru village. See "Don't Miss *Les Roulottes*" (p. 125), for details. You'll also find a few inexpensive snack bars in Avatoru.

Restaurant Lagoon Grill ★ FRENCH When the Hotel Kia Ora closed, assistant food and beverage manager Stephane Croutelle and other former staffers opened this lagoonside restaurant with al fresco tables under large shade trees. There are tables inside in case of rain, but outdoor dining is definitely the way to go here. Stars of the menu are super-tender Kobe beef steaks from the grill, which also braises fresh fish and tropical lobsters. Pizzas are available, too, although mine had too much cheese. A snack-type lunch menu also has burgers and fresh salads.

Main road (east of airport). ✆ **96.04.10.** Free pick-up with reservations. Main courses 2,500CFP–4,500CFP. AE, MC, V. Tues–Sat noon–2pm and 7–9pm, Sun noon–2pm.

Snack-Restaurant Moetua SNACK BAR You'll be snacking over the lagoon at this simple establishment next to the Tiputa Pass dock. It's a local favorite for burgers, sandwiches, *poisson cru,* and grilled steaks and fish served with fries. In other words, it's like a stationary *roulotte.*

At Ohutu Point (end of the main road at Tiputa Pass). ✆ **28.06.96.** Reservations not accepted. Most items 400CFP–1,000CFP. No credit cards. Mon–Sat 11am–4:30pm.

TIKEHAU ★

Separated from Rangiroa by a deepwater channel, Tikehau is much smaller and less developed than its huge neighbor. Its nearly circular lagoon, 26km (16 miles) across, is no more than 30m (100 ft.) at its deepest. The late Jacques Cousteau found in 1987 that the Tikehau lagoon had more species of fish than any other French Polynesian lagoon. Apparently that's still true, which makes this a great destination for snorkelers and novice divers, as well as providing a substantial income for Tikehau's 400 or so friendly residents, who make more money by trapping and shipping fish to Papeete than from black-pearl farms.

Most local residents live in **Tuherahera,** the only village, on a large *motu* on the southern side of the atoll. It's one of the prettiest Tuamotuan villages; hibiscus, frangipani, bougainvillea, and other colorful flowers seem to grow everywhere.

The Tikehau **airport** is on the same island as Tuherahera village; in fact, you can easily walk from the tiny terminal to the village jetty. All of the accommodations will meet you if you have reservations, and all either have, or can arrange, **bicycle rentals** for about 1,500CFP a day. There are no rental cars here since there is simply no place to drive them!

Tikehau is an excellent place to stay at one of the family-run pensions, for several of them stand beside one of French Polynesia's best beaches—a long, curving beach of both white and pink sand on the eastern side of Tuherahera. Unlike Rangiroa, where you must ride a boat for more than an hour to see a pink-sand beach, here it's actually in the village. The atoll is also home to the **Tikehau Pearl Beach Resort,** an excellent luxury hotel, and the charming **Relais Royal Tikehau,** each on a *motu* of its own (see "Where to Stay & Dine," below).

Lagoon Excursions, Snorkeling & Scuba Diving

Tikehau has much better beaches than either Rangiroa, Manihi, or Fakarava, and you can wade from them into the lagoon near your accommodations for excellent snorkeling. The Tikehau Pearl Beach Resort, Relais Royal Tikehau, and the pensions can organize boat trips out on the lagoon to little deserted islets such as **Motu Ohihi,** on the eastern edge of the atoll, where you can swim off a pink-sand beach. Out in the lagoon are **Motu Puarua** and **Motu Oeoe,** the so-called Bird Islands, where noddy birds and snowy-white fairy terns nest. These trips often include stops at a black-pearl farm and one of the fish farms, which provide so much of Tikehau's income. In a modern twist on the ancient stone Polynesian fish traps, such as at Maeva on Huahine (p. 158), the locals use bait to lure fish inside the traps and a

---

 Bring Cash & Don't Drink the Water

You'll find grocery stores, a post office, and an infirmary in Tuherahera, but **no bank.** Bring local currency, especially if your pension does not accept credit cards. (This same advice is true for Manihi and Fakarava.) The post office sells phone cards, which you can use to make local and international calls at a pay phone outside. You can buy Wi-Fi access from the pensions on the main island. As on all the atolls, do not drink the tap water on Tikehau. Bottled water is available at the pensions and from the grocery stores in Tuherahera.

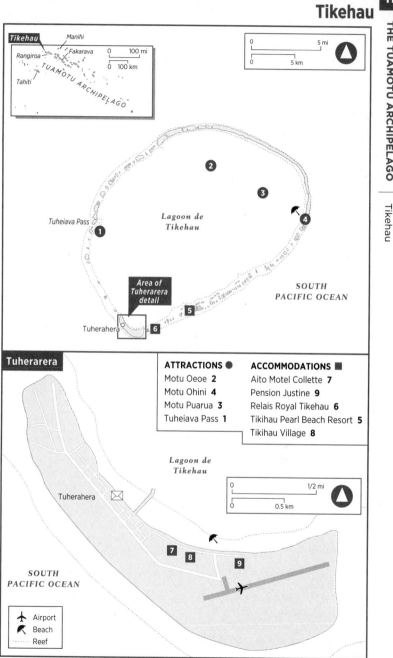

Tikehau

Manihi
Fakarava
Rangiroa
TUAMOTU ARCHIPELAGO
Tahiti

0   100 mi
0   100 km

0   5 mi
0   5 km

Lagoon de Tikehau

Tuheiava Pass

Area of Tuherarera detail

Tuherahera

SOUTH PACIFIC OCEAN

Tuherarera

ATTRACTIONS ●
Motu Oeoe **2**
Motu Ohini **4**
Motu Puarua **3**
Tuheiava Pass **1**

ACCOMMODATIONS ■
Aito Motel Collette **7**
Pension Justine **9**
Relais Royal Tikehau **6**
Tikihau Pearl Beach Resort **5**
Tikihau Village **8**

Lagoon de Tikehau

Tuherahera

0   1/2 mi
0   0.5 km

SOUTH PACIFIC OCEAN

✈ Airport
🏖 Beach
···· Reef

maze of chicken wire to keep them from escaping. Prices vary from about 7,000CFP per person for snorkeling trips to about 11,000CFP for a full lagoon excursion, including a picnic on a small islet.

Tikehau's best diving is in and around **Tuheiava Pass,** the one navigable entry into the lagoon. You will see graytip and blacktip sharks and the occasional manta ray, but the appeal here is the enormous population of colorful fish. **Manihi Blue Nui Dive Center,** based at the Tikehau Pearl Beach Resort (✆ **96.23.01;** www.bluenui.com), is one of the best in French Polynesia, with top-of-the-line equipment and hard-topped boats with ladders. Based at Tikihau Village, **Raie Manta Club** (✆ **96.22.53** or 72.89.08; http://raiemantaclub.free.fr) serves the pensions in Tuherahera village. They charge about 6,500CFP per one-tank dive and teach PADI certification courses. Raie Manta has snorkeling trips for 2,000CFP per person.

Where to Stay & Dine

There are no restaurants or snack bars on Tikehau, and only the **Tikehau Village** pension (see below) welcomes outside guests, so buy a meal plan or pay a room rate that includes at least breakfast and dinner. The pensions listed here have various rates depending on the number of meals provided, so make sure you understand what you're paying for.

EXPENSIVE

Tikehau Pearl Beach Resort ★★★   You may think you have made a horrible mistake as your transfer boat approaches, for rustic Tuamotu-style thatch disguises the luxuries awaiting at this resort, which occupies all of Motu Tiano, a small reef islet a 10-minute boat ride from the village and the airport. Other than a concrete patio separating the lagoonside pool from the conical-roof dining room and bar, everything about it is *très* Polynesian, with lots of thatch, mats, and bamboo. Strong currents in a shallow pass rip in and out beneath some of the overwater bungalows here, which means you can't go swimming from their decks. Consequently, opt for one of the "premium" suites built over quieter water; they do have ladders leading into the lagoon. The beach here has more pink and white sand than you'll find on Rangiroa and Manihi. Every unit is spacious and well-appointed, and the beachside units have large outdoor bathrooms behind high rock walls. The bungalows aren't screened, but the staff closes the windows and turns on the electric mosquito repellents while you're at dinner. Ceiling fans and the trade winds usually provide plenty of ventilation, but opt for a premium overwater or deluxe beach bungalow if air-conditioning is important to you.

B.P. 20, 98778 Tuherahera, Tikehau. ✆ **800/657-3275** or 50.84.54 for reservations, or 96.23.00. Fax 43.17.86 for reservations, or 96.23.01. www.spmhotels.com. 37 units. 46,000CFP–75,000CFP double. AE, DC, MC, V. **Amenities:** Restaurant; bar; babysitting; health club; Internet; Jacuzzi; outdoor pool; room service; sauna; smoke-free rooms; spa; watersports equipment. *In room:* A/C (13 units), ceiling fan, TV, hair dryer, minibar, Wi-Fi (500CFP/hour).

MODERATE

Relais Royal Tikehau ★★★ 🏨   At low tide, you can walk across the reef and another small islet to the village from this charming little hotel, the creation of the delightful Jean-Claude and Monique Varney. Jean-Claude worked in New Zealand for many years, and Monique spent her Papeete career in tourism, so both speak English as well as French. They call this their retirement project, and a fine one it is. Their restaurant-bar building and three of their bungalows stand beside a *hoa*, a shallow pass between theirs and the next *motu*. (I watched from my porch as stingrays trolled for breakfast in the pass just after daybreak.) Four other bungalows are next to a gorgeous beach of white-and-pink sand. The Varneys have four hotel-style rooms upstairs over a monstrous rainwater cistern. Monique decorated each unit with bright, color-matched drapes and *tivaivai* (handmade appliqué quilts). The bungalows and central building are lined with mats and covered with plastic imitation thatch (it lasts five times as long as natural leaves). Every unit has its own bathroom here, but only the bungalows have hot-water showers. The Varneys do not provide Internet access for their guests, but my netbook received a Wi-Fi network from other pensions, for which I had purchased an access card at another resort.

B.P. 15, 98778 Tuherahera, Tikehau. ©/fax **96.23.37**. www.royaltikehau.pf. 11 units. 26,000CFP–20,570CFP double; 32,000CFP–37,000CFP bungalow. Rates include breakfast and dinner. 2-night minimum stay required. MC, V. **Amenities:** Restaurant; bar; watersports equipment. *In room:* Ceiling fan, TV (beachside units), no phone.

INEXPENSIVE

The pensions below are all beside the long white-and-pink-sand beach beginning at Tuherahera village and running east to the end of the main *motu*. They are all cut from the same mold—that is, a few bungalows and a main building, where guests can relax and be fed. The island's airstrip is behind them, but don't worry: At worst only a couple of flights arrive and take off each day, and only during daylight hours.

> ### Fish, Fish & More Fish
>
> Given that fish farming is Tikehau's main industry, forget steaks and chicken. Get used to being served fish for lunch and fish for dinner and fish on your *motu* picnic. The locals even eat fish for breakfast.

Aito Motel Colette The closest pension to the village, Aito Motel Collette is named both for its owner and the *aito* (ironwood, or Australian pine) trees that shade her property. The beach here is wide, although the lagoon on this western end is shallow, especially at low tide. The clapboard-sided bungalows have high thatched roofs, now covered by tin painted green, and the front porches are trimmed with tree-limb railings, which adds a touch of charm. They come with various bed configurations (two doubles, one double, or a double and a single). Each has its own private bathroom with cold-water shower. Fans and mosquito nets are available. Guests gather in a large living room and on a lagoon-facing veranda, where meals are served. Collette speaks no English, so a knowledge of French will be helpful here.

B.P. 43, 98778 Tuherahera, Tikehau. ©/fax **96.23.07**. Fax 96.22.47. pensionaitomotelcolette@mail.pf. 5 units. 8,500CFP per person. Rates include all meals. No credit cards. **Amenities:** Restaurant; bar. *In room:* Fan, no phone, Wi-Fi (500CFP/hour).

Pension Justine Owner Justine Tetua allows campers to pitch tents on the sand, which helps to set her pension apart from the others. Her best units are three individual bungalows with private bathrooms by the beach. Two other buildings each have two bedrooms that share a bathroom. All have front porches and screened windows. All showers dispense cold water. Meals are served in the main house.

98778 Tuherahera, Tikehau. ©/fax **96.22.87** or 72.02.44. 5 units. 8,000CFP–10,500CFP per person in bungalow, 3,000CFP per person camping. Bungalow rates include all meals; camping rates include breakfast. No credit cards. **Amenities:** Restaurant; bar; bikes; Internet (free); watersports equipment. *In room:* Ceiling fan, fridge, no phone, Wi-Fi (500CFP/hour).

Tikehau Village ★   Often booked solid by Tahiti residents, Caroline and Paea Tefeiao's lively little hotel sits near Aito Motel Collette on the widest part of the beach. The lagoon is relatively shallow here, but a pier provides access to deeper water as well as a diving base for Raie Manta Club (see "Lagoon Excursions, Snorkeling & Scuba Diving," above). The bungalows have more Tuamotuan charm than any others here, with natural thatched roofs and walls trimmed with coconut-palm fronds. Each has a front porch, a ceiling fan, and a private bathroom (hot-water showers). Four smaller units are geared for singles and couples, while five larger bungalows attract families. Try to get a beachfront bungalow if you can. Under a big thatched roof, the moderately priced French and Tahitian restaurant is open to all comers, although reservations are strongly advised. Caroline speaks both English and French.

B.P. 9, 98778 Tuherahera, Tikehau. ©/fax **96.22.86.** www.tikehauvillage.com. 9 units. 10,000CFP per person. Rates include breakfast and dinner. MC, V. **Amenities:** Restaurant; bar; bikes; watersports equipment. *In room:* Fan, no phone, Wi-Fi (500CFP/hour).

MANIHI

Known for its black-pearl farms, Manihi lies 520km (312 miles) northeast of Tahiti. In fact, French Polynesia's pearl-farming industry began here in the late 1960s, and although many farms are now closed, the 30 or so remaining seem to sit atop nearly every coral head dotting the lagoon. Great lines of buoys float like crab pots atop the blue water, with long strands of pearl oysters suspended below.

Most of the atoll's 800 or so residents live in the only village here, **Paeua,** which sits beside **Tairapa Pass** on Manihi's southern side, the only navigable entry into the lagoon. (Both the village and the pass are also referred to as Turipaoa.) Manihi has very good diving excursions out on its lagoon; otherwise, I would look to another island for my atoll adventure.

> ## 🖐 Black Pearls
>
> Do not expect to buy the black pearl of your dreams directly from a Manihi farm at a huge discount, for they are all shipped to Papeete to be graded before being sold. Only one farm welcomes guests to see how pearls are produced, and then only on Monday, Wednesday, and Friday. Plan your visit accordingly.

Boats land at Paeua village at the jetty inside Tairapa Pass. From there, head inland for 1 block, turn right, and walk to the pass, where there's a grocery store fronted by a huge shade tree. After sipping a soft drink on a bench beside the tree, stroll along the seawall for a sensational view of the outer reef. You'll pass a small, picturesque Catholic church facing the sea.

The **airport** is on the same *motu* as the Manihi Pearl Beach Resort, which sends golf carts to fetch its guests from the terminal. The resort has bicycles for its guests' use, but there are no rental vehicles available here, nor is there public transportation.

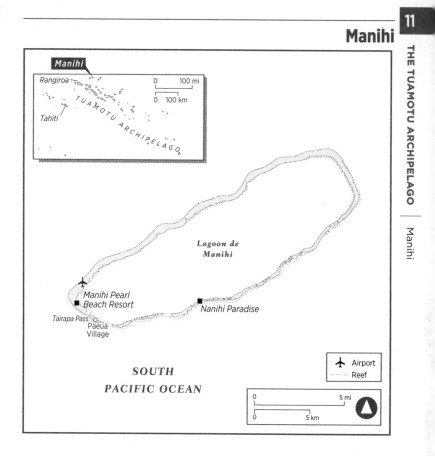

There is **no bank** on Manihi, so bring local currency if you plan to visit the village. The **post office** (which has pay phones) and the nurse-staffed government **infirmary** (© **96.43.67**) are both in Paeua. Do not drink the tap water; bottled water is available at the resort and from the grocery stores in Paeua.

Lagoon Excursions, Snorkeling & Scuba Diving

At 30km (16 miles) long by 5.6km (4 miles) wide, the clear lagoon is bigger than Tikehau's but not nearly as large—nor as deep—as those in Rangiroa and Fakarava. Like Tikehau, it's better for diving among colorful tropical fish, as opposed to the big rays and sharks that make diving at Rangiroa so exciting. That's not to say there are no sharks here; to the contrary, the lagoon seems infested with the small reef varieties, and rays feed on plankton near Tairapa Pass, which is wider and deeper than those at Rangiroa. Its strong-enough current makes "riding-the-rip" diving and snorkeling trips a highlight here. All dive sites are in or just outside the pass.

Manihi Blue Nui Dive Center (© **96.42.17;** www.bluenui.com), based at the Manihi Pearl Beach Resort (see below), provides top-of-the-line PADI diving. It charges about 6,700CFP per one-tank dive. The resort also allows for fishing (both deep-sea and hand-line in the lagoon), snorkeling trips, picnics on deserted islands, and lagoon excursions.

Where to Stay & Dine

Manihi Pearl Beach Resort ★★ This modern resort and the airstrip share a *motu* on the western end of Manihi's lagoon. Like at Rangiroa, the beach here is more pebbly than sandy, but guests can sun themselves on little islets equipped with palm trees and chaise lounges, or on a faux beach beside a lagoonside horizon pool. A thatched-roof bar adjacent to the pool is cozy and conducive to meeting your fellow guests. In addition to diving, activities include swimming, snorkeling (you can snorkel outside the pass), canoeing, visiting pearl farms and the village, lagoon and deep-sea fishing, spending a day on a deserted *motu*, and cruising at sunset. The prevailing trade winds can generate a choppy lagoon under the 19 overwater bungalows here. Both the overwater and beachside units have mat-lined walls, natural wood floors, ceiling fans hanging from mat-lined roofs, king-size beds, writing tables, ample shower-only bathrooms, and covered porches with two recliners. Each beachfront unit also has a hammock strung between two palm trees out front, and their bathrooms are outdoors behind high wooden walls. Although a majority of guests here are European couples, the staff makes English speakers feel at home.

B.P. 1, 99711 Turipaoa, Manihi. ✆ **800/657-3275** or 50.84.54 for reservations, or 96.42.73. Fax 43.17.86 for reservations, or 96.42.72. www.spmhotels.com. 34 units. 30,000CFP–60,000CFP double. AE, MC, V. **Amenities:** Restaurant; bar; free airport transfers; babysitting; bikes; health club; outdoor pool; room service; smoke-free rooms; spa; watersports equipment; Wi-Fi (500CFP/hour). *In room:* A/C (in premium overwater bungalows), ceiling fan, TV, hair dryer, minibar.

Nanihi Paradise You will really be away from it all at this pension, for it resides on a small *motu* on the south side of the lagoon, a 30-minute boat ride from the airport. Also residing here are owners Philippe and Vaiana Dantin and their daughter, Nanihi, for whom they named it. Philippe began his career as a chef in France but later worked for high-end resorts in Fiji, where he perfected his English. Here they have three plywood-and-tin buildings, each with two bedrooms joined by a long front porch and separated by a full kitchen and open-air bathroom (cold-water showers). The windows are not screened but mosquito nets drop over the beds. Philippe both catches and cooks the fish served at dinner. Most of the guests are families from Tahiti. The trip from the airport can be wet if the trade winds are blowing, which is most of the year here.

B.P. 76, 99711 Turipaoa, Manihi. ✆ **93.30.40.** Fax 93.30.41. www.nanihiparadise.com. 3 units. 13,500CFP per person. Rates include all meals. MC, V. **Amenities:** Restaurant; bar; watersports equipment. *In room:* Fan, kitchen, no phone, Wi-Fi (500CFP/hour).

FAKARAVA ★★

Southeast of Rangiroa and about 490km (300 miles) northeast of Tahiti, Fakarava's rectangular reef encloses French Polynesia's second-largest lagoon. This 60×24km (37×15-mile) aquamarine jewel is filled with such a rich variety of sea life that part of it has been designated a UNESCO nature preserve. Needless to say, there is some very good diving and snorkeling here.

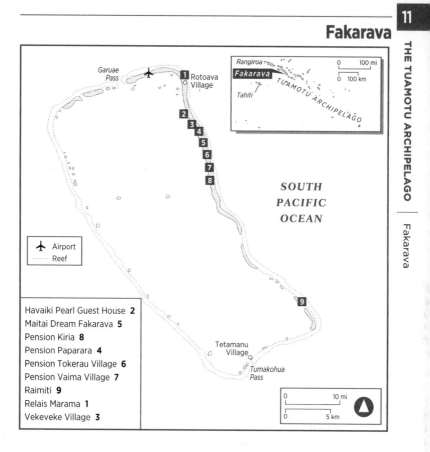

Unlike most Tuamotu atolls, I find Fakarava interesting from a historical stand-point. The airstrip and the main village, **Rotoava,** sit at the atoll's northeastern end, but the first European settlement here was at **Tetamanu,** on the far southern end of the lagoon beside narrow **Tumakohua Pass,** a 1½- to 2-hour boat ride from the airport. Coupled with fine snorkeling and diving in the pass, seeing the crumbling ruins of a prison and a restored 1834-vintage Catholic church make a visit to the ghostlike Tetamanu one of the more fascinating jaunts in the Tuamotu Archipelago.

The administrative center was moved to Rotoava to take advantage of **Garuae Pass,** the widest in French Polynesia. It's so wide and deep, in fact, that ships as large as the *Queen Elizabeth 2* can safely enter the lagoon and anchor off Rotoava. The cruise ship *Aranui 3* pulls in here on its way to the Marquesas Islands (see "Cruising in the Islands," in chapter 3).

From Rotoava, a road—facetiously dubbed "rue Flosse" because former French Polynesian President Gaston Flosse paved part of it prior to a visit by French President Jacques Chirac in 2003—runs for 30km (18 miles) along French Polynesia's longest *motu.* Beautiful beaches border this skinny strip of land that encloses the northern and eastern side of the lagoon (the western and southern sides consist of reefs dotted with a few small islets).

Rotoava has a **post office** (with public phone and ManaSpot Wi-Fi), **infirmary** (℡ **98.42.24**), school, whitewashed church, and three general stores, but **no bank.** The island's only resort, the White Sand Beach Resort, and most of its pensions accept credit cards, but bring local currency if yours doesn't. Do not drink the tap water on Fakarava; bottled water is available at the resort and the grocery stores in Rotoava.

Getting Around Fakarava

The airstrip is on the northern side of the atoll, 4km (3½ miles) from Rotoava. There is no public transportation on the island, so the accommodations meet arriving guests who have reservations. **Relais Marama** (see "Where to Stay," below) rents bikes for 1,200CFP per day. Other pensions have bicycles for their guests. Anyone can rent a scooter or bike from **Faka Location** (℡ **78.03.37**). Scooters cost 5,000CFP for a half-day and 8,000CFP for 24 hours, while bicycles go for 1,500CFP for 8 hours.

Exploring Fakarava

LAGOON EXCURSIONS ★★★

The most enjoyable lagoon excursion I've ever made in French Polynesia was a full-day excursion to the near ghost village of **Tetamanu,** on Fakarava's far southern end. After a 1½-hour speedboat ride from the resort, guide Coco Randal landed us at Tetamanu for a look at its early-19th-century prison ruins and restored 1834-vintage Catholic church. After petting a huge grouper and drift-snorkeling with the current inside Tuamakohua Pass, we went out for a picnic on a tiny islet completely surrounded by brilliantly pink sand. Unlike any other lagoon excursion in the Tuamotu Archipelago, this one adds a bit of history to fine snorkeling and swimming.

The resort and the pensions will organize these trips. They know who the guides are and can call around to see who has space for you. The all-day trips to Tetamanu village are very popular, so make your request as far in advance as possible.

One of the best is **Fakarava Explorer** (℡ **98.42.66;** www. fakarava-divelodge.com), operated by English-speaking Ato Lissant of Pension Paparara (p. 230). Ato takes dolphin-watching and snorkeling cruises to Garuae Pass, *motu* picnics, and fishing trips. He charges 12,000CFP per person for all-day tours to Tetamanu, with a minimum of five persons.

> ### R. L. S. Was Here, Too
>
> Before he arrived in Tahiti during his 1888 South Pacific cruise, Robert Louis Stevenson sailed his yacht *Casco* through Garuae Pass. He liked Fakarava so much that he moved ashore and stayed for 2 months in a house near the whitewashed Catholic church, the village's prime landmark

SCUBA DIVING & SNORKELING ★★★

Garuae Pass is one of the most exciting dive sites in French Polynesia. At nearly a kilometer (⅔ mile) across, it dwarfs all other passes in the Tuamotus and has just about every kind of fish, shark, and ray you're likely to see in French Polynesia; the coral here is very good, too. As at Rangiroa, hammerhead sharks gather here from December through March, manta rays between July and October. July also sees huge schools of marbled groupers. Most dives are of the drift variety; that is, the dive boat takes you beyond the reef and you ride the incoming tide through the 15m-deep (50-ft.) pass back into the lagoon. You had best be an advanced diver to explore Garuae Pass, but those with either advanced or intermediate credentials can dive the much smaller and less challenging Tuamakohua Pass, at the southern end of the lagoon. Novice divers can choose from several sites in the lagoon, much of which is teeming with sea life since it's a protected marine reserve.

TOPdive Rangiroa has a base at the White Sand Beach Resort (© **98.43.76;** www.topdive.com), while **Fakarava Diving Center** is at the nearby Pension Paparara (© **93.40.75** or 77.10.00; www.fakarava-diving-center.com). TOPdive charges about 7,500CFP for a one-tank dive in or near Garuae Pass, while Fakarava Diving Center charges 6,500CFP. A full-day's outing to Tetamanu, including a picnic lunch and diving in Tuamakohua Pass, goes for about 18,000CFP per person. The island's other reputable dive center is **Te Ava Nui Plongé,** in Rotoava (© **98.42.50;** www.divingfakarava.com).

BLACK-PEARL FARMS

You can spend a few hours wandering around Rotoava, a typical Tuamotuan village of about 450 residents, and a few more hours looking at black pearls. **Havaiki Pearl Guest House** (p. 230) operates a pearl farm on the southern end of the village. **Hinano Pearls,** 3km (2 miles) north of the White Sand Beach Resort (© **98.41.51**), also welcomes visitors and will pick up resort guests who call ahead. Neither charges admission to visit. You will have a chance to buy pearls at both, but bear in mind that French Polynesia's wholesalers usually scarf up the cream of the crop before you get a chance to see them. Before shelling out any cash, see "Buying Your Black Pearl" (p. 113). I wouldn't buy set pearls here.

Where to Stay
EXPENSIVE

Raimiti ★★   On a *motu* near the atoll's southeastern corner (a 1½-hour boat ride from the airport), this remote Robinson Crusoe–like getaway is the creation of partners Eric Lussiez and Florian Pilloud, who for many years owned Residence Linareva on Moorea (p. 148). They have two simple but charming bungalows, appropriately named "Fare Robinson" and "Fare Crusoe." On the lagoon side of the motu, Fare Robinson is made entirely of native materials. Its hot-water shower is in a separate thatch building. On the ocean side, Fare Crusoe is larger and more private; it has an indoor bathroom with hot-water shower. Eric was the owner-chef of Moorea's excellent Linareva Floating Restaurant, which sank a few years ago, so the food here is very good. Although their guests are predominately European, both Eric and Florian speak English as well as their native French. Solar panels provide a minimal amount of electricity at their eco-friendly resort.

B.P. 144, 98764 Fakarava. © **71.07.63.** www.raimiti.com. 2 units. 46,500CFP–53,000CFP double. Rates include all meals. AE, MC, V. 2-night minimum stay required. **Amenities:** Restaurant; bar; free airport transfers; watersports equipment. *In room:* No phone.

White Sand Beach Resort Fakarava   Formerly the Maitai Dream Fakarava, this unpretentious resort was showing some wear and tear during my recent visit, but is still the only international-standard hotel here. It sits beside the lagoon, a 15-minute *le truck* ride from the airstrip. A pier extends from the central building out over the multihued lagoon, but there are no overwater bungalows. Instead, the 28 units sit along or facing the pebbly beach, and most of their front porches have lagoon views. Built of timber with peaked shingle roofs, they are spacious and comfortably furnished with king-size and single beds, desks, and ceiling fans, and their ample bathrooms feature open-air showers with their own outside entry. The restaurant serves both indoor and outdoor tables and serves French fare with Polynesian influences.

B.P. 19, 98764 Fakarava. ✆ **93.41.50.** Fax 93.41.51. www.whitesandfakarava.com. 28 units. 27,000CFP–44,000CFP. AE, MC, V. **Amenities:** Restaurant; bar; babysitting; bikes; watersports equipment; Wi-Fi (in lobby; 500CFP/hour). *In room:* A/C, ceiling fan, TV, fridge, hair dryer.

INEXPENSIVE

Havaiki Pearl Guest House ★   Set beside the lagoon on the southern end of the village, this is the most popular pension in Rotoava—and with good reason, since most of its bungalows have front porches right on a lovely white-sand beach. Although they have plywood sides and tin roofs, inside they show traditional Polynesian style, with mat walls and ceilings over their double and single beds. The unscreened windows push out, but each bed has a mosquito net. Every unit has a modest private bathroom with cold-water shower. Owner Clotilde "Havaiki" Dariel makes sure all bungalows have fresh flowers, while her husband, Joachim, a Frenchman who speaks fluent English, tends to the family pearl farm at the end of a long pier out over the lagoon. The restaurant is open to all comers at dinner, and Snack-Restaurant Teanuanua is a short walk away (see "Where to Dine," below).

98763 Rotoava, Fakarava. ✆ **93.40.15.** Fax 93.40.16. www.havaiki.com. 7 units. 18,000CFP–22,000CFP double. Rates include breakfast and dinner. AE, MC, V. **Amenities:** Restaurant; bar; watersports equipment. *In room:* No phone, Wi-Fi (660CFP/hour).

Pension Kiria ★★   Fakarava's most charming pension is the creation of Kareen Langomazino and Kahui Lissant, who named it for their young daughter. They built their four bungalows completely of thatch and other local materials and added many Polynesian touches. My choice is the lagoonside Toau bungalow, which has a floor of crushed coral. Another has a sleeping loft, where you can stash your children. All units have open-air bathrooms with cool-water showers. Most of the shore here is a rock wall, but there is a small area where you can wade into the lagoon, and a white-sand beach is next door. Kareen, who speaks both French and English, serves meals in a dining room under a thatch roof.

B.P. 89, 98763 Rotoava, Fakarava. ✆/fax **98.41.83.** www.pensionkiriafakarava.com. 4 units. 9,500CFP per person double occupancy. Rates include breakfast and dinner. No credit cards. **Amenities:** Restaurant; bar; Internet (free). *In room:* Fan, no phone.

Pension Paparara   A short walk north of White Sand Beach Resort, this is one of the oldest pensions here. Owner Corina Lenior and her English-speaking husband, Ato Lissant, have five A-frame bungalows beside the rocky lagoon shore. Two of these have tiled bathrooms, while the others share toilets and both enclosed and outdoor showers (all showers are cold-water, whether attached to a bungalow or not). If you don't mind walking on a crushed-coral floor, the choice unit has a front porch literally hanging over the lagoon; it also has a second double bed up on a mezzanine. Corina serves meals either in their house or at picnic tables under a thatch pavilion. In addition to owning a pearl farm, Ato operates Fakarava Explorer lagoon tours (see "Exploring Fakarava," above), and Fakarava Diving Center is based here.

B.P. 88, 98763 Rotoava, Fakarava. ©/fax **98.42.66.** www.fakarava-divelodge.com. 5 units (2 with shared bathroom). 16,000CFP–19,000CFP double. Rates include breakfast and dinner. MC, V. **Amenities:** Restaurant; bar; bikes; Internet (500CFP/hour); watersports equipment. *In room:* No phone.

Pension Tokerau Village ★ You can see the pier sticking out from the White Sand Beach Resort, which is a short walk north of this pension, one of the more comfortable ones here. Owner Flora Borders and her daughter, Gahina (both of whom speak both French and English), have four government-backed bungalows separated from a fine beach by a carefully tended garden. Colorfully decorated with Tahitian fabrics, all units have shingle roofs, double beds as well as singles, satellite-fed TVs, private bathrooms with cold-water showers, and front porches with lagoon views. Their walls are hung with Borders family photos, including one of Flora with her father when she was 5 years old. Outsiders with reservations are welcome in Flora's open-air restaurant at the rear of the bungalows.

B.P. 53, 98763 Rotoava, Fakarava. ©/fax **98.41.09.** tokerauvillage@mail.pf. 4 units. 11,000CFP per person. Rates include breakfast and dinner. AE, MC, V. 2-night minimum stay required. **Amenities:** Restaurant; bar; bikes; watersports equipment. *In room:* Fan, TV, no phone.

Pension Vaiama Village Rustic but charming bungalows built entirely of thatch and other natural materials distinguish this pension, south of the White Sand Beach Resort. Their push-out windows are not screened, but mosquito nets hang over their double and single beds. Each has a bathroom (with cold-water shower) in outhouse-like buildings. Meals are served at picnic tables under a thatched roof beside the lagoon. The shoreline here is pebbly. Friendly owner Dorita Amaru speaks French but not English.

B.P. 25, 98763 Rotoava, Fakarava. ©/fax **98.41.13.** www.fakaravavaiama.com. 4 units. 18,000CFP double. Rates include breakfast and dinner. MC, V. **Amenities:** Restaurant; bikes; Internet (1 hour free per day); watersports equipment. *In room:* No phone.

Relais Marama The French term *relais,* which denotes establishments between a pension and a hotel, does not really apply to this lodging set in a coconut grove on the sea side of Rotoava village, where it can be quite windy. As owner Jacques Sauvage says, "It's more like camping out." The accommodations consist of small and basic bungalows with plywood walls, tin roofs, front porches, and push-out windows which are not screened (the double beds do have mosquito nets). You can pitch a tent in the coconut grove next to the ocean and share the communal kitchen and four very clean bathrooms with other guests. A Frenchman who has lived in the South Pacific for more than 40 years, Jacques speaks English fluently. He will take you to a private beach on the lagoon 4km (2½ miles) south of Rotoava.

B.P. 16, 98763 Rotoava, Fakarava. ©/fax **98.42.51.** teavanui@divingfakarava.com. 8 units (all with shared bathrooms). 9,000CFP double; 2,000CFP per person camping. Rates include continental breakfast. MC, V. **Amenities:** Bikes. *In room:* No phone; Wi-Fi (1,000CFP/hour).

Vekeveke Village Although it lacks charm, this pension does have two guest cottages whose front porches extend out over the lagoon, thus giving them the semblance of overwater bungalows. They and two smaller beachside units are built of plywood with tin roofs, and each has a bathroom with cold-water shower. The "overwater" units have a double bed downstairs and a single bed in a loft. Meals are served in a thatched-roof building with outdoor seating. You'll need to practice your French here, since owners Thierry and Lenick Tau do not speak English.

B.P. 149, 98763 Rotoava, Fakarava. ©/fax **98.42.80.** www.pension-fakarava.com. 6 units (all with bathroom). 12,600CFP per person. Rates include breakfast and dinner. MC, V. **Amenities:** Restaurant; bar; bikes; watersports equipment. *In room:* No phone.

Where to Dine

The **White Sand Beach Resort** and all the pensions serve meals to their guests. **Havaiki Pearl Guest House** and **Pension Tokerau Village** welcome outsiders who make advance dinner reservations (that is, before 2pm). As everywhere in the Tuamotu Islands, inquire whether the hotel rate you're paying includes meals.

In Rotoava, the appropriately named **La Roulotte** (© **75.60.49**) adds crepes and waffles to the usual meal-wagon menu of steaks, fried fish, and very fresh *poisson cru.* Most items range from 500CFP to 1,500CFP. Open Monday to Saturday from 11am to 2pm and 6 to 9pm, Sunday from 6 to 9pm. No credit cards.

Snack-Restaurant Teanuanua ★ FRENCH Cecile Casseville's open-air lagoonside restaurant, on the south end of the village and a short walk north of Havaiki Pearl Guest House, is a fine place for lunch while you're touring Rotoava, or for a sunset drink and dinner anytime. Cecile, a Frenchwoman who once was a tour guide on Moorea, speaks English fluently. Her best dishes are fresh fish pan fried and served in butter, vanilla, Roquefort, pepper, or mustard sauces. Nicely spiced tuna tartar is available in starter or main course sizes. For desert she replaces the apple in *tarte tartin* with fresh pineapple; it's a winner.

Rotoava, south end of village. © **98.41.58.** Reservations recommended July–Aug. Main courses 2,000CFP–3,200CFP. MC, V. Mon, Wed, and Thurs 11:30am–2pm; Fri–Sun 11:30am–2pm and 6:30–8:30pm.

THE MARQUESAS ISLANDS

Like most sailors navigating down from California or the Panama Canal, I made my first French Polynesian landfall in the Marquesas Islands, at the country's far northeastern edge. These hauntingly beautiful islands were *really* remote 3 decades ago. Air Tahiti made the 3½-hour flight up here once every 2 weeks, and few cruise-ship passengers ever came close to the Marquesas.

A lot has changed since then. Air Tahiti now flies from Papeete every day to **Nuku Hiva** and **Hiva Oa,** the two main islands; the cruise ship *Aranui 3* comes up here every 3 weeks; and the *Paul Gauguin* occasionally plies these waters (see "Cruising in the Islands," in chapter 3). To my mind, the *Aranui 3* is the best way to explore more than one or two islands up here, including **Ua Pou** and **Fatu Hiva,** two of French Polynesia's most dramatically beautiful islands (see "Exploring the Marquesas on the *Aranui 3*," below).

Some things haven't changed, for the Marquesas still seem a world apart from the rest of French Polynesia. They were the first to be settled by Polynesians, who came from Samoa around 150 B.C. and later went on to colonize Hawaii and Easter Island, the northern and eastern outposts of the great Polynesian Triangle. To this day, the Marquesan language is more like Samoan and Hawaiian than Tahitian. Instead of *"Ia orana,"* up here you are as likely to be greeted with *"Ka'oha"*—the origin of the Hawaiian *"Aloha."*

The Marquesans are proud of their ancient culture with its rich heritage of arts and crafts, especially stone sculpture, woodcarving, and tattooing. As in Samoa and Hawaii, their songs are more melodic and their dances are more graceful and not as suggestive as the hip-swinging versions in the Society Islands. Although more Marquesans now live on Tahiti than up here, those who remain are less stressed than their urbanized brethren.

The geography is different here, too. The islands lie between 7½° and 11° south latitude, placing them much closer to the Equator than Tahiti. The South Equatorial Current brings cool water from South America, however, thus both tempering the climate (it's much drier up here than in the Society Islands) and impeding the growth of coral reefs. As a result, these rugged volcanic islands drop abruptly into the sea. Many of the bays up here have beaches (many infested with biting *no-nos* [sand flies], especially on Nuku Hiva), but with little coral to form lagoons or fringing coastal plains upon which to build round-island roads, getting to them—or anywhere else, for that matter—can be major obstacles in the Marquesas.

In other words, you will be sorely disappointed if you come to the Marquesas expecting a luxurious beach vacation. But adventurous souls who like to shop for exquisite handicrafts, go hiking on spectacular paths, ride the descendants of horses brought here from Chile in the 19th century, and see some phenomenally beautiful scenery will thoroughly enjoy these remote and fascinating islands.

INTRODUCING THE MARQUESAS ISLANDS

Known in French as *Isles Marquises* and in the local dialects as *Te Henua Enata* and *Te Henua Enana* (literally, Land of Men), the Marquesas Islands are a 350km-long (214-mile) chain about 1,400km (850 miles) northeast of Tahiti and some 500km (305 miles) beyond the Tuamotu Archipelago. These distances alone make them seem as if you are visiting another country. In fact, they are farther away from Tahiti than the Cook Islands, the neighboring nation to the west.

The 10 main islands are all high, mountainous, and extremely rugged. They are the tops of extinct volcanoes whose ancient craters are clearly visible on topographic maps. The eroding caldera form high plateaus on some islands, and dramatic ridges fan out like spokes from the craters to form steep valleys on all of them. Black basaltic cliffs, buttresses, and stovepipe peaks seem to leap from the sea in many places.

The islands are administratively divided into northern and southern groups. **Nuku Hiva, Ua Pou, and Ua Huka** are the inhabited islands of the northern group. A deep ocean channel and about 80km (50 miles) separate them from the inhabited southern islands of **Hiva Oa, Tahuata,** and **Fatu Hiva.**

Nuku Hiva is the administrative center of both the archipelago and the northern group, while Hiva Oa is the capital of the southern islands. They are the only islands that are relatively easy to visit—unless you're on a cruise—and the only two with international-level accommodations.

> ### In the Middle of Nowhere
>
> The Marquesas' nearest neighbors to the east are the Galápagos Islands, approximately 3,400 nautical miles away. When you're on a yacht halfway between the two, you are as far away from dry land as you can possibly be on the face of the earth.

About 10,000 people live in the Marquesas today. There were many times that number when Europeans first arrived, beginning in 1595 with the Spanish explorer Alvaro de Mendaña, who named the group for Marques Don Garcia Hurtado de Mendoza de Canete, wife of Peru's reigning viceroy. When de Mendaña departed, the population had been reduced by 200 Marquesans killed in a skirmish on Tahuata. English Capt. James Cook dropped by in 1774 and estimated 100,000

The Marquesas Islands

Map of the Marquesas Islands showing Motu One, Hatutu, Eiao, Nuku Hiva (Hatiheu, Taiohae), Vaipaee, Hane, Ua Huka, Hakahau, Hakahetau, Ua Pou, Fatu Huku, Hiva Oa (Puamau, Atuona), Vaitahu, Tahuata, Motane, Hanavavae, Omoa, Fatu Hiva, with Airport legend and scale bars (50 mi / 50 km). SOUTH PACIFIC OCEAN.

people lived on the islands. Thanks to disease, a brief Chilean slave trade, and economic opportunities elsewhere, only 2,225 people lived here in 1926. The population has been increasing thanks to a high birthrate and the Marquesas' awakening to the modern world during the past 2 decades.

In the absence of coastal plains, more ancient Marquesans lived up in the valleys than down by the ocean. Compared to their seaside relatives in the Society Islands and the Tuamotus, they were mountaineers, and their descendants carry an independent mountaineer streak to this day. Seeing themselves as modern stepchildren of Tahiti, many would like to separate from the rest of French Polynesia and have their own political relationship with France.

Given the steep terrain and no shortage of boulders, the ancients built platforms of stone to make both their *maraes* (*me'aes* up here) and their houses level. Their *me'aes* dwarfed most *maraes* in the Society Islands and contained even larger *tohuas*, or meeting areas paved with stones. Human sacrifices were made at the *me'aes*, for the Marquesans lived an often violent, brutal life that included frequent wars between tribes followed by cannibalistic rituals. (The last known victim on Nuku

EXPLORING THE marquesas ON THE ARANUI 3

Like many folks cursed with wanderlust, my friend Muriel Weber and I had long dreamed of traveling the South Pacific on a tramp steamer, exploring remote, seldom visited islands while the ship loads and unloads its cargo. The notion has been part of South Seas lore since trading schooners started sailing the islands in the 19th century.

When American archaeologist Dr. Robert Suggs headed to Nuku Hiva to conduct research in 1956, the only way to the Marquesas was by a copra schooner that traded dry goods for dried coconut meat. With a schedule determined largely by which islands had copra ready to trade (closely guarded secrets in those days), it took him 2 weeks to sail from Tahiti to Taiohae Bay. He slept in a cramped cabin.

You can still share a cramped cabin or deck space on other interisland freighters from Papeete, but we much prefer the *Aranui 3,* a uniquely designed, 355-foot-long vessel that is half cargo ship and half modern passenger liner. "Cruising in the Islands" on p. 67 has more information.

The *Aranui 3* (the name means "Big Road") is indeed a hybrid. Christened in 2003, it was designed and built in Europe. Its front half carries up to 2,000 tons of cargo, while the rear half accommodates up to 200 passengers. Although not superluxurious, the very comfortable rear has a dining room serving fine French fare, a bar, a boutique, a large guest lounge, a video room, and a small outdoor swimming pool. Accommodations range from a dormitory with 18 bunks to spacious stateroom suites. It's not a big cruise ship with stabilizers, so it does roll a bit on the open ocean.

An expert accompanies most voyages, and on our first cruise it was Dr. Suggs, who lectured about Marquesan history and culture on the ship and led excursions to the *me'aes* and other historic sites, some of which he excavated for the American Museum of Natural History in the 1950s. Among his books are *The Archaeology of Nuku Hiva, Marquesas Islands, French Polynesia* (1961). In 2000, he coauthored (with Burgl Lichtenstein) *Manuiota'a: Journal of a Voyage to the Marquesas Islands,* a highly readable account of their cruise on the previous *Aranui.* It's packed with information about the islands.

We left Papeete on a Saturday and arrived at Fakarava the next morning for 2 hours of snorkeling in that great lagoon. After spending the rest of Sunday and all of Monday at sea we arrived for sunrise behind the phenomenal spires atop Ua Pou, one of the most incredibly beautiful islands I have ever seen. The nimble crew unloaded everything, from Toyota pickup trucks to toilet paper, while we explored Hakahau village on foot (comfortable walking shoes are a must) and were treated to a dance show and lunch ashore. That afternoon, the *Aranui 3* moved around to Hakahetau village on Ua Pou's northwest coast, then sailed to Taiohae Bay on Nuku Hiva for the night.

A few new passengers came aboard at Taiohae, for in addition to Papeete, you can join or leave the ship at Nuku Hiva, Hiva Oa, Fakarava, or Rangiroa. A few came on just to ride from one island to the next.

And so it went for 10 more days as we visited Hiva Oa (twice), Fatu Hiva, Tahuata, Ua Huka, and back to Nuku Hiva and Ua Pou prior to stopping for a half-day's picnic at Rangiroa then returning to Tahiti.

Thanks to the *Aranui 3* and her marvelous Polynesian captain and crew, we lived our tramp steamer dream—in anything but a cramped cabin.

Hiva was a 10- or 11-year-old girl eaten in 1924; her skull is in the American Museum of Natural History in New York.)

Stylized stone **tikis** representing ancestors and tribal gods adorned the *me'aes*. (Tiki is spelled and pronounced *ti'i* up here, but I'll keep the *k* in it for simplicity's sake.) The remaining tikis are the largest examples of the Marquesans' extraordinary skills as stone carvers and woodcarvers. Unlike the puritanical 19th-century Protestant missionaries in the Society Islands, who made the Tahitians destroy their idolatrous stone tikis, the Catholic missionaries had more faith in the heathens up here. The priests let them keep most of their tikis, but made them break off the genitalia. The castrated tikis add a delightfully ancient aspect to many Marquesan *me'aes*.

While some *paepaes* (stone housing platforms) are still in use, you will see hundreds of them deserted and overgrown up in the valleys. Coupled with the breadfruit, pandanus, and other trees the ancients planted near their platform homes, these depopulated valleys make the Marquesas Islands seem mysteriously haunted.

Getting To & Around the Marquesas

The remoteness of the islands and the scarcity of interisland transportation deserve special attention when planning your trip. It's easy to get to Hiva Oa and Nuku Hiva, since **Air Tahiti** flies to both from Papeete almost daily. One of these flights, usually on Saturday, stops in Rangiroa before going on to Hiva Oa and Nuku Hiva (in that order), so you can also fly here after visiting the Tuamotu Archipelago without having to return and connect in Papeete.

Air Tahiti's small planes connect Nuku Hiva, Hiva Oa, Ua Huka, and Ua Pou (no other Marquesan island has an airstrip), so don't be surprised if you are ferried on a smaller plane between Nuku Hiva and Hiva Oa to catch your return flight to Tahiti.

Otherwise, there is no scheduled transportation system among the Marquesas Islands. You will be on your own in tracking down one of the small boats or trading ships that irregularly connect the islands. This is relatively easy between Hiva Oa and nearby Tahuata, but not elsewhere. For this reason, I recommend taking a cruise on the *Aranui* 3 or another ship to see more than Nuku Hiva and Hiva Oa in any reasonable amount of time and with as few hassles as possible.

See "Getting Around Tahiti & French Polynesia" and "Cruising in the Islands," in chapter 3, for more information.

Visitor Information

Tahiti Tourisme in Papeete distributes information about the Marquesas (see "Visitor Information," in chapter 3). Nuku Hiva and Hiva Oa both have local tourism

---

Be Prepared to Be Flexible

Some of Air Tahiti's flights from Papeete to the Marquesas stop first at Hiva Oa before going on to Nuku Hiva. The airstrip on Hiva Oa sits high up on a ridge and can be closed due to fog or rain, especially from March through August. When that happens, the plane skips Hiva Oa and goes directly to Nuku Hiva. Accordingly, pay close attention to the airline's schedule when planning your trip. And always be prepared to be flexible up here.

committees, which have joined together to host a website at **www.marquises.pf**. The committees have visitor information offices on both islands (see the "Fast Facts" sections for Nuku Hiva, below, and Hiva Oa, later in this chapter).

NUKU HIVA ★★

Although it appeared on the world's television screens in 2002 as the setting of the fourth *Survivor* series, Nuku Hiva first became famous in the 1840s, when Herman Melville jumped ship and was befriended for several weeks by the otherwise ferocious Taipi tribe in the rugged **Taipivai Valley.** Based on that adventure, Melville's first novel, *Typee,* launched his illustrious writing career.

Then as now, Nuku Hiva is the largest of the Marquesas Islands and the second largest in French Polynesia. It is so rugged that a majority of its 330 sq. km (127 sq. miles) surely go straight up and down. Two volcanoes formed Nuku Hiva. The large central crater has eroded away on one side, leaving in its bottom the high, cool **Toovii Plateau,** now devoted to farms and pastureland. On the southern coast, half of another crater fell into the sea, creating deep **Taiohae Bay,** the largest harbor in the Marquesas and a favorite port for cruising yachts. On the northern side of the crater, **Mount Muake** abruptly rises for 864m (2,834 ft.), forming an awesome backdrop to the town of **Taiohae,** the capital of the archipelago, and its half-moon harbor. Other than arriving by water, the only way into Taiohae is to descend Mount Mauke's clifflike face.

The central mountains cut off what trade winds blow at this latitude, leaving the western third of Nuku Hiva a desert, known as the **Terre Déserte (Deserted Land).** Rather than being lush and green, the valleys here are dry canyons reminiscent of the American Southwest and the Australian Outback. With the exception of a few cattle ranches and homes near the airport, this area is quite literally deserted.

Getting Around Nuku Hiva

The **Nuku Ataha Airport** is on Nuku Hiva's dry northwestern corner, 48km (29 miles) from Taiohae. A vehicle will be sent from your accommodations to meet you for about 8,000CFP per person round-trip. From the airport, it's a ride of about 1 hour on the winding road that climbs up and down two steep mountain ridges and across the Toovii Plateau before descending into Taiohae. Add that to the 3½-hour flight from Papeete, and you can easily eat up a day just getting to Taiohae. There is some great scenery along the way, however, so I look at the ride from the airport to Taiohae as just another sightseeing excursion.

Nuku Hiva is not a good place for those prone to carsickness. All of its few roads are narrow, winding, and often treacherous, especially when wet. In places, they are literally blasted into the sides of cliffs. If you miss one of the many 180-degree hairpin curves, you could plunge more than 1,000 feet to your ultimate demise. For this reason, I recommend exploring by guided tour rather than rental vehicle (see "Exploring Nuku Hiva," below). If you insist on taking your life into your own hands, **Pension Moana Nui** (© **92.03.30;** http://pensionmoananui.ifrance.com), in Taiohae, rents four-wheel-drive vehicles for about 12,500CFP per day. I warned you, though, so don't sue me if you drive off a cliff.

There is no regular taxi service on Nuku Hiva as such, but several locals will take you about in their four-wheel-drive vehicles. The arrangements can be made through

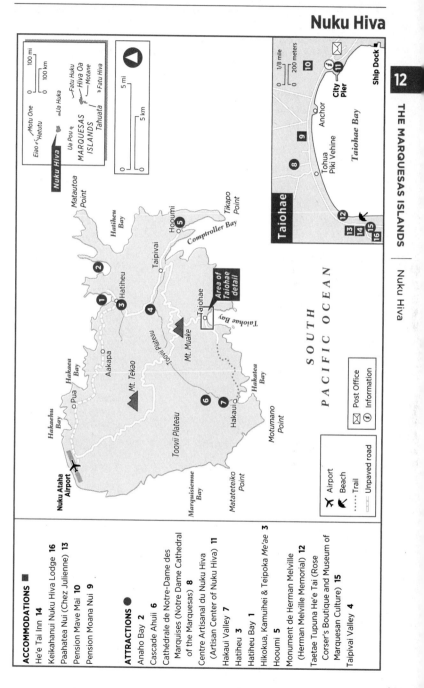

ACCOMMODATIONS ■

He'e Tai Inn **14**
Keikahanui Nuku Hiva Lodge **16**
Paahatea Nui (Chez Julienne) **13**
Pension Mave Mai **10**
Pension Moana Nui **9**

ATTRACTIONS ●

Anaho Bay **2**
Cascade Ahuii **6**
Cathédrale de Notre-Dame des
  Marquises (Notre Dame Cathedral
  of the Marquesas) **8**
Centre Artisanal du Nuku Hiva
  (Artisan Center of Nuku Hiva) **11**
Hakaui Valley **7**
Hatiheu **3**
Hatiheu Bay **1**
Hikokua, Kamuihei & Teipoka Me'ae **3**
Hooumi **5**
Monument de Herman Melville
  (Herman Melville Memorial) **12**
Taetae Tupuna He'e Tai (Rose
  Corser's Boutique and Museum of
  Marquesan Culture) **15**
Taipivai Valley **4**

your accommodations, or contact **Nuku Hiva Transports** (✆ **92.06.08**), **Huku Tours** (✆ **92.04.89**), or **Rose Marie Tours** (✆ **92.05.96**). Fares depend on how far you want to go, so be sure to agree on a price before setting out.

Residents of the outlying villages are as likely to travel by **boat** as they are by vehicle. Several individuals rent crewed boats to take you from place to place, such as from Taiohae around to the Hakaui Valley, or from Hatiheu to Anaho on the north shore. Ask at your accommodations to arrange a boat, or contact the local tourism committee for advice (see "Visitor Information" under "Fast Facts: Nuku Hiva," below). The boats moor at the marina on the eastern side of Taiohae Bay.

[FastFACTS] NUKU HIVA

The following facts apply specifically to Nuku Hiva. For more information, see "Fast Facts: Tahiti & French Polynesia," in chapter 13.

Currency Exchange
Banque Socredo has an office with ATM on the waterfront in Taiohae. Hours are Monday through Friday from 7:30 to 11:30am and 1:30 to 4pm.

Drugstores
Pharmacie Nuku Hiva, on the western side of Taiohae (✆ **91.00.90**), is open Monday through Friday from 8:30am to noon and 3 to 5pm, Saturday from 9 to 11am.

Emergencies & Police
The **emergency police** phone number is ✆ **17.** The phone number of the **gendarmerie** in Taiohae is ✆ **92.03.61.**

Healthcare Taiohae has a government **hospital** (✆ **91.02.00**), and Haitiheu and Taipivai villages both have **infirmaries.**

Internet Access The island's hotels and pensions have Internet access for their guests, and the post office has ManaSpot Wi-Fi.

Post Office The post office in Taiohae is uphill between the small boat marina and the cruise-ship port. It's open

Monday through Thursday from 7:30 to 11:30am and noon to 3:30pm, Friday to 4:30pm.

Visitor Information
The **Office du Tourisme de Nuku Hiva,** B.P. 32, 98742 Nuku Hiva (✆/fax **92.08.25;** www.marquises. pf), is in the municipal market, on the waterfront opposite the Taiohae *mairie* (town hall). It's open Monday to Friday from 7:30am to 3:30pm, Saturday from 7:30am to 12:30pm.

Water Don't drink the tap water on Nuku Hiva. The grocery stores sell bottled water.

Exploring Nuku Hiva

Given the sometimes dangerous condition of the roads and the difficulty of finding things on Nuku Hiva, I recommend seeing the sights on a guided tour. The best are offered by the **Keikahanui Nuku Hiva Lodge** (p. 246), which offers a full-day tour to the Taipivai Valley and Hatiheu for about 9,000CFP per person, including lunch at Chez Yvonne. It also has a half-day version that goes as far as the Taipivai. The lodge's guides speak English.

Other options are Deane Richard Temarama of **Temarama Tours** (✆ 28.08.36 or 24.66.42; temarama.tour@hotmail.pf), and **Jocelyn Henua Enana Tours** (✆ **92.00.52** or 74.42.23).

TAIOHE

It's easy to explore the town of Taiohae on foot, since its main street follows the curving shoreline of Taiohae Bay for about 3.5km (2 miles).

While most other cruise ships anchor out in the harbor, the *Aranui 3* docks at the main wharf on the eastern side of the bay. Between it and town is **Tu Hiva,** a hill where U.S. Navy Commodore David Porter built a fort in 1813. Porter used Taiohae as a temporary base from which he raided British shipping in the Pacific during the War of 1812. He named this outpost Fort Madison, in honor of then U.S. President James Madison. The French renamed the spot Fort Collette after they took over in 1842. Nothing remains on the hill today except wild goats and a navigation marker.

The town hall, wharf, post office, and hospital are in the original French settlement on the eastern side of the bay. Beside the bay is a modern complex housing the visitor information office, a day-time snack restaurant, a small vegetable market, and the **Centre Artisanal du Nuku Hiva** (**Artisan Center of Nuku Hiva;** no phone), where some very fine handicrafts are on sale Monday to Saturday from 7:30am to 4pm.

Most commercial activity is in the middle of town, or just east of where the airport road comes down off the Mount Muake cliff. The junction is marked by a large seaside cross in honor of the first Catholic mission here.

Follow the next road west inland into the Meau Valley and you'll see the *Cathédrale de Notre-Dame des Marquises* (**Notre Dame Cathedral of the Marquesas).** The gate to the compound was part of a wall from the original 19th-century church, but this modern version was built in 1977. Be sure to go inside and see the marvelous stone carvings and woodcarvings that each island donated to the cathedral. The pulpit and Stations of the Cross are elaborately carved from single trunks of *tamanu* (ironwood, or Australian pine). The artists gave the biblical stories a Marquesan touch. St. Paul holds a spear instead of his Sword of Damascus, the breadfruit substitutes as the olive tree, and Hinano beer is depicted as one of the seven deadly sins!

Farther up the valley is a restored *me'ae.*

On the west side of the bay, you'll pass a large park and then the *Monument de Herman Melville* (**Herman Melville Memorial),** a terrific wooden sculpture executed in 1991 by noted local artisan Kahee Taupotini. There's a fine view from here back along the bay. This side of the bay is skirted by a black-sand beach, where locals go swimming and launch their racing canoes. For a bit of refreshment and another excellent view, head up the hill to the Keikahanui Nuku Hiva Lodge (p. 246).

THE TAIPIVAI VALLEY ★★

My most memorable day on Nuku Hiva was spent traveling to the rugged northeastern side of the island in the company of a tour guide. Although it's hardly more than 25km (15 miles) to the end of the road, this excursion required a full day, a good part of it spent just getting from place to place. This is the top trip for anyone to make, since most of Nuku Hiva's key sites are here, especially Melville's **Taipivai Valley** and the highly picturesque northeast shore village of **Hatiheu.** From Hatiheu, you can hike or take a boat to one of the few coral reefs in the Marquesas, at **Anaho** on the island's northeastern corner.

After climbing up Mount Muake out of Taiohae (there's an unbelievably beautiful view of Taiohae Bay from the top), the road follows a mountain ridge, from which you can see one of the beaches used in *Survivor*. It then steeply descends down to **Taipivai** village, at the head of Controller Bay. From there, another coastal road goes southeast to **Hooumi,** a small village on yet another bay. Since access across Hooumi's white-sand beach is easy, some cruise-ship passengers land here rather than at Taipivai, beside the shallow Taipivai River.

The paved road retraces Herman Melville's footsteps up into the steep **Taipivai Valley.** Your guide will stop about halfway up the valley at restored *paepaes* (stone platforms), the only remnants of the village where Melville reputedly stayed for a few weeks after he deserted an American whaler in 1842. In *Typee,* Melville has his protagonist fall in love with a local beauty, Fayaway, after being captured by the powerful Taipi tribe. Instead of sticking around, he escapes after watching a cannibal ceremony. In reality, the Taipi were friendly and treated Melville well. You'll see several waterfalls off in the distance as you climb higher into the valley.

HATIHEU ★★★

Once out of the valley, you will soon be looking down at **Hatiheu,** one of my favorite villages in all of French Polynesia. It sits in a little bay beside a curving black-sand beach. A Moorea-esque ridge topped by basaltic stovepipes dramatically looms over the western end of the beach, creating a quintessentially South Seas scene. Dating to 1872, a white statute of the Virgin Mary stands atop a cliff overlooking the bay. The best view of the bay is from the stone wharf on the eastern side (follow the dirt road along the shoreline).

Like me, Robert Louis Stevenson was quite fond of Hatiheu and its spectacular setting when he sailed here in 1888. (Great minds do think alike!)

HIKOKUA, KAMUIHEI & TEIIPOKA ME'AES ★★★

Among several restored *me'aes* in the Marquesas, three of the most impressive are **Hikokua, Kamuihei,** and **Teiipoka,** on the Taipivai road above Hatiheu. **Hikokua** is a large open area used for ceremonies, dances, and human sacrifices. Restored for the 1999 Marquesas Festival of the Arts, it has impressive tiki statues. The Kamuihei and Teiipoka sites flank the road higher up in the valley. The expansive Kamuihei part is definitely worth exploring, for it has well-preserved tikis, petroglyphs carved

Lunch at Yvonne's

Whether on a tour or on your own, plan to have lunch in Hatiheu at **Restaurant Hinako Nui,** at Yvonne Katupa's **Chez Yvonne** pension across the road from the beach (ⓒ **92.02.97;** hinakonui@ mail.pf). This thatched-roof charmer specializes in fresh seafood, including delicious shrimp beignets and char-grilled tropical lobster. Everything comes with fresh local vegetables and breadfruit fritters, and dessert is often flambéed bananas. Main courses range from 1,500CFP to 3,000CFP. If you decide to stay overnight, Yvonne has five simple bungalows to rent in the gardens behind the restaurant for 18,000CFP double, including all meals. Bring cash, since Yvonne does not accept credit cards.

into huge boulders (no one knows what they mean), and a pit under an enormous banyan tree, in which human sacrifices were said to have been restrained prior to being dispatched (it's more likely they were used to store food for feasts or to ferment breadfruit *poi,* one of the Polynesians' favorite desserts, which kept well in times of drought). Dr. Robert Suggs, the American archaeologist who often serves as guest lecturer on the *Aranui* 3 and the *Paul Gauguin,* discovered human skulls and leg bones in the banyan tree when he excavated the site in 1956 and 1957. The large sizes of these structures are a testament to how many people once lived in this now-deserted valley.

ANAHO ★★

Across a ridge east of Hatiheu, the small village of **Anaho** sits beside a palm-fringed, white-sand beach in yet another bay visited by Robert Louis Stevenson in 1888. Anaho is unusual, however, because it has one of the few coral formations in the Marquesas, a fringing reef off the beach over which you can snorkel. The sand beach has the usual contingent of biting sand flies, so I wear both insect repellent and sunscreen.

> ### Be Careful Around this Tiki
>
> If you are thinking of infertility treatments, you can save a bundle by visiting Hikokua, the restored *marae* near Hatiheu village. Hikokua has a carved tiki in the shape of a phallus. Any woman who touches it, legend says, will soon become pregnant.

Although seldom used by ships these days, **Anaho Bay** is one of the best natural harbors in the Marquesas. In October 1943, an accidental fire severely damaged the cruiser USS *Concord,* which anchored here while carrying Rear Admiral Richard Byrd—of arctic exploration fame—on a mission to find World War II anchorages and potential airfields for the U.S. Navy. Byrd and the *Concord* survived, but 26 American sailors killed in the fire were given seamen's burials in the bay.

You can hire a boat at Chez Yvonne in Hatiheu (see "Lunch at Yvonne's," above) for the 10-minute ride around to Anaho, or hike over the saddle between the two bays. The path starts at a crossroads about 100m (328 ft.) east of the restaurant. The rather strenuous hike takes about 45 minutes each way, but you'll have a nice view of Anaho Bay from atop 218m-high (720-ft.) Teavaimaoaoa Pass.

HAKAUI VALLEY & AHUII WATERFALL

Over Mount Muake to the west of Taiohae, the **Hakaui Valley** is home to the **Cascade Tevaipo,** one of the world's highest waterfalls at 350m (1,159 ft.). The waterfall pours off a high plateau at the head of the valley. This area was a prime set for the *Survivor* television show. The trail from Taiohae into the valley is too dangerous for hiking, but your accommodations can arrange a boat to take you around to Hakaui, from where an ancient stone trail goes upriver to the falls, about a 2-hour walk. Or you can ride horseback from Taiohae (see "Hiking & Horseback Riding," below). Bring food, water, and insect repellent, and wear shoes suitable for fording the river.

Hiking & Horseback Riding

Nuku Hiva has a number of fine beaches, such as those at Hatiheu and Anaho (see "Exploring Nuku Hiva," above), and there's a black-sand beach on the western side of Taiohae Bay. Unfortunately, they are all infested with biting *no-nos* (sand flies). These nearly invisible pests are particularly aggressive at dusk. If you do go swimming, try to pick a day when the wind is blowing in from offshore, and always lather up with insect repellent.

HIKING

You will have a pretty good hike just walking along the shoreline of Taiohae village. For something a great deal more strenuous, climb the airport road to the top of Mount Muake for its view down over the bay.

In the old days, Marquesans got around by boat or by trails up and over the mountains. Many of these old tracks still exist. One of them begins at the Taetae Tupuna He'e Tai (see "Rose Corser & Marquesan Art," p. 245), just downhill from the Keikahanui Nuku Hiva Lodge (p. 246), and goes for 3.5km (2 miles) into **Collette Bay.** The usually deserted beach over there is a fine place for a picnic, but remember to bring—and apply!—your insect repellent.

Marquises Rando (✆ **92.07.13** or 21.08.74; www.marquisesrando.com) provides professional guides for individuals or groups. Its prices range from 6,600CFP per person for a 2½-hour hike to 12,000CFP for a 6½-hour trek, including lunch and transportation to and from the trail heads.

HORSEBACK RIDING

In the 19th century, European whalers and traders brought horses to the Marquesas—plus cattle, pigs, and goats—which soon became wild and had a serious impact on native flora and fauna. You are unlikely to encounter a wild pig on Nuku Hiva these days, and most cattle are confined to ranches on the Toovii Plateau, but you will see horses along the roads and goats prowling the rocky mountainsides.

The strong, capable Marquesas horses are prized throughout French Polynesia, and you horse devotees will have ridden their cousins on Moorea and Huahine. You can ride them here on many of the ancient trails, such as to Hakaui Valley and the Ahuii waterfall.

Up on the plateau just north of Taiohae, Patrice Tamarii of **Le Ranch** (✆ **92.06.35;** danigo@mail.pf) rents horses, leads trail rides, and has 1- to 3-night horseback trips to the north shore, where you camp on beaches. **Alphonse and Sabine Teikiteetini** (✆ **92.01.52** or 21.24.15; tourisme@marquises.pf) lead half- and full-day rides; contact them for reservations and prices.

Where to Stay & Dine

During my recent visit, Rose Corser had almost finished building **He'e Tai Inn** (✆ **92.03.82;** marquesasrose@gmail.com), an eight-unit hotel next to her museum on the western side of Taiohae Bay (see "Rose Corser & Marquesan Art," p. 245). The motel-style rooms will have air conditioners, ceiling fans, TVs, private bathrooms, and wireless Internet access. The inn will have a restaurant and bar—the latter with daily happy hours for cruising yachties and other visitors. Rose said she

ROSE CORSER & marquesan art

Rose Corser and her late husband, Frank, sailed their yacht from California to Nuku Hiva in 1972 to study Marquesan art and culture for a master's degree Rose had in the works. It was a great subject to study, since the islands are justly famous for both their unique cultures and their long history of extraordinary art and handicrafts.

More than any other South Pacific islanders, the ancient Marquesans were masters at carving tikis from stone and wooden war clubs and spears from local hardwoods, adorning the latter with the same intricate geometric designs used in their tattoos (which covered most of their bodies) and on the tapa cloth they made from the bark of the paper mulberry tree. Their carving skill was evident even in everyday items such as bowls, axes, pestles, and fishhooks.

The old crafts have been preserved to a remarkable degree, especially carvings made of stone, wood, and bone. The Cathédrale de Notre-Dame des Marquises and the Monument de Herman Melville in Taiohae both are terrific examples (see "Exploring Nuku Hiva," above).

You will come across artisans carving away in their shops in both Taiohae on Nuku Hiva and Atuona on Hiva Oa, and many villages have *centres artisanal*

(artisan centers) where the crafts are for sale, especially when cruise ships are in port. The best items are often sold in Papeete, however, especially during the *Heiva Nui* festival in July and at special Marquesan art exhibitions.

Rose and Frank Corser went back to the United States after their 1972 voyage, but they returned for good in 1979. Rose never finished her master's degree, but she founded the marvelous **Taetae Tupuna He'e Tai ★★★** (© **92.03.82**), also known as Rose Corser's Boutique and Museum of Marquesan Culture, just downhill from the Keikahanui Nuku Hiva Lodge in Taiohae. Not only is it the best place to buy Marquesan art, but it's also a terrific museum. Here you will see artifacts dating from the Polynesian settlement period of about A.D. 150 to the 1800s. Many of the ancient pieces are on loan from Marquesan families, who have owned them since the dawn of Polynesian time. The carvings, tapa-cloth paintings, grain-seed necklaces, and *kumu hei* (a local lei made of fragrant plants) and other items on sale are all unique pieces of art, not handicrafts. Indeed, Rose's museum is a required stop on your visit to the Marquesas Islands. Hours are Monday to Friday from 8:30 to 11:30am and 2:30 to 5pm, Saturday 8:30 to 11:30am.

plans to charge 10,000CFP for a double, including continental breakfast, and will accept MasterCard and Visa credit cards.

You can stay away from Taiohae at **Chez Yvonne,** in Hatiheu village, home of the charming Restaurant Hinako Nui (see "Lunch at Yvonne's," p. 242).

All accommodations here have meal plans. The restaurants at **Keikahanui Nuku Hiva Lodge** and **Pension Moana Nui** are open to the public, but reservations are advised.

For inexpensive fare, a *roulotte* sets up on the waterfront next to Magasin Kamake (look for the big "Lotto" sign). See "Don't Miss *Les Roulottes*" (p. 125) for more information.

EXPENSIVE

Keikahanui Nuku Hiva Lodge ★   Sitting on a hill with a fine view of Taiohe Bay, this is one of the two international-level hotels in the Marquesas Islands, its sister on Hiva Oa being the other. The entire complex blends so well into its natural setting that you hardly notice the shingle roofs when looking this way from Taiohae Bay. Local artisans contributed woodcarvings and tapa cloth to the central building and to each of the 20 bungalows, thus giving the entire property a distinctly Marquesan character. The high-ceiling central building with restaurant, bar, and swimming pool overlooks the bay, as do most of the bungalows (room rates here vary by the quality of each unit's view). Each bungalow has a full picture window in front to take advantage of the bay or garden view, plus a covered porch with wooden lounge chairs. All are equipped with king-size beds and bathrooms with tiled showers. The restaurant, understandably, is the best on the island.

B.P. 53, 98742 Taiohae, Nuku Hiva (western side of Taiohae town). © **800/657-3275** or 92.07.10. Fax 92.07.11. www.pearlresorts.com. 20 units. 28,500CFP–39,900CFP bungalow. AE, MC, V. **Amenities:** Restaurant; bar; bikes; outdoor pool; room service; smoke-free rooms. *In room:* A/C, ceiling fan, TV, fridge, hair dryer, Wi-Fi (500CFP/hour).

INEXPENSIVE

Paahatea Nui (Chez Julienne)   Also opposite the black-sand beach on the western side of Taiohae, Julienne and Justin Mahiatapu rent three rooms in their house and have six shingled-roof bungalows in their tropical gardens. All of the bungalows and one of the rooms have private bathrooms with hot-water showers, while two in-house rooms share toilets and showers. Guests here are served breakfast, but no other meals.

B.P. 201, 98742 Taiohae, Nuku Hiva. ©/fax **92.00.97.** paahateanui@mail.pf. 6 units 9,800CFP bungalow. Rates include continental breakfast. No credit cards. *In room:* No phone, Wi-Fi (500CFP/hour).

Pension Mave Mai   On a hillside between the boat docks and the center of Taiohae, Régina and Jean-Claude Tata's pension boasts some of the better-equipped rooms here, with air-conditioning, ceiling fans, balconies or patios, and small private bathrooms with hot-water showers. They occupy a modern, two-story motel-like building, with half the units upstairs, half down. Two units have kitchens. Guests can lounge and have meals on a large patio overlooking the bay.

B.P. 378, 98742 Taiohae, Nuku Hiva. ©/fax **92.08.10.** pension-mavemai@mail.pf. 8 units. 9,000CFP double. AE, MC, V. *In room:* A/C; kitchen (2 units); no phone, Wi-Fi (660CFP/hour).

Pension Moana Nui   Across the main drag from the bay in the center of Taiohae, this pension is sometimes called the Hôtel Moana Nui, and with good reason, since it doubles as Nuku Hiva's commercial hotel for business types who can't afford the Keikahanui Nuku Hiva Lodge. The rooms have televisions, narrow balconies, and private bathrooms with hot-water showers. Four of them are air-conditioned. The owners also rent an air-conditioned bungalow. The pleasant, open-air restaurant serves good pizzas and French fare, but I was not impressed with the island-style dishes such as shrimp in coconut-curry sauce.

B.P. 33, 98742 Taiohae, Nuku Hiva. ©/fax **92.03.30.** http://pensionmoananui.ifrance.com. 8 units. 8,800CFP double. Rates include continental breakfast. AE, MC, V. **Amenities:** Restaurant; bar. *In room:* A/C (4 units), ceiling fan, TV, no phone.

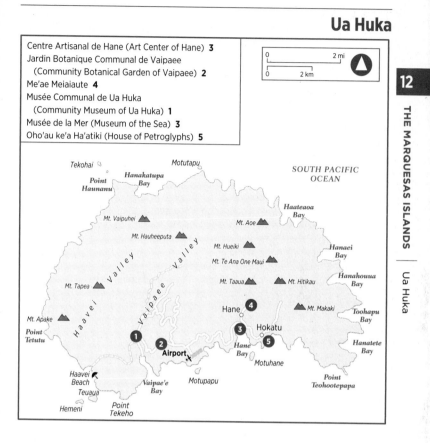

Centre Artisanal de Hane (Art Center of Hane) **3**

Jardin Botanique Communal de Vaipaee
  (Community Botanical Garden of Vaipaee) **2**

Me'ae Meiaiaute **4**

Musée Communal de Ua Huka
  (Community Museum of Ua Huka) **1**

Musée de la Mer (Museum of the Sea) **3**

Oho'au ke'a Ha'atiki (House of Petroglyphs) **5**

UA HUKA ★★

Sitting 42km (26 miles) due east of Nuku Hiva and one-quarter its size, Ua Huka may be the least visually appealing of the major Marquesas Islands, but to my mind it is one of the more interesting from both artistic and cultural standpoints. Some of the most talented woodcarvers and sculptors in French Polynesia live and work on Ua Huka, and the island's 600 or so local residents are so proud to be Marquesan that they have established not one but *four* museums explaining their indigenous culture. They also have planted the territory's only botanical garden beyond Tahiti.

The success of its carvers and sculptors has made Ua Huka one of the most prosperous islands in the Marquesas. An acquaintance of mine told me of her sculptor brother coming from Ua Huka to Tahiti to buy a new vehicle. When he and the dealer had agreed on a price, he opened his backpack and counted out the purchase price—in cash! Despite its not having a bank in which to deposit his money, Ua Huka has three times more motor vehicles per capita than any other Marquesan island—and its only road is fully paved.

Ua Huka is the top of an extinct volcano, whose southern half either exploded or fell into the sea, leaving two-thirds of a small crater and half of a large one. Only the tops of the mountains along the craters' rims get reliable rainfall, and only their upper slopes and the river- and stream-fed valleys are green. It wasn't like this in 1813, when American Admiral David Porter described lush vegetation and fertile, populated valleys.

All of the island's inhabitants live along the desertlike southern shore, which is made even more brown and barren than it would naturally be by wild horses and feral goats. Together they have destroyed much of the native vegetation outside the valleys. (The flip side of that coin is that horseback riding is easy to arrange, and some of the goats wind up in a decent local curry.)

Exploring Ua Huka

Ua Huka's three villages and all of its points of interest are on or near its south shore. A paved road runs the 13km (8 miles) from **Vaipaee** village in the west through **Hane** to **Hokatu** in the east. Vaipaee is the administrative center, although Hane is the larger of the villages. The post office and main infirmary are at Vaipaee, but I repeat: There is no bank on Ua Huka.

Nor is there public transportation, although many locals will gladly take you around the island in their ubiquitous vehicles. The **Ua Huka Airport** sits elevated above sea level on a plateau about halfway between Vaipaee and Hane. Your pension will arrange to meet your flight if you have reservations.

Your pension also will arrange horseback riding.

VAIPAEE

Ua Huka's only safe harbor is at Vaipaee, and quite a harbor it is. A narrow fjord leads from the sea, and virtually hides the village and its black-sand beach at the head of a small bay. The bay is so shallow that the *Aranui 3*—but not larger vessels, which are too long to do it—must pivot completely around and moor out in the fjord with its bow facing back out to sea. There is barely enough room for the *Aranui 3* to turn around without hitting the cliffs on either side of the fjord. We all got up early to watch this remarkable maneuver, a testament to the skipper's ability with the helm and throttle.

A short walk inland leads to the island's post office and administrative offices, behind which is the small but exceptional **Musée Communal de Ua Huka**

💬 An Offshore Ruckus

One way ancient Polynesian navigators discovered islands in the vast Pacific Ocean was to follow birds to their land-based nests. This must have been true of Ua Huka, for millions of sooty terns (*kaveka* in the local language) nest on **Teuaua** and **Hemini,** small islands just off its southwestern coast. These huge avian flocks create such a ruckus that you can hear them from ships as you pass nearby—and if the wind is right, you can smell them, too! Locals have installed a rope ladder up Teuaua's clifflike sides so they can collect *kaveka* eggs, which reportedly taste like sardines, from nests on the flat top. Cone-shaped Hemini, however, is off-limits.

(Community Museum of Ua Huka) ★★★ (✆ 92.60.13). Here is a remarkable collection of artifacts such as *adzes* (primitive stone axes), fishhooks, drums, war clubs, earrings, and necklaces. Be sure to go to the back, where one exhibit displays a prehistoric Polynesian kitchen and another re-creates a remote burial cave complete with an original canoe (which held the deceased's bones) and a wooden vase (which held the skull). The seashell collection is notable. Best of all are several tikis carved by Joseph Tehau Vaatete, the museum's custodian and Ua Huka's most noted carver. Since many of the best original tikis were removed from the island by collectors or traders, Joseph painstakingly re-created them based on photographs taken during a 1920s expedition by the Bishop Museum in Hawaii. Some of those photos are on display, too. An adjacent handicrafts shop sells some of the best woodcarvings I have seen in the Marquesas. The museum and shop are always open when cruise ships are here; at other times, ask at your pension about arranging a visit. Admission is free, but donations are accepted.

At Papuakeikaha, between Vaipaee and the airstrip, **Jardin Botanique Communal de Vaipaee** (**Community Botanical Garden of Vaipaee;** ✆ 92.61.51) was created in 1974 in an effort to protect and preserve the native flora, which was quickly disappearing into the mouths of Ua Huka's wild goats. The collection has steadily grown to include exotic plants from elsewhere, plus groves of citrus trees. Unfortunately, the examples are not labeled. There's a small aviary here, and this is a good place to watch for several native species of birds. The garden is open Monday to Friday from 6:30am to 4:30pm, on weekends by request. Admission is free.

HANE

The attractive village of Hane begins at a dark sand beach and climbs into a valley created by its own volcanic crater. Archaeologists have dated pottery fragments found in a sand dune near the beach to about 150 B.C., making this one of the earliest examples of human habitation in French Polynesia. A paved road and shady parks now skirt the shore of this picturesque half-moon bay. The beach fringing the bay here is good for swimming and snorkeling, or just sitting back and watching local men carry heavy bags of copra out to whale boats sent ashore by trading boats.

At the T-intersection near the center of the bayside promenade, the **Musée de la Mer** (**Museum of the Sea;** ✆ 92.60.13) displays ancient canoes, fishhooks, and nets, plus re-created examples of canoe prows. It shares a building and phone number with the **Centre Artisanal de Hane** (**Art Center of Hane**), where you can buy excellent woodcarvings and stone carvings as well as *tivaivai,* the handmade appliqué quilts local women have been making since missionaries taught them how to sew in the 19th century. Both the museum and crafts shop are open when cruise ships are here; otherwise by appointment. Admission is free.

Super carver and community museum custodian Joseph Tehau Vaatete has his open-air studio on the paved road heading inland from the museum (✆ 92.60.13). Joseph accepts commissions and will ship your piece to you.

Keep walking about 30 minutes uphill on the paved road, a dirt path, and then concrete stairs to **Me'ae Meiaiaute,** the most important ancient temple on Ua Huka. Although its stone platforms have not been restored, and some of its four tikis are damaged, the site commands a splendid view back down over the coastline.

HOKATU

From Hane, the main road reduces to one paved lane and climbs around a steep headland (if one vehicle meets another on this stretch, one must either back up or fall off a cliff!) before descending into another small bay and picturesque little Hokatu. The village's main street is lined with hibiscus, bougainvillea, and other flowers, but the beach consists entirely of black rocks and gravel. Rather than trying to swim, spend your time at the local handicrafts shop known as **Huau Ote Papatuhuna** (no phone), which has a wide selection, and observing the remarkable plaster re-creations of ancient petroglyphs found on Ua Huka in **Oho'au ke'a Ha'atiki** (**House of Petroglyphs**; ✆ **92.60.55**). Explanatory labels under the petroglyphs are written in both French and English. The shop and petroglyphs museum are open when cruise ships are in port; otherwise by appointment. Admission is free to both.

Where to Stay & Dine on Ua Huka

Ua Huka has no hotels, only four family-run pensions. All serve meals, but none accepts credit cards, nor do they have post office boxes. Write to them simply at 98744 Vaipaee, Ua Huka, or you can make reservations at www.haere-mai.pf.

Le Réve Marquisien (✆/fax **92.61.84;** revemarquisien@mail.pf) is in Pahataua Valley about 1km (a half-mile) from Vaipaee. Owners Marie-France and Charles Aunoa have four bungalows with private bathrooms and TVs. They charge about 12,500CFP double for these luxuries, including all meals.

Karen Taiaapu-Fournier's **Pension Mana Tupuna Village** (✆/fax **92.60.08;** manatupuna@mail.pf), on a hillside overlooking Vaipaee, has three bungalows with private bathrooms (hot-water showers). Karen charges about 11,000CFP double, including all meals.

Auberge Hitikau (✆/fax **92.61.74**), in Hane village, is more like a motel than the others. It has three rooms (with shared bathrooms) adjacent to the open-air **Restaurant Chez Fournier,** where Celine Fournier serves lunch to cruise-ship passengers, including goat curry and an unusual *poisson cru* made with mayonnaise instead of coconut milk. Rates are 6,500CFP per person including all meals.

In Hakatu village, Maurice and Delphine Rootuehine have five bungalows with private bathrooms at their **Chez Maurice et Delphine** (✆/fax **92.60.55**). Their tin-roof bungalows have fine views from their porches down over Hakatu's narrow valley and small bay. They charge 5,900CFP per person including breakfast and dinner.

UA POU ★★★

About 40km (25 miles) south of Nuku Hiva, Ua Pou is one of the most dramatically beautiful islands in French Polynesia. I was awe-struck when I first saw it from the deck of the *Aranui 3* as we approached at dawn from the southwest. Before us, the triangular, cloud-topped peak of **Mount Oave** stood 1,203m (4,042 ft.) high in the middle of Ua Pou, but most spectacular were a dozen basaltic thumbs protruding from ridges descending from the peak. This jagged outline of Moorea-esque spires justifiably appears in many promotional photographs, and it led Jacques Brel to write his song, "La Cathédrale." The first Marquesans also must have been impressed, for the name Ua Pou means "the Columns."

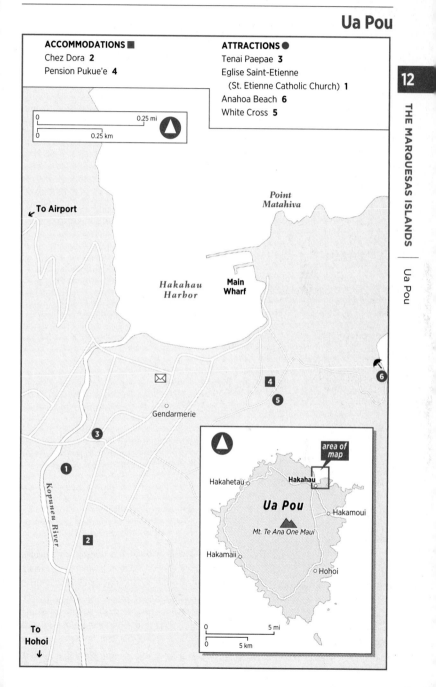

ACCOMMODATIONS ■
Chez Dora **2**
Pension Pukue'e **4**

ATTRACTIONS ●
Tenai Paepae **3**
Eglise Saint-Etienne
   (St. Etienne Catholic Church) **1**
Anahoa Beach **6**
White Cross **5**

To Airport

Point
Matahiva

*Hakahau
Harbor*

**Main
Wharf**

Gendarmerie

Kopunen River

Hakahetau

Hakahau

Ua Pou

Hakamoui

Mt. Te Ana One Maui

Hakamaii

Hohoi

area of
map

To
Hohoi

The volcano that created Ua Pou, the third largest Marquesan island, was different from others in the group, for it created both phonolite, a hard rock that was excellent for flaking into cutting tools, and so-called **flower stones,** or pebbles whose imbedded crystals formed flowerlike designs in the dark rock. Found only on Ua Pou, flower stones are excellent, easy-to-carry souvenirs.

Exploring Ua Pou

Although a rough dirt road circles the island, most of Ua Pou's population of some 2,200 lives on the northern coast in and between the villages of **Hakahau** and **Hakahetau.** Hakahau is the administrative center, with a gendarmerie, infirmary, post office, and a Banque Socredo branch with an ATM. The post office broadcasts a ManaSpot Wi-Fi signal.

There is no public transportation system on Ua Pou. The pensions pick up guests who have reservations at **Aneou Airstrip,** on the north shore about equidistant between the two villages. With the sea at one end of the airstrip and a mountain at the other, Air Tahiti's small planes land uphill headed inland and take off downhill in the opposite direction, regardless of which way the wind is blowing.

HAKAHAU

Ua Pou's basaltic spires form a picturesque backdrop to Hakahau, which sits beside a black-sand beach in a gorgeous half-moon bay on the northeast coast. A breakwater protruding halfway across the bay protects the local dock from the sea swells and makes it possible for the *Aranui 3* (but not larger vessels) to come alongside here. From the dock, a paved street runs along the bay past a large, thatched-roof pavilion—under which locals sell handicrafts when ships are in port—to the town hall, post office, bank, and island school.

The street beside the school leads inland to **Tenai Paepae,** the ancient gathering place restored for an arts festival in 1995. Locals stage dance shows on the *paepae* for cruise-ship passengers.

Facing the *paepae* is **Eglise Saint-Etienne (St. Etienne Catholic Church),** a stone structure erected in 1981 on the site of the first church in the Marquesas. In addition to spectacular woodcarvings, the church is worth visiting for the view of the mountainous spires framed by a triangular window above its southern nave. Carved from a single tree trunk, the pulpit symbolizes the bow of God's ship splitting the stormy seas of life.

A partially paved, partially dirt road leads through dry scrub brush from the eastern side of the bay across a ridge to **Anahoa Bay,** site of a lovely beach. It's good for swimming in the surf, but cover yourself with insect repellent to ward off the *no-nos,* and be on the lookout for jellyfish in June and July. It's worth the 20-minute hike up to the large **white cross** standing atop the ridge, where you will have a marvelous view down over Hakahau.

HAKAHETAU

Unlike arid Hakahau, which sits in the dry rain shadow of Mount Oave, the charming little village of **Hakahetau** is green and lush. Its little bay is unprotected from the sea swells, and the village dock—at the base of a sheer cliff—is often buffeted by waves. The eroding beach has been replenished with black stones. Although the bay is picturesque, Hakahetau's charm is along the paved street following a stream inland. It passes a small **Catholic church** built of river stones in 1859. One of the oldest in the Marquesas, its roof is supported by posts carved with likenesses of the Apostles and the Polynesian transliterations of their names. Cross the bridge farther upstream to a pavilion where **stone carvers** work and sell their handicrafts.

Keep going past the pavement to a natural, open-air copra-drying platform, where locals lay out coconut meat to dry in the sun. It commands an excellent view of the village and bay. On the way up, you will pass a sign for the **Manfred Cascade,** a waterfall about a 45-minute walk upstream via a track best negotiated on foot or in a four-wheel-drive vehicle. The cascade is like a swimming hole in the jungle, but lather up with insect repellent against the hordes of mosquitoes living up here.

Where to Stay & Dine on Ua Pou

There is no international-standard hotel on Ua Pou, only pensions run by local families.

The best view and most attractive digs are at **Pension Pukue'e** (✆/fax **92.50.83;** http://chez.mana.pf/~pukuee), on the road to Anahoa Bay. Owner Elisa Kautai has four rooms sharing two bathrooms (both with hot-water showers) in her chalet with a grand porch overlooking an outdoor swimming pool and Hakahau village. Her tattooed French husband, Jérôme, speaks both French and English. Rates are 8,800CFP per person including breakfast. Wi-Fi is free.

There's also a decent view from **Chez Dora** (✆/fax **92.53.69**), up in the valley south of Hakahau village. Dora Teikiehuupolo rents three bedrooms in her two-story house, one of which has a private bathroom with hot-water shower. More private are two government-issue bungalows out in the yard. The bungalows have fans and TVs, but their showers dispense cold water. Dora charges 7,000CFP per person including breakfast and dinner.

Neither pension accepts credit cards.

Rosalie Tata, who makes a delicious *poisson cru,* opens her **Restaurant Chez Rosalie** (no phone) when cruise ships are in port.

HIVA OA ★★★

Just as Nuku Hiva has had its famous guests in Herman Melville and the sand-fly-bitten contestants and crew of television's *Survivor,* so has Hiva Oa, for here lie the remains of French artist Paul Gauguin and Belgian singer-poet Jacques Brel. Gauguin arrived in 1901 to escape what he saw as harassment by French colonial officials on Tahiti. He died here in 1903. Brel sailed his yacht here in 1975 and just plain fell under the spell of Hiva Oa's beauty, serenity, and friendly people. Brel was planning to build a spectacular home here when he died in 1978.

The second largest of the Marquesas Islands, Hiva Oa is indeed a place of beauty and serenity. Its rugged scenery was created by a series of volcanoes on an east–west line. One of the craters partially fell into the sea, forming huge **Taaoa Bay** on the south shore and leaving the fishhook-shaped island we see on today's maps. Another crater dominates the center of the island, while a third, on the northeastern coast, also partially collapsed to form **Puamau Bay,** upon whose banks sit one of French Polynesia's most important archaeological sites. In fact, Hiva Oa is pockmarked with the remains of ancient *me'aes,* many of them restored.

Gauguin and Brel both lived in **Atuona,** the island's only town—and my first landfall when I sailed to French Polynesia in 1977. Their graves and an excellent museum dedicated to both of them are highlights of any visit to Hiva Oa. Atuona isn't as physically impressive as Taiohae on Nuku Hiva, but it retains more of a French colonial ambience, with some buildings still standing from Gauguin's day.

Getting Around Hiva Oa

The **airport** is at an altitude of 500m (1,650 ft.) up on the Tepuna Plateau, 13km (8 miles) northeast of Atuona. Fog or rain can unexpectedly close the airstrip here, so be prepared to enjoy an extra night or two on Hiva Oa. *Always* plan to fly back to Papeete a few days before your international flight home.

Your accommodations will arrange to pick you up if they know you're coming, or look for **Vaite Transport** (**Ida Clark Taxi;** ✆ **92.71.33** or 72.34.73). Despite her *anglais* name, Ida Clark speaks scant English, but she will take you into Atuona for about 1,500CFP.

Atuona Rent a Car (✆/fax **92.67.07** or 72.17.17), **Hiva Oa Location** (✆ **91.70.60** or 72.83.83), and **David Location** (✆ **92.72.87**; davidkmk@mail.pf) all rent four-wheel-drive vehicles for about 13,000CFP a day. The main road is paved from Atuona past the airport going northeast, but be extremely careful when driving here. The north-shore road around Motuua is so dangerous that I strongly recommend taking an organized tour to see Puamau (see "Exploring Hiva Oa," below).

[Fast FACTS] HIVA OA

The following facts apply specifically to Hiva Oa. For more information, see "Fast Facts: Tahiti & French Polynesia," in chapter 13.

Currency Exchange

Banque Socredo has an office on the main road in Atuona. The ATM on the side of the building is open only during banking hours: Monday through Friday from 7 to 11:30am and 1 to 4pm.

Drugstores **Pharmacie Atuona** (✆ **91.71.65**) is in the Taiohae *mairie* (town hall) complex in the center of town. It's open Monday through Friday from 8am to noon and 2 to 5:30pm, Saturday from 8:30 to 11:30am.

Emergencies/Police The **emergency police** phone number is ✆ **17.** The **gendarmerie** in Atuona (✆ **92.73.61**) is a major landmark in the middle of town.

Healthcare The Atuona government **infirmary** (✆ **92.73.75**) and **dental clinic** (✆ **92.73.58**) are in the Taiohae *mairie* (town hall) complex in the center of town.

Internet Access The island's one hotel and some of its pensions have Internet access for their guests. The post office has ManaSpot Wi-Fi access.

Post Office Like most things official in Atuona, the post and telecommunications office is in the *mairie* (town hall) complex.

It's open Monday through Thursday from 7:30am to noon and 12:30 to 4:30pm, Friday to 2pm. Puamau village also has a post office.

Visitor Information The **Comité du Tourisme de Hiva Oa,** B.P. 273, 98741 Atuona, Hiva Oa (✆/fax **92.78.73**; www.marquises-hivaoa.org.pf), has a visitor information office in a small building near the Gauguin museum. It's open Monday through Friday from 8 to 11:30am and 1 to 3pm.

Water Don't drink the tap water on Hiva Oa. The grocery stores sell bottled water. The town of Atuona can run short of water, so don't be surprised if the tap water is suddenly shut off at 8pm.

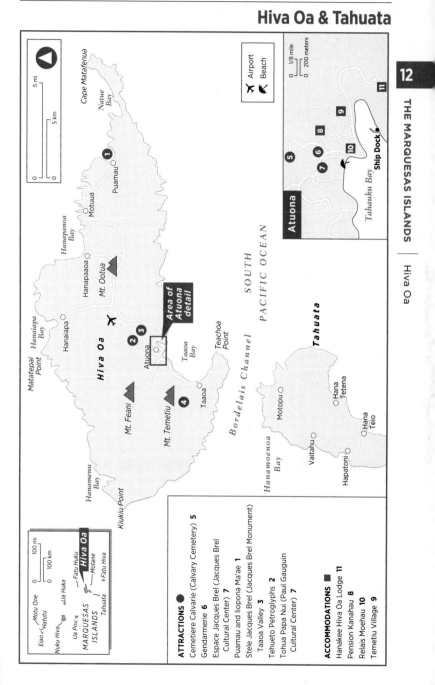

ATTRACTIONS ●

Cemetiere Calvarie (Calvary Cemetery) **5**
Gendarmerie **6**
Espace Jacques Brel (Jacques Brel
Cultural Center) **7**
Puamau and Iipona Ma'ae **1**
Stele Jacques Brel (Jacques Brel Monument)
Taaoa Valley **3**
Tehueto Petroglyphs **2**
Tohua Papa Nui (Paul Gauguin
Cultural Center) **7**

ACCOMMODATIONS ■

Hanakee Hiva Oa Lodge **11**
Pension Kanahau **8**
Relais Moehau **10**
Temetiu Village **9**

Exploring Hiva Oa

A rocky headland divides the town of **Atuona,** on the northern shore of **Traitors Bay,** into two parts. Cargo ships and cruising yachts put into **Tahauku Bay,** a narrow cove on the east flank of the headland. Other than the black-sand beach and a freshwater faucet emerging from a cliff, there was little there when I sailed into the harbor back in 1977. Today, a man-made breakwater protects the concrete town dock and small boat marina. From the black-sand beach, the **Faakua Valley** goes off to the northeast.

On the western side of the headland, the original village borders another curving black-sand beach and follows the Vaioa River up into a valley. Unlike Taiohae on Nuku Hiva, where the main road follows the shoreline, here the main street is a block inland, separated from the beach by houses, churches, and parks. Sunset comes early to Atuona, for to the west looms the pointed peak of **Mount Temetiu,** tallest in the Marquesas at 1,190m (3,927 ft.). Atuona's other key landmark is the **gendarmerie,** at the center of town. Two blocks west on the main road is the town's **Tohua Pepeu,** a restored ancient meeting ground where locals stage dance shows and sell handicrafts to visiting cruise-ship passengers.

ATUONA'S TOP ATTRACTIONS

Cimetière du Calvaire (Calvary Cemetery) ★★   Paul Gauguin and Jacques Brel are both buried in this cemetery, on a hill overlooking Atuona. On the way up, you'll pass Brel's home, to the left when the road bends. The large basaltic tombstone above his grave bears a plaque with Brel's likeness and that of his mistress and companion, Maddly Bamy (she and Brel's family reportedly are in a constant struggle over the plaque!). I am always amazed at the number of flowers and shell necklaces left on the grave by Brel's fans. Gauguin's tomb is two rows up to the right. You'll recognize it by the sign at his feet and the replica of his *Oviri* statue standing over his head. Frangipani trees constantly deposit their fragrant flowers on the grave. Stop for a few minutes before the cemetery's tall white crucifix and take in the fine view over Atuona and Taaroa Bay.

Atuona, uphill from gendarmerie. Free admission. Daily 8am–sunset. From gendarmerie, follow the signs and climb the inland road uphill.

Espace Jacques Brel (Jacques Brel Cultural Center)   Behind Tohua Papa Nui (the Gauguin Cultural Center; see below), this hangarlike museum recounts the singer's life. From the rafters is suspended his Beechcraft Twin Bonanza airplane, *Jojo,* which he used to go back and forth to Tahiti, often on missions of mercy. You will see displays of traditional Marquesan arts and crafts as well. The shop sells CDs and tapes of his albums. The Brel and Gauguin cultural centers share a ticket office.

Atuona, 1 block west of gendarmerie. Admission 500CFP adults, 250CFP children 12–18. Mon–Fri 8–11am and 2–5pm; Sat 8–11am.

Stele Jacques Brel (Jacques Brel Memorial)   Brel had intended to build a home on a ridge near the airport, in a spectacular overlook of Tahauku and Taaroa bays. Construction had not begun when illness cut his life short in 1978 at age 49, but the site is marked by this black rock bearing his portrait and a line from his song "Marquesas." It's not easy to find, so see it on a tour or ask directions from one of the locals.

Atuona, 5km/3 miles northeast of town on airport road. Free admission. Daily 24 hr.

> ## A Debt Left Unpaid
>
> **Magasin Gauguin,** an old clapboard general store beside a huge mango tree near the Gauguin Cultural Center on Atuona's main street, is a relic of the days when Paul Gauguin lived here. In those days it was owned by American merchant Ben Varney, himself the founder of a large mixed-race family.
>
> The painter bought his supplies here, including bottles of liquor that he kept cool in a well beside his house (he would fetch them with a long bamboo pole). It is said that when Gauguin died on May 8, 1903, he owed Varney a considerable debt.

Tohua Papa Nui (Paul Gauguin Cultural Center) ★★★ A block west of the gendarmerie is this fine museum, located on the site of Gauguin's last residence. It was opened in 2003 on the 100th anniversary of his death, so discount earlier reports about it not being open or not being very good. Start by watching a 2-minute video about Gauguin's life and then take plenty of time to see the reproductions of his paintings by the wife-and-husband team of Viera and Claude-Charles Farina (who could make an illegal fortune as forgers!). Instead of using old copra bags made of jute, as did Gauguin, the Farinas executed these stunningly accurate replicas on real canvas. The exhibition starts with his self-portraits and then follows chronologically. His French Polynesian works, therefore, are near the rear of the building.

Out back is a replica of Gauguin's last residence, which he called his **Maison du Jouir (House of Pleasure)**—an apt name, apparently, since he painted *Barbaric Tales,* one of his best nudes, while living here.

Be sure to shop for Marquesan handicrafts in the boutique, which the center shares with *Espace Jacques Brel* (see above).

Autuona, 1 block west of gendarmerie. Admission 600CFP adults, 300CFP children 12-18. Mon-Fri 8-11am and 2-5pm; Sat 8-11am.

TEHUETO PETROGLYPHS

Reaching northeastward from Traitors Bay, the Faakua Valley is known for its **Tehueto Petroglyphs,** or stone carvings in basaltic rock. Done eons ago, these figures depict human beings with their arms in the air. The site is within hiking distance of Atuona, but the road is so rough that I do not recommend the walk. You can see it on a tour (see "Organized Tours," below), but your time will be better spent at Puamau.

PUAMAU & TE ME'AE TEIIPONA ★★★

Like an excursion to Hatiheu on Nuku Hiva, seeing **Puamau** and its archaeological site is the top trip to make on Hiva Oa. Be prepared for a long day, for it takes 2½ hours to get here from Atuona. The road is paved from town past the airport onto the Tepuna plateau, a cool region with ferns and pines and wild orchids, but it soon turns to gravel and gradually descends to the north shore, where it is literally blasted into cliffs above the serrated coastline. The views are spectacular on this winding road, but it is the most dangerous stretch on Hiva Oa, especially during or just after rain. For this reason, I highly recommend taking an organized tour to Puamau.

lunch WITH MARIE-ANTOINETTE

Many tours stop for lunch in Puamau village at **Pension Peheku'a (Chez Marie-Antoinette; ℭ 92.72.27**), which has two simple rooms to rent. On the grounds is **Tohua Pehe Kua,** the grave of Puamau's last Polynesian queen before the French took over in 1842. She lived until the early 20th century. A popular but unfounded legend says she's buried here with her two bicycles. For sure, Marie-Antoinette's family-style lunches are pure Polynesian: *poisson cru,* goat roasted with onions in coconut milk, boiled mountain bananas, deep-fried breadfruit, and sugary *po'e* (the local version of Hawaiian poi). Lunch is often included in the price of a tour; if not, expect to pay about 2,200CFP for a full meal—in cash. You can stay overnight for 7,000CFP per person, including all the *po'e* you can eat.

On the northeastern side of the island, picturesque Puamau village sits beside a black-sand beach and is surrounded on three sides by the steep walls of an extinct volcanic crater. Depending on the height of the surf and the amount of jelly fish present, the beach is good for swimming on its eastern side.

You may meet some of Paul Gauguin's descendants here, but Puamau's highlight is the restored **Te Me'ae Teiipona.** One of the most significant ancient temples in French Polynesia, it is famous for the largest stone tiki in all of Polynesia other than the mysterious figures on Easter Island, far off in the eastern South Pacific between here and Chile. In fact, some anthropologists believe the Polynesians who first settled Easter Island came from Puamau. The tallest figure here, a rendition of a Polynesian chief named Taka'i'i, is much smaller than those on Easter Island, but still stands 2.4m (8 ft.) tall. The most unusual is of a woman lying on her stomach with her hands lifted skyward behind her back, said to be the likeness of a woman giving birth. Admission is 300CFP per person.

TAAOA VALLEY

About 7km (4¼ miles) by dirt road southwest of Atuona, the **Taaoa Valley** has the largest concentration of ceremonial sites in all of French Polynesia. Some of the more than 1,000 *paepaes* (stone platforms) have been restored, but many more still lie in the jungle. Archaeologists believe one of the stone tikis here was used to prepare humans to be sacrificed. Although you can find your way to Taaoa easily enough, the remains occupy most of the valley, so a tour is the best way to see it all.

HANAIAPA

The paved cross-island road from Atuona descends through the narrow Vaipeehia River valley and terminates at the beach in the pleasant north coast village of **Hanaiapa.** You can swim in the bay off the canoe shed near the river's mouth, and if the sea is calm, snorkel off the concrete dock (bring your own gear). Residents of Atuona like to escape to Hanaiapa on the weekends, for in addition to the beach, a plethora of fruit trees and flowers make this one of the more attractive villages in the Marquesas. There are no restaurants or other facilities, but a handicrafts shop opens when cruise ships are here.

ORGANIZED TOURS

The best tours with English-speaking guides are organized by the **Hanakee Hiva Oa Lodge** (℃ 92.75.87), the island's only international-level hotel (p. 260). It charges about 10,500CFP per person for an all-day excursion to Puamau, including lunch at Pension Chez Marie-Antoinette. Half-day trips to Taaoa cost about 4,000CFP per person. One of its guides will take you to the *Stele Jacques Brel* (Jacques Brel Memorial) or to see the Tehueto Petroglyphs for about 7,600CFP each.

Outdoor Adventures

When you've had enough of Paul Gauguin, Jacques Brel, and ancient archaeological sites, you can hit the great outdoors on Hiva Oa.

DIVING

With cliffs plunging into the sea and no fringing coral reefs, the waters off Nuku Hiva present a very different diving experience from that found anywhere else in French Polynesia. The cool South Equatorial Current makes these waters rife with plankton, while limiting visibility to 10 to 20m (33–66 ft.). On the other hand, you may well encounter scalloped hammerhead sharks, melon-headed whales, and other creatures not seen elsewhere in the islands. And even novice divers can enter caves, one of which has a sandy floor populated by stingrays.

At this writing, Eric Le Lyonnais' **SubAtuona** (℃ 92.70.88 or 27.05.24; eric. lelyonnais@wanadoo.fr), is the only dive operator in the Marquesas. Bring you own mask, flipper, full wet suit, underwater flashlight, and diving computer. Book well in advance. He charges about 7,000CFP for a one-tank dive.

FISHING

There's some pretty good hunting for tuna, mahimahi, and other deep-sea game fish in these waters. A charter boat can be arranged through your accommodations, or you can contact Gabriel "Gaby" Heitaa, owner of the **Pua O Te Tai** (℃ 91.70.60; heitaagaby@mail.pf). His is one of the boats that also provides transportation between Hiva Oa and Tahuata.

HIKING

You can hike from Atuona to the Tehueto Petroglyphs and to Taaoa, but I think it's best to go with a guide. The **Hanakee Hiva Oa Lodge** (℃ 92.75.87) organizes hiking excursions, or you can contact Bonno Henry of **Hiva Oa Rando-Trek** (℃ 92.74.44) or **Hiva Oa Trek** (℃ 20.40.90).

HORSEBACK RIDING

Another way to see the Tehueto Petroglyphs or Jacques Brel's intended home site is on the back of a strong Marquesan horse. Up on the plateau near the airport, **Hemau Ranch Tahauku** (℃ 92.70.57) leads excursions to both sites for about 7,000CFP and 14,000CFP, respectively.

MOUNTAIN BIKING

In addition to horseback rides, the **Hanakee Hiva Oa Lodge** (℃ 92.75.87) also organizes mountain-bike excursions to various points in and near Atuona. Contact the hotel for particulars and prices.

Shopping

You will see several "Sculpture Traditionnelle" signs around Atuona and Puamau directing you to the workshops of local carvers who are here and at work. The **Comité du Tourisme de Hiva Oa** knows where they are (see "Visitor Information" under "Fast Facts: Hiva Oa," p. 254). The boutique at the **Tohua Papa Nui (Paul Gauguin Cultural Center)** usually has some top-quality pieces and is well worth exploring (p. 257). There's another good handicrafts shop across the road from the center.

Where to Stay

All of Hiva Oa's hotels and pensions offer various meal plans. If available, I would opt for a rate that includes breakfast only. You will likely have lunch on an excursion or at a "snack" in town while seeing the sights, so there is little point in paying for that in advance. I also like to dine out while here, so I don't pay for dinner, either.

The most remote place to stay is **Pension Peheku'a (Chez Marie-Antoinette)**, in Puamau village on the far northeastern shore, at least 2½ hours by road away from Atuona (see "Lunch with Marie-Antoinette," p. 258).

EXPENSIVE

Hanakee Hiva Oa Lodge ★   With a stupendous view out to sea from its perch on a ridge above the eastern side of Tahauku Bay, this is the island's top place to stay—and along with its sister, the Keikahanui Nuku Hiva Lodge, it's one of the two international-level hotels in the Marquesas. You will be welcomed into the main building by a large and quite immodest Marquesan tiki. It and other carvings throughout the complex will not let you forget where you are. The main building opens to a small infinity-edge pool with a 200-degree view up the Tahauku Valley all the way around to the Bordelais Channel and (on a clear day) Tahuata island in the distance. Virtually identical to those at Keikahanui Nuku Hiva Lodge (p. 246), the guest bungalows step downhill below the pool. The most expensive have sea views, while the least expensive face the valley (*Tip:* Bungalow no. 7 looks toward both the sea and the valley.) Each unit was decorated by a Marquesan woodcarver and has a king-size bed, a porch, and a tiled bathroom with shower. The dining room shares the view and serves very good French fare—it's far and away the best restaurant on Hiva Oa. The hotel offers its guests a wide range of activities (see "Organized Tours" and "Outdoor Adventures," above).

B.P. 80, 97742 Atuona, Hiva Oa (on airport road 3.5km/2 miles northeast of town). © **800/657-3275** or 92.75.87. Fax 92.75.95. www.pearlresorts.com. 14 units. 22,800CFP–39,900CFP bungalow. AE, MC, V. **Amenities:** Restaurant; bar; bikes; outdoor pool; smoke-free rooms. *In room:* A/C, ceiling fan, TV, hair dryer, minibar.

INEXPENSIVE

Pension Kanahau ★★   One of the better pensions in French Polynesia, this fine little inn sits on the ridge between Atuona town and Faakua valley. Marquesan-born owner Tania Dubreuil learned English while dealing with all the yachties who put in at Atuona, and she got the idea of building a restaurant where they could come and have dinner overlooking the small boat harbor in Tahauku (Traitors) Bay. Later she installed four standard government-backed bungalows and decorated them in island style, with *tivaivai* (handmade appliqué quilts) on the beds and colorful fabrics on the windows. They also have televisions, ceiling fans, mosquito nets over queen-size beds, sofas that convert to single beds, writing tables, and private bathrooms with hot-water showers. Two of the front porches look across Tahauku Bay to the sea, while the other two face the valley. Most meals are taken under a large shade tree on a patio beside the main house, which has a television lounge. Guests with children can use the kitchen inside. Tania's is a relaxed, friendly establishment that can become quite lively when the yachties are in town from April through September.

B.P. 101, 98741 Atuona, Hiva Oa (Tahauku valley, 2km/¼ mile east of town). ℭ **91.71.31** or 70.16.26. Fax 91.71.32. www.pensionkanahau.com. 4 units. 12,500CFP double. No credit cards. **Amenities:** Restaurant; bar; Jacuzzi. *In room:* Ceiling fan, TV, no phone, Wi-Fi (2 hours free, then 400CFP/hour).

Relais Moehau ★ This modern, two-story white building with a green-tile roof is the best choice within easy walking distance of Atuona's top attractions. It sits up on a hillside overlooking the black-sand beach of old Atuona. The rooms are all upstairs and open to a veranda that wraps around the building, so you can sit out and admire the view. Although not extravagant, the units are clean and comfortable, each with a ceiling fan, a double or two single beds, and a private bathroom with hot-water shower. Open to all comers, the downstairs restaurant specializes in wood-fired pizzas as well as French fare. Owners Georges and Gisèle Gramont are originally from the Tuamotu Archipelago. A bit of French will come in handy here.

B.P. 50, 98741 Atuona, Hiva Oa (east side of town). ℭ **92.72.69.** Fax 92.77.62. www.relaismoehau.com. 8 units. 12,100CFP double. Rates include continental breakfast. MC, V. **Amenities:** Restaurant; bar. *In room:* Ceiling fan, TV, no phone.

Temetiu Village ★ Like Pension Kanahau, this is a good establishment on the eastern side of the ridge separating the town from the harbor. Friendly owner Gabriel "Gaby" Heitaa operates the Pua O Te Tai fishing boat (see "Outdoor Adventures," above), while his equally friendly wife Feli speaks English. Their seven hillside bungalows all have a view of the bay. Three of them have two bedrooms with three single beds in each. All have televisions and private bathrooms with hot-water showers.

B.P. 52, 98741 Atuona, Hiva Oa (east side of town). ℭ **91.70.60.** Fax 91.70.61. www.temetiuvillage.com. 7 units. 8,735CFP double. AE, MC, V. **Amenities:** Restaurant. *In room:* TV, no phone.

Where to Dine

The **Hanakee Hiva Oa Lodge** has the best restaurant on the island and a fine view to go with its excellent French and Continental fare. The best pension dining rooms—with the best views—are at **Relais Moehau** (especially if the pizza oven is lit) and **Temetiu Village.** Reservations are essential at both.

Restaurant Hoa Nui MARQUESAN You will have a Marquesan feast at this large restaurant, across the road from the Vaioa River. As at Chez Marie-Antoinette in Puamau, the chow is deliciously local, with the likes of goat with onions and coconut milk, fried breadfruit, and sweet banana *po'e.* You can get breakfast and lunch here without a reservation, but bookings are required a day in advance for dinner.

Atuona (in Vaioa Valley). ℭ **92.73.63.** Dinner reservations required 1 day in advance. Full dinner 2,500CFP. No credit cards. Daily 6am–10pm.

Snack Make Make REGIONAL East of the gendarmerie, this gaudy green building is another landmark in old Atuona. The menu is typically Tahitian, with burgers, grilled steak or chicken with french fries, *poisson cru,* chow mein, and shrimp in coconut curry sauce. You can order to go. The hours can vary here.

Atuona, east of gendarmerie. © **92.74.26.** Reservations not accepted. Snacks and meals 600CFP–2,500CFP. No credit cards. Mon–Fri 11am–2pm and 6–8pm; Sat 8am–2pm.

TAHUATA ★★

Lying less than 4km (2½ miles) south of Hiva Oa across the Bordelais Channel, lush and lovely Tahuata is the smallest inhabited island in the Marquesas. Most of its creating volcano dropped into the sea, leaving only the northwestern rim of its crater still standing. The old caldera wall forms Tahuata's steep southeastern coastline, while sharp ridges fan out and create beautiful valleys to the north and west.

Although Fatu Hiva was first to be sighted, Tahuata was the first of all Polynesian islands to be visited by Europeans. Spanish explorer Alvaro de Mendaña "discovered" it in 1595 and sailed into the little bay at **Vaitahu,** then and now the island's main village. He named it *Madre De Dios* (Mother of God). Capt. James Cook stopped here in 1774. Admiral Dupetit-Thouars claimed the island for France in 1842, but a local chief named Iotete resisted. Several French sailors were killed in the ensuing skirmish and are buried on a hill above Vaitahu. The admiral built a fort overlooking the valley; although overgrown, it's still here, too. The French prevailed, but the Tahuatuans are still fiercely independent.

They also are the best bone carvers in French Polynesia, making this the best place to shop for scrimshaw and other such items.

Exploring Tahuata

Vaitahu has a post office, but there is neither a bank nor an airport on Tahuata. Access is strictly by boat from Tahauku Bay on Hiva Oa. The Hanakee Hiva Oa Lodge (p. 246) and other accommodations on Hiva Oa will organize day trips to Tahuata, and the island's lone pension arranges transfers for its guests. There are no car rentals; in fact, there are few vehicles on Tahuata since its only road (linking Vaitahu to Motopu in the north and Hapatoni to the south) is barely more than a dirt track. Most folks get around here by boat.

You will definitely need a boat or yacht to reach the beautiful white-sand beaches skirting **Hanamoenoa** and **Ivaiva bays** north of Vaitahu. Unfortunately, both of these idyllic spots have *no-nos.*

VAITAHU

Midway on the island's west coast, historic **Vaitahu** sits in a narrow valley. There is no harbor here, only a wharf on the north side of the bay, where boats from the cruise ships land their passengers (it's a sight to see a big yellow backhoe removing cargo from barges sent ashore by the *Aranui 3*). From there a paved road runs around the bay past a small, wooden Protestant church to the town hall, post office, school, and a large thatched-roof pavilion used for meetings and the sale of handicrafts to cruise-ship passengers. Definitely worth examining are museum-quality bone carvings by **Teike Barinas** (© **92.93.24**).

In front of the town hall stands a monument declaring, in French, that after 1995 the Marquesas Islands shall be known to the world by their original name, *Fenua Enata* (Land of Men). Another commemorates Chief Iotete's rebellion against the French in 1842. As I said, the Tahuatans are independent-minded.

In the school, the small **Musée de Vaitahu (Vaitahu Museum; ✆ 92.92.19)** tells of expeditions in the valleys and displays fishhooks, *adzes* (primitive stone axes), and other items discovered during the digs in the 1990s. Organized by archaeologist Barry Rolett of the University of Hawaii, the captions are in French, English, and Marquesan. The museum is open Monday to Friday and on cruise-ship days from 8am to 4pm. Admission is 200CFP.

Facing the bay from a large open space stands the impressive **Eglise Sainte Mère de Dieu (Holy Mother of God Catholic Church),** built of stone with Vatican backing in 1988, the anniversary of the arrival of the first Catholic priests in 1838. The name also evokes Mendaña's visit in 1595. Look up at the church steeple, where a woodcarving by noted sculptor Damien Haturau depicts the Virgin Mary holding the baby Jesus, as does an impressive stained-glass window inside the church.

A paved street follows an often-dry streambed inland from the beach. You will pass a number of wood-frame houses dating from the early 20th century. Across a bridge is the studio of **Felix Fii** (✆ 92.90.42), one of the best tattoo artists in French Polynesia.

HAPATONI

About 15 minutes by boat south of Vaitahu, **Hapatoni** is one of the most pleasant and friendliest villages in the Marquesas. Enormous *temanu* trees and the **Royal Road** skirt the little bay, making for a picturesque stroll. The middle of the village is dominated by the restored **Me'ae Anapara** and **Me'ae Eia,** two large meeting and worshiping sites. Next to them, a gray stone Catholic church and cemetery offer a contrast of ancient and modern worshiping methods.

Hapatoni seldom sees foreign visitors except when the *Aranui 3* pulls in every third Sunday. Then the entire village turns out to offer fresh fruits, a meal of Marquesan cuisine, and handicrafts for sale.

Where to Stay & Dine on Tahuatu

The only place to stay is **Pension Amatea** (✆/fax **92.92.84**), where Marguerite Kokauani rents five rooms in her modern house. Guests share a bathroom and shower. Marguerite charges about 5,000CFP per person. She also serves meals and will arrange horseback riding and other excursions. Book well in advance, for Marguerite must also arrange your boat transfer from Hiva Oa.

FATU HIVA ★★★

Lying 56km (34 miles) southeast of Tahuata, remote Fatu Hiva is one of the most dramatically beautiful islands in French Polynesia. Like Moorea, it's half a bowl formed by the remaining third of a volcanic crater that rises steeply from the sea, resulting in many cliffs plunging precipitously into the surf. Rising from the middle of the original crater's floor, rugged **Mount Teamotua** is flanked on either side by narrow valleys in which the island's 560 residents live. On the south side, **Omoa** is the administrative center, while to the north, **Hanavave** is the most unusual valley in the Marquesas.

The island came to the world's attention in 1938 when Thor Heyerdahl published *Fatu Hiva: Back to Nature,* describing the year he and his bride, Liv, spent here trying to live a totally natural life. It didn't work. Nearly emaciated, he and Liv were evacuated by local missionaries. While here, Heyerdahl developed the theory that the Polynesians came originally from South America, which led to his sailing the balsa raft *Kon Tiki* from Peru to the Tuamotu Archipelago in the late 1940s.

Today Fatu Hiva (whose name is sometimes spelled Fatu Iva) is French Polynesia's leading producer of **tapa,** the natural cloth made from the bark of paper mulberry, banyan, and other trees. Geometric designs were tattooed on the bodies of the wearers in ancient times, not on the cloth, but the modern version is decorated with a multitude of designs. Local women show cruise-ship passengers how bark is beaten into cloth and then painted. Fatu Hiva is the best place in the territory to buy tapa.

Exploring Fatu Hiva

There is no airstrip on Fatu Hiva, and the only sensible way of getting here is on the *Aranui 3,* which anchors first at picturesque **Omoa** village beside a small bay. Omoa has a post office and an infirmary. There is no bank on Fatu Hiva; hence, credit cards are useless here.

Omoa's prime attractions are large, back-to-back tikis standing at the waterfront and **Musée Grelet** (**Grelet Museum;** no phone), on the first level of a colonial-era house built by François Grelet. A Swiss man, he settled here in the 19th century, married a local woman, and began collecting Marquesan art. Carried on by his descendants, the museum contains war clubs and spears, *adzes,* tikis, and stone pestles used to pound breadfruit into poi. Most impressive are intricately carved wooden *koka'a* bowls, from which poi is served. Many modern items are very much for sale. The museum is open on cruise-ship days, other times by appointment. Admission is free.

From Omoa, a 17km (11-mile) dirt road scales the central mountain and down into **Hanavave.** It's much faster and easier to go between the two villages by boat, but four-wheel-drive vehicles use this road, which was built to service the electric power lines linking the two settlements. It's a popular 4- to 5-hour hike, especially for *Aranui 3* passengers since they rejoin the ship at Hanavave. Although usually passable, the track has sections of slippery mud that can stick to the bottom of shoes and hiking boots. It can be a hot walk, too, so bring ample supplies of water, snacks, and sunscreen. The first half of the walk is a steady incline—like walking uphill on a treadmill for 1½ to 2 hours!—so you should be in good health before making this hike.

The road gradually climbs out of Omoa Valley, crosses the central mountain, then descends very steeply into Hanavave. The views from the switchbacks are awesome; at one point, it seems as if you are looking straight down into the **Baie des Vierges** (**Bay of Virgins**) at Hanavave. The valley itself is punctuated with tiki-shaped spires protruding from sharp ridges descending from the old crater wall. No other place in French Polynesia is this ephemeral.

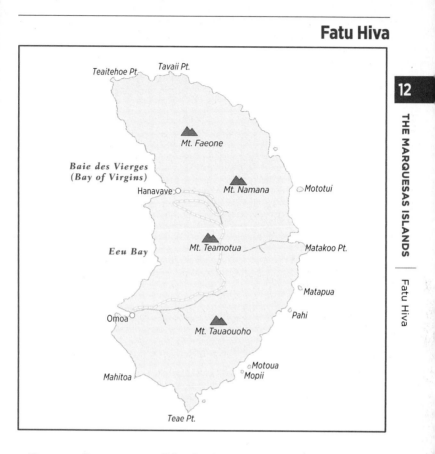

Hanavave village sits on a small flat plain beside a beach of black rocks and boulders. Its backdrop consists of huge black pillars standing like the posts of a giant gate between it and the valley. The phallus shape of these posts has given rise to humorous conjecture that the 19th-century French missionaries added an "i" to *Baie des Verges* (Bay of Phalli, let us say), thus renaming it *Baie des Vierges* (Bay of Virgins). The Marquesan name means "Surf Bay."

Hanavave attracts scores of cruising yachts, in part because the setting sun invariably paints this gorgeous valley with an enormous variety of changing colors.

Where to Stay & Dine on Fatu Hiva

You must be an intrepid traveler to get to Fatu Hiva on your own, but you can stay at Bernadette Cantois' **Chez Lionel** (*C*/fax **92.81.84;** chezlionel@mail.pf), in the village about 1.5km (1 mile) inland from the Omoa wharf. Bernadette has a kitchen-equipped bungalow whose private bathroom has a hot-water shower, plus two rooms in her house (with shared facilities). She charges about 9,000CFP double for a bungalow, 8,500CFP double for a room, including breakfast, but she does not accept credit cards. Bernadette will arrange horseback riding, fishing, and excursions.

FAST FACTS: TAHITI & FRENCH POLYNESIA

The following facts apply to French Polynesia in general. For more specific information, see the "Fast Facts" sections in the specific island chapters.

Area Codes French Polynesia does not have domestic area codes. The country code for calling into French Polynesia is **689.**

Business Hours Although many shops in downtown Papeete stay open over the lunch period, general shopping and business hours are from 7:30 to 11:30am and from 2 to 5pm Monday to Friday, 8am to noon on Saturday. In addition to regular hours, most grocery stores also are open from 2 to 6pm on Saturday and from 6 to 8am on Sunday.

Cellphones (Mobile Phones) See "Staying Connected," p. 70.

Drinking Laws The legal drinking age is 21. Most grocery stores sell beer, spirits, and wines. Hinano beer is brewed locally and is less expensive than imported brands. I bring a bottle of duty-free liquor with me.

Driving Rules See "Getting Around Tahiti & French Polynesia," p. 54.

Drug Laws Plenty of pot may be grown up in the hills, but possession and use of dangerous drugs and narcotics are subject to long jail terms.

Drugstores The main towns have reasonably well-stocked pharmacies, or chemists. Their medicines are likely to be from France.

Electricity Electrical power is 220 volts, 50 cycles, and the plugs are the French kind with two round, skinny prongs. Most hotels have 110-volt outlets for shavers only, so you will need a converter and adapter plugs for other appliances. Some hotels, especially those on the outer islands, have their own generators, so ask at the reception desk what voltage is supplied.

Embassies & Consulates The **United States** has a consular agent on Tahiti (✆ **42.65.35;** www.usconsul.pf). The nearest U.S. embassy is in Suva, Fiji. Other consular representatives include **Australia/Canada** (✆ **46.88.53;** marc.j.siu.petropol@mail.pf), **New Zealand** (✆ **27.25.43;** www.nzembassy.com/newcaledonia), and the United Kingdom (✆ **42.00.50**).

Emergencies If you are in a hotel, contact the staff. Otherwise, the emergency **police** phone number is ✆ **17** throughout the territory.

Etiquette & Customs Even though many women go topless and wear the skimpiest of bikini bottoms at the beach, the Tahitians have a sense of propriety similar to what you find in any Western nation. Don't offend them by engaging in behavior that would not be permissible at home.

Firearms   French Polynesians can own shotguns for hunting, but handguns are illegal.

Gasoline (Petrol)   Service stations are common on Tahiti, but only in the main villages on the other islands. Expect to pay about 120CFP per liter of gasoline (*essence* in French). One U.S. gallon equals 3.8 liters or .85 imperial gallons.

Holidays   For more information on holidays, see "When to Go," p. 42.

Insects   There are no dangerous insects in French Polynesia. The only real nuisances are mosquitoes and tiny, nearly invisible sand flies known locally as *no-nos*, elsewhere as *no-seeums*. They appear at dusk on most beaches here. Wear trousers or long skirts and plenty of insect repellent (especially on the feet and ankles) to ward off the *no-nos*. If you forget to bring insect repellent along, look for the Off or Dolmix Pic brands at the pharmacies.

Insurance   Since my health insurance policy does not cover me outside the United States, I always buy a travel insurance policy that provides evacuation if necessary. For information on traveler's insurance, trip cancellation insurance, and medical insurance while traveling, please visit **www.frommers.com/tips**.

Internet Access   See "Staying Connected," p. 71.

Language   French is the official language. Most residents also speak Tahitian, and English is widely spoken among hotel and restaurant staffers.

Measurements   French Polynesia is on the metric system. Metric measurements in this guide are listed first, followed by non-metric conversions in parentheses. Conversions for metric to non-metric, and vice versa, are available online at www.online conversion.com.

Mail   All the main towns and many Papeete suburbs have post offices. Letters usually take about a week to 10 days to reach overseas destinations in either direction. Mailing addresses in French Polynesia consist of post office boxes (*boîtes postales* in French, or B.P. for short) but no street numbers or names. Local addresses have postal codes, which are written in front of the city or town. (If you send a letter to French Polynesia from the U.S., do *not* put the postal code behind the name of the town; otherwise the U.S. Postal Service may dispatch it to a zip code within the United States.)

Passports   All visitors to French Polynesia must have a passport that will be valid for 6 months beyond their stay in French Polynesia. See "Embassies & Consulates," above, for whom to contact if you lose yours while here.

For other information, contact the following agencies:

For Residents of Australia   Contact the Australian Passport Information Service at ✆ **131-232**, or visit www.passports.gov.au.

For Residents of Canada   Contact the central Passport Office, Department of Foreign Affairs and International Trade, Ottawa, ON K1A 0G3 (✆ **800/567-6868;** www.ppt.gc.ca).

For Residents of Ireland   Contact the Passport Office, Setanta Centre, Molesworth Street, Dublin 2 (✆ **01/671-1633;** www.foreignaffairs.gov.ie).

For Residents of New Zealand   Contact the Passports Office, Department of Internal Affairs, 47 Boulcott Street, Wellington, 6011 (✆ **0800/225-050** in New Zealand or 04/474-8100; www.passports.govt.nz).

For Residents of the United Kingdom   Visit your nearest passport office, major post office, or travel agency or contact the Identity and Passport Service (IPS), 89 Eccleston Square, London, SW1V 1PN (📞 **0300/222-0000;** www.ips.gov.uk).

For Residents of the United States   To find your regional passport office, check the U.S. State Department website (travel.state.gov/passport) or call the National Passport Information Center (📞 **877/487-2778**) for automated information.

Police   The emergency **police** phone number is 📞 **17** throughout French Polynesia. The territory has two types of police: French *gendarmes* and local *commune* police. Both enforce traffic laws.

Safety   Do not leave valuables in your hotel room or unattended anywhere. Street crimes against tourists are rare, and you should be safe after dark in the busy parks along boulevard Pomare on Papeete's waterfront. Friends of mine who live here, however, don't stroll away from the boulevard after dark. For that matter, stay alert everywhere after dusk. Women should not wander alone on deserted beaches any time, since some Polynesian men may still consider such behavior to be an invitation for instant amorous activity.

Smoking   Inside most public buildings including restaurants are smoke-free. The hotels must have nonsmoking rooms.

Taxes   Local residents do not pay income taxes; instead, the government imposes stiff duties on most imported goods, and a value-added tax (VAT, or *TVA* in French) is included in the price of most goods and services. Only the TVA on set pearls is refundable in the European fashion (see "Buying Your Black Pearl," p. 113). Another 12% tax will be tacked onto your hotel bills (including restaurant and bar expenses) and another 50CFP to 200CFP per night for the Tahiti, Moorea, and Bora Bora communities.

Telephone   See "Staying Connected," (p. 72).

Time   Local time in the most-visited islands is 11 hours behind Greenwich Mean Time. That is 5 hours behind U.S. Eastern Standard Time or 2 hours behind Pacific Standard Time. Add 1 hour to the Tahiti time during daylight saving time in the U.S.

The Marquesas Islands are 30 minutes ahead of the rest of the territory.

Since French Polynesia is on the east side of the international date line, Tahiti has the same date as the United States, the U.K., and Europe, and is 1 day behind Australia and New Zealand.

Tipping   Although tipping is considered contrary to the Polynesian custom of hospitality, it's a widespread practice here, especially in Papeete's restaurants (credit card forms now have a "tip" line here). Nevertheless, tipping is not expected unless the service has been beyond the call of duty. Some hotels accept contributions to the staff Christmas fund.

Toilets   Public toilets are present in the parks along Papeete's downtown waterfront and at the port facilities on Raiatea and Bora Bora. Large hotels and restaurants are often the best bet for clean facilities.

Visas   See "Entry Requirements," p. 44.

Visitor Information   The best source of up-to-date information in advance is **Tahiti Tourisme,** B.P. 65, 98713 Papeete, French Polynesia (📞 **50.57.00;** fax 43.66.19; www.tahiti-tourisme.pf).

The Website has links to Tahiti Tourisme offices in Australia, New Zealand, the United Kingdom, and several countries including the United States at 300 N. Continental Blvd.,

Visitor Information

Ste. 160, El Segundo, CA 90245 (📞 **310/414-8484;** fax 310/414-8490; www.tahiti-tourisme.com).

Once you're in Papeete, you can get maps, brochures, and other information at the Tahiti Tourisme's **Fare Manihini** visitor bureau (📞 **50.57.12;** www.tahiti-manava.pf), located in the cruise-ship welcome center on the waterfront, on boulevard Pomare at rue Paul Gauguin. See "Fast Facts: Tahiti," in chapter 5.

Be sure to pick up the ***Tahiti Beach Press,*** a free weekly English-language newspaper that lists special events and current activities. Copies are available in most hotel lobbies.

Tahiti Tourisme distributes free maps of each island. Each weekly edition of the free *Tahiti Beach Press* carries artistic maps of the island and Papeete.

The Tahiti-based **Agence Tahitienne de Presse** (www.tahitipresse.pf) is the best source for breaking local news as well as events and weather. Click on the "English version" link.

The East-West Center at the University of Hawaii gathers news from French Polynesia and other islands on its **Pacific Islands Report** website, http://pidp.eastwestcenter.org/pireport. It includes links to newspapers, news services, and universities.

Other useful websites include:

○ **www.airtahitimagazine.com**, with articles from Air Tahiti's in-flight magazine.

○ **www.diving-tahiti.com**, for general information and links to dive operators in all of the islands.

○ **www.frommers.com**, especially the message boards, where you can read what other travelers have to say about Tahiti and French Polynesia.

○ **www.meteo.pf**, the official site of Météo France, the local weather service.

○ **www.tahitiguide.com** is one of the most comprehensive commercial sites and has a booking engine for many hotels and pensions.

○ **www.tahiti-nui.com**, where you can see what the weather is doing in Papeete and on Bora Bora through Tahiti Nui Travel's live webcams.

○ **www.tahitisun.com**, with links to several other sites that offer a host of information about each island.

Water   Tap water is consistently safe to drink only in Papeete and on Bora Bora. Well water in the Tuamotu islands tends to be brackish; rainwater is used there for drinking. You can buy bottled water at every grocery store. The local brands Vaimato and Eau Royal are much less expensive than imported French waters.

Index

See also Accommodations and
Restaurant indexes, below.

General Index

A

Abercrombie & Kent, 66
Accommodations, 73–75. *See
also* specific destinations; and
Accommodations Index
    best, 3–7
Active vacations, 68–70
Adventure Eagle Tours, 109
Aehautai Marae (Bora Bora), 187
Afareaitu (Moorea), 135
Aguila (ship), 103
Air, 46
Air Moorea, 51
Air Tahiti, 52, 237
Air Tahiti Airpass, 51
Air Tahiti Nui, 46
Air travel, 45–51, 54
Albert Rent-a-Car (Moorea), 129
Albert Tours (Moorea), 129, 131,
    136
All Saints' Day, 43
Aloe Cafe (Bora Bora), 184
Anaho, 241, 243
Anahoa Bay (Hakahau), 243, 252
Anau (Bora Bora), 187
Anini Marae (Huahine), 160
Ann Simon Boutique (Moorea),
    141
Antibacterial ointment, 45
AO Api New World (Huahine),
    157
Aora, Mount (Tahiti), 93
Apia Tehope, 168
Apooti Marina (Raiatea), 70, 170
Aqua socks, 45
Arahoho blowholes (Tahiti), 101
Arahurahu Marae (Tahiti), 93, 107
Aranui 3 (cargo ship), 54, 67,
    236
Archipel Croisièrs, 70
Area codes, 267
Arehahio Locations, Rangiroa,
    212
Aremiti, 52
Arioi, 30, 108
Art Center of Hane, 249
Atimaono (Tahiti), 106
Atiraa Waterfall (Moorea), 135
ATMs (cashpoints), 57
Atuona (Hiva Oa), 254, 256–257
Atwater, Dorence, grave (Tahiti),
    106
Australia Escorted Tours, 66
Austral Islands, 78–79
Avapeihi Pass (Huahine), 162
Avatoru Pass (Rangiroa), 211, 216
Avatoru (Rangiroa), 211, 212

Avea Bay (Baie Avea; Huahine),
    156, 160
Avea Beach (Huahine), 162

B

Baggage allowances, 47
Baggage storage, 50
Baie Avea (Avea Bay; Huahine),
    156
Baie des Vierges (FatuHiva), 264
Bain Loti (Loti's Pool; Tahiti), 100
Bali Hai Boys (Moorea), 144
Banks. *See* Currency and
    currency exchange
Banque de Polynésie, 50
Banque Socredo, 50
Bathy's Dive Center (Tahiti),
    110, 111
Bathy's Diving (Moorea), 139
Bay of Tapuraha (Tahiti), 104
Bay of Virgins (FatuHiva), 264
Belvedere Lookout (Moorea),
    134
Biking and mountain biking, 69
    Bora Bora, 183
    Fakarava, 228
    Hiva Oa, 259
    Moorea, 130
    Tikehau, 220
Billabong Pro Surfing, 42
Bird Island (Rangiroa), 214
Bird Islands, 220
Bird Quest, 66
Birds and bird-watching, 27,
    65–66
Birdwatching Breaks, 66
Black-pearl farms, Fakarava, 229
Black pearls
    Manihi, 224
    Moorea, 141
    Raiatea, 175
    Rangiroa, 216
    Tahiti, 112, 113
Bligh, William, 19–20
Bloody Mary's Restaurant & Bar
    (Bora Bora), 187
Blue Glue (Papeete), 114
Blue Lagoon (Rangiroa), 214
Books, recommended, 34–37
Bora Bora, 182–200
    accommodations, 192–197
    brief description of, 77
    currency exchange, 184
    drugstores, 184
    the east coast, 187
    emergencies, 184
    getting around, 183–184
    healthcare, 184
    Internet access, 184
    nightlife, 200
    north and west coasts,
        187–188
    restaurants, 197–200
    shopping, 191
    watersports, 190–191
Bora Bora I Te Fanau Tahi, 191

Bora Bora Lagoonarium, 189, 190
Bora Bora Parasail, 190
Bora Pearl Company, 191
Botanical Gardens, Harrison W.
    Smith (Tahiti), 105
Botanical Gardens (Papeete), 95
Bougainville, Antoine de, 15
Bougainville's Anchorage
    (Tahiti), 102
Bounty, HMS, 19–21
Boutique Bora Bora, 191
Boutique d'Art Marquisien
    (Moorea), 140
Boutique Gauguin (Bora Bora),
    191
Brando, Marlon, 108
Briac, Olivier, 137
Bugs, 59
Buses, 52
Business hours, 91, 267

C

Calendar of events, 42–43
Calvary Cemetery (Atuona), 256
Captain Bligh Restaurant and
    Bar (Punaauia), 126
Carbonfund, 65
Carnival, 43
Carrefour supermarket (Tahiti),
    121
Car rentals, 54
Car travel, 54–55, 90–91
Cascades de Faarumai (Tahiti),
    102
Cascade Tevaipo, 243
Cathédrale de Notre-Dame des
    Marquises, 241
Cathédrale de Papeete Notre-
    Dame de L'Immaculée
    Conception, 99
Cave de Rangiroa, 217
Caverne de Maui (Tahiti), 104
Cellphones, 70–71
Centre Artisanal de Hane, 249
Centre Artisanal du Nuku Hiva,
    241
Centre d'Experimentation du
    Pacifique, 25
Centre Moana Nui (Tahiti), 111
Centre Vaima (Papeete), 96
CFP (French Pacific franc), 56
Champion supermarket (Tahiti),
    121
Charles W. Morgan (whaling
    ship), 205
Chinese New Year, 42
Chinese people, 31
Christian, Fletcher, 19–20
Christian missionaries, 22–23, 32
Cimetière du Calvaire (Atuona),
    256
Circle Island Tour (Tahiti),
    100–109
Climate, 40–42
Clinic Paofai (Tahiti), 92
Clinque Cardella (Tahiti), 92

273

Restaurants